The Traveling Economist

The Traveling Economist

Using Economics to Think about What Makes Us All So Different and the Same

Todd A. Knoop, PhD

An Imprint of ABC-CLIO, LLC
Santa Barbara, California • Denver, Colorado

Library of Congress Cataloging in Publication Data

Names: Knoop, Todd A., author.
Title: The traveling economist : using economics to think about what makes us all so
    different and the same / Todd A. Knoop, PhD.
Description: First Edition. | Santa Barbara : Praeger, An Imprint of ABC-CLIO,
    LLC, [2017]
Identifiers: LCCN 2016051279 | ISBN 9781440852367 (hard copy) |
    ISBN 9781440852374 (eISBN)
Subjects: LCSH: Economics. | Economics—Sociological aspects. | Economic policy. |
    Technological innovations—Economic aspects. | Globalization—Economic aspects.
Classification: LCC HB171 .K626 2017 | DDC 330—dc23
LC record available at https://lccn.loc.gov/2016051279

ISBN: 978-1-4408-5236-7
EISBN: 978-1-4408-5237-4

21   20   19   18   17   1   2   3   4   5

This book is also available as an eBook.

Praeger
An Imprint of ABC-CLIO, LLC

ABC-CLIO, LLC
130 Cremona Drive, P.O. Box 1911
Santa Barbara, California 93116-1911
www.abc-clio.com

This book is printed on acid-free paper ∞

Manufactured in the United States of America

Copyright Acknowledgments

All images courtesy of Todd A. Knoop, PhD

To my Fellow Travelers, particularly
Rhawn, Sunil, Eric, Brian, Deb, Edie, and Daphne

Contents

Preface   ix

Chapter 1   Why Do the Haves Have and the Have-nots
                Have Less?   1

Chapter 2   Why Are Drivers in Other Countries
                So Much Worse Than Back Home?   31

Chapter 3   Why Are There More Workers Than Patrons
                at This Coffee House? The Tradeoff between
                Capital and Labor   61

Chapter 4 $50 Billion to Ride the Bus!?! How Governments
                Can Kill Growth or Help It to Thrive   95

Chapter 5   Nothing Needs Reform as Much as Other People:
                Culture and Economics   131

Chapter 6   What's a Landline? Technological Diffusion
                around the World   167

Chapter 7   Best Price for You! The Economics of Haggling   197

Chapter 8   I Think That I Shall Never See Any Economics
                as Lovely as a Tree: Nature and Economics   225

Chapter 9   Who Owns the Space Behind My Seat? Traveling
                Economics   245

Chapter 10 Coming Home   271

Notes   287

Bibliography   307

Index   319

Preface

The point of going somewhere like the Napo River in Ecuador is not to see the most spectacular anything. It is simply to see what is there. We are here on the planet only once, and might as well get a feel for the place.

—Annie Dilllard[1]

Why is something as difficult as travel also one of the greatest joys of life? People find delight in travel for many reasons: to encounter new people and new places, to investigate novel cultures and diverse ways of living, to experience beauty (both man-made and natural), and to simply break out of the routines of ordinary life. But what all of these reasons have in common is that we enjoy travel because it allows us to experience difference. As humans, we have a predilection toward homogeneity. We have an inborn desire to be tribal and associate with those who are similar to us, and we yearn for home and the places that are most familiar. But humans are also evolutionarily hard-wired to enjoy the thrill of experiencing the uncommon. It is this desire that has led to exploration and the expansion of humans across the planet (and even off it). The lure of the new and interesting—the appeal of the exotic—is a desire that is as inborn as the need for social interaction or comfort. Travel is the way we explore difference and "scratch the itch" of experiencing the unusual.

So what does economics have to do with travel? At a superficial level, it might seem very little. The traditional definition of economics is that it is the study of how societies distribute scarce resources. Nothing about travel in that. But an alternative definition of economics has been gaining wider acceptance recently, a definition of economics that the father of economics Adam Smith had in mind when he said: "It is not from the benevolence of the butcher, the brewer, or the baker that we expect our dinner, but from their regard to their own interest."[2] In this modern view, economics is really about the study of how people respond to incentives in order to further their own interests. This modern view shifts the focus of economics away from scarcity—on what people don't have—and toward incentives—on what people actually receive when they take specific actions. The recasting of economics as the study of how people respond to incentives has three radical implications for how economics can help us better understand the ways that people behave, think, and interact across the globe.

First, this new definition emphasizes the fact that different people live in different environments and face a diverse set of rewards and punishments at varying times. These diverse incentives motivate different behaviors across people and even in the same person over time—not just economic behaviors but social and personal as well. Unfortunately, many of these actions profit one person but hurt everybody else—robbery, for instance. So when economists study incentives, we are not only interested in how certain incentives prod people into taking certain actions, but we are also interested in how governments and societies can shape incentives in ways that encourage people to behave in ways that benefit both themselves and society as a whole. For instance, one of the primary challenges of economics is to develop policies, laws, and enforcement systems that incentivize people to produce their own goods (where everyone stands to benefit) and not just steal the goods of others (where someone benefits only at a cost to others).

Second, the economic focus on incentives does not mean that incentives are only financial rewards or penalties. They could also be social incentives, such as the approval or the condemnation of peers, or physical incentives, such as avoiding punishment or gaining comfort. The key is that these incentives are rewards or punishments that people care about.

The third, and most important, implication of this modern definition of economics is that because the incentives that impact human behavior are so much broader than the narrow financial incentives that are typically associated with economics, economics has expanded the scope of its investigations well beyond the study of how people trade goods and services. Economics focuses not only on supply, demand, income, unemployment, etc., but also has extended its reach into the study of a much wider array of individual and societal interactions. Modern economics has something to say about why family structures have evolved over time, how political special interests impact public policy, what factors influence crime rates, why religious practices differ and change, how parents choose the names of their babies, how to foster better public health practices, and many other topics that don't explicitly relate to narrow business transactions.

Using this innovative perspective, economists have gained new insights into the determinants of difference across people, cultures, societies, countries, and time. Economics has become a powerful tool that can be used to make each of us much more perceptive observers. As a result, developing a deeper understanding of economics is an important part of becoming a better traveler. Travelers who have fostered their economic insight will be those who get the most out of their travels because they will be better able to appreciate their experiences. If we travel to observe beauty and experience alternative lifestyles, then a lack of economic sense leads to a blindness that prohibits us from seeing these things as they actually are. Such a lack of perception deadens our experiences and makes them less enjoyable. Learning the insights of modern economics and appreciating how economists view the world can help travelers better comprehend their experiences, and with better comprehension, many deeper truths will reveal themselves. In effect, a deeper understanding fostered by a better awareness of economics can allow a tourist (someone who sees what they know is there) to become an explorer (someone who learns anew each and every day from what they see).

For example, consider this picture. To the casual tourist, the Dunky Investments/Security/Detective business in Botswana, Africa (Dunky means "donkey" in the local language of Setswana) might seem a somewhat eclectic and amusing mix of activities for a small business. An ordinary

Jack of all trades, master of none?

tourist in Botswana would note that when they read the popular detective book series set in Botswana, *The No. 1 Ladies' Detective Agency*, they never read about the excellent detective Mma Romotswe taking time out of her busy mystery-solving business to manage someone's retirement portfolio or provide bodyguard services to local celebrities. An ordinary tourist might also compare this small business with those from the developed country that they come from and say that this kind of "jack of all trades" business simply reflects the overall poverty in Botswana. But the traveling economist observes something quite different because they have a theory that provides them with a lens through which to see the world more clearly. When the traveling economist sees this picture, they see not the results of poverty, but the causes of poverty. The traveling economist sees a motivated entrepreneur, but one who has started a business that cannot specialize because it is too small and operates in a risky business setting, forcing it to emphasize diversification over specialization. Without specialization, the traveling economist sees a business that cannot invest in the capital and technology needed to become more productive and more profitable. The traveling economist sees the many risks associated with living on the edge of poverty, and the impact that this risk has on people's stress levels, their health, their ability to plan for their future, and their ability to provide for their children's future. The traveling economist sees a businessperson providing informal lending (pejoratively, "loan sharking") because he or she knows that most people are unable to get financial services—loans and savings accounts—from traditional banks. The traveling economist sees the importance of trust, or the lack of it, in both our economic and personal interactions, and how important it is to have reliable information (even that provided by a detective) so that people can verify the trust that they place in others. The traveling economist sees a business that is offering services not provided by the police or the legal system because of a lack of public spending, poor laws, corruption, and general inefficiency. Finally, the traveling economist sees how all of these factors—and many others—interact to determine the economic environment that each of us live in. It is this economic environment that affects incentives and influences behavior. This economic environment shapes our quality of life in so many different ways, not just through its impact on economic factors such as employment and income, but also through its impact on our social interactions, health, well-being, and happiness.

Of course, other disciplines of study—such as political science, anthropology, sociology, history, and the natural sciences—also provide useful insights into the reasons why people and places differ. But many of the insights from these disciplines are better understood by most people. The subject of economics still tends to be perceived as an intellectual black box by many, despite the fact that when fundamental economic concepts are clearly explained, the most common responses become "That makes sense," "I never thought of it that way before," or "That's interesting!" Very few things in economics are counterintuitive, but intuition must first be nurtured before the immense explanatory power of economics is unleashed. (An explanatory power that, I would argue, rivals or exceeds that of any other academic discipline. But hey, I'm biased. I'm an economist.) An ignorance of economics not only makes you a less informed traveler, but it makes you vulnerable to the media biases and political misrepresentations that often surround discussions of why people behave in the ways that they do.

In this book, I want to introduce you to a few simple economic concepts that will help you to think differently and more deeply about the differences between the people and the places you visit during your journeys. The fundamental perspective that motivates this book is that a little economics can reveal profounder truths to the perceptive traveler about all of the novel things that they are observing, as well as influence their outlook on life long after the journey is over. In the words of Samuel Johnson, "The use of travelling is to regulate imagination by reality, and instead of thinking how things may be, to see them as they are."[3] This is exactly what economics aims to do as well, and it is the reason why using economics to enrich our travel can magnify the value of both. The great economists that we talk about in this book—Adam Smith, David Ricardo, Thomas Malthus, John Maynard Keynes, Friedrich Hayek, and others—were heavily influenced by the things they observed on their own travels; seeing things as they really are stimulated them to think about why it had to be.

You will notice that I spend more time talking about my experiences traveling in the less developed world than in developed countries. Why, you might ask, not spend more time talking about Europe or the United States? Isn't it an interesting question to ask why France has so many outdoor cafes and what economics can tell us about this? Let me be clear: I have nothing against travel in developed countries. If anyone plans on traveling to France in the near future, I would happily tag along and sip some wine along the Champs-Élysées while ruminating about the economic implications of *haute couture* or about why a certain, *je ne sais pas*, "sharpness" in French attitudes exists toward tourists.

However, most of the world is not currently rich, although it is getting more so. As economic development spreads across the globe to places like China, India, Central and South America, and Africa, the gravitational center of the world we now live in is changing. The world's economy and its politics are increasingly interrelated, and now it's not just the rest of the world that has to adjust to what is happening in the developed world, but often vice versa. The rise of the second and third world is not just the result of the skyscrapers sprouting like grass in Mumbai, or the fact that luxury watch stores are as numerous as Starbucks in Shanghai. It is also because there is a growing sense of dynamism and optimism in these places, even though it remains true that most of the world lives under conditions that are still chaotic and humble. Economics has a lot to say about why these global changes are occurring, and developing countries are often the places that provide the best illustrations of the power of economics to explain the modern world that all of us live in. But regardless of where you go, a basic understanding of economics is crucial to the education of any modern, well-rounded traveler, whether it be travel to the world's poorest places or its richest.

In his book *The Art of Travel*, the philosopher Alain de Botton (2002) describes how training in the art of drawing can make someone a better traveler. It does this by conditioning the artist to notice details. When forced to focus and think about the minutiae of any object, the artist must see and appreciate the parts that make up the whole. It also allows the artist to stop and purposely see the seemingly ordinary as well as the extraordinary. In this sense, training as an artist is primarily about learning how to see what is important, not just representing the easily observable. According to de Botton, the 19th-century artist John Ruskin told students at the end of his drawing course "Now, remember, gentlemen, that I have not been trying to teach you to draw, only to *see*."

Economics can perform this same function for everyone, but particularly for the traveler. A grasp of economics can help each of us see what is really going on around us during our trips. There is an old joke that "an economist is someone who sees what works in practice and asks if it also works in theory." Yes, exactly! That is what each of us should be doing when we are traveling. Only by thinking more carefully about why things work as they do can we actually come to appreciate the beauty and complexity of the world around us.

According to Friedrich Nietzsche, learning how to maximize what we learn from our experiences is the key to self-improvement. In his words: "When we observe how some people know how to manage their experiences . . . then we are in the end tempted to divide mankind into a minority (a minimality) of those who know how to make much of little, and a majority of those who know how to make little of much."[4] A good traveler and a good economist will be a member of the former—those who know how to make much of little—and this book will help the reader learn how much more can be made from the little things seen on our journeys.

CHAPTER ONE

Why Do the Haves Have and the Have-nots Have Less?

The whole of science is nothing but a refinement of everyday thinking.
—Albert Einstein[1]

Faith, hope and money—only a saint could have the first two without the third.

—George Orwell[2]

An important motivation for travel is to learn about how the other half lives. For those of us who live in developed countries, the other half is actually the much larger half. We live in a world with huge differences between a relatively small number of rich and a much larger number of poor. Roughly 80 percent of the world's population lives on less than $10 a day, and 21 percent (or 1.2 billion people) live on less than the astonishing low level of $1.25 a day, which is the World Bank's official yardstick for measuring poverty. While there are an estimated 800 million people who are underfed across the world, more than 100 million people in the United States are on diets.[3]

What does it mean to live on $10 a day? Or to live on $1.25 a day? This is a very difficult question for anyone to answer without actually being forced to live on such amounts for an extended period of time—a fact-finding mission that even the most curious, or masochistic, traveler is unlikely to undertake. But traveling in poorer countries does provide a glimpse into the incredible challenges associated with living on so little.

In order to see extreme poverty firsthand, I recommend that you take a tour of a slum during your next trip. The act of visiting a slum is a difficult proposition for most travelers. The idea of visiting an area to witness other people's misery seems disquieting at best, unethical at worst. The author and travel writer Paul Theroux explained his experience touring a township slum outside of Cape Town, South Africa, in this way:

> It seemed that curious visitors, of whom I was one, had created a whole itinerary, a voyeurism of poverty, and this exploitation—at bottom that's what it was—had produced a marketing opportunity: township dwellers, who never imagined their poverty to be of interest to anyone, had discovered that for wealthy visitors it had the merit of being fascinating, and the residents became explainers, historians, living victims, survivors, and sellers of locally made bead ornaments, toys, embroidered bags, and baskets, hawked in the stalls adjacent to the horrific houses. They had discovered that their misery was marketable. That was the point.[4]

Residential housing in the Dharavi slum.

In contrast with Theroux, I see no reason why visiting a slum should be any more or less acceptable than touring affluent neighborhoods filled with mansions—something that all of us have done. Part of the motivation for travel is to see the reality of how people live, not how we would like to believe they live. The fact of the matter is that a huge portion of the world's population—an estimated 860 million people—live in slums worldwide. In Sub-Saharan Africa, 62 percent of the urban population lives in slums and these numbers are growing by nearly five percent a year.[5] As a result, the population density in many slums is simply astonishing. In Manhattan, the population density is roughly 26,000 people per square kilometer, while in the Dharavi slum within Mumbai, India—made famous by the movie *Slumdog Millionaire*—the population density is conservatively 293,000 people per square kilometer.[6] To put it another way, between 700 and 1,000 people live in every 900 square meters of housing space (about the size of a McMansion in the United States) within Dharavi. Nearly 4,000 people live on every acre.

What makes a slum a slum? Slums suffer from too many people, but they also suffer from three fundamental shortages: too little investment, too few public goods, and an absence of public health services. First, there is the investment shortage. Low-quality housing becomes a self-fulfilling trap; there is little reason to try to improve the value of your house when it is surrounded by others that are in similarly poor shape. In addition, most people who live in slums do not own but rent, and renters don't have the same incentives to make improvements on their residences as owners do. Why should a slumlord invest in a property when renters are already paying more than one-fourth of their income in rent and have few other housing alternatives? The lack of investment in slums also discourages business and job creation. Those businesses that do exist in slums tend to be very small, undercapitalized, and labor-intensive.

The second shortage slums face is in public goods and services. Slums not only lack urban planning and public infrastructure, but also suffer from a lack of education, legal systems, safety standards enforcement, and social safety nets. Shortages of public services in slums persist because slum residents are consistently underrepresented in the political process. Not only do the poor lack the ability to buy influence, but many of the people living in slums are migrants who do not have the right to vote in local elections or are purposefully undercounted by local politicians and slumlord elites who stand to gain from disenfranchising the poor.

The third shortage is closely linked to the first two shortages, but might be the most important: the shortage of public health services within slums. Poor health—due to a lack of sanitation and overcrowding—can lead to a health trap that keeps many slum residents from working productively and, as a result, keeps them trapped in poverty and sickness. According to one study of slums in Bangladesh, 82 percent of residents had been debilitated as a result of sickness within the last 30 days.[7] In Dharavi, 78 percent of the more than 3 million residents do not have access to private latrines, and more than half of the total Indian population defecates outdoors. The result is persistent, recurring illness. Despite increases in income and food consumption levels in India, more than 65 million children remain malnourished. In fact, one-third of middle-to-high-income children are malnourished in India, reflecting the fact that poor health has as much to do with a general lack of sanitation and health as the amount of food eaten.[8]

It is often hard to see a place with fresh eyes, even when visiting it for the first time. The traveler always brings their own baggage of personal experiences and preconceived notions with them on their visits. I could not help but bring Charles Dickens's eyes with me on my first visit to a slum. Dickens described the slums of 19th-century London in these dire and, to me, unforgettable terms:

> It is a black, dilapidated street, avoided by all decent people . . . these tumbling tenements contain, by night, a swarm of misery. As, on the human wretch, vermin parasites appear, so, these ruined shelters have bred a crowd of foul existence that crawls in and out of gaps in the walls and boards; and coils itself to sleep, in maggot numbers, where the rain drips in; and comes and goes, fetching and carrying fever, and sowing more evil in its every footprint . . .[9]

But after I had actually visited one, I saw that Dickens only portrayed a small part of what is actually going on in slums. My first trip to a slum was in Soweto, South Africa. Soweto is the township close to Johannesburg where many blacks—including Nelson Mandela during his formative years—were forcibly segregated by apartheid laws from nearby, largely white Johannesburg. While the apartheid system ended in 1994, the segregation remains. Soweto has an official population of 1.3 million people, but its actual population is nearly three times that when counting the migrant workers from rural South Africa and Zimbabwe that live there for large parts of the year. The slums in Soweto and in many other large slums across the world exist as a place to live, not to work. There is little industry in Soweto, or really any economic activity at all beyond basic retail shops. People live in Soweto so that they can gain access to jobs outside Soweto. In that sense, it is not only a racial ghetto but also an economic ghetto; a place where living is kept separate from work and where economic opportunity can only be found by leaving.

Today there are more and more middle- and even upper-class neighborhoods in Soweto as more blacks have found economic success in the major economic hub of Johannesburg but want to enjoy the vibrant cultural life and social dynamism that exists in Soweto. (This evolution from slum to gentrified neighborhood has occurred in New York, London, and most modern rich metropolises.) However, when visiting one of the poorest areas of Soweto, called Kliptown, the real implications of segregation from larger economic development become apparent. Small shacks built of corrugated metal and spare wood—meant to be temporary but remaining all too permanent—lined narrow dirt lanes and water and trash-filled ditches. Only one public toilet and one water tap had been built by the government for every 100 people in Kliptown. As night was falling, a steady rain began and as lightning flashed, I looked up to see only the netting of jury-rigged electrical wires between the shacks and tilting power poles. With no sewage system, rainwater overflowed the ditches and the muddy lanes, pooling in front of and then into many of the lower-lying shacks. Invited into one of these shacks, I saw that the dirt floors were so damp that the furniture was slowly sinking right into it. School-aged children struggled to read under a single, low-wattage bulb that faintly lit only a third of the room in a rough circle. Thick smoke hung in the air from wood stoves, dimming the room to such an extent that it was hard to see the faces of my hosts as they talked about the challenges they faced living where they do.

All of the cooking and heating in Kliptown was done in wood stoves. The dangerous health implications of indoor air pollution from charcoal cooking stoves is one of the clearest examples of how much different it is to live in the rich world than in the poor. In the poor world, indoor air pollution is one of the leading causes of death by causing cancer and cardiovascular disease, and by promoting lower respiratory infections, such as tuberculosis and pneumonia, which are the most frequent causes of death in developing countries. Interestingly, the next most common killers in less developed countries are diarrhea, HIV, malaria, low birthrates, neonatal infections, and birth trauma. All of these are diseases are preventable, to one degree or another, with sufficient medical resources and behavioral changes. To say this another way, the poor tend to die of things directly linked to their lack of income.

But people are not wholly defined by their income levels, poverty is not always hopeless, and slums are not just prisons of misery. As I spent more time in Soweto, including a second trip that I made later with my family, we repeatedly had heartwarming experiences with the incredibly open and friendly people who live there. On a bike tour of Soweto, which became more of a parade than a tour, people from up and down the lanes came out to wave and say hello. Kids ran after us slapping our hands and waving and singing (for those few hours I felt as if I knew what it was like to be a member of the British royal family). So many people stopped us to talk that it was overwhelming, but also life-affirming. Grandmothers came out of nowhere, kissing the tops of our kids' heads. An older woman came up to my wife and said "Now that you have visited, you have to come here and live! You can be my neighbor, and we will love you and cook for you!!"

It took me a few more visits to different slums in different parts of the world such as Argentina, Belize, China, Botswana, Namibia, and even in the United States to fully understand that slums are not always the inescapable poverty traps that Dickens described and that I first saw. On a trip to the Dharavi slum in Mumbai, I observed that in contrast to Soweto, Dharavi is a place where people both live and work. Here, people are regularly using their homes as their workplace, engaged in jobs that are either too dirty, too hard, too regulated, or require too many bribes to do in other areas of the city; for example, sorting and recycling plastics and metal waste, tanning leather, and making earthen pottery and bricks. In effect, Dharavi is an economic empowerment zone, a place largely separate from the reach of dysfunctional Indian laws, public corruption, shocking bureaucracy, and stifling social norms such as caste prejudice. Because of this relative freedom, the dominant fact of life within Dharavi is activity. Everyone and everything is in constant motion. Piles of plastics are assembled and moved, bricks are hauled from where they are kilned to where they are shipped, and chemicals for processing leather are lugged to the poorest areas of Dharavi where people with few other job options work diligently while breathing in the stinking, toxic fumes.

The fact that Dharavi has become a booming entrepreneurial center has increased rents there to developed-world levels. In 2014, the rent for a 4-meter by 4-meter room (the standard size of a bedroom in an American house) was more than $200 a month (monthly per capita income in India is only $125 a month). Rents in Dharavi are higher than outside of Dharavi because of the greater freedom the owner has in how the space can be used. Of course, the negative impacts of many of the activities that go on within Dharavi, such as pollution, are felt everywhere else in Mumbai.

Slums can serve as poverty traps for many residents because of the shortages of investment, public services, and public health that can create a vicious circle of poverty: The poor are poor in part because they live in a slum, but the poor can only live in slums because they are poor. By tracking the people who live in slums, researchers have found that those who have lived in a slum the longest also tend to be the poorest. In the slums of Kolkata, India, over 70 percent of its residents have lived in the slums for over 15 years.[10] However, living in a slum can also serve as a potential springboard to getting ahead and then getting out. People are attracted to slums because they represent greater economic opportunity than elsewhere. The fundamental truth about slums is that their existence reflects the fact that the urban poor are richer than the rural poor.[11] People choose to live in slums because things are relatively good there. Slums similar to Dharavi existed in the United States and Europe as they made a similar evolution from rural to urban-centered economies during the Industrial Revolution. With all of these factors in mind, slums are best viewed as staging areas for the painful transformation that rural migrants must make in order to obtain a higher quality of life in urban areas, and represent a choice to pursue a better life, not necessarily an inescapable trap in a bad one.

Despite the economic opportunities that slums present, and beneath the sense of happiness that many residents gain by living in these close-knit communities, there is also a palpable sense of unease within the slums I have visited. Not unease because of any real physical danger—in fact, many of the world's slums are also some of the most statistically safe places to live in terms of crime. The unease was due to the fact that to live in poverty is not only difficult, but it is also risky. One reason is that the poor get sick more often. The poor often lack access to safe drinking water, public sanitation, and adequate medical care. In addition, persistent hunger plays a role in poor health, impacting 15 percent of the population in developing countries but nearly one-third of its children. As a result, the average life expectancy of those living in extreme poverty is 20 years less than it is among those living in developed countries.[12] How many children growing up in extreme poverty live long enough to see their children raised to adulthood and then see their grandchildren? Not nearly enough.

But the most important, and often ignored, sources of risk in the lives of the poor is the fact that when you live on a dollar or two a day, you likely do not actually get a dollar or two each and every day. Some days you might earn $10, and for the next five days you get nothing. This is because those who live in extreme poverty often do not have regular employment, but instead are typically self-employed entrepreneurs, offering their services as day workers or street vendors without a regular source of income. Even when the poor have regular employment, they do not have access to many of the services that those of us living in developed countries have that give us a measure of security. Often there is no social safety net, no public health facilities, no unemployment insurance, no disability insurance, or no retirement insurance, etc. Even more importantly, most of the poor do not have access to financial services, such as credit cards, loans, savings accounts, or life insurance. One study finds that 40 to 80 percent of people in emerging economies lack access to formal banking services.[13] As a result, any negative event—a family member getting sick, a natural disaster, someone losing their job, a theft—threatens to tip even the most financially stable households into crisis. While many households can rely on informal means of finance—such as wage advances, store credit, not paying bills on time, borrowing from neighbors, and pawning their goods—these methods are undependable and expensive.[14] Informal loans typically have annual interest rates between 40 and 200 percent a year in less developed countries. As a result, life is more stressful for the poor, not simply because of their low levels of income but because of the instability of their income and the risk that comes along with it.

While the level of poverty in many countries is often shocking, it is magnified by the disparity in incomes both between and within countries. First, there is great disparity in average incomes between people in different countries. The richest 20 percent of the world's population earn 75 percent of the world's income, while the poorest 20 percent earn only 5 percent of the world's income. It has not always been this way: Significant income disparities between countries have only existed since the Industrial Revolution in the mid-1700s. This "great divergence" was not the result of poor countries getting poorer; instead, it was the consequence of poor countries growing slowly while rich countries grew much more rapidly. In the year 1000 CE, the less developed world of today was actually slightly richer than the developed world of today—the two richest regions of the world at that time were China and the Middle East. Today, per-capita income in the five richest countries is more than 100 times that of per-capita income in the five poorest countries.[15]

The income disparity within the population of poorer countries can be just as shocking. As ranked by their Gini coefficients, which is a statistical measure of income inequality between people within a country, only 3 of the 50 countries with the worst income inequality in the world are developed countries (Hong Kong with the 11th, Singapore with the 26th, and the United States with the 41st worst income inequality). The 10 countries with the most unequal incomes are all in Sub-Saharan Africa or Latin America.[16]

Mumbai is often referred to as THE megacity of the 21st century, a growing economic center of a rapidly emerging market economy. Mumbai is mammoth: Greater Mumbai's population in 2012 was over 20 million, and is expected to be over 28 million by 2020—it's adding a million new people per year. Already the largest city in the world, its population will add the equivalent of New York City's population in less than a decade. Mumbai is also the richest city in India, with income nearly twice as large as the rest of India on a per-capita basis, and it accounts for a disproportionate amount of India's international trade and financial transactions. Unfortunately, Mumbai is also an example of the sad trend toward worsening income inequality. In this city of Bollywood movie stars and international financiers, a remarkable 55 percent of the population currently lives in unregistered housing or in slums such as Dharavi. Over 6.5 million people in Mumbai have no permanent shelter.

I talked previously about how expensive rents are in Dharavi and other slums in India. Mumbai is also the most expensive city for purchasing real estate in the world. Mumbai is an island with little transportation infrastructure linking it to larger areas of land, creating a shortage of space and housing. But prices are also driven up by skyrocketing demand, primarily because there are so many poor living so close to a growing number of super-rich. It is estimated that it would take more than 300 years for an average Indian citizen to pay for a 100-square-meter piece of real estate (about the size of a studio apartment) in Mumbai.[17] However, for many of the rich, these high prices are nothing but an investment opportunity.

Within sight of Dharavi and other slums stands Antilia, the world's first billion-dollar (that "b" is not a typo) private residence. It was built by the petrochemical mogul Mukesh Ambani, the fifth richest man in the world according to *Forbes* magazine. The 40-story tower houses his wife, three children, and a few of the 600 full-time workers needed to maintain the residence within its 38,000 square meters of space. It includes a six-story

The billion-dollar Antilia mansion that overlooks Dharavi (the black building on the left).

parking garage, three helipads (I have never seen one helicopter in Mumbai), and a few other necessities such as an ice room with man-made snowstorms to help the family cool off in the face of Mumbai's oppressive heat.

Of course, you don't have to travel to a place as poor as India to experience inequality. As mentioned above, the United States has one of the most unequal income distributions in the world. In 2011, the top 1 percent earned as much income as the bottom 50 percent (and 20 percent of all income).[18] Worsening income inequality is worrying for a number of economic, political, and societal reasons. However, one important difference between inequality in rich and poor countries is that the living conditions of everyone across the distribution are higher in the developed world. Developed countries largely experience relative poverty, not absolute poverty along the lines of the World Bank's $1.25 a day standard. Using definitions of poverty based on the income needed to "consume those goods and services commonly taken for granted by members of mainstream society," the poverty line in the United States in 2012 was $23,050 for a family of four (or slightly less than $16 a day per person). By these standards, 16 percent of the U.S. population was living in poverty in 2012. Poverty ranges from 8.8 percent of individuals in New Hampshire to 21.3 percent in Mississippi.[19] The poverty rate in the United States is similar to the average poverty rate in the European Union. However, poverty rates vary quite a bit across Europe, in part because different countries use different measures of relative poverty.

How do economists measure income in the first place so that they can determine who is living in poverty and who is not? Typically, economists use a measure of total income called Gross Domestic Product, or GDP, which is an imposing-sounding name for what is a pretty simple concept. GDP is simply the value of all the goods and services produced within a country over a period of time, where value is measured by using market prices. The difficulty in calculating GDP is not in understanding what it is, but in hunting down the quantities and prices of all of the goods and services produced within an economy. This leads to one of the problems GDP has in accurately measuring actual income in a county: Many goods get missed in GDP, particularly goods and services that are not produced within formal markets. Such informal production is common across the world, but particularly in less developed countries where many people don't have regular jobs and most work on a piecemeal basis or for themselves. Economists estimate that 40 to 60 percent of GDP is missed in less developed countries because of our inability to directly measure informal production. The upshot of all this is that income as measured by GDP is significantly underestimated in less developed countries. It also means that the income disparities between rich countries and poor countries are often exaggerated by using GDP alone as a measure of well-being.

Another problem with GDP is gender bias. GDP is seen by many critics as being explicitly biased against women because women spend twice as much time working in informal markets as men. These critics argue that by ignoring "household work," GDP diminishes women's contribution to household income, and also ignores the incredible inequality that exists because women do most of the unpaid but important work—such as raising children—in any society. By one estimate, including unpaid work by women would boost GDP in the United States by 25 percent in 2010, although this amount is significantly less today than in the past because so many women have entered the formal labor force since the 1950s.[20] Looking at a broader group of 27 countries, estimates of unpaid household work range between 15 percent (in Canada) and 43 percent (in Portugal) of GDP.[21]

Sometimes GDP is used not just to measure income in a country, but also as a measure of the "well-being" of its citizens. But GDP is an imperfect measure of well-being because GDP encompasses a very narrow conception of what matters to people: Its focus is on market income alone. As a result, GDP by itself does not consider things such as income distribution. It says nothing about what goods and services are actually being produced: guns or food, it is all the same. Finally, GDP focuses only on production and ignores the side effects, both positive and negative, of this production. For example, if a rain forest in Brazil is clear cut, the value of the trees is added to Brazilian GDP, but the pollution or lost environmental benefits of those trees is not subtracted from GDP in Brazil or anywhere else. The negative side effects of production that impact people other than just the buyers and sellers is what economists refer to as *negative externalities*. On the other hand, GDP also ignores many positive side effects of production (*positive externalities*). For example, money directly spent on education is included in GDP, but the many positive societal and family benefits that come from having a more educated population— more informed citizens, more creative ideas, more stable families, better health—are ignored by GDP.

Economists regularly use GDP as a way to compare income levels across countries—but again, there are problems with doing this. GDP is measured in terms of market prices, but market prices in India are expressed in Indian rupees, and in China they are expressed in Chinese renminbi (RMB). An adjustment needs to be made in order to account for differences in the value of the two currencies in which local prices are expressed. The simplest way to do this would be just go and look up the current market exchange rate between the rupee and RMB. The problem with this easy solution is that market exchange rates vary greatly on a day-to-day basis, as any experienced foreign traveler can well attest. During the East Asian financial crisis in 1997, the Indonesian currency (the rupiah) declined by 40 percent relative to the U.S. dollar in a matter of days. If you were using this market exchange rate to compare GDPs, Indonesian income relative to U.S. income fell by 40 percent despite the fact that the actual production and standards of living within the two countries had not changed. This makes economists hesitant to use current market exchange rates to compare GDP if we are trying to accurately assess the relative standards of living of people across countries.

Another limitation of using current market exchange rates when comparing GDP has to do with the fact that exchange rates are often manipulated by governments. They do this through monetary policy (changing the supply of their currency) or through currency controls that restrict who can hold their currency outside of the country. Take China, for instance. In an effort to keep the international price of their exports cheap, China has used monetary policy and currency controls to keep the RMB undervalued. This has a number of important effects on growth in China and across the world, but most significantly for this discussion, using China's undervalued exchange rate to compare GDPs makes China look a lot poorer than it actually is—at least 50 percent poorer relative to the United States according to some estimates.

One final problem with using current market exchange rates when comparing GDP is evident to both economists and to any traveler. Within any country, there are goods traded on international markets—e.g., cell phones, brand name clothing (not rip-offs), cars—and there are local goods that are not traded internationally—e.g., restaurant meals, local clothing, and personal services. Because the prices of internationally traded goods are determined by world markets, they do not differ very much between countries (although they will differ at the margin because of taxes and transportation costs). In fact, exchange rates over time tend to adjust to reflect the fact that internationally traded goods should sell at roughly the same price across countries. For example, if internationally traded goods are cheaper in Mexico than they are in the United States, smart entrepreneurs will buy more of these goods in Mexico and ship them to the United States, eventually putting upward pressure on the peso exchange rate until the price differences begin to disappear. This idea—that internationally goods that are freely traded between countries should also have similar prices across countries—is often referred to in economics as the *law of one price*.

There is solid evidence that the law of one price is a good, but rough, description of how prices and exchange rates move over long periods of time between countries. However, the law of one price only applies to internationally traded goods. The prices of local goods are likely to be much lower in poorer countries because of lower labor costs, which is one reason why local food, services, and housing in less developed countries usually seems dirt cheap to those of us traveling from developed countries. As a result, if you use market exchange rates to value the local currency, you are using exchange rates that are adjusting to make internationally traded goods similar in price, not the cheap local goods. This means that using market exchange rates to place a value on the local currency typically creates a downward bias for poor countries (i.e., their currency buys less in U.S. dollars on international markets than it actually buys in local markets). As a result, market exchange rates for the local currency tends to make the cost of living look higher and people look poorer in less developed countries than they actually are. Using market exchange rates to make cross-country comparisons in GDP will consistently make richer countries look better and poorer ones look worse.

To correct for the problems with market exchange rates, economists calculate what is referred to as *purchasing power parity (PPP) exchange rates.* Here, the PPP exchange rate is the exchange rate that makes the price of the same basket of commonly consumed goods the same across two countries. In other words, the PPP exchange rate is the exchange rate that actually compares the cost of similar goods across countries, not the market exchange rate that only reflects the price of internationally traded goods. PPP exchange rates better reflect true standards of living in poor countries and form the basis of a more accurate comparison of income across countries. Often the differences are large—many poorer countries will become 50 percent richer using PPP exchange rates than market exchange rates. For example, in 2013, Mexico's per-capital GDP in U.S. dollars was nearly 50 percent higher ($15,563 vs. $10,629) using PPP exchange rates to calculate GDP instead of current market exchange rates.

Of course, PPP exchange rates have their problems as well. One of the biggest is that no two countries consume the same baskets of goods—samp (ground corn kernels) and pap (sorghum porridge) would be relatively heavily weighted in the basket of Botswana goods, while beans and tomatoes would be relatively heavily weighted in the basket of Mexican goods. Also, many goods—take, for example, health care services—differ widely in quality across countries. But economists have devised technical ways of minimizing these biases in the baskets consumed so that GDP measured according to PPP exchange rates gives an imperfect but roughly accurate measure of relative incomes between countries. As a result, when I talk about income levels across countries in this book, I will be using PPP exchange rates so that we can have the most accurate comparisons.

You might be asking yourself why I am spending so much time talking about the wonky details of calculating GDP as opposed to a topic that might be even mildly interesting. My objective here is, in part, to give you a sense of the many small but important things that economists have to think about when it comes to actually measuring even the seemingly simplest of concepts. Economics is not always the easy, sexy, fun-loving science that most people think it is. But most importantly, I think that one of the best things that you can learn from economics is a skepticism about everything, and particularly of quantitative data. There is a common perception that "the numbers don't lie," but the truth lies closer to the saying popularized by Mark Twain that there are "lies, damned lies, and statistics."[22] No concept as complex as "well-being" or "standards of living" can be captured in a single statistic; to attempt to do so is necessarily going to give an incomplete, and often inaccurate, picture. An important part of thinking like an economist is to not just accept the numbers at their face values, but to recognize that they are inherently two-faced.

Why don't economists just focus on some other measure of economic well-being, such as life expectancy or infant mortality or some psychological measure of happiness? There are two reasons why economists are reluctant to abandon GDP despite its limitations. First, these other measures of development have their own problems and focus too much on their own very narrow aspects of well-being. As I just said: any number used in isolation is potentially misleading. For example, while life expectancy is important, it is influenced by many factors that have little to do with the quality of people's lives while they are actually living. Second, economists have confidence in GDP because GDP is strongly related to a very wide variety of alternative measures of development. Countries with high levels of GDP also have higher life expectancy, lower infant mortality, better health, and higher literacy among other measures of well-being.

The Nobel Prize–winning economist Amartya Sen contends that possessing freedom, not things, is the best measure of a country's development.[23] He argues that countries need to be evaluated "in terms of their actual effectiveness in enriching the lives and liberties of people—rather than taking them to be valuable in themselves." In his opinion, countries make a mistake when they attempt to sacrifice personal freedoms, or democracy, in an attempt to spur economic growth through brute force. But measuring freedom and using it as a proxy for well-being suffers from many of the same limitations as using GDP. Freedom is a qualitative characteristic that cannot be easily quantified. There is also the problem of weighing which freedoms are most important to society. For example, is religious freedom more important to society than political freedom or access to health care? Finally, many freedoms are in conflict: one person's freedom to practice their religion, such as forcing people to obey the Sabbath and close businesses, infringes on another person's economic freedom to earn extra income or hit the shopping malls on the weekend. In the end, the fact of the matter is that, as Sen recognizes, GDP is closely correlated with many different types of freedom. Higher incomes open up a broader range of choices for people to make; more income increases people's "capabilities" in Sen's terminology. Higher incomes mean greater freedom to choose the job you want, not just a job that you need to survive. Higher incomes allow for more mobility and freedom through travel. Higher incomes also enable education, which allows people to make more informed choices and which improves their quality of life in many different ways. Higher incomes also increase access to health care, increasing health and life expectancy. As a result, GDP is likely to be as good a measure of freedom as any other imperfect measure of freedom.

Economists also continue to stick with GDP because we observe that countries with higher GDPs are, in fact, more satisfied with their lives. According to the Gallup World Poll, people in countries with higher GDPs have higher self-reported levels of life satisfaction. In fact, a doubling of GDP doubles the mean level of life satisfaction within a country.[24] Of course, measures of life satisfaction have their own limitations because it is always unclear exactly what "satisfaction" is capturing. A few psychologists have instead attempted to estimate levels of self-reported "happiness" across countries and have found that the richer you are, the happier you are.[25] The problem with happiness, however, is that it is an emotion, not a state of being, as illustrated by the speech of Mr. Micawber in Charles Dickens's *David Copperfield*: "Annual income twenty pounds, annual expenditures nineteen pounds nineteen and six, result happiness. Annual income twenty pounds, annual expenditures twenty pounds ought and six, result misery."[26]

We also know that GDP is a useful tool for measuring economic development because GDP growth is closely related to changes in poverty. Many studies have validated the argument that faster GDP growth reduces poverty rates among those living in extreme poverty.[27] One comprehensive study by the World Bank reports that in the 1990s across 14 poor countries, a 1 percent increase in GDP reduced poverty by 1.7 percent—an amazingly large impact.[28] The fact that GDP growth in the less developed world has risen over the last three decades is the primary reason behind one of the biggest stories in the entirety of human history: the precipitous fall in the number of people across the globe living in extreme poverty. In 1990, 43 percent (1.9 billion people) of the population in developing countries lived in extreme poverty. This number fell to 21 percent by 2010, and is projected to fall to 4 percent ("only" 200 million) by 2030.[29] This fall in poverty is directly related to a dramatic increase in GDP growth; GDPs in developing countries grew 1.5 percent faster from 1990 to 2010 than they did from 1960 to 1990. The most dramatic example of the relationship between rising GDP growth and falling poverty is China. Between 1981 and 2010, while GDP growth averaged 8 percent a year, China lifted 680 million out of poverty—twice the population of the United States! But even outside of China, GDP growth has risen, and the number of people living in extreme poverty has fallen by an additional 280 million over this same time. Faster income growth, as measured by GDP, is remaking the lives of billions of people and is one of the happiest, and often overlooked, developments shaping the world that we travel in today.

Along with alleviating poverty across the world, rising global GDP has also driven dramatic improvements in health. If we take a long view of history, higher incomes have not always led to healthier lifestyles. The first massive step toward economic development in human history was the Neolithic Revolution 10,000 years ago when humans in the Fertile Crescent region of what we refer to today as the Middle East moved away from hunter-gatherer societies and toward stationary agriculture and animal husbandry. Because agriculture increased disease (most human diseases mutate from animals), reduced hygiene (because of increased population density), and reduced the diversity of diets, the Neolithic Revolution may have increased food production at the cost of worsening health and life expectancy. However, this first step in economic development eventually led to the Industrial Revolution in the mid-1700s, when dramatic increases in income, knowledge (such as the development of germ theory), and technology (public sanitation, antibiotics, and vaccinations) allowed for remarkable improvements in health. For example, in the United States, average life expectancy has increased from 47.3 years for children born in 1900 to 78.8 years for children born in 2014. Along with these increases in the quantity of life, there have also been other important increases in the quality of life: lower disability rates, higher IQs, and increasing adult height attests to our improved fitness.

Today, global health has improved, even in those countries that have seen little growth in their own incomes. Every country in the world has seen its infant mortality rates fall since 1950, and nearly every country in the world has increased its life expectancy. In fact, increases in life expectancy have been largest in poor countries. However, low income is still closely related to poor health. Life expectancy in Sub-Saharan Africa, for example, still remains 26 years below that of rich countries, and more than one-fourth of all children in the region die before they reach five years of age; these are worse health statistics than the United States had in 1900 before the general acceptance of germ theory. Today, the average Indian male is 15 centimeters shorter than the average Englishman. While average height is growing in India, it will take more than 200 years for the average height of Indian males to catch up with English males, and 500 years for the same thing to happen for Indian women.[30]

While income and health are clearly related, the relationship is not as simple as it might first seem. Economists have identified a turning point in the relationship between health and income referred to as the *epidemiological transition*.[31] In countries with lower income levels, most deaths occur among the young and are the result of infectious diseases, such as malaria, tuberculosis, and the flu (the things that people in rich countries were dying from 200 years ago). At higher income levels, most deaths are among older adults and are the result of chronic diseases such as heart disease and cancer. This epidemiological transition point is approximately at per-capita GDP levels of $10,000 a year; roughly where China, Egypt, and Indonesia are today. The good news for countries below this transition point is that future improvements in health are within their grasp because the most common causes of illness are preventable with existing medicines, improved public health, and more vaccinations. A dollar spent on health in countries below this transition point has a much bigger impact than a dollar spent on health above this point. The bad news is that these dollars are hard to come by in poor countries. Per-capita health expenditure in Sub-Saharan Africa is $100 a year, compared to England and the United States where they are $3,470 and $8,300 a year, respectively.[32] Such vast differences are hard to comprehend and even harder to accept.

In sum, higher GDP means more freedom, less poverty, better health, and more life satisfaction among many other measures of quality of life. While GDP is not a perfect measure of well-being, it gets as close as any single statistic can.

Even as the number of people living in extreme poverty falls and average global incomes rise, a great deal of income inequality still exists between countries. So how is the traveler to understand all of this disparity between the haves and have-nots? What are the most important factors that make rich countries rich and poor countries poor? This last question has puzzled philosophers since the Age of Enlightenment. One of the earliest and most influential attempts to answer this question was the theory of mercantilism. Mercantilism predates economics as a discipline and asserts that countries become rich when they export more than they import and accumulate reserves of gold in the process. According to mercantilism, the existence of poverty is one of the most important factors that serve to make a country rich; poverty provides a source of cheap labor that merchants can exploit to produce inexpensive exports that are the foundation of wealth. In the words of the Dutch mercantilist philosopher Bernard de Mandeville, "In a free nation where slaves are not allow'd of, the surest wealth consists in a multitude of laborious poor."[33] Mercantilist thinking played a huge role in justifying the repressive colonial policies and domestic labor regulations adopted by many European countries before the Industrial Revolution. Mercantilism was a pre-growth theory in that it viewed trade as a zero-sum activity: everyone who gains must do so at the expense of someone else. The rich become rich because they exploit the poor, but overall wealth is stagnant.

Economics as a discipline of study began when Adam Smith debunked mercantilism and its justification for economic oppression as the primary source of wealth. Smith's book *An Inquiry into the Nature and Causes of the Wealth of Nations*, as the title makes clear, focuses on this question of why rich countries are rich and poor countries are poor. Before he wrote this book, Smith served as a tutor and spent three years traveling in Europe. What he saw on his travels greatly informed the writing of his *magnum opus*—illustrating that traveling and observation have always been at the heart of economics. All of the most influential economists since Adam Smith—economists that we will talk about later in the book such as David Ricardo, Thomas Malthus, John Maynard Keynes, Friedrich Hayek, and others—added to our understanding of this question about why incomes differ so much across countries and across people. In each case, the thinking of these great economic minds was informed by their own travels and the observations they made during them.

Like all great inquiries into the human condition, there is no simple answer to this question of why the rich are rich and the poor are poor. The best way to think about answering this question is to first understand the determinants of wealth and poverty from an elevated, broader perspective, then drill down to the deeper causes of economic inequality. I want to begin at the highest, or "helicopter," level, not with Adam Smith (more on him later), but by introducing you to three other economists: Karl Marx, Alfred Marshall, and Robert Solow.

Karl Marx was the ultimate ivory tower academic: a German intellectual who found it difficult to deal with actual humans. Marx did little traveling and never visited any businesses or factories despite spending most of his life in England during the dawn of the Industrial Revolution. Instead, he spent most of his time in cafes and the British museum library (seat G7). In the words of the writer-historian Sylvia Nasar, "He shut out the messy, confusing, shifting world of facts so that he can contemplate the images and ideas in his own head without these bothersome distractions."[34]

Marx made some critical assumptions about economics that were consistently violated in the real world, and Marx failed to notice because he failed to move about and look around. While Marx recognized the incredible increases in production going on around him in England, he viewed it all as unsustainable because he believed that profits could only be generated by increasingly exploiting labor. Marx essentially adopted the mercantilist view that economics is a zero-sum game and that profits can only be made at the expense of workers. As a result, the only way a firm can increase productivity, in Marx's mind, is by getting each worker to work more hours for the same wages. Because making profits through getting workers to work more hours is an unsustainable strategy in the long run (there are only 24 hours a day), the only other way businesses could continue to be profitable is to continually reduce wages. In Marx's reading of history, falling wages would eventually lead to resentment, civil strife, and a revolution that would overthrow the capitalist system and replace it with one in which labor would eventually be in charge and distribute resources equitably.

Setting aside his predictions of revolution, there are many problems with Marx's analysis, the biggest problem being that Marx refused to recognize a crucial fact about the world around him: Wages were rising throughout the late 1800s in England at the same time that Marx was writing about the inevitable collapse of wages. The Marxist/mercantilist view that winners require losers failed to explain what was really going on in the industrializing world. The fact of the matter is that Marx generated a theory of why capitalist economies could not sustain growth while living at a time and in a country that was experiencing dramatic sustained growth. It is a great lesson that should motivate all bookish, academic types to look around them more, and particularly to travel.

The Englishman Alfred Marshall might be thought of as the first modern economist: He was the first to synthesize the insights of early economists such as Adam Smith into a cohesive and comprehensible framework suitable for consumption by the masses. For example, the supply and demand graphs that every undergraduate economics student must grapple with come directly from Marshall's seminal textbook *Principles of Economics*.[35] The desire to understand and deal with poverty, as opposed to simply accepting it as a fact of life like many of his contemporaries, was the primary motivation for Marshall's interest in economics. Marshall wrote in his letters: "The desire to put mankind into the saddle is the mainspring of most economic study."[36] Marshall's active view of economics was also reflected in his active life as a traveler and diligent observer of the economic behavior around him. Marshall visited hundreds of factories and businesses throughout his life (unlike Marx), and his tour of America in 1875 was an important influence in writing his *Principles* book.

If poverty is the result of low wages, Marshall asked himself this: Why then are wages so low? The insight that Marshall gained from his travels was that wages are low when workers are unproductive. When workers do not produce very much, then firms cannot afford to pay them very much either. This is the reason why skilled labor pays more than unskilled labor. The only way that the productivity of labor can increase is for businesses to implement incremental changes to its production processes over time. It is the sum of these persistent changes that creates sustained increases in labor productivity, wages, and standards of living. These incremental changes include purchasing new capital and equipment, incorporating new methods of organization, adopting new technologies, and using accumulated knowledge to produce more with less. In Marshall's view, the primary force driving these incremental changes is competition. During his many visits to firms, Marshall observed how firms were constantly forced to adjust their processes and become more efficient over time in order to stay profitable in the face of competition from other firms making similar changes. Competition is about survival through adapting to the market environment better than other businesses. This requires businesses to continuously provide better and cheaper goods and services that people want and are willing to pay for.

Why don't firms attempt to exploit workers by lowering wages to increase profits, as Marx suggests they will, instead of increasing productivity? In Marshall's view, competition is not about exploitation because there is limited upside in racing to the bottom. Firms cannot sustain profits only by cutting wages, and they know it. Instead, firms try to grow the overall size of their market by competing for the best workers and attracting more customers. The way that they do this is to provide cheaper, better products while at the same time paying higher wages to attract and keep their best workers. Without competition, there are no incentives to make the difficult changes that profit everyone in the end. Competition creates incentives for everyone to attempt to finish first, benefiting society as a whole, as opposed to racing to the bottom and dragging everyone down with them.

Marshall was also one of the first economists to understand the power of compounding, or how small changes, when sustained, build on one another and lead to big differences in levels over time. In his words, the compounding of small advancements is a force that "becomes a little seed that will grow up to a tree of boundless size."[37] Albert Einstein referred to compounding as the greatest mathematical discovery of all time. To illustrate the incredible power of compounding, consider two countries that have similar income levels today, but one is growing at 1 percent a year and the other at 2 percent a year. In 70 years—a little over two generations—the country growing at 2 percent will be twice as rich as the country growing at 1 percent.[38] Compounding means that small differences in economic growth rates lead to big differences in income levels over time. It is an important reason why there is so much income inequality across the globe today—any country that began to grow slightly earlier and/or grew slightly faster finds that the income gap between itself and other countries has expanded over time. It is also the reason why, as Marshall observed, small incremental changes in productivity accumulate into big differences in wages and standards of living if they can be sustained through competition.

In his quest to understand growth and poverty, Marshall placed his aim squarely on the productivity of labor, and it was a bull's-eye. As I will illustrate throughout this book, labor productivity is the cornerstone of standards of living. In the 1950s, MIT economist Robert Solow stepped back and asked a bigger-picture question: Can we more carefully identify exactly where increases in labor productivity come from? Solow's self-effacingly titled paper "A Contribution to the Theory of Economic Growth" won him a Nobel Prize and established the benchmark for how modern economists think about economic growth.[39] In this paper Solow argues, quite unsurprisingly, that there are three aggregate sources of growth within any economy: the quantity of labor, the quantity of capital, and technology. This doesn't seem quite worthy of a Nobel Prize, does it? But Solow's real contribution was in arguing that one of these three factors was far and away the most important in explaining increases in the productivity of labor and economic growth. Let's consider each of the candidates one at a time.

First, let's think about the quantity of labor. There are limits to how much a country can grow *on a per-capita basis* by getting people to work more, to enter the labor force, or to work harder—eventually it is bound to hit a limit because there are only so many hours in a day and only so many people who can work. The more sustainable way to increase labor and growth is to increase the quality of labor. But there are two significant difficulties in increasing the quality of labor. First, spending more money and time on education does not necessarily translate into improving the quality of labor. The relationship between the quantity and quality of education is one of the most pondered, but still remarkably unclear, puzzles in economics. Across countries, there is no relationship in the data between public expenditures on education and aggregate income levels.[40] Note that we are talking about aggregate spending on education, not about the actual quality of the education provided with this spending. The lack of a relationship between education spending and income likely reflects the fact that it is difficult to measure a good education, and that using education spending is not a particularly good proxy for quality. The second constraint on increasing the quality of labor is that that time itself is limited. There are only 24 hours in a day, seven days in a week, 52 weeks in a year, and 78 years in a life (20 years less than that, on average, if you live in a poor country). There are physical limits to the amount of time that can be spent increasing the quality of labor, and every hour spent on education is an hour that is not spent earning income.

Just to be clear: the argument here is not that disparities in labor are unimportant in explaining income differences. It is that there are good reasons to think that differences in the quantity and quality of labor are not the most important factors in explaining differences in income.

Next, let's consider the role of physical capital in generating income growth. To the eye of a traveler, one of the most obvious differences between rich and poor countries is that the rich workers have access to more equipment that makes them more productive. It's not surprising that the farmer in Iowa is richer than the rural farmer in China, as one is using tractors and combines while the other is using shovels and ox-drawn plows. However, there are good reasons to think that differences in physical capital are not the most important factor in explaining differences in income. Once again, there are limits to the role that physical capital alone can play in generating income. One limit is that most capital is costly, and every unit of capital that is produced represents consumption that cannot take place. Every tractor that is made can be thought of as a car that is not produced. So making more capital goods does not by itself increase income; it only does this over time if these capital goods increase productivity.

However, having more capital alone does not always increase productivity and increase income. One reason is that capital is often not allocated to its most efficient uses (this is what economists call *malinvestment*, which we will talk more about later). But right now let's focus on the biggest limit to growth driven by physical capital alone: the *Law of Diminishing Marginal Returns*. There are few laws in economics—some might say because most of what economists say is criminal. The real reason is that there are few principles in economics that are uncontradictable. Diminishing Marginal Returns is one of these principles. So bear with me as I discuss its subtleties, because a grasp of Diminishing Marginal Returns is one of the most effective means of refuting lazy economic thinking about why different countries grow at different rates.

The Law of Diminishing Marginal Returns says that as the amount of physical capital increases, everything else being equal, the productivity gains from adding more physical capital begin to fall. This concept is quite intuitive: The first tractor that a farmer buys is very productive, but the second and third tractors are less and less so. At some point, adding more and more capital to production, keeping the other inputs to production the same, will lead to fewer and fewer benefits in terms of increasing productivity and income.

The crucial implication of the Law of Diminishing Marginal Returns is that while a country might be able to increase income for a time by adding more physical capital alone, it can't do it forever. In fact, growing by adding capital alone is less likely to generate growth than increasing the quality of labor alone. Why? Because physical capital is less important in production than labor. If we average across countries, roughly two-thirds of income is paid to labor in the form of wages and salary, while only one-third is paid to physical capital. These relative payments tell us that labor is about twice as important as physical capital in the production process. Why else would businesses be paying twice as much to labor as they pay to capital? As a result, differences in physical capital cannot be the largest determinant of differences in incomes between countries. Trying to grow by increasing physical capital alone is like trying to make a larger pizza by only adding more cheese without adding more crust or toppings. It might work up to a point, but eventually you are just going to be left with the same amount of pizza but a lot of excess cheese. Likewise, trying to expand incomes through capital investment alone is likely, at some point, to leave a country with little additional income and a lot of excess and unproductive capital.

The Law of Diminishing Marginal Returns says that differences in physical capital are not the most important determinant of differences in *income levels* across countries. However, in the short run, differences in capital investment rates can play a large role in explaining differences in *income growth rates*. This is because, according to the law, the first units of capital should be more productive that the last units of capital within a country. In a poor country with relatively little capital, increasing capital investment will increase productivity and growth more than it will in a rich country that is already saturated with capital. This is why the fastest-growing countries in the world are also some of the poorest—they are growing because they have been able to increase their investment rates and build on extremely low levels of physical capital. As these countries obtain more physical capital and become richer, new capital will become less productive and their income growth rates will decline.

Here is the big takeaway: High growth rates are not so much a sign of great economic success as they are signs of past economic failure; likewise, growing more slowly over the long term is one of the consequences of being rich, and it is a small price to pay. The only way that rich countries in Europe could grow at the rates experienced in China and India would be for these countries to destroy their existing stocks of physical capital. This is obviously an idiotic economic policy. It is always better to have high levels of income and slower growth rates than vice versa.

To the extent that differences in income do reflect differences in physical capital, the Law of Diminishing Returns says that these differences should disappear over time; in other words, there should be convergence in income. This is, in fact, what we observe among developed countries: Developed countries that were the poorest 50 years ago have grown the fastest since that time, narrowing the gap between the income levels of rich countries. A good example of how this occurred can be seen in comparing Europe and the United States after World War II. Because the war was largely fought on European territory, it was Europe's physical capital that was destroyed, creating significant differences in income that have disappeared over time as capital has been rebuilt in Europe and the Law of Diminishing Returns has done its work. But when we compare rich countries to poor countries, we see no convergence. That tells us that differences in income levels cannot be the result of differences in capital alone.

In our quest to determine which factor plays the most important role in determining differences in income, having ruled out labor and capital, we are left with one: technology. To paraphrase the Bible, now these three things remain: not faith, hope, and love, but labor, physical capital, and technology. But the greatest of these is technology. Technology is the one factor that does not suffer from natural limits or the constraints of diminishing marginal returns. In fact, technology is the way that economies offset the diminishing marginal returns to capital and labor. The only limit to technology is our own creativity. It is technology that allows us to produce more outputs with the same number of inputs. Technology is the most important factor in driving economic growth.

The primacy of technology in determining income is a difficult proposition for many people to accept. They look around and see the need for oil, steel, engines, equipment, and computers, and they say "Doesn't this mean that natural resources and physical capital are the key to being rich?" But the fact of the matter is that we don't really need these things—what we need is energy, transportation, means of communication, and ways to store information. Satisfying our needs is not always a matter of having more *things*; it is a matter of generating *ideas* that transform the way that we provide for these needs. Fifty years ago, who would have thought that our desire for human interaction could be met with the tiny cell phones we have in our pockets? New ideas embodied in new technologies allow us to meet our needs in ways that do not require as many physical resources, essentially allowing us to produce more with less. We have found ways to turn water and wheels into transportation, the sun into energy, electromagnetic waves into means of communication, and sand into silicon that in turn can be turned into computer chips to store information. In the words of Paul Romer:

> Every generation has perceived the limits to growth that finite resources and undesirable side effects would pose if no new recipes or ideas were discovered. And every generation has underestimated the potential for finding new recipes and ideas. We consistently fail to grasp how many ideas remain to be discovered. The difficulty is the same as we have with compounding. Possibilities do not add up. They multiply.[41]

But while we know that technology is important, the problem for economists becomes measuring just how important it is. Technology is not directly measurable; we can't go out and quantify technology growth as it is happening. In fact, the way that Solow chose to measure technology's contribution to higher incomes was as a residual: Take total income and subtract out the measurable contribution of labor and capital. He called what is left over *total factor productivity* (TFP), which is a fancy term for "everything that contributes to growth that we can't really measure." TFP does capture the contribution of technology to growth. But it also captures many other factors which impact growth that may or may not be related to technology.

What Solow found in his empirical results is that TFP accounts for roughly two-thirds of income growth in the United States, with changes in capital accounting for most of the remaining one-third. Labor contributed relatively little, with almost all of the changes in the labor force in the United States related to the increase in the number of women who entered the work force after World War II. Economists after Solow have tried to refine these estimates. For example, economists have tried to more accurately measure labor and capital and have attempted to better separate the impact of higher quantities of capital from improvements in the quality of capital that result from technology. But as a generalization, this two-thirds number associated with technology's contribution to income is a solid rule of thumb for the United States.

What about in other countries? Despite all of its limitations, measured TFP is strongly related to levels of income across countries. Poor countries have low TFP, and rich countries have high TFP. TFP varies much more across countries than the levels of capital and labor. In fact, differences in TFP explain as much as 90 percent of the differences in income between the richest and poorest countries. To the extent that TFP accurately measures technology, then the rich are rich primarily because they have better technology. In fact, the economic historian Deirdre McCloskey has argued that "capitalism" is a misnomer because capital plays a relatively small role in our market economies. She suggests a better term would be "innovationism."[42]

After decades of economic research on this topic, the preeminence of technology in explaining economic growth might not seem like the most earth-shattering conclusion. However, when one stops to think about the primacy of technology, the implications for economic growth and public policy are profound. What can poor countries do to increase the technology available to its citizens? Why can't the poor simply adopt the technology that already exists in rich countries? If technology is so important, where does it come from? Is technology produced, or does it just occur by happy accidents?

I will repeatedly return to examining the answers to these questions throughout the rest of this book. As travelers, if we want to understand what is going on around us, we have to understand the material conditions that are the basis upon which different ways of living are built. You can't understand the Egyptian pyramids or the Great Wall of China and why they were built, or the British Museum in London and why so many of the world's great artifacts are located there and not in their places of origin, or the Mayan ruins across Central America that attest to the rise and collapse of a great empire, or the chaos of traveling in Zimbabwe to see natural wonders such as Victoria Falls, without first understanding why differences in technology, productivity, and income are so great across countries.

Let's go back, and let me remind you of the way that I defined the study of economics in the preface of this book. The modern view of economics is that it is the study of how people respond to incentives of all sorts, not just financial incentives, but those that satisfy our innate desires to earn positive feedback (or avoid negative feedback). Economists have adopted the term *institutions* to refer to the structures created by societies, families, and governments that shape incentives and influence individual behavior. The use of this word "institutions" is somewhat problematic as it brings to mind an imposing building with marble columns and tall leaded-glass windows—as something that is set in stone and permanent. But this is not what economists mean with they use the word institutions. Economists use the word institutions to mean the laws, rules, practices, and beliefs that influence incentives which, in turn, govern behavior. Because society, culture, and government practices can change over time, so do institutions. And as institutions change, so do the incentives and behaviors they encourage.

To put this view of the world in another way, the perspective of economics is one in which people are not innately different. Human nature is universal, a claim that is widely supported by biological studies that find that the amount of genetic variation found among *Homo sapiens* is very small relative to other species.[43] The incredible varieties of human behavior that we observe in the world are not created by our inherent dissimilarities but are the result of the diversity of our social environments. Poor countries are not poor because they have a heavy dose of "poor" genes in their gene pool. They are poor because they live under a set of institutions and incentives that do not encourage people to engage in productive behaviors that, over the long run, increase income. Their people do not sufficiently invest in education, or save to accumulate capital, or invest in creating and adopting technologies, or start businesses. They do not do these things because these options are blocked and the proper incentives (such as societal pressures or financial payoffs) to get people to do these things are lacking. Likewise, rich countries are not rich because they are genetically superior. Instead, they have developed, or inherited, a set of institutions that create incentives that encourage their people to engage in productive behaviors. These productive behaviors—such as investing in education, physical capital, and particularly technology—have led them to increase their productivity and incomes over time.

This institutional view of economics essentially argues for the importance of nurture over nature when it comes to economic outcomes. It is not what you are born with that is most important but the environment in which you live. It is a view that radically rejects racist explanations of why people are different. It also rejects the social Darwinist view that the rich are somehow the "fittest." Instead, it is a decidedly positive view of humanity: with the proper institutions and incentives in place, any country can develop and improve its standards of living and the welfare of its people.

One point on which I think that every well-traveled person will agree—in fact, it might be the single most important thing that I have learned during my own travels—is that poor countries are not poor because there is a shortage of good, intelligent, hard-working people. In fact, just the opposite. I am consistently amazed at how hard-working most poor people are, working many more hours and at much more demanding jobs than the vast majority of those living in rich countries. Likewise, many poor people have an amazing ability to scheme, think outside the box, and figure out creative workarounds to deal with almost any situation. As one Argentinian businessman once told me: "Argentineans are born entrepreneurs. You have to be entrepreneurial just to make it to work in the morning. Once you are at work, the challenges there seem simple by comparison." But these chaotic societies that constantly demand entrepreneurial skills are also the same chaotic societies that prevent these skills from being put to productive uses. For the billions living in poverty, their entrepreneurial skills are primarily devoted to trying to work the system (for example, avoiding repressive taxes, corruption, and heavy-handed bureaucracy) in order to piece together a day-to-day living instead of trying to produce more and better goods and services, which is the ultimate source of income in any economy.

To put this in another, maybe more colorful, way, we are all entrepreneurs. We are all trying to earn an income to provide for the wants and desires of ourselves as well as our families. Both Mark Zuckerberg and Genghis Khan were trying to earn a living. But for one, the institutions that existed in society rewarded those who had computer programming and social networking skills. For the other, the institutions that existed at the time ensured that the rewards went to the powerful who could organize armies and thrive in warfare. Entrepreneurs are not innately "good"; they can be prodded into constructive or destructive behavior based on the institutions that are in place.

Of course, arguing that institutions are the meta-cause of wealth and poverty doesn't fully answer the question of why the rich are rich and the poor are poor. We'll come back to this big question as the book moves along. For right now, it is enough to establish the primacy of institutions and to be clear about what economists mean when they use this word. Once again, institutions simply mean the factors that influence incentives, which in turn shape behavior.

In order to think a little more deeply about how institutions shape behavior, the next chapter turns to one of the first things that any traveler notices about the place they are visiting: that everyone there is a horrible driver.

CHAPTER TWO

Why Are Drivers in Other Countries So Much Worse Than Back Home?

No place works any different than any other place, really, beyond mere details. The universal human laws—need, love for the beloved, fear, hunger, periodic exaltation, the kindness that rises up naturally in the absence of hunger/fear/pain—are constant, predictable, reliable, universal, and are merely ornamented with the details of local culture. What a powerful thing to know: that one's own desires are mappable onto strangers; that what one finds in oneself will most certainly be found in The Other—perhaps muted, exaggerated, or distorted, yes, but there nonetheless, and thus a source of comfort.
—George Saunders[1]

I can honestly tell you: I am an above average driver. Other people are incompetent and drive erratically. I just occasionally make mistakes. Other people drive aggressively as if they own the road. I am just going with the flow of traffic. Other people never pay attention to what they are doing when behind the wheel. I just get occasionally distracted.

This difference between "I" and "other people" is always brought into the starkest relief when traveling the roads of a foreign country. More likely than not, our first experience when we visit a country outside of the generic, climate-controlled environment of the airport is the time we spend on the road either being chaperoned to our hotel or anxiously trying to drive there ourselves. On the road we see people following different laws, abiding by some of these laws and ignoring others, behaving according to unique customs, and using different modes of transportation than we see back home.

For me, there has been no travel experience quite as discombobulating as my first visit to Mumbai, India. It somehow seemed inhospitable that first-time visitors are so efficiently swept out of a modern airport and immediately placed in the crucible that is Indian traffic. Before I arrived in India, I had read that there are 46 distinct modes of road transport, but my first impression of an actual Indian road was that they missed quite a few. Cars, rickshaws, buses, trucks, combis, bikes, scooters, motorcycles, ox carts, goat carts, cows, horses, pedestrians, and many more, competed for space on a very narrow road bounded by buildings, not guardrails or sidewalks. Arms and legs popped out of many vehicles, while entire families—dad, mom, and up to four kids—rode on one motorcycle. The competition for space was so severe that people had to fight for the space that they already occupied—making progress in the melee seemed almost secondary. Bicycles, pedestrians, and even hawkers (selling to stalled drivers) flowed into the small openings that sporadically appeared amongst the larger cars or trucks like water in a densely bouldered stream. An occasional cow or broken cart served as an additional speed bump to slow traffic. Along the outer edges of the road where footpaths would normally be located, people slept, sold, bought, sat, and begged. Open green space was unimaginable. Pedestrians walked with a purpose, never empty-handed but carrying boxes, food, pots, wood, and children.

In his classic *On the Road*, Jack Kerouac said that "the road is life," and in India that is true.[2] However, while Kerouac envisioned an open road symbolizing freedom and exploration, an Indian road symbolizes man battling against and adapting to his environment. No one in Mumbai appears to be driving with a Kerouacian sense of exploring the open road and appreciating new experiences; driving is more something to be endured and, hopefully, survived. Moving even a few hundred yards in this mess could take hours, and progress was so slow that many businessmen have mobile offices in their cars, complete with a secretary in the back seat with a computer and a printer. Horns of varying pitch, loudness, and duration were deployed so consistently that they quickly became droning background noise, like amplified crickets in a field. Everyone seemed to be following some unique—and from my perspective—unfathomable strategy for getting through the mess. Progress could only be made by employing guile and accepting the possibility of damage to your car. There did not appear to me to be any rules of the road, only suppositions.

There are popular stereotypes about the prowess of drivers in other countries: Latinos drive emotionally; Asians drive erratically; Southern Europeans drive aggressively; and Northern Europeans always follow the rules of the law to the letter, whether they make sense or not. However, these widely held driving stereotypes are just Rorschach tests for the stereotypes one group of people often makes about different groups of people. In fact, it is easy to find many examples of countries in which defining cultural characteristics are inconsistent with their behavior on the roads. I once taught in Botswana in Southern Africa. The Batswana are generally community-minded and laid-back. The country is a quiet, homogenous democracy that has a relatively high level of GDP and low levels of corruption—it's often referred to as Africa's version of Scandinavia. The Batswana are generally relaxed, and the typical pedestrian walks so slowly that it often looks as if people are napping on their feet. But when Batswana get in the car, they drive as if their hair is burning and they are looking for a fire station. Batswana drivers view zebra pedestrian crossings the same way the lions that live there view actual zebras: as a good chance for an easy kill. Every time I got behind the wheel in Botswana, I felt like I was in a stock car race in which I was the only one not trying to win, just to finish. This behavior is difficult to explain by appealing to culture alone.

Are there factors more important than culture that determine the social behaviors that govern the road? What can economics tell us about why no two roadways are exactly alike?

According to one United Nations survey, nearly two-thirds of Americans and Russians reported being the victims of aggressive driving behavior in the last year, roughly 50 percent more likely than in Europe.[3] These aggressive behaviors include speeding, reckless passing, ignoring traffic regulations, being followed, and being subjected to verbal abuse. Interestingly, the people who admitted to engaging in reckless driving behaviors were also more likely to claim to be a victim of it; maybe because it takes one to know one. According to another study, aggressive driving, driving errors, and traffic accidents are more common in Southern European countries than in Northern European countries.[4]

Studies that examine aggressive driving can be biased by the fact that what is perceived as an aggressive action by one person might not be perceived that way by another person with a different perspective. For example, passing on the right on roads where you drive in the right-hand lane might be considered an aggressive action in some places but prudent conduct in others. Likewise, drivers often unintentionally insult other drivers because of different expectations regarding what constitutes polite driving behavior. No form of driving communication is more fraught with the possibility of misunderstanding than the use of the car horn. In Northern Europe and in much of the United States, the horn is primarily intended to express displeasure. However, in pleasant New Zealand where many things are seemingly upside down, drivers restrict horn use to a warm beep of "thank you" after you have allowed them to pass or yielded the right-of-way. New Zealanders express their displeasure by being uncommunicative and not honking—a passive-aggressive method for dealing with bad driving, for sure. In India, the passing vehicles are responsible for making themselves known, hence the ubiquity of horn use ("horn please!" signs are posted on many trucks), and the fact that Indian drivers largely remain indifferent to the fact that their side mirrors have been shorn off in traffic.

No place on Earth presents a wider range of car horn communication possibilities—and opportunities for miscommunication—than urban China. Chinese dialects are tonal in nature: The same sounds expressed with different intonations can mean very different things depending on whether they are spoken with a tone that is flat, rising, falling and rising, or falling sharply. The simple sound *ma* could mean mother, horse, help, or scold depending on its intonation when spoken. When going into a restaurant, asking for take-away is just a tone away from asking for a hug. As one of my students in China found out the hard way, saying you like pandas is just a tone away from saying you like chest hair. As someone who has never developed a subtle ear for intonation, many Chinese words sound alike to me. Likewise, during my first trips on Chinese roads, the constant cacophony of horns seemed to communicate nothing to me other than the fact that I was in a country with more than 1 billion people. The answer to every stimulus when driving seemed to be a honk. It was as if every Chinese driver had their horn hooked up to their cardiac pacemaker so that it would blast with each beat of their heart. But with time, I came to realize that horn usage in China can be every bit as informative as Mandarin—in fact, in linguistically diverse China, the horn might be the only dialect that everyone can understand. Short, solid honks ask for recognition (particularly when preparing to pass the car ahead) or as a brief interrogation of another driver's intentions. Long honks demand attention from all of the cars in the immediate area, but are as polite as an "excuse me" when moving through a crowd. Double honks indicate irritation; double long honks indicate anger bordering on insanity. Repeated machine-gun honks indicate that the driver no longer finds this traffic game fun and is hoping that using their horn will transport them to their happy place. And there is always the simple honk indicating that yes, the driver is still alive.

Variations in driving behavior across countries are matched by variations in traffic fatalities. Traffic accidents caused an estimated 1.25 million deaths worldwide in the year 2013. While this number is down slightly from 2000, the World Health Organization expects the number of global deaths to reach almost 2 million a year by 2030, at which point traffic accidents will have supplanted HIV/AIDS as the most common cause of death in poor and middle-income countries. Ninety per cent of road traffic deaths occur in low- and middle-income countries despite the fact that they only account for half of the world's registered vehicles.[5] The risk of dying as a result of a traffic accident is highest in Africa (26.2 per 100,000 population), which has 40 of the 50 most dangerous countries for traffic accidents. The lowest accident rates are in Europe (9.3 per 100,000), with the world average being 17.5 deaths per 100,000. Roughly half of global traffic fatalities are not to the drivers of four-wheeled vehicles but to vulnerable road users such as pedestrians, cyclists, and motorcyclists.[6]

Road fatalities are a tragedy at the human level because of the loss of life, but they are also an economic misfortune. Every lost life means additional expenses and lost income, which in turn leads to lower levels of health, education, and other measures of well-being within the victim's families. When aggregated, studies suggest that road injuries cost poorer countries roughly 3 percent of their GDP a year—a significant loss of income for countries where income is not very high in the first place.[7]

How can we understand the deeper causes of these differences in driving behaviors, road conditions, and road fatalities across countries? I will argue that the forces that make us different drivers are the same forces that explain why levels of income are so different across countries: the key to both is institutions.

In the last chapter I introduced the economic concept of institutions. Once again, institutions simply means the structures created by societies, families, and governments that shape incentives and influence individual behavior. Institutions change incentives, which in turn influence people's actions in regard to saving, working, investing, developing technology, engaging in entrepreneurship, and many other economic activities in ways that we will explore as the book moves forward. As an introduction to developing a deeper understanding of what institutions are and how they work, let's consider the ways in which different societies create different institutions and incentives that influence people's behavior behind the wheel.

In every country there are rules of the road. Some of these rules of the road are written laws that define what we should do when we drive. These *de jure* ("according to the law") rules reflect the values that society places on specific social interactions. A social scientist would say that *de jure* laws typically reflect *injunctive norms*: norms that specify how society agrees we all should behave. But there is often a difference between what society says people should do and what people actually do. There are *de jure* laws and there is *de facto* ("in practice") behavior. Social scientists would refer to the generally accepted ways that people actually behave as *descriptive norms*, recognizing the fact that the ideals that a society sets for itself with its injunctive norms are often not practiced in daily life.

Consider one example to illustrate: jaywalking. In Western countries, most cities outlaw jaywalking and give pedestrians the right of way only when in a crosswalk. Of course, these *de jure* laws are followed more closely in certain places (Copenhagen and Hamburg), while *de facto* behavior allows for regular jaywalking in many other places (New York and Shanghai). In Hanoi, Vietnam, the *de jure* law is that pedestrians always have the right-of-way at pedestrian crossings, but the *de facto* behavior is that it is always the responsibility of drivers to avoid pedestrians, period, regardless of where they cross the street. The implications of this are to be expected: Pedestrians cross wherever they want and drivers pay no attention to crossings or traffic lights—they just try to avoid hitting pedestrians. As a result, crossing the street in Hanoi is something akin to an extreme adventure sport, and stepping into traffic feels like stepping off the top of a cliff. Cars race up and down streets with no pause until a collision with a pedestrian is imminent. The pedestrian is expected to cross the road at a point of his or her choosing but do it at a constant speed so that drivers can avoid them, not vice versa. The worst thing a pedestrian can do is to make eye contact with drivers for fear of showing any indecision, or to slow down or speed up for any reason lest the driver's calculation of how to blow by you at full speed is thrown off.

Consider another example: speed limits. Most countries have *de facto* laws that limit speeds on the road. These laws recognize the injunctive norm that says that an individual does not have the right to endanger other drivers by driving at excessive speeds. Of course, the safety benefits of speed limits must be balanced against the cost of people's time spent on the road, and many societies choose different balance points for this trade-off. Some countries set higher speed limits because they value their time more heavily or because they place a premium on an individual's own right to monitor their driving behavior. On the other hand, some countries set lower speed limits because they weigh the communal public safety benefits of a lower speed limit more heavily than the costs of going slower.

In setting the speed limit, one of the key institutions that impact *de jure* laws is how the injunctive norms of the society balance communal responsibilities versus individual freedoms. Societies that are more collectivist in nature—Scandinavian countries being a commonly used example—tend to emphasize an individual's responsibility to society more heavily than an individual's personal rights. Collectivist values in Scandinavian countries and elsewhere are a complex function of their history, culture, social evolution, and political environment. As a result, you would expect lower speed limits in such countries because of the higher value they place on public safety. In societies that place more value on individual freedom—say, the United States—you would expect that there would be higher speed limits and faster travel times, but at a cost to public safety. And Scandinavian countries do, as a general rule, have lower speed limits than the United States and also lower traffic fatality rates. (This is complicated somewhat by the fact that in the United States, each state sets its own speed limits, but under some influence from the federal government. As a result, you would also expect state-by-state variations in speed limits and fatalities in the United States to reflect differences in the way their residents choose to balance the trade-off between communal responsibilities and individual freedoms.)

Having said this, nearly every country in the world has *de jure* speed limits (although there are areas in some countries without them, such as the Autobahn in Germany and some Native American reservations in the United States). In fact, there is surprisingly little variation in legal speed limit laws across countries. What differs much more across countries is how closely the posted speed limits are actually followed in practice. In other words, the *de jure* speed limit is often not reflected in *de facto* speeds, and the differences among *de jure* laws are small relative to the variation in *de facto* behavior. It seems that while most societies have injunctive norms that value the safety of the entire community, many countries also have descriptive norms that say that the individual can still drive as fast as they want; in other words, that injunctive norms are for other people to follow, but not necessarily for me.

For many behaviors, coordinating *de jure* with *de facto* behavior takes care of itself. Take, for example, the choice of which side of the road people drive on in any particular country. Failing to drive on the same side as everyone else has immediate and costly consequences, forcing strict adherence to the law. It reminds me of a joke about a commuter who is driving home from work when he gets a panicked call from his wife. "Careful, darling! I heard on the radio that there is a crazy person driving on the wrong side of the highway!" To which the husband replies, "One crazy person! There are hundreds of them!"

De jure and *de facto* behavior, injunctive and descriptive norms, are often inseparable in certain countries. The Germans are well-known for having a rules-based society that also places a great deal of emphasis on following the rules exactly as written. There is a German saying that "Everything is forbidden. Apart from that, do what you like." German roads reflect these values: lots of traffic signs and rules are posted, people stop early when the light turns yellow, speed limits are closely followed, and people don't try to jump ahead of other cars when merging in traffic but patiently queue.

In other countries, the unwritten rules of the road are much different than the written rules of the road. In many American states, there is a widely accepted 5–10 mile "leeway" in the speed limit that is demanded by motorists and granted by police. In other words, you can speed—just not too much.

In many areas of China, *de facto* and *de jure* standards are not close enough to even be considered kin to each other. China's transportation system has undergone an almost unfathomable transformation over the last 30 years. China has built some 2.6 million miles of roads, half of these since 2002. (In fact, at one time the Chinese government considered turning the Great Wall into a road.) These new roads have generally been built according to Western standards and the Chinese have generally adopted Western *de jure* driving laws in regard to speed limits, passing and turning rules, right-of-ways, etc. But the driving behaviors exhibited on Chinese roads are very different from what is found in Western countries because, as in many other aspects of Chinese life, *de jure* laws are not reflected in *de facto* behavior. One of the most popular Chinese sayings is "Green means go, yellow means go, and red means find another way around." Likewise, one of the fundamental facts about China is reflected in the well-known aphorism "The mountains are high, and the emperor is far away." Both of these sayings capture the descriptive norms of everyday Chinese life: if you think you can get away with it, then it is not necessarily frowned upon to try.

Consider one more example of the chasm that can exist between injunctive and descriptive norms that pertains not to driving, but to public transportation. Tickets to ride the trains on Mumbai's enormously overcrowded passenger rail system are typically uncollected because of the immense traffic (more than six million passengers a day) that swamps Mumbai stations. As a result, many passengers who ride the train in Mumbai every day don't pay for tickets. However, conductors do perform spot checks and issue large fines when they catch people riding trains without tickets. In order to avoid these fines, groups of "ticketless travelers" in India have banded together to provide fine insurance for members. If caught riding without a ticket, a member fraudster can use their written citation to gain a full reimbursement from the organization's pooled membership fees. It's a classic example of the disconnect in many people's minds between injunctive and descriptive norms: it's not really wrong if I can get away with it.

In summary, differences in institutions can explain differences in driving behavior. Different emphases on individual rights versus communal responsibilities shape the injunctive norms that describe how drivers should behave. However, much more importantly, different expectations regarding how closely posted laws should actually be followed in practice play the most important role in explaining why driving differs dramatically depending upon where you are. As travelers, we have inculcated our home institutions and bring with us a different set of expectations regarding how closely descriptive behavior should match injunctive norms, and *de facto* conduct should match *de jure* behavior. As a result, when we leave our home, we tend to believe that the people we are visiting are almost always worse drivers than we are. In actuality, they are simply different drivers than us. While the laws in the new location are usually similar to those from where we come, the institutions on the ground, the behaviors they favor, and the resulting variations in *de facto* behavior from *de jure* behavior are so completely different that they feel wrong to us travelers.

How do some societies enforce injunctive norms so that they match descriptive behavior? In particular, how do societies ensure that the needs of the community are balanced against the freedom of individuals so that everyone doesn't just do only what is best for themselves to the exclusion of everyone else? Economics can give us some insight into these questions, specifically using a branch of economics known as game theory. Game theory attempts to understand strategic decision making, meaning decisions in which two or more individuals have some knowledge of the choices available to other people and whose actions impact these other people in a positive or negative way. In other words, game theory is really about understanding the strategic interactions between people. When what I do impacts you and when what you do impacts me, and when both of us are aware of this, then game theory can help us to understand the decisions that each of us will make.

While game theory was originally developed as a method for helping military decision makers understand and evaluate military strategies, it is now used to understand all sorts of societal interactions, from how to raise your children to how Apple should set the price of its iPhone. Given that highway driving involves a long series of interactions between you and other drivers—where their behavior impacts you and vice versa—driving is a great example of how the insights of game theory can be used to explain observed behavior.

One well-known game theory experiment is referred to as the ultimatum game. In the two-person version of this game, the first person is given some money and instructed to share it with the second person. If the second person accepts the offer, they both keep the money; if the second person rejects the offer, then neither player gets to keep anything. The supremely rational way to play this game is for the first person to offer the second person a small amount only slightly greater than zero and keep the rest. This is best for the first person who makes the offer, and the second person should still accept this seemingly bad deal because getting something is better than nothing. However, when this game is actually played by real people, most people playing the role of the second person will reject any offer less than 50 percent of the total, punishing the first person as well as themselves if they don't receive a "fair" offer.

Why do people punish others when they also hurt themselves in the process? There is a deeply ingrained sense within each of us which demands that we be treated fairly, but which also encourages us to treat other people fairly. This sense is part of what makes *Homo sapiens* so successful as a species: We have a strong sense of community and are social creatures. We rely on reciprocity among members of our group in order to ensure the success of the group in harsh environments. This sense of community is maintained when members who violate the rules that help all of us are punished for doing so. The way that injunctive social norms are drilled into us so that they become descriptive norms is through punishment. This occurs even when "it hurts me as much as it hurts you," as the saying goes. It appears that most people are allowing their communal instincts and injunctive norms of fairness to guide their actions when they play the ultimatum game.

Societies that are able to keep descriptive norms in line with injunctive norms are good at consistently punishing those who disobey the rules, even when it hurts everyone else. This will lead to the "cooperative equilibrium," where everyone follows the rules. But game theorists also recognize that "multiple equilibria" are possible in this game. Another outcome is that individual members of society lose confidence that other members will enforce the rules and incur the costs that come with consistent punishment of those who violate cooperative behavior. In other words, people are conditional cooperators.[8] In this case, no one punishes rule-breakers, there is no enforcement of communal values, and injunctive and descriptive norms begin to differ from each other.

One example of this that I have seen in my travels is in crossing one-lane bridges in rural New Zealand versus in rural northern India. When crossing a one-lane bridge, the second car to arrive should give way to a car already crossing the bridge coming from the other direction. This is the cooperative outcome, and it is also faster and safer for everyone. In New Zealand, it is very common for drivers to play what I call "Not Chicken": cars on either side of a bridge act as if they were the last to arrive, politely trying to wave the other car over the bridge until someone finally crosses, allowing the other car to "win." In India, there were no such niceties. Cars would inevitably try to cross the bridge simultaneously, not only risking life and limb but inevitably taking a much longer time to do so because they each had to inch across in order to avoid shaving off each other's fenders. This uncooperative equilibrium is inefficient, but it is also an equilibrium that no driver by themselves can improve upon: any driver that would choose to yield to a car already on the bridge might end up having to wait there forever.

It is not surprising that countries in which laws are rarely violated are countries that more strictly punish deviations from accepted societal behavior. In Europe, Northern European countries actually issue more tickets for traffic violations than Southern European countries, even though the data suggests that Northern Europeans drive less aggressively and their roads are safer.[9] This is consistent with the argument that enforcement creates incentives for people to abide by *de jure* laws. This is what is hinted at in this photo from Botswana, where a fierce-looking man says "Don't

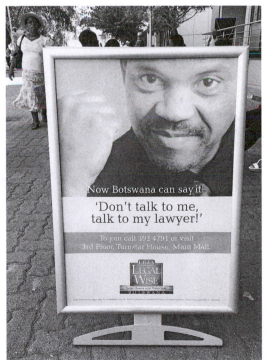

The rule of law in Botswana.

talk to me, talk to my lawyer!" as if a lawyer is a much more imposing means of enforcement than any fist. But lawyers alone don't work—you need an entire legal system and police force to back them up. In addition, it is not just the efficacy of enforcement that matters but also the size of the penalties imposed on violators. In Finland, speeding tickets are assessed as a percentage of the driver's income, increasing the penalties on richer drivers (often into the tens of thousands of dollars), so that everyone experiences proportional and significant financial consequence when they are caught breaking the law. Not surprisingly, Finnish roads are some of the safest in the world.

Other countries lack the means to punish scofflaws because the government or collective society is incapable of doing so. Consider traffic lights in two countries: Sierra Leone and Argentina. There were no traffic lights in Sierra Leone for 14 years until a single one was reinstalled in 2016. Every traffic light had been stolen and scrapped in the country during a brutal, anarchic 14-year civil war in which the government essentially disintegrated. Today, this single traffic light is seen as a symbol of hope that the government of Sierra Leone is now functioning and, even more importantly, is serious about enforcing *de jure* law by limiting the corruption of the country's crooked traffic police who use the drivers in the intersections they monitor as their own moving ATM machine. It is interesting how something as simple as a traffic light can capture the importance of having some impartial and uncorrupted enforcement mechanism to help coordinate *de jure* and *de facto* behavior.

Of course, just because you have traffic lights does not mean that people obey them, as Argentineans can attest. Following traffic lights not only helps to avoid collisions in intersections—the most dangerous sections of any roadway—but also facilitates faster travel times by allowing traffic to flow more freely as long as everybody follows the light and awaits their turn. Traffic lights seem like something everyone should support. But in Argentina, traffic lights are designed differently and specifically in ways that reflect the public's desire to flout injunctive norms. Argentinean traffic lights go from green to yellow to red—like other lights I was familiar with in the United States—but then go from red TO YELLOW to green. In other words, drivers are given a warning to slow down in anticipation of a red light, but they are also given encouragement to get started and leave early in anticipation of a green light. The result is that every time the traffic light turns yellow, Argentinean intersections become a dangerous mass of cars trying to sneak through on the last green light or get ahead on the next green light. Argentinean traffic lights—coupled with Argentinean *de facto* norms—are dangerous and inefficient. Unfortunately, they are also indicative of how Argentina works, a society that glorifies an individual's prerogative to get away with something as opposed to following the rules. In Argentina, the word for entrepreneur (*empresario*) is also used as a synonym for criminal. Argentinean institutions disincentivize consideration of the communal good, which not only makes it a difficult place to drive, but also a difficult place to reap the benefits of productive behavior. In the 1930s Argentina was one of the 10 richest countries in the world. Today, the IMF ranks Argentina as having only the 51st highest level of per-capita GDP in the world despite remarkable endowments of energy, raw materials, agriculture, and a highly educated population. If you want a brief illustration of why, look at their traffic lights.

How can we explain why some societies have institutions that enforce social responsibility and incentivize following the rules, while other countries have institutions that encourage individuals to ignore their communal commitments and incentivize descriptive norms of behavior that are very different from their injunctive norms? This, of course, is a multi-trillion-dollar question, the answer to which not only helps us understand differences in driving behavior but also differences in income levels across countries. But it is not an easy question to answer because institutions are shaped by a wide variety of factors that are not easy to delineate. In theory, any factors that impact incentives—even things as intangible as widely shared beliefs—are part of institutions. However, let me discuss four of the most important causal factors that economists and other social scientists have identified as playing an important role in determining institutions, particularly those institutions that influence our behaviors on the roadways.

The Enforcement of Laws and Corruption

The most obvious way to make sure that *de jure* is the same as *de facto* is to have law enforcement and judicial systems that are efficient, fair, and honest. When *de jure* laws cannot be effectively enforced, then people will often ignore them to the detriment of society as a whole.

The inefficiency and inequity of the legal and judicial systems in many countries is well known to many travelers—hopefully you have only heard of the stories, not experienced them. Law enforcement is often arbitrary in many places and, as a result, the law is arbitrarily followed. Also, justice delayed is justice denied: In many countries, the legal and judicial system proceeds so slowly that it becomes almost irrelevant. For example, there are currently over 22 million cases backlogged in the Indian legal system, with roughly one-third of these cases being over five years old.[10] There are roughly 25,000 cases pending to the Indian Supreme Court (taking between 8 and 20 years to be resolved).[11] The result is a general and outright disregard for the law. According to one English police study, there are more than 110 million traffic violations in the city of Delhi each day, and only about 10 percent of drivers can be expected to comply with traffic laws.[12] Not surprisingly, one out of 10 global road deaths take place in India—over 240,000 fatalities in 2011 alone, or nearly one person every two minutes.[13]

The worst way that law enforcement can fail is as a result of corruption among government officials: bureaucrats, police officers, and judges. Corruption is costly not only because of the thievery. Corruption also reduces the perceived legitimacy of the law and provides everyone else with the justification to engage in corruption because "everyone else is doing it." Corruption first limits opportunities to get ahead, but then comes to be seen as the best way for the victims to get ahead themselves. It is this violation of the basic notion of fairness that makes societies with rampant corruption more accepting of illegal behavior. When the rules are seen as illegitimate, there is no reason why society should demand that descriptive norms be enforced so that they match injunctive norms.

The five-step approach to policing.

This is the reason I was so intrigued by the sign that adorned the Chinese traffic police station that is pictured here. The English translation offered on the sign is "complaints acceptance," but I was puzzled by what exactly this sign was intending to communicate. Was this a place where complaints were to be shared with the police? If so, where do you go for complaints to actually be dealt with? Or, was this a place where people who have complaints may come to gain acceptance of the fact that nothing will be done about them? In this case, it would be a kind of five-step approach to policing, but here the last step—acceptance of what you cannot change—is the first step. Regardless, my confusion over how to interpret this sign is probably only exceeded by the confusion that most Chinese have when it comes to dealing with the indiscriminate and unfair policing policies that are common throughout China.

Similarly, I have always enjoyed the fact that in Italy, you file police reports for traffic accidents at the Ufficio Denunce (the "Office of Denunciations"). Given the questionable reputation of Italian police, it is only natural to ask who is being denounced, and whether these denouncements occur after crimes or after visits to this office.

The corruption of traffic policing may be the most insidious form of corruption because it is so capricious and almost everyone is forced to deal with it on a daily basis. The fact that traffic corruption takes place at a very personal level, with the bribe-taker directly confronting the bribe-payer, reduces the perceived legitimacy of the law much more than higher-level corruption that the general public is not forced to grapple with on a daily basis and which largely takes place among faceless officials.

Stories of the ubiquitous police corruption on the roads of many countries are all too common. For example, more than 80 percent of Nigerians report that they have paid a bribe to the police in the last 12 months.[14] If you want specific examples, check out BribeNigeria.com, a Web site in which the victims of corruption in Nigeria share their stories, or IPaidABribe.com, a similar Web site for India. Here, victims of corruption attempt to increase transparency regarding corruption and try to shame corrupt officials. Based on the stories shared on BribeNigeria.com, police corruption from ignored or imaginary traffic violations is the most common form of corruption experienced by Nigerians. The utter routineness of police corruption on the roads has shaken the confidence of most Nigerians in their country—not only in their legal and police systems, but in their entire political system.

Because people often do not trust the law or the police who enforce it, they are forced to find workarounds and alternative strategies in order to avoid formal legal systems and law enforcement. On the streets of China, it is common for the aggrieved party in any accident to sit in the middle of the road and prevent the other party from moving their car until they can negotiate a payoff and settle the dispute in cash on the spot. While traffic is tied up for miles, the two drivers will haggle in the middle of the road, each with a phone to their ear, shouting over the blaring of car horns, calling their friends on their mobile phones to come quick and join them in the middle of the road—and to bring cash. There is a great deal to be said in favor of the efficiency of this judicial process for those involved in the crash, as it allows them to avoid the capricious and costly Chinese legal system. However, it makes life miserable for everyone else.

One clever economic study examining the relationship between traffic corruption and people's tendency to disregard the law focused on parking tickets issued by New York City police to United Nations diplomats between 1997 and 2002.[15] Because these diplomats have immunity from parking tickets, they have an incentive to flaunt New York parking laws. Over the period of this study, the authors looked at 150,000 parking violations issued to vehicles with generic diplomatic plates. Not surprisingly, those countries that incurred the most parking tickets in New York came from countries with the highest levels of perceived corruption back home. Many countries—including the Scandinavian countries and Japan—were issued no tickets despite the fact that they would never have to pay for any parking violations. This is a clear example of how people internalize institutions, specifically the idea that people's actual behavior should match injunctive norms. Once institutions are instilled in a person, they have a long-lasting impact on how that person behaves even when they leave their country of origin and live under a different set of institutions.

By failing to punish, or by even outright rewarding, reckless behavior, corruption is one of the most important factors determining road fatalities in any country. One economic study found that measures of corruption are the strongest predictor of road fatality rates in a county; more important than income levels.[16] Countries with the lowest levels of perceived corruption, such as New Zealand, Singapore, and the Scandinavian countries, also have the safest roads.

Corruption can also reduce safety on the roads by reducing the efficacy of driver training and licensing. One study of the driver licensing process in Delhi, India, found that those prospective drivers who had the highest expressed desire to quickly obtain a driver's license often obtained one by hiring a license "fixer" (i.e., bribe arranger) to avoid driver training.[17] When all licensed drivers were later tested, 69 percent of the drivers who had used a fixer failed the test as compared to only 11 percent of those who actually went through driver training. In fact, the researchers found that among all drivers, the better an individual's driving skill, the less their actual chance of getting a license. Being a better driver reduced your chances of obtaining a driver's license in Delhi because everyone who used a fixer got a license; some of the people who went through training failed to pass the test.

Political Dysfunction

The inability of certain countries to enforce injunctive norms and limit corruption is often the result of political systems that don't serve the public welfare. In any society there is always conflict. Typically, this conflict is of one of two types: First, the rights of the individual must be balanced against that of society as a whole, and second, the rights of one group of people must be balanced against the conflicting rights of other groups of people. Maintaining checks and balances between these competing interests is something that efficient and fair political systems that are viewed by its citizens as legitimate do well. On the other hand, in dysfunctional political systems, conflict turns into hostility, and individual or group interests begin to supersede the interests of society as a whole. It can get to the point where people fail to see themselves as part of a broader society, only as members of a smaller interest group.

One important way in which dysfunctional political systems are dysfunctional is that they create institutions that excessively favor the few over the many. In authoritarian political systems, political elites—those with inordinate influence because of their wealth or political power—benefit from political systems that they have designed specifically to favor themselves. Political elites dictate policies and institutions that maximize their personal benefits and not the welfare of society as a whole. Under authoritarian political systems, non-elites are disempowered. As a result, they feel it is appropriate to disregard the law and injunctive norms because they view them as fundamentally unfair and illegitimate. According to the British playwright Kenneth Tynan, "Bad driving—i.e. fast and reckless driving— tends to exist in inverse ratio to democratic institutions. In an authoritarian state, the only place where the little man achieves equality with the big is in heavy traffic. Only there can he actually overtake."[18]

On the other hand, driving can't be left to simple majority rule, either. Minority rights, including those of elites, must be protected. If they are not, then a tyranny of the majority can allow the many to exploit the few, and society can descend into chaos. For example, if a law is passed in California saying that every out-of-state driver must pull to the curb when being followed by a car with a California license plate, no one's interest will be served in the long run because every state could pass similar laws, and overall driving will be made significantly slower and more miserable. For this reason, pure democratic systems are unlikely to create institutions that lead to safer and more efficient roads. India, which is the largest democracy in the world and also has one of the most democratic political systems, would be an example of this type of political dysfunction. The chaos on India's roads is often matched only by the chaos of its politics, where every driver and every voter acts like their own special interest group in which their interests take precedence over everyone else's. Functioning republics—which have democratically elected representatives along with checks and balances on power aimed at limiting the influence of both political elites as well as the political power of majorities—are most likely to encourage productive behavior, economic growth, and good driving.

Political dysfunction is also an important factor in determining the kinds of corruption that exist in a society and how costly that corruption is. Not all forms of corruption are the same or are equally as costly. In some countries, corruption is decentralized in that it takes place at an individual level, and each bribe is independent from other acts of corruption; for example, the police officer who demands a personal payment for a traffic violation, or a road block set up to extort payments from passing motorists. Decentralized corruption is more likely to take place in countries with dysfunctional governments where central authority is lacking and where everyone acts in their own self-interest (once again, think India). On the other hand, centralized corruption is top-down corruption that is organized by powerful elites. This often includes organized crime and political corruption; for example, when a bureaucrat demands a kickback for their boss in order to process a driver license, or a politician demands a bribe in order to approve spending on a road building project. Centralized corruption is more likely in autocratic political systems where elites have the power to organize and enforce coordination among officials so that bribes make their way up the chain of command. In its extreme, centralized corruption can lead to *kleptocracy*, where the primary objective of government becomes maximizing the graft collected by a small number of elites.

While both forms of corruption are costly and frustrating, it is decentralized corruption that is the most damaging.[19] When corruption is centralized, there are incentives for officials to act like a "corruption monopolist." Monopolists maximize their revenue by keeping competitors out, limiting the overall amount of corruption in order to increase the price of each individual act of corruption. With decentralized corruption, there are no limits on the amount of corruption, and every police officer, bureaucrat, and politician attempts to maximize the amount of their own bribes that they can collect. At its worst, decentralized corruption devolves into what we see on the roadways in failed states, where every stretch of road becomes clogged with roadblocks, creating an endless series of successive bribes that effectively ends anyone's actual ability to use the road. This is why it is better to drive in China, which is autocratic but the corruption is more centralized and limited in volume, than it is to drive in government-free Somalia (although I have never actually tested this hypothesis myself).

Many empirical studies confirm these observations and find that countries with more political stability—even if it is created through authoritarian institutions—tend to have less overall corruption.[20] It also explains why countries that have moved from centralized to decentralized corruption— such as in Iraq after the fall of the dictator Saddam Hussein and the subsequent sectarian unraveling of the country—have much costlier corruption than before under the autocratic regime (and also lower growth and more dangerous roads).

Historical Path-Dependence

Another factor in why institutions differ across countries and societies is that current institutions reflect the long-lasting effects of the different historical legacies of these societies. In the words of William Faulkner: "The past is not dead. It's not even past."[21] Events from the past influence today's institutions and norms because institutions and norms are very slow to change.

One of the most widely cited studies in economic development over the last 20 years was conducted by Darin Acemoglu, Simon Johnson, and James Robinson.[22] They argue that colonization has had a long-lasting legacy on colonized countries in more important ways than just which side of the road people drive on. In their study, these authors argue that the wide variety of institutions in former colonies today reflects the different colonization strategies that were followed in different places hundreds of years ago. Where the climate and health environment, as measured by settler mortality rates, was conducive for the permanent settlement of immigrants, colonization strategies focused on establishing institutions that matched injunctive and descriptive norms, *de jure* and *de facto* behavior, just like the colonizers had back home. This includes establishing representative political systems and building equitable and effective legal systems. This was most likely to be the case in colonies within temperate climate zones, such as in North America, Australia, and New Zealand. However, in most other colonies, immigrant mortality was so high that few colonizers actually intended to permanently live there. In Nigeria in the mid-1800s, roughly 2,000 deaths occurred each year to sustain a constant level of 1,000 settlers in the country! In these countries where mortality was high, primarily in Latin America, Southeast Asia, and Sub-Saharan Africa, the economic incentives faced by immigrants encouraged extractive colonization policies, such as mineral exploitation and slavery, which were not consistent with the creation of quality institutions or with people following injunctive norms.[23] The authors show that settler mortality rates that existed in the mid-1800s are closely related to various measures of institutions that still exist today, including the risk of government corruption and autocratic political systems. The authors argue that this is evidence of the importance, and persistence, of the historical origins of institutions.

And why were some countries colonizers and other countries colonies in the first place? When European and Asian societies first interacted with those in the Americas, Sub-Saharan Africa, and the Pacific, it was the Eurasian societies that dominated and were able to impose their visions for institutions on these "new worlds." Jared Diamond argues that this occurred because of the "Guns, Germs, and Steel" advantages Eurasia had, which resulted from natural ecological advantages.[24] Because of superior climates for food production (more land in temperate zones), foodstuffs (wheat and potatoes), and animals that were more easily domesticated (such as having the horse and not the zebra), Eurasia was able to begin their Neolithic Revolution and establish agrarian societies at a much earlier period of history than the rest of the world. These Eurasian farming societies allowed for more food production, facilitating faster population growth, political organization, technological development, and more disease immunity. (Human diseases typically originate in other animals; living in close proximity to domesticated animals is the way that most diseases make the jump to humans. As a result of their earlier transition to agriculture, Eurasian countries were exposed to more diseases in earlier eras, helping them generate disease immunity that New World societies did not develop.) As a result, Eurasians were more advanced than the rest of the world when they first interacted and were less vulnerable to disease. The aftermath of these first contacts has had consequences that persist to this day, as Eurasians often imposed self-serving institutions in the Americas and Africa that continue to impact incentives and behavior in a number of subtle and unforeseen ways.

In summary, the proponents of these path-dependent theories of institutions might argue that differences in driving rest not in our genes but in the unforeseen legacy of our past. Or, to twist Shakespeare, the fault of our bad driving is not in ourselves, but in our stars.

Cultural Differences

Of course, the reflexive explanation of differences in driving behavior is that driving reflects culture because culture instills deeply ingrained beliefs that each of us is a slave to. Culture is such a commonly offered answer to so many questions regarding the differences between societies—from driving behavior to income differences to political interactions—that I will devote an entire chapter to taking an economic look at culture, in Chapter 5.

Let me say a couple of things for now about how culture impacts institutions. First, there is no doubt that cultural differences play a role in shaping institutions. This is particularly true in regard to how culture determines injunctive norms, or beliefs about how people should behave. As we discussed earlier, it is not surprising that cultures that are more communitarian tend to adopt stricter *de jure* laws and more strictly enforce *de facto* behavior that is consistent with these laws.

However, I, along with many (but not all) other economists, am fairly skeptical of cultural determinist arguments that insist that most of the differences in behavior between people can be boiled down to variations in culture. The problem with cultural determinism is that cultural explanations can often be used to argue either side of any debate. For example, why are Chinese roads so dangerous and why do Chinese drivers fail to obey traffic laws? Is it because Chinese culture is too antiauthoritarian? To support this, one can point to the importance of Confucian philosophy, which emphasizes personal ethics over *de jure* law and one's responsibility to their own family over that to society as a whole. The popular Chinese adage "it is easier to ask forgiveness than permission" captures the fact that there is an antiauthoritarian strain in the culture. Or is the problem that Chinese culture is too authoritarian? To support this, one can argue that Chinese culture has for millennia coexisted with political systems characterized by dynasties, dictatorial emperors, centralized corruption, and little regard for individual freedom. In this unjust system, the only way that many individuals can survive is to disobey the law. Both of these cultural arguments are plausible, but they are also contradictory. The difficulties posed by these questions of culture are why I want to give the topic of culture a fuller examination in a later chapter.

While institutions play a very important role in shaping road behavior, it is also worth asking whether being poor itself is a cause of more dangerous roads. According to one economic study, the answer is both yes and no.[25] Countries with the safest roads are actually very poor countries (with levels of per-capita GDP below $1,200 a year) and rich countries. It is in the middle-income countries (particularly in countries with per-capita GDPs of between $1,200 and $4,400) where fatalities skyrocket to more than 300 percent of what they are in poor countries. Why the difference? Much of it has to do with the number of new drivers in these middle-income countries. In poor countries, few people drive. Most are forced to use less costly, and safer, modes of transportation such as buses, trains, bicycles, scooters, and walking. In middle-income countries, the number of new cars—and more importantly, the number of new drivers—booms. Rich countries have even more drivers, but they also have more experienced drivers (and also spend more on driver training, licensing, and on road safety, as we will discuss in a moment).

Ground zero for the explosion of new drivers hitting the roads is China. In 1977 there were only 1 million registered vehicles on Chinese roads. By 1997 there were more than 15 million. Today, more than 260 million registered vehicles populate Chinese roads. Last year alone more than 15.1 million new cars and 26 million new drivers were added to Chinese roads, which by itself is more than the total number of licensed drivers that existed 15 years ago.[26]

The transition from walking to driving in China has coincided with the largest human migration in history: more than 250 million Chinese have moved from rural to urban areas. Constantly reciting statistics when talking about China is a hard thing to avoid because the numbers you find are all so astounding. But this one is truly astonishing: a population nearly the size of the entire United States has moved from their traditional homeland to booming urban Chinese cities over the last generation. What has driven this migration? As Greek philosophers, economists, and Broadway musicals say: Money makes the world go around. Urban areas—where higher-paying manufacturing, private sector, and export-oriented jobs are located—have income levels that are more than five times what they are in rural areas of China. At the same time, advances in Chinese agricultural production have allowed China to feed itself with 200 million fewer farmers than in the 1970s.

Today, China is one of the most dangerous places in the world to drive, with 20.5 fatalities per 100,000 residents, nearly twice the fatality rate of the United States. China's roads are dangerous in part because *de facto* and *de jure* behaviors are so different from each other for reasons discussed earlier, particularly because of the ubiquity of corruption in the country. In fact, there have been numerous stories of Chinese drivers who accidentally hit pedestrians, then back up and hit them again in an attempt to intentionally kill them.[27] Why? Corruption and incentives. These "double-hit" accidents are driven by the fact that killing a pedestrian can cost between $30,000 and $50,000 if a lawsuit is filed against the driver (whether the driver was in the wrong or not), but paying for the lifetime care of a disabled victim can cost many times that. In the few cases where drivers have been caught attempting a "double-hit," many have gotten away with little punishment by bribing police officials and judges. Because of this, there have also been examples of vigilante justice (an extreme way of enforcing injunctive norms) in which crowds have beaten drivers to death who have tried to "double-hit" a pedestrian.

China also has dangerous roads because almost all of its drivers are so new at it. Car crashes are now the leading cause of death for Chinese between the ages of 15 and 29.[28] In fact, last year there were more road fatalities in China than there were vehicles in China in 1970. Peter Hessler brilliantly captures the chaos of Chinese roads that has resulted from this rapid change from a rural, pedestrian society to an urban, motorized society:

> In China, the transition has been so abrupt that people drive the way they walk. They like to move in packs, and they tailgate whenever possible. They rarely use turn signals. Instead they rely on automobile body language: if a car edges to the left, you can guess that he's about to make a turn. And they are brilliant at improvising. They convert sidewalks into passing lanes, and they'll approach a round-about in reverse direction if it seems faster. If they miss an exit on a highway, they simply pull onto the shoulder, shift into reverse, and get it right the second time. They curb-sneak in traffic jams, the same way Chinese people do in ticket lines. Tollbooths can be hazardous because a history of long queues has conditioned people into quickly evaluating options and making snap decisions. When approaching a toll, drivers like to switch lanes at the last possible instant; it's common to see an accident right in front of a booth. Drivers rarely check their rearview mirrors. Windshield wipers are considered a distraction, and so are headlights.[29]

The migration of people from rural to urban areas is not taking place in China alone. In 1960, about one-third of the world's population lived in cities. Today, roughly half, and by 2050 nearly 70 percent of the world's population, will live in urban areas. This migration is most pronounced in poorer countries because this is where the gap between urban and rural wages is the largest. Of the 23 megacities (more than 10 million in population) that exist in the world, 18 of them are in poor and middle-income countries. With urbanization comes a driving culture. In Mexico, the number of cars is rising at twice the rate of urban population growth, and in

India three times the rate. For the foreseeable future, all of these new drivers will mean very dangerous roads.

Another reason why driving is so dangerous in many countries is that the quality of the roads themselves is bad. Roads are a classic example of what economists call a *public good*: They provide positive benefits to everyone in society, not just to the drivers themselves. By making transportation easier, roads also facilitate trade, economic efficiency, public safety, and growth. Public goods create *positive externalities*: They generate benefits for those who didn't pay for the road and don't even directly use it. As a popular Chinese saying goes, if you want to get rich, build a road. The problem with building public goods, such as roads, that benefit everyone is that no one wants to pay for the costs of building and maintaining these roads. It is easy for individuals to free-ride off public goods in the hope that someone else will pay for the roads they are enjoying the benefits from for free. However, if everyone is a free-rider, no roads will be built. This is a classic example of a *market failure*, or a situation when the free market will not provide an optimal outcome for society as a whole. One way to overcome this market failure is through government intervention; specifically, it is a justification for governments to tax the public in order to pay for roads to be built, allowing us to collectively do what we won't do by ourselves.

To build and pay for these public goods, effective government is needed. But some countries have government bureaucracies that are weak, dysfunctional, corrupt, or all of the above. Bureaucrats often lack the skills necessary to plan, finance, and build road projects. The quality of roads in many countries is horrendous, falling apart moments after being built, because shoddy materials and poor workmanship are the easiest ways to cut corners to pay for graft. Governments in some countries have a problem with raising tax revenue to pay for these roads because there are too few honest bureaucrats to collect the taxes and make sure that the money goes into government coffers and not into the pocket of some corrupt official. Even when bureaucratic corruption is nonexistent, many governments have weak tax laws, little tax enforcement, and rampant tax evasion among the populace. They also have weak legal systems that make it difficult to enforce zoning laws and to use *eminent domain* in order to compel individuals to sell land to the government for projects in the public's interest.

Even when the resources do exist to build public goods such as roads, the public goods that are needed may not be the ones that bureaucrats want because of special interest considerations or corruption. Consider China's record of massive public capital projects: the Terracotta Warriors, the Great

Wall, the Forbidden City, and Empress Dowager Cixi's marble boat—beautiful cultural relics with modern-day tourist value, but also some of the most unproductive uses of resources in human history. In addition, there is the problem that once these projects are built, the incentives are often missing to get bureaucrats to administer and maintain public goods properly. Why is the Department of Motor Vehicles in most places so notoriously difficult to work with? Because workers at the DMV have no incentive to get more customers, only fewer customers.

Dhaka, the capital city of Bangladesh, is not high on many people's travel bucket list, and with good reason. The road conditions there are some of the worst in the world. As the 20th largest city in the world with a population density nine times that of Paris, you would expect to see something more than an unplanned village of more than 12 million people—but you would be wrong. Only 7 percent of the city is covered in roads (compared to a planned urban area such as Chicago with 40 percent). While there are 650 major intersections in the city, only 60 have traffic lights. There is a noticeable lack of small, feeder roads, so there is usually only a single road to get to a specific destination, and this single road is inevitably jammed. There is also a distinct lack of cross-town roads, only north-south roads. By one estimate, the cost of traffic delays and pollution to the poor citizens of Dhaka is about $300 per person per year, or roughly one-fifth of per-capita income.[30]

What can be done when such a road infrastructure disaster exists? In most poor countries, the majority of fatalities are actually incurred by pedestrians and those on two-wheeled vehicles, not in cars. The single best way to improve safety and reduce congestion would be to spend money on separate pathways for pedestrians and animals while finding ways to separate car traffic from bicycle, motorcycle, and rickshaw traffic. Of course, this is easier said than done given the scarcity of economic resources and general government ineffectiveness.

Applying economic thinking to roadway management can also help solve the problem of congestion. While public goods create positive externalities that benefit everyone, they can also create negative externalities that cost society as a whole. Because public goods can be used and enjoyed by all, they tend to get overused. When I choose to drive, I do not incorporate the costs of the increased congestion I am helping to create that is borne by the other drivers on the road. Other drivers don't extend me this courtesy, either. We also overuse our roads in other ways: cheap gas in the United States has encouraged Americans not only to drive more, but to drive bigger cars, imposing negative externalities in the form of more dangerous accidents and more pollution. As a result, we all over-drive because it is really "too cheap" to drive, in the sense that we only think about the costs we personally incur when we drive, not the costs we create for others. This phenomenon is often referred to as the *tragedy of the commons*: public goods that are owned by everyone tend to get treated as if they are owned by no one, hence they get overused.

Once again, we can appeal to game theory to help us understand why the tragedy of the commons occurs and what can be done to overcome it. Consider the following game in which there are two players, "You" and "Others." We can express the outcomes, or "payoffs," from driving less or driving more in the following matrix, where the first number in each cell represents the payoff to you and the second the payoff to others, as shown in the table below.

		Others	
		Drive Less	Drive More
You	Drive less	(2,2)	(0,3)
	Drive more	(3,0)	(1,1)

The payoffs in this game reflect the costs of having to share the road with other drivers. Note that the best payoff for you personally is to drive more while others drive less—you get there faster. (This outcome reminds me of a joke: one hundred percent of New York drivers think that New Yorkers should use public transportation more frequently.) However, when viewed from the perspective of overall society, the highest total payoff (four total) is for everyone to drive less but get there faster. We can call this the cooperative outcome. The worst societal payoff is for everyone to drive more (two total) and suffer through traffic jams. We call this the noncooperative outcome.

In this game, what can we expect the actual outcome to be? The Nobel Prize–winning economist John Nash (the subject of the Oscar-winning movie *A Beautiful Mind*) identified the expected outcome to this game—what today we refer to as a Nash equilibrium. An outcome is a *Nash equilibrium* if everyone is doing what is best for themselves, not necessarily what is best for society. In this game, notice that the best choice for you is to always drive more; no matter what others choose to do, you always get a higher payoff by driving more. Unfortunately, the same is true for others as well. As a result, the Nash equilibria to this game is for everyone to drive more, for the payoff to society to be lower than it could be, and for traffic to be horrible. In other words, we will be stuck in the noncooperative outcome. The cooperative outcome, where everyone drives less, might be an appealing utopia, but it is not a rational strategy for people to follow given the incentives to drive that are in place.

The tragedy of the commons is a big reason for the tragedy of driving in many places. The fact that Indian roads are not just for transportation but are really the only "free" sources of space for many people who are homeless or who own farm animals is the reason that roads are so crowded with cows, traders, sleepers, and the homeless. The same phenomenon is common in many parts of Africa. You might have heard of the Big Five for African hunters: buffalos, lions, leopards, rhinos, and elephants. But the five animals you are most likely to kill when visiting Africa are the animals you are most likely to hit with your car because they are living or being transported on African roads: goats, cattle, chickens, dogs, and donkeys. The fact that everyone owns the road—including the animals—means that nobody can drive very safely or quickly on them.

The tragedy of the commons doesn't just impact roads in poorer countries—it is a fact of life on roads in developed countries as well. However, one important difference in richer countries—other than the quality of the road infrastructure itself—is the fact that governments in developed countries are usually strong enough to enforce safety regulations in order to reduce the danger of these congested roads. Rich countries have improved road safety, even in the face of an ever-increasing number of drivers, by spending money to enforce higher vehicle safety standards as well as seat belt, helmet, speeding, and drunk driving laws. Not only do governments spend money on enforcing these laws but they have honest police who can effectively conduct enforcement and make sure that *de jure* and *de facto* behaviors match.

Stronger and more effective governments in many rich countries have also taken to dealing with the tragedy of the commons by using one of their most powerful tools for changing incentives: taxation. Many governments have increased vehicle registration fees in order to discourage car ownership at the margin. Big cities such as Singapore (all the way back in 1975), London, Milan, and Stockholm have taken things further, forcing drivers to pay an additional toll to enter and drive on city roads (and also to park their cars) during peak traffic times. The intuition behind these congestion taxes is to "internalize" the negative externality by increasing the personal costs of driving closer to the social costs. In essence, drivers are being forced to consider whether the benefits of the car trip they are about to make, and the time at which they are making it at, are greater than the "true" cost of driving. According to one study, congestion taxes in London (about $19 per trip) have reduced car traffic during peak times by roughly 13 percent as more people have been sufficiently incentivized to take public transportation.[31]

To better understand how congestion taxes work, let's return to our Nash equilibrium example from before, but now assume that everyone who drives more is forced to incur a penalty of -2 points, reducing their payoffs so that they are now the following, as shown in the table below:

		Others	
		Drive Less	*Drive More*
You	*Drive less*	(2,2)	(0,1)
	Drive more	(1,0)	(−1,−1)

Notice that the Nash equilibrium has now changed. It is now a best strategy for you and for others to drive less because driving more now has a lower payoff. In this case, this congestion tax has actually allowed the government to increase the overall payoff to society by making the cooperative outcome more attractive at the individual level. It is a good example of how a strong and informed government can use the tools at its disposal to change incentives and improve institutions in ways that can benefit everyone.

Congestion taxes have been taken to the extreme in China, like so many other things there. The Chinese government has tried to discourage driving and limit congestion by imposing huge registration fees on cars in the "first-tier" cities of Beijing, Shanghai, Guangzhou, and Shenzhen. For example, registering a new vehicle in Shanghai costs $9,000, significantly more than average annual income in the country. In Beijing, permits are rationed not only by price but by lottery. In 2014, more than 1.74 million people applied for only 150,000 new vehicle permits.[32] Of course, the immediate question on the lips of most Chinese was whether this is a true lottery or whether the dice are loaded in favor of government officials and party members who, unsurprisingly, seem to be having a great deal of "luck" getting car permits. In other countries, imposing such large taxes and fees is politically infeasible. After extensive discussion and frequent complaints from constituents, New York City rejected a congestion tax similar to that of London. In Dhaka, attempts to limit the number of rickshaws—which employ 1.5 million of the city's poorest residents—only resulted in massive protests and increased bribery opportunities for the city's police.

Are there good reasons to believe that driving skills will improve and roads will become dramatically safer over time? While it is nice to think about some utopia where accidents, traffic jams, reckless driving, and car fatalities have become historical events like chariot collisions, there is at least one good reason to think that bad and reckless driving will permanently be with us: Unfortunately, as driving gets safer, drivers tend to take more risks. This phenomenon is often referred to as the Peltzman effect after the economist Sam Peltzman, who argued that safety innovations and regulations in the 1960s and 1970s—such as seat belts, air bags, and auto insurance requirements—had not reduced vehicular death rates.[33] While there was some decline in driver fatalities, they had been offset by higher death rates for those not protected by these safety innovations, such as pedestrians and bicyclists. This is because drivers who feel safer tend to drive less cautiously. It is, inevitably, human nature to disregard what is not foremost in our minds. As a result, reductions in the dangers associated with driving have not fallen by as much as one would expect based on the benefits of new technologies in isolation. We humans have a way of defeating our own best intentions.

The new technologies of the future such as driverless cars are unlikely to make us perfectly safe because the human element will still exist. And for that reason, a road in India will in all likelihood still be Indian and a street in China distinctly Chinese because of the distinctive institutions that exist in each place. This will be considered normal for the Indian in India and the Chinese in China; for visitors, these unique driving experiences will be a source of frustration and fascination, which is part of what makes travel worth the hardship.

Why Are There More Workers Than Patrons at This Coffee House? The Tradeoff between Capital and Labor

When some people travel, they merely contemplate what is before their eyes. When I travel, I contemplate the process of mutability.
—Lieh-Tzu[1]

In 2009, I went with my wife and children to live in Botswana while I served as the director of a study abroad program. I applied for this job because I felt that it was a chance to contribute to the educational experience of University of Botswana students and to put into action my deep commitment to the international education of American students. In reality, I spent most of my time dealing with an endless series of managers and bureaucrats. For example, the modest university-owned apartment my family moved into was initially missing a few things: water and electricity, chief among them. In order to get these services, I had to deal with the university's maintenance department. When I visited the maintenance building, the head man in office #13 told me to take copies of my request to the men in offices #7, #8, and #10. The man in #7 told me I needed to go to #6, which I did. The man in #8 gave me copies to take to #4 and #5. The man in #10 was not there, so I took the request to his secretary in #9. She told me to come back tomorrow.

I spent my first week in Botswana daily visiting my new friends in offices #6, #7, #8, #9, and #13. To an observer, it must have looked as if I was trapped in a life-sized game of "Whack-a-Mole" as I popped in and out of offices. The head man (in office #13) always seemed to be taking my case very seriously—at least that is how I chose to read the concerned look he got on his face whenever I knocked on his door. The gentleman in office #8 could not help me in getting my water heater working, but he enthusiastically worked on trying to get me to participate in a get-rich-quick scheme he had devised where I would go back to the states, buy a bunch of iPhones, and ship them back to him so he could sell them in South Africa at a much higher price. I felt like the nameless author in Franz Kafka's *The Trial*, who was trapped into endlessly petitioning hundreds of seemingly random people in a fruitless attempt to learn what crime he had been charged with.[2] I knew what would lie at the end of this entire process: when I finally found the right person, I wouldn't have the right form.

Occasionally, a team of laborers would show up at my apartment to tinker with my maintenance problems: two men to work and two men to supervise. Interestingly, they never brought power tools, only the most basic hand-powered tools. I assumed that the reason why so many workers were needed was that without much equipment, even the easiest of jobs became physically demanding.

Sometimes I needed a break from working the endless bureaucratic maze and retreated to the local coffee shop at the American-style shopping mall. It had the three things that Westerners most desired: coffee, air conditioning, and Internet access. Every time I was there, regardless of the time of day, there were as many workers as patrons in the shop. The coffee shop manager desperately tried to find things for the workers to do—one day I saw him assign a couple of servers to polish the *bottom* of the tables. Periodically, a customer would walk into the shop and would immediately be surrounded by a circle of waiters or waitresses seeking something to do to help them fill up their work hours. Inevitably, the employees spent most of their time engaged in chit-chat with customers about the latest doings in the English Premier League (that customer was most likely me). This was all much different than my coffee shop experiences back home, where only two baristas regularly hustled to quickly serve wave after wave of impatient and caffeine-starved patrons with the help of an industrial espresso machine as big as a refrigerator.

One dependable measure of a country's level of economic development is the number of people paid to stand around and do very little, or to do much less than what they could be doing if they had better tools at their

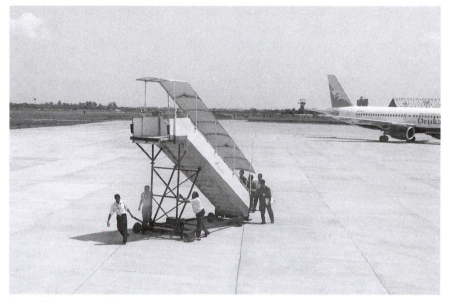

Lots of men at work.

disposal. The examples are ubiquitous to any traveler in the less developed world: Indian day-laborers breaking rocks into gravel with a hammer; South Africans cutting grass along the roadsides with scythes; a Belizean police officer flagging traffic at an intersection in place of a traffic light. In many economies, everything that can be done by hand is done by hand. In the above photo, a group of men in Nepal are pushing an airplane ladder across a runway instead of having one man move it with the help of a motorized vehicle (not shown is the similar-sized group of workers standing outside of the picture watching these men push the ladder). Production in poor countries is very labor-intensive, and little capital is used even when that capital is available and relatively cheap.

Why is this the case? You will commonly hear—you might have even said it yourself during your own travels—that there are just too many people in poor countries. One hypothesis is that surplus labor encourages firms to do things in labor-intensive ways. But there are problems with this explanation. What do you mean by "too many people"? The population density in many poor countries (e.g., southern Africa) is among the lowest in the world, while many rich countries have very high population densities. And producers don't make decisions based on how many people they employ, but upon how much profit they can generate. European farmers are not saying to themselves: "Unemployment is high right now, so I am not going to buy that tractor. Instead, I am going to hire some more workers to dig in the dirt with a shovel."

Another hypothesis is that capital is just not available in some areas of the world. Labor is used intensively in poor countries because often, there is no other choice. Once again, however, there are problems with this explanation. If capital is so hard to come by, why are Chinese peasants planting seeds by hand just miles away from Beijing where billion-dollar public infrastructure projects are announced weekly? Also, it's not just the expensive and technologically advanced capital that is missing in less developed countries, but cheap and easily obtainable capital as well; think back to those Batswana maintenance workers working without power tools. Here's another problem with the hypothesis that capital is unavailable: If poorer countries were simply capital-starved, wouldn't profit-driven investors seek to remedy that? Simple supply and demand analysis says that the return on an asset increases as it becomes increasingly scarce. Those with wealth to invest should be able to find many potentially profitable uses for capital in capital-scarce countries. But in reality, this often does not happen, particularly in the poorest of poor countries.

In this chapter, I want to examine the labor–capital tradeoff and how it differs across countries, richer and poorer. What is the relationship between population growth, capital investment, and economic growth? Do poor countries suffer from a surplus of people or a shortage of capital? Or both? Or neither?

One of the great novels in English literature also provides us with some of the best insight into the productivity of labor and the process of economic growth. The book is *Robinson Crusoe*, published in 1719 by Daniel Defoe. In this well-known novel, a man stranded on a desert island is forced to live on his own wits. He has to be a jack-of-all-trades, growing his own food, making his own clothes, and building his own house. Crusoe is resourceful and clever, but there is one thing that Crusoe cannot be: productive. Because he needs to do everything for himself (until a native he names Friday shows up), he can't specialize in doing anything very well. He does not get the benefits of repetition, of building specific tools for certain jobs, or of figuring out better methods of doing specific jobs over time.

Defoe clearly anticipated the fundamental insights of Adam Smith's *The Wealth of Nations*, written roughly 50 years later. In Smith's conception of the "invisible hand of the marketplace," it is the gains from specialization coupled with the power of markets that drive increases in the productivity of labor over time and ultimately generate higher standards of living.

Specialization is crucial to growth because it is impossible to be an expert at producing everything. By specializing in certain activities, each individual can develop specific skills that increases their productivity. But humans also crave variety, and this is where markets come in. Markets allow us to trade what we are good at producing for an infinite variety of goods that we are not so good at producing. This means that we can have the best of both worlds—variety and volume—without being trapped in a Robinson Crusoe economy where we have to make everything for ourselves and are not very good at doing any of it. While Smith's ideas on specialization and trade are simple, they are also powerful; after 250 years, they remain the most succinct explanation of how people increase their productivity and quality of life over time.

Next to Adam Smith, the next most influential thinker from economics' first century is probably Thomas Malthus.[3] Unlike Adam Smith, who was an academic philosopher with a predilection towards utopian thinking, Thomas Malthus was a dour English cleric with a bent toward the dismal. If they had a modern favorite film, Adam Smith would choose Star Trek and Thomas Malthus a zombie movie. Malthus's pessimistic view of the future has influenced generations of doomsayers. Just as in those zombie movies, Malthus lurks around every corner, his ideas refusing to die, ready to consume brains.

The cornerstone of Malthus's theory is one of the most important—and broadly applicable—ideas in economics. This is the law of diminishing marginal returns to labor. (We introduced its cousin, diminishing marginal returns to capital, in Chapter 1.) Assume for the sake of simplicity that only two things go into production: capital and labor (forget, right now, that not all labor and capital are the same, or that technology advances over time). The law of diminishing marginal returns to labor says that if I add more and more labor to a fixed amount of capital, holding everything else the same, the productivity of these new laborers is going to fall. Because I am asking each new worker to work with less and less capital per worker, each new worker will be less productive. For example, consider that coffee shop in Botswana, which daily demonstrated the applicability of diminishing returns to labor. As more and more workers were added to a fixed amount of capital (the coffee shop itself), the productivity of each worker got lower and lower.

Malthus's theory of economic growth is based on an understanding of the diminishing marginal returns to labor coupled with his real-world observations as a cleric living in rural England in the late 1700s. Malthus witnessed two things that shaped his vision of the future. First, the English population was growing. In fact, the level of the population was growing exponentially in England because of the power of compounding. Today's children will eventually have children of their own, and so on; as a result, the level of the population will explode over time. Malthus's second observation was that while the population was growing exponentially, the methods of production and the amount of capital were not. In late 18th-century England, people were working in much the same ways that they had for centuries: Most people were farmers, most capital was land (which in the island nation of England was not growing), and the capital used to farm this land had not changed in any appreciable ways since the Iron Age. The result is that standards of living in England were very low. During the late 1700s, the average British farmer consumed only 1500 calories a day, one-third less than primitive hunter-gatherer tribes, mostly in the form of bread. But even at these low levels, English farmers were better off than those on the continent, the French and Germans, who had enjoyed even less improvement in their methods of agricultural production.[4]

Putting these two observations together, Malthus came to the conclusion that one plus one was something less than zero. As population continued to grow, the result would be more and more labor added to a relatively constant amount of capital. Because of the law of diminishing returns to labor, labor productivity would steadily fall. Eventually, labor productivity and standards of living would drop below what is needed to provide subsistence-levels of consumption. In other words, the population would increase to such a point that it would not be sustainable. Massive famines would inevitably occur.

While famines are horrible, there is a bright side (who said Malthus was a dismal, glass-half-empty kind of guy?). Famines would reduce the size of the population, increase labor productivity (diminishing returns working in reverse), and improve standards of living (for those who survived). Unfortunately, these good times would not last long. Malthus was skeptical about humans' ability to exert self-control. He argued that any increases in income that resulted from a falling population would inevitably lead to higher population growth rates as people became healthier and went right back to their procreative habits, leading to another lap on the same vicious population cycle.

Malthus influenced generations of development economists and policymakers. His influence on Karl Marx, which we discussed in Chapter 1, is obvious. Both believed that wages would have to fall over time in a capitalist economy—Malthus because the supply of labor was increasing, Marx because the only way to increase profits was to exploit workers. In hindsight, however, it is clear that Malthus's influence on economic thinking is similar to Justin Bieber's influence on pop music: most unfortunate.

Malthus has been used to justify forced sterilizations of the poor. For example, between 1975 and 1976, 21 percent of Indian couples (more than 8 million people) were sterilized, most forcibly, with the encouragement and financial support of international aid agencies such as the World Bank and the United States government.[5] Malthus played an important advisory role in China's adoption of its one-child policies in 1980. Such policies have trampled over individual rights and led to millions of involuntary abortions and infanticides, particularly of girls. Policymakers at the national and international levels have pushed "cash for condoms" policies based upon Malthusian thinking, but which did little to reduce birth rates because most births in poor countries are the result of intended pregnancies, not accidental.[6] Malthus has also been used to justify huge aid-based capital construction programs under the rationale that the primary reason the productivity of labor is so low in poor countries is that they have too little capital. These capital-building programs have generally been ineffective, and billions of dollars have been wasted, saddling many countries with oppressive levels of debt.

It is curious that Malthus continues to garner so many admirers because Malthus's predictions regarding population growth are clearly refuted by experience. For most of human history, neither sustained population growth nor sustained income growth occurred. The average rate of population growth between 1 million BCE and 1800 CE was only .02 percent a year. Per capita growth during this period was only .05 percent a year, but it was highest where population growth was the highest, in direct contrast to the claims of Malthus. Beginning in the late 1700s, population began to grow at a much faster rate, as Malthus observed. But world population has continued to grow since that time and has not contracted as Malthus predicted. It took 250,000 years for the world's population to reach 1 billion in 1804, but it took only a little more than one additional century to reach 2 billion (in 1927), and only 33 more years to reach 3 billion (in 1960). It took only 12 years to get from 6 billion to 7 billion, which occurred in 2011. But despite this exponential population growth, global per-capita income is higher now than it has ever been. In fact, today obesity is a larger global public health problem than famine. The World Health Organization reports that obesity has doubled across the globe since 1980, and 65 percent of the world's population lives in countries where more people are dying from medical complications associated with obesity than are dying from health problems associated with malnourishment.[7]

Malthus was wrong. Understanding why Malthus was wrong—and the things that he was right about—is a great way to come to a deeper understanding about why poor countries tend to use more labor-intensive production methods and why rich countries use more capital-intensive production methods.

Here is the first, and most obvious, problem with Malthus's analysis: He did not consider the role of improvements in technology. Technology has played a key role in increased food production, and in the production of all goods and services. Technology does this in two ways. First, technology changes the nature of inputs by creating new forms of capital and labor that had not previously existed. Technology has created many new forms of capital and other inputs that have greatly increased agricultural production: tractors, combines, fertilizers, pesticides, and genetically modified seeds (both naturally and engineered), to name a few. As a result, modern agricultural production is about much more than land and brute effort. Although Malthus was writing during a time when the Industrial Revolution was well under way in England, he failed to see how the innovations being made in manufacturing would eventually make their way into the agricultural sector of the economy.

Second, technology has also changed production processes so that we get more output with the same amount of inputs. For example, consider Henry Ford's idea of the assembly line. Instead of keeping the cars in one place and asking the workers to move, Ford set up a system where the workers remained stationary and the cars moved. When stated that way, it doesn't sound like such a radical idea, but this small insight allowed Ford to dramatically increase the number of cars he could produce with the same levels of workers and capital.

The most important change in the agricultural production process in the modern era is that new technologies have allowed for the creation of larger farms that rely much more upon physical capital and much less upon labor. Agricultural innovation has freed more people to move off the farm and into the production of other goods. In Malthus's world view, most people could only find work as farmers, meaning that population growth chained more and more people to a fixed amount of land. But what has actually happened is that higher agricultural labor productivity created surplus labor, which encouraged people to migrate to urban areas to work in industries that are less dependent upon land. In 1600, 70 percent of the United Kingdom's population lived in rural areas, but today this number is less than 2 percent.[8] This urban migration fueled the Industrial Revolution in Britain (just as it is doing today in China), and it also meant that more people were not helplessly tied to the ups and downs of agriculture but became part of an increasingly diversified and fast-growing economy.

Technology is the most important way that economies overcome the limits of diminishing marginal returns. Growth driven by capital or labor effort is necessarily constrained. Improving labor productivity by only increasing inputs is limited by the amount of resources people can save and accumulate to build new capital. Improving labor productivity by working harder or working more is limited by physical restrictions such as the fact that there are 24 hours in a day. But technology can increase without bounds. It is not limited by the natural resources you have, by how much land you have, or by the size of your population. Technology is only limited by the size of our collective imagination. Today an American worker can earn in only 17 weeks what it took a American worker in 1915 an entire year to earn.[9] Malthus's failure was an inability to conceive of the relative utopia that we live in today. Because he was unable to imagine a world in which people would do more than farm, eat, and have sex, he failed to foresee the diversity, robustness, and growth that characterizes modern life.

Malthus's second failure is also related to technology, but in a different way. Malthus never considered the possibility that population growth is not just a drag on productivity because of diminishing returns. In fact, having more people creates more ideas; this leads to faster technological growth and rising productivity levels, not lower standards of living.

There are a number of reasons why having a larger population actually increases innovation and economic growth. To understand these reasons, we first need to talk about the economic characteristics of technology and how new technologies are created. This is such an important and interesting topic that I would like to devote a full chapter to it later in this book (Chapter 6). So I am going to build some anticipation and make you wait for some answers. (Is it working?) But for now, even without a full understanding of the technological creation process, there is one simple reason that explains why a larger population leads to more technology growth: Having a larger population increases the chances that you will have more geniuses, which in turn increases the likelihood of a "great invention" being created. Now, as we will talk about later, the picture of innovation that many of us have in our heads—where technology is created in a laboratory by a solitary mad scientist working frantically—is generally a bad way to think about where most technology comes from. But undoubtedly genius does play a role in some new technologies, and the odds favor having more of these geniuses as the population grows in size. I will add more reasons as to why larger populations might facilitate more technological innovation when we return to this discussion in Chapter 6.

The third problem with Malthus's dire predictions about population growth leading to economic calamity is that Malthus failed to consider an alternative hypothesis: that it is changes in income that cause population growth rates to change, and not vice versa. While rich-country policy-makers often fret about high birth rates in less developed countries, they turn around and worry about the low birth rates in their own countries. Today, half of the world lives in countries in which birth rates are lower than mortality rates, meaning that their population is shrinking. The countries that have made this demographic transition include most of Europe, Japan, Canada, and China.[10] In fact, the national and local governments in many of these countries, such as Italy and Germany, have taken to providing financial incentives to couples in an attempt to incentivize people having more children.

However, given the high price of having a child, it is unlikely that the modest financial incentives offered by governments will be enough to significantly increase birth rates. What Malthus failed to consider is that as income rises and people move to urban areas, the opportunity cost of having more children has increased greatly relative to the benefits of having more children. Today, when a woman decides to have a child, she has to forfeit professional opportunities and income—these were not considerations when most women worked at home. In addition, children cost more today because we are preparing them for a skill-intensive workforce. Education is costly, and the time spent on education is time that a child cannot spend providing income to the family through work. Finally—and it is somewhat crass to say this so bluntly—declines in infant mortality associated with rising standards of living make it more likely that parents will be rewarded for any investment that they make in a child. When so many children die as infants in poor countries, many parents have large numbers of children as a form of insurance, hoping that a few will survive to adulthood in order to provide income for the rest of the family. For example, the 20-year increase in average life expectancy that India experienced between 1955 and 2005 was associated with a 50 percent drop in fertility.

As a result of these factors, fertility rates are declining dramatically in countries that are experiencing economic growth. For example, fertility rates in Vietnam have fallen from 7.5 births per woman in 1970 to a little more than 2 today. Many emerging market economies such as Turkey, Brazil, and Thailand have already seen their birthrates fall below replacement levels. These changes in the developing world will continue to slow world population growth rates for generations, and global birthrates have already fallen from 6.0 births per woman to 2.9 births per women between 1972 and 2008.[11] The United Nations predicts that by 2040, world population growth will fall to levels not seen since before the Industrial Revolution, and by 2070 world population growth will be less than 0.2 percent a year.[12] The fact is that the most effective method of birth control is getting richer.

Let's continue to pile on poor Mr. Malthus—particularly given that he is no longer here to defend himself. The fourth and final problem with Malthus's view of economic growth is that it ignores what is at the heart of growth: incentives and institutions. As we have already talked about throughout this book, when governments and societies are able to build institutions that incentivize people to invest in education, capital, and new technologies, people become individually richer and contribute to improvements in the living standards of society as a whole.

One good example of how institutions impact the relationship between population and income is in the freedom each society grants to women to make their own fertility decisions. When women are free to work, get an education, have a legal right to divorce, hold property, and use contraception, then higher incomes are most likely to reduce birth rates. In many cases, however, all of the decision-making power in a family is controlled by the person that bears the smallest share of the costs of birth: the man. This is often the result of cultural, religious, and social norms, and also because men have a disproportionate share of economic and political power. When women's costs and benefits are not fully considered in family planning decisions, birthrates are likely to be high.

The best example of how institutions, not population levels, create poverty can be found by taking a closer look at the economics behind famines. Contrary to the claims of Malthus, famines are NOT about shortages in food production. They are instead about problems with food distribution. In other words, while nature causes droughts, distorted markets cause famines. The Nobel Prize–winning economist Amartya Sen lived through the Bengal famine of 1943. The conventional thinking for a long time was that this famine was the result of Bengal having too many people and not enough food; Bengal has one of the highest population density rates in the world. But what Sen was able to show is that total food production in Bengal was higher in 1943 than it was in many prior non-famine years.[13] It was not total food production that changed. What did change was that there was a war in the region in 1943. As a result, the wealthy and other elites began to hoard food, driving up its price to exorbitant levels beyond the ability of the rural poor to afford it. This unequal distribution of food was facilitated by poor distribution systems and, most importantly, by the inordinate power of political and economic elites that allowed them to gain access to food before it came to markets, often through corruption. Sen documents how other famines throughout history have followed similar scripts and are always the result of institutional failures, not failures of production. Similar institutional failures are evident in the most famine-plagued nations today: North Korea and Somalia.

Sen has gone on to argue that a famine has never taken place in a democracy because democracies limit the power of elites and tend to create better institutions that ensure inclusive food distribution. Autocracy, on the other hand, undermines inclusive institutions and creates political environments in which famines can take place. This was true during famines in India during the 1800s, blamed on the boom in English cotton and the collapse of the Indian cotton industry (discussed later in this chapter). Why didn't India mechanize cotton production and increase efficiency in the same way that England did? Because of a whole range of policy decisions taken both by Indian officials and their British colonizers aimed at keeping Indian manufacturing inefficient and the country a captive market for British exports.

Another example of how institutions institutionalize famines is the Great Chinese Famine of 1958–1961, during which upwards of 40 million people died. Under the Great Leap Forward program, food production and distribution was taken away from individuals and communalized, greatly reducing agricultural output and also placing food distribution in the hands of corrupt political officials. Corrupt local officials then lied to higher-level officials about what food production actually was. For example, grain production fell by 25 percent between 1958 and 1960, but local officials reported that it doubled. Rural farmers were forced to meet food quotas based on these inflated production statistics that eventually lead to their own starvation. At the same time that millions of people were starving, China actually exported food to Russia in an effort to pay for the military buildup desired by Mao Zedong.[14]

Similar institutional failures are at the heart of why many economists are skeptical of large foreign aid programs. Many foreign aid initiatives, particularly those dating back to the 1950s and 1960s, were based upon the Malthusian rationale that there are too many poor people and that the only way to increase the productivity of labor is to increase the amount of capital per worker. This "capital fundamentalist" approach claimed that growth was a linear function of a country's investment rate. If you double investment in capital, the thinking went, you will double income growth. As documented by William Easterly in his book *The White Man's Burden*, numerous construction projects for new dams, roads, schools, airports, etc., in the less developed world greatly contributed to the coffers of a few political elites, but created little long-lasting benefit for the general public.[15] The reason is clear: Much of the money was lost through corruption, and most of what was not stolen was wasted through general inexperience, lack of planning, and poor maintenance. Just giving a country capital without the appropriate complementary inputs—such as knowledge, technology, and productive institutions—is a very effective way of fostering corruption, but an ineffective way of fostering economic growth.

Now that I have spent many pages badmouthing poor Malthus, I do want to concede one point to him. Here it is: Just as Malthus argued, whenever conditions exist so that there is a persistent excess supply of labor, then labor will be inexpensive and the demand for capital will be low. Or to put it another way, whenever labor is never fully employed, it will be cheap, and when labor is cheap, it will discourage businesses and governments from investing in the capital and technology that can make labor more productive.

Let me explain this very important point in more detail. Many countries suffer from chronically high unemployment rates. For example, in South Africa unemployment has not fallen below 22 percent at any time during the last two decades; in Spain, it has not fallen below 16 percent. These high unemployment rates actually *underestimate* the true number of people unemployed because many workers who become discouraged by their inability to find work give up looking and drop out of the labor force. Once they are out of the labor force, they are no longer counted as unemployed by the statisticians. The result of having such a large and persistent mismatch between the number of people who want jobs and the number of jobs created is that there is also going to be downward pressure on wages, making labor inexpensive.

However—and this is the key—inexpensive labor reflects unproductive labor. When labor is so cheap, there is little incentive for firms to invest in capital, training, or technology in order to make labor more productive. Instead, firms employ lots of labor and ask them to do their jobs in labor-intensive ways. In other words, they use labor as a substitute for capital and technology, not as complementary inputs into production. We can call this outcome the Malthusian trap. As a result, labor stays cheap, unproductive, and largely unemployed in a continuation of a vicious cycle.

But this is not what we see in countries where there is no persistent surplus of labor. In these countries, labor is in demand and its price is bid up. Labor becomes the most expensive aspect of production. As a result, firms have an incentive to try to reduce their dependence on labor by making it more productive through spending more on capital, education, training, and technology. Thus, labor is destined to become more productive the more expensive it becomes. Economists have collected data to show that the extent to which machines are substitutes for labor is vastly outweighed by the complementarities between labor and capital that increase productivity and wages.[16] As machines replace the routine and codifiable, labor is then freed to engage in more productive activities that rely more upon creativity and problem-solving, and which also pay higher wages.

Consider one historical example of the complementarity between capital and labor: the cotton industry in late 1700s England, the epicenter of the Industrial Revolution. A key reason the Industrial Revolution started in England was because of its high wages. Labor costs were six times higher in Manchester, England than what they were in India in the mid-1700s, when India was the center of the global cotton trade. These high wages in England created incentives for English cotton firms to develop and invest in the creation of machines—such as the spinning jenny—in order to use cheaper capital to replace expensive labor. But instead of replacing labor, this mechanization only increased the aggregate demand for workers in the cotton industry by making labor more productive and growing the overall size of the cotton market. Employment in the English cotton industry went from 2.6 percent of the labor force in 1770 to 22.4 percent by 1830, employing 1 out of every 6 workers in the country, despite the incredible mechanization of textile making.[17] How did this happen? Higher cotton profits led to more capital investment and newer ways of organizing production. Higher productivity led to falling prices for cotton and textiles, increasing the demand for cotton and creating new jobs in England in the process. Unfortunately, lower cotton prices didn't help everyone. The Indian cotton industry, strangled by unproductive institutions, remained labor-intensive and capital-poor. Eventually, the Indian cotton industry was devastated by English competition, shrinking by more than 50 percent (and contributing to localized famines, as we discussed earlier).

Consider a modern example of the complementarity between capital and labor: ATM machines. You would think that if there was any new form of capital that killed jobs, it would have been the spread of ATM machines in the 1990s. ATMs seemingly made the vast majority of bank tellers obsolete. However, as the number of ATMs in the United States increased from 100,000 to 400,000 between 1995–2010, the number of people employed as bank tellers actually increased. Why? First, while fewer tellers were needed at each branch, banks opened more branches (40 percent more) because each branch could operate with fewer tellers and became cheaper to maintain. Second, bank tellers were freed by ATMs to do different jobs other than just cash transactions and focus on activities that machines cannot do, such as relationship building and providing financial advice—activities that significantly contribute to a bank's profitability and increased the demand to hire more tellers.[18]

The fact that labor and capital are complements, not substitutes, is an absolutely fundamental insight into the economics of development, but yet one that very few people fully understand. Many people reflexively accept the Malthusian view and think of labor and capital as substitutes—i.e., the more capital you use, the less labor you employ. But instead, capital and labor are complements in countries where growth is occurring. When you have more capital, labor becomes more productive and, hence, more valuable. This incentivizes the accumulation of capital, which increases wages and employment. Higher employment and wages then incentivize the accumulation of more capital in a virtuous circle.

The problem in countries with persistently high unemployment rates is that incentives are consistently skewed towards using labor in quantity, not in quality. Hence, people are employed with scythes along African roadways to cut the grass and with straw brooms along walkways—labor is so cheap that there are no incentives to invest in lawnmowers or blowers. In fact, grass-cutting and street-sweeping teams are seen as a way to put surplus labor to some use, however inefficient this use is. There are no financial incentives to incentivize efficiency. On the other hand, in

Street sweepers in Africa.

countries where labor is relatively scarce, investing in labor-saving capital and technology not only benefits the firm, but it also benefits each worker by making them more productive and increasing their wages.

The simplistic Malthusian view that capital and labor must always be substitutes, not complements, is one of the bad ideas that have dominated economic discourse for centuries. In England, Queen Elizabeth I banned knitting machines in England in 1583, and a group of 19th-century textile workers known as the Luddites smashed mechanical looms in a fight against improving the productivity of labor. In the view of Queen Elizabeth and the Luddites, anything that increased the productivity of labor also discouraged employment. The problem with Luddite thinking is that they assumed that labor-saving machinery would be used to produce the same amount of output, just using less labor. Instead, what we have observed throughout history is that labor-saving capital and technology are used to produce *more* of these goods, and many other new goods, using *more* labor overall. In other words, technology and capital have not been used to replace jobs, but to generate more and different jobs devoted to meeting our unlimited desires for new forms of consumption. Of course, the transition from old jobs to new jobs in different industries is often costly to certain individuals. This is the reason for the short-sighted resistance to new methods of production that has existed throughout history, from the Luddites nearly 200 years ago to those people today who fear that robots and international trade will leave us all unemployed in the future.

How then do countries break out of this Malthusian trap and make capital and labor complements, not substitutes? Importantly, the Malthusian trap has nothing to do with the size of the population itself. A country can have a high level of population but still have low unemployment as long as job creation is sufficiently rapid. Likewise, countries with relatively low populations—here, you can think of most Sub-Saharan African countries where population density is quite low—can still have a large surplus of labor if there is little job creation. Countries escape the Malthusian trap when they can increase the rate of job creation above the level of population growth for a sustained period of time. When it comes to the question of how countries create more jobs, the discussion has to return to—I know, I am beginning to sound like a broken record—institutions. When a country has incentives in place that encourage productive behavior, labor will be utilized efficiently and jobs will be created. These will, in turn, incentivize labor-saving investments in capital and technology that will raise standards of living over time and help an economy break from the Malthusian trap. But when these incentives are not in place, surplus labor begets low wages, labor productivity remains stagnant, and the Malthusian trap becomes a Malthusian prison.

How did institutions first come into place that allowed certain regions to break out of their Malthusian traps? In the predevelopment age, people were unable to produce more than subsistence-level amounts of food. When everyone was barely producing enough to stay alive, it was difficult to save towards building new capital, devote labor towards organizing society in more efficient ways, or spend time on developing new methods of production. As argued by Jared Diamond, whom I discussed in the previous chapter, Eurasia (which includes the Fertile Crescent) escaped from the Malthusian trap earlier than other regions because of the many ecological advantages that it possessed.[19] As a result, Eurasia was the first to evolve away from a migratory society loosely organized around hunter-gatherers and begin the Neolithic Revolution towards a more complex society built on agriculture and capital investment. These more tightly organized and productive societies were the first to make important institutional advances such as building political systems and organizing armies, which are crucial to protecting and acquiring capital. They were also the first to enforce laws that governed financial transactions and protect the property rights of individuals.

One of the oldest surviving writings in the world is the Code of Hammurabi, the Babylonian code of law that dates back to 1700 BCE and survives on a stone stele in the Louvre. Much of this code is devoted to proscribing the laws that shaped the economic institutions of the day. It specified things such as how contracts can be enforced, what is a legal interest rate to be paid on a loan, who should be held liable and for how much when someone does not fulfill their contractual obligations, and how capital should be passed on through inheritance. Writing and enforcing such laws was not possible until societies were able to develop a state bureaucracy. Creating the structures of a state government only became possible when labor and agriculture became productive enough to generate the income to pay for it and generate the excess labor to operate it.

Changing institutions were also at the heart of ending feudalism and the beginning of the Industrial Revolution in England. Many historians trace the downfall of feudalism in England to one of the most tragic events in European history: the Black Plague. On the negative side of the ledger, the plague killed roughly half of the population of Europe. On the positive side, it drove up wages for those who survived. Higher wages and general social unrest led to a revolution among the laboring classes in England, known as the Peasant Revolt, which took place in 1381. As a result of this revolt, labor markets were eventually freed by allowing workers to leave their places of birth without the permission of landholders. The fact that people were not tied to the land in the same ways that they were in other countries meant that labor migrated to urban areas earlier in England than elsewhere; this is one of the important but often ignored reasons why the Industrial Revolution began in England.

During the colonial era, distinctive ecologies as well as different colonization strategies served to create many varied conditions for labor across the globe. Consider the differences between the colonial institutions established in North America versus those in Latin and South America. Latin and South American economies relied heavily on imported slaves from Africa and enslaved indigenous peoples. In part, this was because the kind of crops that could be grown in most of these regions, such as sugar cane and cotton, were best produced at scale, demanding large farms and a small number of owners. (For this reason, the development of the southern United States should be considered closer to that of Latin America, while the development of the southern part of South America is actually closer to that of the northern United States). Institutions in different colonies were also a function of the settler mortality in each colony, as we discussed in the last chapter when we talked about the work of Acemoglu, Robinson, and Johnson.[20] The existence of heat and disease in the American South discouraged colonists from working the land by themselves and instead they relied on slave labor, both indigenous and trafficked from Africa. Slavery not only created a permanent surplus of labor, but it also removed incentives for producers to be concerned about the well-being of their laborers. In other words, it created institutions that imposed a Malthusian existence on the vast majority of the population.

On the other hand, in more temperate regions where the climate was less conducive to disease, settlers tended to emigrate with their families and work their own land. This was easier to do in North America because English colonies were organized under a land system that favored the establishment of a large number of small landholders. Not so in the Spanish and Portuguese colonies, which were organized under the *encomienda* system, which literally granted the ownership of indigenous people to landowners; in exchange, the landowner was responsible for their religious well-being (but not necessarily their physical well-being). One implication of these different systems is that squatters were given significant rights in the North but almost none in South and Central America. Many northern colonies adopted systems in which squatters were allowed to buy title to land at a price set by a jury if the legal owner would not pay for improvements made by squatters. In addition, government-owned land was widely distributed among the population in North America through a long series of land laws, such as the Homestead Act of 1862 in the United States. As a result, capital in the form of land was freely available, but surplus labor looking for work was not. Labor shortages were a consistent fact of life in the North American colonies where slavery was banned and population density was always much lower, even before colonization. (For example, the population density of indigenous peoples in the United States was only about one-fifth of that in Mexico.) Because of this labor shortage, labor-saving capital and technology was always more quickly adopted in the north. Not surprisingly, it is in the north where the Industrial Revolution first took hold in the Americas.

What about Africa? Obviously, the extractive institutions set up by colonizers to plunder the minerals and labor of Africa played a disastrous role on the continent just as they have done in Latin America. However, one important difference in Africa is that a huge fraction of the African population was actually shipped out of Africa. Many areas in West Africa saw population declines of between 10 and 40 percent during the Atlantic slave trade. When England lost half of its population during the Black Plague, it served to raise wages and increase labor productivity, and eventually it sparked improved institutions. In Africa, because the slave trade destroyed institutions as well as lives, the population collapse only created more competition for capturing new slaves, producing regional power vacuums that sparked generations of civil conflict between different groups trying to steal larger pieces of a shrinking economic pie.

What about today? What are some of the factors that shape today's institutions and which keep many countries stuck in a Malthusian trap of surplus labor, low labor productivity, and low standards of living? Let me focus here on five ways that dysfunctional institutions contribute to the continuation of the Malthusian trap today.

Labor Markets and Investment Decisions Are Often Distorted by Governments

Many policymakers think that the best way to reduce the surplus of labor and raise wages is to regulate these problems away. Unfortunately, these sorts of regulations are usually counterproductive. Take, for example, the simple matter of registering a business so that it can legally hire workers. Some argue that this process needs to be lengthy and exacting because workers can be exploited. However, reasonable regulation can quickly grow into excessive red tape that gets wrapped around the neck of job creation. According to the annual World Bank publication *Doing Business*, in the United States it takes an average of 6 days to complete and process the paperwork to start a small business at a cost equivalent to roughly 1.4 percent of per-capita GDP.[21] In India it takes 29 days at a cost of 50 percent of per-capita GDP; in Nigeria, 34 days and 63 percent of per-capita GDP. The harder it is to open a business or close a business, hire a worker or fire a worker, change a wage or resist wage changes set by the government, or avoid paying a bribe, then the less likely it is that businesses will hire new workers.

This is a big reason why so many businesses in countries with persistently high levels of unemployment are family-owned or one-person operations. In the words of the development economists Abhijit Banerjee and Esther Duflo, most of the world's poor are "reluctant entrepreneurs."[22] The unemployed are often forced to be their own bosses because it is their only way to get work. Roughly 50 percent of the urban poor have their own businesses.[23] Many poor are forced to start their own small businesses because of a lack of job opportunities. These small businesses tend to operate in the informal sector of the economy and are undercapitalized, lack economies of scale in production, and have difficulty sustaining over-time. Informal production accounts for 40 to 80 percent of GDP in less developed countries, and the poorer the country, the larger the informal markets.

Without access to capital and education, the logical choice for most small entrepreneurs is to do jobs with no barriers to entry, no start-up costs, no oversight, and no paperwork. Many street vendors in China offer services such as ear cleaning and knife sharpening; in India, you can get basic dental work (such as tooth removal) done at your bus stop (and no appointment necessary!). Although the market for these services might be limited, the appeal of these jobs is that every cent earned is a cent of profit. It is a hard way to earn a living, but the only way that makes sense and cents. Some of my most prominent memories of traveling are of the women in many countries who fill sidewalks selling street food in the morning, fruit and mobile phone minutes in the middle of the day, and street food again as people return home from work at the end of the day. In the evening, they collect recyclables and wood from the streets and fields. Their work effort is humbling; their inability to convert this hard work into higher incomes is heartbreaking.

It is not just poor countries that overregulate labor. The misguided 35-hour work week adopted in France in 2000 did not increase the demand for labor or add to people's *joie de vivre*. What French politicians don't understand about economics could fill the Louvre. The shorter work week only served to increase the cost of labor and disincentivize hiring more workers (one of the reasons why unemployment in France is consistently above 10 percent), while also failing to reduce the number of hours worked a week by those lucky to still have a job as firms cut back on breaks and free time. Likewise, unemployment benefits in other Western European countries are so generous that workers often work "under the table" in informal labor markets so that they can continue to collect unemployment benefits. For example, unemployed workers can earn nearly three-fourths of their previous salary while collecting unemployment insurance in the Netherlands.[24] Not surprisingly, countries that have the most generous benefits are also the countries where labor is most tightly regulated and it is hardest to find a job.

Capital is also highly regulated by governments in many ways. One of the most important barriers to capital creation is a lack of finance. Businesses need finance in order to obtain the resources needed for investment, but finance is often difficult to obtain in many countries, rich and poor. Many lack access to borrowing because, according to the old adage, "only those that don't need loans can get them." However, it is also true that there is a great deal of variability in finance that is not tied to income levels. In the Middle East, only 25 percent of firms have access to formal finance as compared to 38 percent in Sub-Saharan Africa, 45 percent in Southern Asia, and 55 percent in Latin America.[25]

Why so little finance? In many countries, governments use their financial systems as a cash cow to fill the public coffers. Banks are heavily taxed and regulated towards serving the interests of the government or elites, but at the cost of the overall level of finance being repressed. The microfinance movement, in which small loans are made available to groups of individuals, particularly groups of women, is aimed at trying to find sustainable ways of providing financial access to those that have traditionally been forced to live without it because of a shortage of financial services from traditional banks.

Poor Education Keeps People Poor

When labor is labor—when it is a commodity, as opposed to a specialized input—it is destined to be cheap. Poor countries typically have poor educational systems. Walking the city centers of Buenos Aires, Johannesburg, or Mumbai, you can occasionally forget you are not in Chicago, Hamburg, or Osaka. But when you visit the public schools in Buenos Aires, Johannesburg, or Mumbai, you will never forget where you are. The schools are dark and crumbling, classes are large (three to five times more students per teacher in poor countries), the teachers have education levels that are only marginally above their students (only 10 percent of teachers in many poor countries have formal training), and often the teachers and students are not even there at all (student and teacher absenteeism is roughly 50 percent in some countries such as India).[26]

Exactly what makes for a good education system is a very difficult question to answer.[27] But by most any measure, one of the largest and most persistent differences between rich countries and poor countries is in the quality of their educational systems. Consider just one data point: Only one of the top 50 universities in the world is in a country with per-capita GDP less than $30,000 a year (Tsinghua University in China).[28]

When labor becomes specialized, it is no longer the quantity of labor that matters, but the *human capital* that is in this labor. It is human capital that gets paid a premium. Human capital in the United States is a huge source of wealth and a principal reason why labor productivity and wages are high. According to economists, the value of human capital in the United States is four times the value of its physical capital.[29] This is a surprising figure to many, but one that shouldn't be to those of us who have spent more money on our college education than our house and almost as many years in school as we have spent working. People in developed countries spend almost twice the amount of time (12.4 years vs 6.7 years on average) in school as compared to less developed countries.[30]

These differences in schooling are not caused by differences in school access, or the supply of education. Today, 99 percent of the world's population has access to public schooling. Instead, the biggest problem is the demand for schooling, which in turn reflects a lack of perceived value. In some countries, the quality of schooling is seen as being so poor that it is not worth the fees or the time. For others, poverty combined with the attraction of earning a wage incentivizes child labor over schooling.

Programs that pay families small stipends for every child that regularly attends school, such as the PROGRESSA program in Mexico (which pays between $5 and $20 a month to families of school-aged children), have shown great promise in increasing school attendance, particularly among the poorest of the poor.[31] But history has shown that the most effective way of reducing child labor is to increase the overall productivity of labor. More productive labor decreases the demand for child labor, which is unproductive and low-skilled, while increasing wages for those adults in the family that are of working age, reducing the need for child wages.

Dysfunctional Legal Systems Fail to Protect Property Rights and Encourage Investment

As discussed in the last chapter, dysfunctional legal systems are often unfair because they are operated by judges and enforcement officials who are corrupt. Bad legal systems also delay justice so long that it fails to matter. When firms and entrepreneurs have little confidence that contracts will be honored and promises can be relied upon, they are reluctant to start businesses and engage in the kinds of long-term investment in physical and human capital that drive employment and wage growth.

Property rights are at the heart of incentivizing investment. When property rights are not sufficiently protected, people have no reason to make the sacrifices and take the risks associated with investing in physical and human capital. When a government, a bureaucrat, a mobster, a soldier, or an opportunist can take what is yours without recourse, no one will create things worth taking.

Economic historians, such as the Nobel Prize winner Douglas North, have argued that the spark that ignited the Industrial Revolution was not new technologies, as is taught in many high school textbooks.[32] The fact of the matter is that most of the technologies that we now associate with the Industrial Revolution, such as the steam engine, had already existed for years—the Romans had steam engines. What initiated the Industrial Revolution was the gradual recognition of a single idea: that individual property rights should be respected. According to this view, it is no coincidence that the Industrial Revolution began in England, the place where the first limits on the government's ability to expropriate personal property were adopted. The Declaration of Independence, the French Universal Declaration of Human Rights, the Bill of Rights, Adam Smith's *The Wealth of Nations*, David Hume's *A Treatise on Human Nature*—each of these seminal documents are from the mid-18th century, and each attests to a change in mindset away from vesting power and ownership rights in the state and towards vesting power and ownership rights in individuals. All great journeys begin with a step, and this seemingly simple idea of individual property rights helped transform unproductive institutions into productive institutions, starting countries that accepted it on the path of rapid economic development.

Yet despite the obvious successes of countries that have made enduring commitments to honor individual property rights, many countries find it difficult to protect property rights for a host of political, sociological, and historical reasons. The failures of property rights regimes could fill many books, but let me discuss just one here: the failure of many countries to provide adequate legal title to privately held land. Hernando De Soto argues in his book *The Mystery of Capital* that the fundamental cause of underdevelopment in many places is that it is too expensive and time-consuming for the poor to obtain legal title to the assets that they informally own.[33] De Soto documents just how extreme some of the obstacles to obtaining legal title can be. For example, in the Philippines, obtaining legal title to untitled urban land involved completing 168 bureaucratic steps that take between 13–25 years to complete. In Haiti, purchasing government land involved 176 steps that would take 19 years to navigate. De Soto estimates that the total value of real estate without proper legal title in the emerging world was more than $9 trillion in the year 2000. To put this number in some perspective, this is 93 times the amount of foreign aid given to the developing world over the last three decades. Without legal title and formal ownership, this land and capital cannot be used as collateral in order to gain access to finance. It also reduces the incentives to improve upon this land in an effort to make it more productive. This "dead capital" cannot be used to increase labor productivity, employment, and wages in the ways that it could if it existed under a legal system that more effectively assigned ownership rights to it.

Another source of unproductive property rights has to do with allocating land communally as opposed to individuals. In 31 of Africa's 54 countries, less than 5 percent of rural land is owned privately by the farmers who work it.[34] Similarly, if you have ever traveled through a Native American reservation in the American West, you will notice the high number of mobile trailers that people are living in and the scarcity of houses and business structures. The reason is that that the land is owned by communities and not individuals. Without personal ownership, individuals have few incentives to make a big investment in land that can be easily taken away. In addition, getting a mortgage to buy permanent housing is almost impossible without the land title to serve as collateral to back the loan.

A Lack of Macroeconomic Stability Leads to Employment Instability

In developed countries, the default assumption of investors is one of stability. In poorer countries, the default assumption is "prepare for ensuing disaster." Economic crises are so common that risk avoidance becomes as important as profit-making. In other words, the focus shifts to protecting what you have, not creating jobs and building wealth. Macroeconomic calamity is a regular fact of life in many countries: debt crises, hyperinflations, currency crises, banking crises, repressed financial systems, and expropriatory tax rates, to name just a few of the regular sources of disaster. By creating macroeconomic environments that are full of risk, policymakers reduce the microeconomic incentives for people to take additional risks and make the costly investments needed to accumulate physical and human capital as well as create jobs. Governments kill the incentives to make labor more productive and create jobs in so many ways that this topic deserves its own chapter—Chapter 4.

Closing Markets to International Trade

As mentioned before, Adam Smith and the other early masters of economics realized that specialization and trade are the keys to increasing the productivity of labor while still enjoying the benefits of diversity. These same insights also hold for countries as a whole. Countries can increase the productivity of their labor force by specializing in the goods that they are most productive in making. Countries that have certain natural advantages, technological advantages, or just large populations can specialize in producing goods that make the most of these advantages, then trade for other goods that they are less productive at making. International trade is a way of turning what you have into what you want. As a result, international trade is a key channel through which labor productivity, employment, and standards of living increase over time.

International trade is also crucial to attracting the human and physical capital that makes labor more productive and increases wages. International trade does not simply involve trading goods; it also involves exchanging ideas, knowledge, and technology that directly increase human capital. One of the secrets of the Asian economic "miracle" was a simple recognition that the best way to create human capital was to learn by doing. In other words, focus on making labor-intensive goods in a few targeted industries that could be sold in foreign markets with an eye towards, over time, building the physical and human capital resources needed to make goods that are globally competitive across a broader range of industries. Growth in Asian economies such as Japan, South Korea, and China attest to the power of export-oriented growth.

International trade also increases the amount of physical capital within an economy. With trade in goods come inflows of international capital to build factories and equipment. Also, access to larger foreign markets allows countries to increase the scale of their production and mechanize many processes—things that they could not afford to do if they were only producing for their own smaller domestic markets. Producing for a global market is often a prerequisite to being efficient. An automotive firm cannot make 5,000 cars a year and still afford to invest in the technology and equipment needed to stay at the forefront of productive efficiency. A firm needs to be making 100,000 cars to justify these huge investments. The necessity for such a large scale in production means that smaller countries, such as South Korea, would never be able to have domestic firms in these industries except for the fact that international trade provides them with a much larger number of customers than they have at home.

The benefits of international trade are clear from the data. To highlight just one result, countries that were always open to international trade between 1965 and 2000 have an average per-capita GDP of roughly $23,000; those that were always closed during this time only $5,000.[35] This relationship between openness to international trade and higher income is one of the strongest and consistent empirical facts that explain why some countries are rich and others are poor.

The benefits of international trade, and the costs of protectionism, can clearly be seen by any traveler. One of the real joys of traveling to places like India and Africa is to see people engaged in traditional methods of production. The mind's eye can easily call up an idyllic picture of an African village where women are weaving baskets by hand and sweeping their yards with straw brooms while the men are watching their cattle or picking their crops by hand. These activities appeal to the sentimental western tourist because they harken back to an era that many of us have a certain fondness for, primarily because none of us have ever actually had to live this way. The problem with traditional production is that it preserves traditional productivity and traditional income levels, which are all very low. The simplest answer to why many Sub-Saharan African countries have per-capital GDPs at similar levels to what they had generations ago is because their methods of production have not changed. Production continues to be labor-intensive, uses little physical capital, and requires little specialized knowledge. A big reason for this lack of development is that firms throughout Sub-Saharan Africa have largely been shielded from international trade, either through formal barriers imposed by governments or informal barriers from geographical isolation and poverty. They have not been encouraged to evolve their methods of production through competition, nor have they received the technology and knowledge benefits that come from engaging others in the global marketplace.

Much the same can be said about rural India. One of my fondest travel memories is an overnight train ride I took across rural Uttar Pradesh, the poorest state in the country. I had the luxury of waking up to see the sunrise out the window and watch rural Indians rise to go to their fields or their wells on foot, on bike, or by oxcart. It felt as if I had slipped back in time to an earlier age, because I had. Rural India still lives in a time where global markets, competition, and technology are but a rumor, in large part because of the protectionist policies India has long clung to. But this idealized picture of an earlier, simpler time masks the complexity of these people's lives. Finding a way to live on a couple of dollars a day or less is not simple; it is extremely complicated, and it puts the hard work that most of us claim to do in our developed-country jobs to shame.

Traveling in many areas of East Asia, you see something completely different. Many people bemoan the loss of traditional industry and methods of production throughout Asia because life today is completely different than it was for most Chinese, South Koreans, or Thais just a generation ago. Here, modern production and manufacturing has largely replaced traditional methods everywhere you look—except, of course, in the agricultural sector, which is the last bastion of protectionist policies in throughout Asia. The most dynamic and fast-growing industries are those that engage in the most international trade. While these changes have come at a price—a loss of traditions, culture, dislocation, and environmental degradation—they have also come with huge benefits. Higher standards of living have brought with them better health, longer life expectancy, better education, more leisure, and more happiness.

A surprising fact to many of today's travelers is that these differences between Sub-Saharan Africa and Asia are a relatively new phenomenon. Incredibly, in 1900, Africa as a whole was actually about 25 percent *richer* than East Asia. But today, East Asia is approaching the point where it will soon be *three times richer* than Africa. While there are many differences in the economic policies followed in these two regions, the starkest, and I would argue most important, would be their polar opposite approaches to international trade. There is a history behind these different approaches. Both Asia and Africa were subjected to a long and painful history of colonization between the 15th and 19th centuries. However, there can be little doubt that the worst horrors of colonization were experienced in Africa, particularly the trans-Atlantic slave trade. As many Asian and African countries gained their independence in the 1950s and 1960s, the lingering aftereffects of these global interactions shaped trade policy.

In Africa, independence led to the wide adoption of "import substitution" policies aimed at rejecting foreign goods. (While newly independent African governments rejected international trade, many of the expropriative policies followed by the colonizers were accepted with open arms by a group of home-grown dictators). African countries set up extensive systems of trade barriers and tariffs aimed at protecting and promoting domestic production at the expense of foreign competition. While the goals of import substitution are understandable, the results have been disastrous for Africans. The residents of the 54 relatively small countries that make up Africa have too often found themselves without access to global markets and global technology, and limited by small domestic markets that do not allow for economies of scale in production. Because they are protected from competition, there are few incentives for firms to increase the productivity of labor, which ultimately leads to stagnant wages and low employment growth. Higher food prices because of tariffs have not only reduced standards of living, they have encouraged more subsistence agriculture and even increased fertility rates in Africa, making it more difficult for these countries to escape the Malthusian trap. In an effort to reject "economic re-colonization," as the proponents of import substitution policies have called globalization, the interests of Africans have been abused for a second time.

While colonization in Asia was not benign, it was much less extensive and heavy-handed. In fact, it can be argued that the worst colonizers in Asia were other Asians (Japan in Korea and China in Vietnam, for instance). As Asian countries became independent, they were much more willing to take an outward-oriented approach to economic development referred to as "export promotion": a focus on export industries in order to take advantages of specialization, economies of scale, foreign investment, technology transfer, and knowledge sharing. While it has been costly to tradition and the environment, this approach has also sparked growth that has raised more people out of poverty in a shorter period of time than at any other time and place in human history. The consequences for human welfare have been enormous. While traveling to Asia might be slightly less interesting for those travelers looking to experience the old ways of life, the visitor's loss is clearly the resident's gain.

The modern economic approach to the surplus-labor argument is to see persistent unemployment, high population growth, and labor-intensive production as a symptom of a larger problem, not the cause of the problem itself. Unlike Malthus, today's economists don't see people as the problem; we see the institutions that they create and the behaviors that they incentivize as the ultimate cause of poverty. Whenever conditions exist so that labor cannot be specialized, when labor has no capital at its disposal, and when the production processes used by labor are stagnant, then labor will just be a commodity. It will be cheap, it will be plentiful, and there will be few incentives to invest in it.

According to this view, focusing on population control is focusing on the symptoms rather than the disease. Instead, the best way to reduce population growth is to reduce the incentives to have more children. The best way to do that is to help everyone become richer. And getting richer involves, first and foremost, building better institutions so that you can incentivize productive behavior.

Having said this, there are many in the economic development community that continue to place their primary emphasis on population control in an effort to avoid what they see as the likelihood of a Malthusian future. Certain NGOs and nonprofits have been formed around the idea that population control has a technocratic solution: If the right policies can be adopted, such as broader access to birth control, then population growth will go down regardless of what is happening to income.[36] The problem with this approach is that most pregnancies across the world are planned pregnancies, not the result of a lack of access to birth control. Until more women are more empowered to make their own fertility choices and have greater access to jobs and education—which come with overall economic development—then the balance will always be tilted toward having more children and investing less in each one of them.

Likewise, it is easy to refute the Malthusian argument that the world can't sustain a greater population because our capacity for food production is limited. The fact of the matter is that the share of income devoted to land—a measure of how important land is in production—has fallen dramatically. Today, less than 5 percent of land is used for agriculture in developed countries such as the United States. While we are using less land, world food productivity rose by 350 percent between 1970 and 2010, more than enough to support the world's growing population.[37] However, there is a caveat here: Most of this growth in agricultural production has been in the developed world, where investment, education, and technology have been used to increase the productivity of agricultural labor. Today, Americans spend only about 5 percent of their incomes on food, and agriculture employs less than 2 percent of the workforce; this is a testament to how productive agriculture has become in the United States. In Sub-Saharan Africa, however, nearly 50 percent of income is spent on food and the majority of the labor force is in agriculture, reflecting the low productivity of agriculture in the region. While food production in the rest of the world has risen by nearly 150 percent since 1960, in Africa it has actually declined by 10 percent.[38]

The low productivity of agricultural labor in less developed countries is, in part, the result of food being heavily subsidized in these countries. Many countries, such as India and Indonesia, have food programs that distribute subsidized rice to the population at a small percentage of its market price. Government distribution not only creates a great deal of waste (by one estimate, one-third of the food distributed by the Indian government is wasted through theft and spoilage, or is eaten by rats), but low prices reduce the incentives to increase the productivity of agricultural labor by keeping farming unprofitable.[39]

Proponents of population control are not only concerned about the narrowly defined economic costs of population growth, but also with the environmental consequences of such growth. Here, the example everyone points to is China, a relatively densely populated country that is growing fast and which also has some of the most polluted air, water, and land in the world. By one estimate, nearly 1.3 million Chinese die each year from air pollution alone.[40] The economic costs of this pollution in terms of increased health care costs, shorter life expectancy, and sick days range between 3 to 9 percent of GDP—upwards of a thousand dollars per person.[41]

I was lucky enough (?) to be in Shanghai in December of 2013 during what was at that time the worst air quality day in its history (the "airpocalypse" as one English-language Chinese broadcaster referred to it on television). Particulates in the air were 40 times the safe level recommended by the World Health Organization. Walking around the city, the smog was so thick that I felt like I was a roadie operating the fog machine at a 90s heavy metal rock concert. Not only was it difficult to see any distance ahead of you when you were outside, you couldn't see very far inside either. When walking in a local mall, I could barely see from one store to the next.

Legitimate concerns about environmental degradation should be balanced by an additional consideration, however, and that is history. What is happening today in China has occurred before. For example, Tokyo had sulphur-dioxide readings in the 1960s similar to those of China today. London in the 18th century was famous for its "pea-souper" fogs that would roll in, not from the coast, but from inland, the result of burning high-sulphur coal. However, today air particulates in Tokyo and London are a very small fraction, less than 5 percent, of what they were 150 years ago. The reason for this cleanup is simple: A healthy environment is what economists call a normal good, meaning that as our incomes rise, we are willing to spend more on it. In the early stages of development, incomes are so close to subsistence levels that people cannot afford to care about the environment, and production takes place in the cheapest ways possible, which are usually the dirtiest ways possible. However, as income begins to rise above poverty levels and more people find themselves with discretionary income, they become willing to spend some of this income on the higher taxes and increased regulation needed to protect and clean up the environment. The data strongly suggests that airborne particulates and carbon dioxide emissions fall as countries become richer. This evolution from dirty to clean production is often not quick, but it does happen. This process is now happening in China as the government has begun to respond to pressure from its increasingly prosperous population to do something about the environment, even at the cost of slower growth.

Growth not only brings with it higher incomes, but better technology than we have had in the past. Technology also allows us to develop new energy sources that are less destructive to the environment, solar and nuclear energy being good examples. In many cases, new technologies are more energy efficient. In the United States, the number of BTUs (a measure of energy) used per dollar of GDP has fallen by 60 percent since 1950 and 30 percent since 1990.[42] In the American manufacturing sector, total pollution emissions fell by 60 percent while production rose by 70 percent in the 30 years between 1972 and 2002.[43] The continued evolution of economies away from manufacturing goods and towards service-based economies bodes well for this trend to continue, as service goods are typically less energy-intensive.

However, even given all of this economic happy-talk, we cannot count on economics alone to solve all of the world's environmental problems. One daunting challenge to dealing with many of the world's environmental challenges is that pollution has become increasingly global, not just local. While polluted water and acid rain are largely the result of pollution tied to local production, increasing carbon levels and global warming have no boundaries. While everyone is contributing to the problem, the costs of global warming will not be felt equally by all, and most of the costs will not be borne by those who are the largest generators of carbon emissions.

Consider Kiribati, a Pacific island nation in the Gilbert Island chain. I have never been there, but I would encourage any traveler looking for an idyllic, Pacific island vacation in Kiribati to visit as soon as you can, because it will not be here much longer. Kiribati is composed of 32 low-lying island atolls (the remnants of dormant volcanoes), each of which are less than three feet above sea level on average. Kiribati is expected to be the first nation to entirely disappear as global warming increases sea levels and these atolls are gradually claimed by the ocean. In 2013, the Kiribati government officially began educating its population and encouraging it to emigrate to other countries before this occurs. I-Kiribati (as the residents are called) would certainly be willing to pay a significant fraction of GDP to slow future global warming, but other nations have less to lose and, as a result, are much less willing to pay.

The biggest challenge in dealing with global environmental problems such as global warming is the that the environment is a global public good—it is enjoyed by everyone, regardless of whether you have actually contributed to preserving the environment or not. And just like roads, which we talked about in the previous chapter, there is always an incentive to free ride when it comes to paying for public goods. Most every country in the world would be happy to see other countries incur the costs of limiting their carbon emissions, but few countries are willing to take these costly steps unilaterally. As a result, coordination failure makes it difficult for countries to cooperate. As long as one or two countries fail to make the costly commitment to reducing carbon emissions, other countries see no reason to do so themselves. There is no mechanism, as there is within a single country, to make sure that everyone pays their fair share at the global level (say, for example, through imposing a global carbon tax). The absence of a global government means that global public goods, such as the environment, will be insufficiently provided for. For this reason, the threat of global warming is likely to persist in the future regardless of the amount of future population growth. It is ultimately a political problem, not necessarily a Malthusian problem.

Population control policies that are externally imposed, as compared to those that are the natural result of changes in people's incentives to have children as their standards of living change, often have unintended consequences. Consider China's one-child policy, which has created an impending demographic disaster for the country; this may be the most important challenge that any emerging market economy will face over the next generation. Because of the draconian implementation of this one-child policy in the 1980s and 1990s, which routinely forced couples to abort pregnancies after their first child, China now faces a future with a shrinking workforce and a growing number of older dependents. In 2013, the Chinese government announced that the number of working-age Chinese actually fell by nearly 3.5 million from the previous year; this in an economy where growth has been driven by vast increases in the labor force associated with migration from rural to urban areas.[44] The dependency ratio, which is the number of children and retirement-age people per 100 working-age adults, will nearly double in China from 38 today to 64 by 2050.

Today, even a casual visitor to China can feel the implications of this dramatic change. Public spaces seem almost eerily quiet without the screeching of small children (but the constant honking of cars helps to fill the void). In parks and play areas, you can see upwards of six adults (two grandparents on both sides and the parents) tending to a single offspring. While the potential economic costs of such a dramatic decline in the labor force are significant, there are also potential benefits to China; in particular, a contracting labor force will create powerful incentives in China to stop relying on its rural excess supply of labor and focus on increasing the productivity of labor more than it has had to do in the past.

There are also important social implications of these changing demographics. One is that there are now multiple generations of Chinese who have been raised as only children, often like little emperors and empresses. Most worrying for both the future economic and social structure of China is the gender imbalance that has been created because of the strong cultural preference for male over female children and the economic incentives to have boys that result from China's dowry traditions (the families of brides traditionally pay the families of grooms before marriage). As a result, the one-child policy has made sex-selected abortions routine as many families have decided that if they can only have one child, it has to be a boy. More than 15 million Chinese women are missing from the cohort between the ages of 20 and 29, and 50 million are missing from the entire population. This imbalance is so great that the families of potential brides have begun to reject tradition and demand dowries from potential grooms, a classic example of supply and demand at work. This gender imbalance threatens the stability of families and overall social cohesion, which could undermine the famed Chinese commitment to a "harmonious society" and damage Chinese institutions.

China has recently loosened its population control policies. Beginning in 2015, couples can now legally have two children. However, most experts agree that eliminating the policy now will do little to correct these demographic imbalances. China has become much richer and the incentives for having children have changed. In Shanghai, the average fertility rate is 0.7 children per women, well below the rate mandated under the one-child policy, and significantly below replacement birth rates. Taiwan is a good indicator of China's future; there, birth rates are now lower than they are in mainland China and have fallen to these levels without coercive population control policies.

In most other countries, the demographic transition from larger families to smaller families has been much more gradual because it has been voluntary. The social and economic impacts of changing demographics can be adjusted to more easily given time and, in many cases, will benefit these countries as labor becomes scarcer and the incentives to increase labor productivity grow. Most importantly, voluntary demographic transitions in birth rates do not impinge upon anyone's freedom or violate people's human rights, as China's Malthusian one-child policy has done. Malthusian population control policies throughout history, such as Britain's Poor Law of 1834 (adopted on the theory that charity only hurts the poor because it encourages their reckless procreation) and the Irish potato famine of the 1840s (seen as an effective mechanism for reducing surplus population by British officials), have only served to punish the victims. Only by rejecting such policies and giving people the freedom to make their own reproductive choices will societies promote productive institutions and spur sustained economic growth.

When it comes to understanding "the population problem," travelers often are convinced by their first impressions. When traveling in many countries, particularly booming megacities like Mumbai or Nairobi, it is hard to avoid Malthusian thinking. It just *feels* like there are too many people there. But what I hope I have convinced you of is that population is only a small part of the entire story of labor. Instead we must focus on the productivity of labor. Thinking about labor productivity means that the demand for labor matters, not just the supply of labor. In many places there are too many people, but this is only true because of the ways that most people are working, which is in subsistence agriculture, labor-intensive manufacturing, and informal markets. Because labor is unproductive, it is in low demand relative to its supply. It seems counterintuitive, but only when you make labor more valuable and incentivize using less of it will you see surplus labor disappear. It is at this point that economic development begins in earnest. Employing fewer workers at every task is great for the local population because it means that these workers are more productive, work in a wider variety of jobs, have more and better tools at their disposal, and will be paid more; this increases the demand for everything in an economy, fueling more economic and employment growth. However, it may also mean that you as a traveler will have fewer wait staff to talk with about football while you enjoy your beverage at the local coffee shop. That is a small price we all should be willing to pay.

$50 Billion to Ride the Bus!?! How Governments Can Kill Growth or Help It to Thrive

The right to enjoy property without unlawful deprivation, no less than the right to speak out or the right to travel is, in truth, a "personal" right.

—Justice Potter Stewart[1]

Great nations can often act with a degree of folly which we should not excuse in an individual.

—John Maynard Keynes[2]

Zimbabwe is one of the world's great travel destinations: a unique and vibrant culture, tropical jungles, mountains, African wildlife, and maybe the greatest wonder of the natural world: the stunning Victoria Falls. Once, Zimbabwe was also an economic success story. It was, for a time, "the bread basket of Africa" and its largest food exporter. Unfortunately, Zimbabwe was also notable for its race-based inequality and repressive government under white minority rule. Today, Zimbabwe is one of the largest food importers in Africa and is still notable for its unequal society and repressive government under black majority rule. Some things have changed in Zimbabwe, but its bad government has not. The story of Zimbabwe is one of unending conflict; a testament to the bad things that occur when those in power face few barriers to taking all that they can while they can, leaving little for tomorrow and for everyone else.

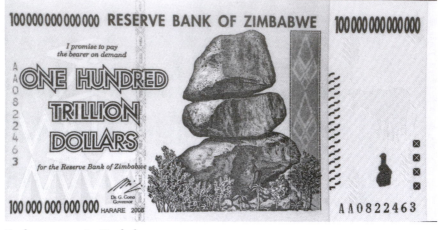

Pocket money in Zimbabwe.

When I visited in 2009, Zimbabwe was in the middle of a historic hyper-inflation. Prices were doubling every day (an implicit inflation rate of 7.9 billion percent a year). A bus ride cost 50 billion Zim dollars today and 100 billion tomorrow. One hundred trillion dollar notes were the most popular unit of Zimbabwean currency—although people avoided using Zim dollars everywhere except when forced to by the government or when going to the toilet (smaller denomination Zim currency was commonly used as toilet paper). Something that cost one Zim dollar on January 1st cost 7.5e+109 Zim dollars by the end of the year—for those of you who forget how to read scientific notation, this is a very big number. Zimbabwe was a nation of multitrillionaires who were starving to death. Nearly 80 percent of the population was living in poverty, and unemployment had risen above 90 percent. It was difficult at that time for foreigners such as myself to walk the streets, both physically and emotionally, as people frantically harassed anyone who didn't look as desperate as they were. Waves of emaciated people would surround me, offering to sell trinkets for the shirt on my back and the shoes on my feet. Women street vendors were selling cooking oil by the spoonful. Shops had few goods on their shelves. The only goods that were available for sale were expensive imports that could only be purchased in return for U.S. dollars at prices much greater than would be found in the United States.

Zimbabwe had been a relatively rich country when it was known as Rhodesia in the 1960s. However, most of its wealth was in the hands of a minority of white farmers (20 percent of the population) who owned

90 percent of the land and controlled all of the levers of government. Blacks were forced to live on homelands (also known as townships) where land was communal and few individual property rights existed. Blacks could not live outside of their homeland unless they had government-approved jobs working as laborers on white-owned land.

A long civil war began in 1965, eventually ending in 1980 with the country's first democratic election. The newly renamed Zimbabwe elected Robert Mugabe, a rebel military leader, as its first president. In the ensuing 20 years, Mugabe consolidated his political power by killing political opponents, increasing the power vested in the office of the presidency, and establishing one-party rule. However, he largely left the structure of the agricultural and manufacturing sectors of the economy untouched. White farmers continued to own most of the productive land in the country, and agricultural productivity remained among the highest in Africa. Black Zimbabweans enjoyed better access to some public services, such as health care, but experienced flat or falling incomes.

Things began to change for the worse in 2000. The first sign of impending disaster occurred when—surprise!—Mugabe won the National Lottery ($100,000 Zim dollars, or about five times the per-capita GDP of the country at the time). It seems that Mugabe had consolidated enough power that he was no longer afraid to openly take what he wanted. Mugabe built political support for his kleptocracy by encouraging war veterans and criminals to chase white farmers off their land. Nearly every white farmer left Zimbabwe (or was murdered) by the mid-2000s, a huge loss in human capital and technology. Agricultural production fell by half, and Zimbabwe went from being Africa's largest exporter of food to one of its largest importers. In 2007, Mugabe established a grain marketing board (the only market to which farmers could sell their crops) that paid farmers only 10 percent of world prices, the difference going to corrupt officials. The government also ordered that any business of sufficient size had to be majority owned by an "indigenous Zimbabwean," hounding many firms out of the country, even those owned by other Africans. Manufacturing fell from more than 20 percent of GDP to less than 1 percent. In 2008, Mugabe forcibly took control of newly discovered diamond fields, saying—I don't think the pun was intended—"Zimbabwe is mine."[3] As the economy contracted, the black educated middle class—doctors, teachers, accountants—seeing no future in Zimbabwe, left. Today, income in Zimbabwe is less than half of what it was in 1980, back to where it was in the 1960s, and life expectancy is down to 36 years of age. However, always optimistic, Zimbabweans joke that they now have the highest IQs in the world: I queue for bread, I queue for sugar, I queue for gas.

As the economy collapsed in 2007, the only way the Mugabe govern-ment could continue to pay for the promises it made to its supporters was to print currency to pay the bills. Things got out of hand amazingly quickly. The central bank went from issuing 5 Zim dollar notes in 2007 to 100 tril-lion Zim dollar notes by 2008. These larger notes were referred to as "Fer-raris" because no one wanted to hold them, so they moved around very fast. A governor of Zimbabwe's central bank said that "traditional econom-ics do not fully apply in this country."[4] (Did he mean "do not fully apply" or "were not applied"?) As inflation rose, many prices and wages that were controlled by the government did not rise. For example, by 2008, the fixed wages public school teachers were earning in Zim dollars were worth the equivalent of only 72 U.S. cents *each month*. Public employees stopped showing up for work, and school, health care, and legal systems fell apart.

By early 2009, Zimbabwe had dollarized, meaning that only the U.S. dollar or other stable foreign currencies were being used in trade. Even the government began paying wages in U.S. dollars in order to get people to show up for work. Deposits in Zimbabwean banks were converted at a rate of $1 U.S. for every 35 quadrillion Zim dollars. Unfortunately, the fact that Zimbabwe was producing almost nothing that it could export abroad meant that it was difficult for the government to earn U.S. dollars to pay its workers despite an extortionary system of currency controls. Falling production, a heavy reliance on imports, and a shortage of currency means that Zimbabwe today still has one of the highest costs of living in the world despite the fact that it also has one of the lowest levels of per-capita GDP (roughly U.S. $950). As a result, most Zimbabweans are living at income levels barely above subsistence. Most trade is conducted in barter within informal markets, most food is grown in backyard vegetable patches, and almost every green space in urban areas has been turned into small gardens.

Good governments can nurture growth, and bad governments can kill it. I hope that I have already convinced you of the importance of institutions—and their importance in shaping incentives that influence behavior—in explaining differences across the globe. If I have, then I have also convinced you that governments are important because of the crucial role they play in influencing institutions. The philosopher Max Weber famously stated that the government of any state "successfully claims the monopoly of the legitimate use of physical force within a given territory."[5] While explicit force is clearly an important source of government power, governments can also impact incentives through financial enticements (through, for example, taxes) and influencing social norms (through, for example, public education). In other words, government power can be in the form of car-rots, or in the form of sticks.

Governments can promote public welfare by incentivizing people to do things that they wouldn't ordinarily do but which have positive exter-nalities on those around them. Legitimate uses of government power that promote social welfare would include things such as imposing taxes to fund public goods such as education, enforcing the rule of law, protecting national defense, redistributing income, and breaking up monopolies. Of course, government power also brings with it the potential for the abuse of power. Too often, governments use their legitimate power toward ille-gitimate ends: enriching elites, extending monopolies, expanding military clout beyond what is necessary for national defense, and manipulating laws to centralizing influence in the hands of a select few. Centralized power can lead to empowering corruption. The illegitimate use of government power is aptly summarized in one apocryphal quote from a South Ameri-can dictator: "For my friends, anything; for my enemies, the law."

Obviously, differences in government institutions explain many of the differences a traveler sees across countries. Take one example: urban slums. A closer look at slums across the world (see our previous discussion in Chapter 1) illustrates how government incentives both push and pull people into different behaviors. The slums of Soweto illustrate how governments can push people into slums. Soweto originated during the apartheid era when black South Africans were forced into townships in order to rob them of their property rights, exploit their labor, and segregate them from the white population that controlled all of the economic and political power in the country. (This process was not dissimilar from the process in which Native Americans were pushed into reservations in the American West.) Although in today's democratic South Africa it is possible for blacks to live wherever they choose, many stay in the townships because of social ties and because they still have too few economic opportunities outside of the townships. The slums of Soweto represent the historical legacy of expro-priative institutions created by government.

The Dharavi slums of Mumbai, India, are a counterexample of how people can be pulled, not just pushed, into slums by the actions of their government. Here, slums are a place of great economic activity and entre-preneurship because here it's possible to escape the heavy hand of a cor-rupt and repressive government bureaucracy. While there is little private investment and few public goods like sewers, roads, and efficient legal sys-tems in Dharavi, there is more freedom: more freedom to start a business without paying a huge bribe, more freedom to avoid paying unreasonable taxes, more freedom from caste prejudices, and more freedom to hire and fire whom you want. The massive amount of informal production that takes place in many countries—often 40 to 60 percent of total economic activity—is most likely to take place in slums. This is not because informal production is most efficient; informal production is inefficient because it is undercapitalized, underspecialized, and very risky. But it is often the only kind of production that can avoid the choking hand of government. Many poor people are pulled into slums because slums are often a relative sanctuary for economic freedom.

There are a great many ways that good governments are good and bad governments are bad. I have already talked about some of the productive and perverse incentives created by governments in earlier chapters, and my intention in this chapter is not to repeat myself. Instead, I want to share some thinking from economists about the bigger picture in order to see more clearly how exactly governments influence people's incentives to work, to invest, to get an education, and to take entrepreneurial risk. I also will examine case studies of natural experiments in governmental institutions: Places where arbitrary borders have created a rift in institutions with huge economic consequences (e.g., North and South Korea), or places where institutions within a country have changed precipitously (e.g., China in 1978). Finally, I want to discuss the fundamental characteristics of governments that effectively promote public welfare, and discuss why democracies are generally more consistent with productive institutions and sustainable economic development than any other form of government.

Probably the most famous travel book in the English language doesn't go to anywhere that actually exists. *Gulliver's Travels* by Jonathan Swift takes its hero to many imaginary places.[6] One constant across each of the places Gulliver visits is that governments, as we like to say around my house, put the fun back into dysfunctional. The governments of Lilliput and Blefuscu are constantly at war over how to properly crack eggs; fierce political debates in Lilliput are held between those who wear high heels and those who wear low heels; the government of the horse-like Houyhnhnms runs an apartheid system that exploits the labor of the human-like Yahoos; and the government-free oceans are filled with thieving pirates. Jonathan Swift has an opinion of government that is lower than that of many modern-day libertarians (or even the modern-day traveler stuck in a visa processing line). Among the giant Brobdingnagians, Gulliver is quizzed by its king about his English government and its penchant for running up debt and fighting wars. The King of Brobdingnag is amazed that thousands of books on the art of government have been written in England because, in his opinion, governing is a matter of common sense and should simply strive to encourage the productivity of the people. According to Gulliver: "And (the King) gave it for his opinion, that whoever could make two ears of corn or two blades of grass to grow upon a spot of ground where only one grew before, would deserve better of mankind, and do more essential service to his country than the whole race of politicians put together."

While the king of Brobdingnag is naïve, he is on to something. One of the most important functions of government is to help increase the productivity of its people. But how does a government go about accomplishing this? In the broadest possible terms, governments that foster productive economic institutions provide two basic services: First, they *ensure an environment of stability and freedom* under which markets can work efficiently. Second, they *correct market failures* when free markets don't work efficiently. Let's talk about each of these characteristics of productivity-enhancing government in more detail.

Ensuring a stable and free environment includes providing for the national defense, protecting citizens against crime and corruption, preventing property seizure (by criminals and by the government itself), and ensuring fair and efficient legal systems. One important way to think about this broad role for government is that good governments find ways to avoid and mitigate conflict, either external conflict with other countries or internal conflict between citizens. For example, having a legal system that allows for the fair enforcement of contracts is one important mechanism for minimizing conflict and enforcing *de jure* laws so that they are equivalent to *de facto* laws. Also, having a system of well-defined property rights helps avoid conflicts over questions related to "who owns what?" At a broader level, mitigating conflict involves having political structures that encourage stability and cohesion among the population, regardless of the income, ethnicity, ideology, or special interests of any particular group.

Government must deal with one conflict in particular, and that is the conflict between elites and other powerful minorities and the broader majority. On one hand, political systems have to protect the masses against elites amassing too much power and manipulating institutions in their favor. For example, elites cannot be allowed to use government to create barriers to competition in order to gain monopoly profits for the businesses they own. Likewise, small groups of highly motivated individuals organized around a single special interest often have big advantages over larger groups in furthering their agendas. Why? Because larger groups are harder to organize and have to share their rewards among many people. Somewhat counterintuitively, small groups are likely to be the most successful in pursuing their special interests because they are easier to organize and each member gets a bigger slice of the payoff pie. A good example of the power of small interest groups can be seen in the relationship between the number of farmers in a country and the size of the agricultural subsidies its farmers receive. In rural and agricultural-intensive countries like India, farmers are actually taxed at relatively high rates and food prices are kept artificially low to the benefit of a smaller group of urban customers. This is driven by special interest politics, as urban residents tend to wield more political influence than the vast number of rural and unorganized Indian farmers. The opposite tends to happen in the United States and Europe, where a small number of farmers are heavily subsidized by the vast majority of the population because farmers are highly organized, active, and focused on this single issue.

On the other hand, if the power of elites and small special interests are thwarted by policies determined by simple majority rule, the institutions put into place may not be favorable to economic or political development. For example, given that there are more poor people than rich people and more borrowers than lenders, a simple majority-rule political system might vote to invalidate all outstanding debt. This would benefit the majority of the population, who are borrowers, in the short run. However, such a policy would put a halt to savings and lending and make everyone a loser in the longer term. This phenomenon is often referred to as the "tyranny of the majority." For these reasons, well-functioning political systems must protect the rights of minorities and the majorities as well as the rights of elites and those who are disadvantaged.

Good governments that effectively manage the conflict between the elites (as a shorthand I will use the term "elites" to also include special interest groups) and the majority share two characteristics. First, they are able to centralize and control power—in other words, they have a monopoly on force, in the words of Weber. In countries where this is not the case, governments fail to function, and all that is left is anarchy and decentralized corruption. This typically occurs in countries caught in a conflict trap, where external conflict, civil wars, and violent crime undermine stability and reduce incentives to invest in the future. From the drug wars in Central America to religious insurgencies in the Middle East to warlord conflicts in Central Africa, it is estimated that more than 1.5 billion people—one-fifth of the world's population—live in a country with armed conflict or excessive levels of criminal violence. No one should be surprised to learn that economists have found that higher levels of violent conflict reduce growth and worsen poverty.[7] The causation also works in reverse because poverty also fosters more instability by making people desperate: In the words of the writer Pearl Buck, "Hunger makes a thief of any man."[8] Too often a vicious circle between poverty and instability is the circle of hell many people find themselves trapped within.

The second characteristic that good governments share is that while they centralize power, they are also pluralistic, meaning that a broad range of voices are included in the policy-making process and, as a result, feel invested in the outcome. When governments are not pluralistic, it inevitably leads to extractive institutions: elites (or special interests) that have few limits placed on their power inevitably proceed to rig the rules of the game so that they always come out the winner.

Governments run by unconstrained elites are unlikely to generate sustained economic development. This is because elites don't always want broad growth; they just want profits. To put this another way, the historian David Landes says that when examining the economic policies adopted in different places throughout history, the best question to ask is not "What would have worked best?"[9] but "Who would have benefited?" Growth is often not a good thing from the perspective of elites. Economic growth often undermines existing technologies and profitable monopolies. Growth demands transparency, which threatens elites by shining a light on corrupt power structures. Historically, economic growth has also increased the economic power of manufacturers and migrant laborers while weakening the power of the aristocracy and landowners (which is one reason why the Industrial Revolution began in England, where these groups held less power than in other areas of Europe).

A perfect illustration of how growth can threaten the interests of elites was provided by Mobutu Seso Seko, the long-time dictator of the Congo (then known as Zaire) who stole an estimated $5 to $10 billion during his tenure from the poorest country in the world. When talking to the president of neighboring Rwanda about an armed military insurgency there, Mobuto said "I told you not to build any roads . . . Building roads never did any good. I have been in Zaire for 30 years, and I have never built one road. Now they are driving down them to get you."[10]

It is possible for growth to occur, for a time, under a government ruled by elites. This can happen when the elites also own the most productive industries and use the government to channel resources to these industries. Slave plantations, manufacturing in the Soviet Union, and Middle Eastern oil kingdoms are all examples of how growth can occur under extractive institutions. The problem is that growth driven by increasing inputs alone, as we have talked about in previous chapters, is not sustainable over the long run because of diminishing marginal returns. Eventually, growth slows as these industries become saturated with capital and labor, but the institutions that incentivize technological innovation don't exist. This has happened or is already happening in all three of the examples mentioned above. Growth can also occur under elite rule when elites co-opt political institutions but allow some inclusive economic institutions. Because these powerful elites impose centralized corruption and not decentralized corruption (see the discussion from Chapter 2), they act like monopolists and limit the overall level of corruption so that it does not completely choke growth. Chile, South Korea, and China are all examples of countries that were or are dictatorships of the elite with centralized corruption but that have allowed enough economic freedom to incentivize economic growth. Interestingly, as Chile and South Korea became richer, their political institutions became more inclusive as well, encouraging sustainable economic growth. Will the same hold true for China?

Correcting market failures is the second important goal that good governments achieve. For example, governments should provide for public goods that are not sufficiently provided by the market. Anyone looking for a public restroom (indoors) in India knows what I am talking about. Too few public goods are provided by markets because people have an incentive to free-ride off goods that benefit everyone in society. I have already talked in detail about three types of public goods that are often in short supply within countries burdened by ineffective governments: health care (Chapter 1), roads (Chapter 2), and education (Chapter 3). Good governments are also able to collect the taxes needed to pay for these public goods in an equitable and efficient way. One study found that emerging market economies collect only 18.2 percent of their GDP in taxes compared to the developed country average of 37.9 percent.[11] This is partly because the informal sector is much larger in poorer countries, which is more difficult to tax. But inefficient tax bureaucracies, weak legal systems, and ancient accounting and information systems are also to blame. Finally, rich elites with a great deal of political power often shape tax systems to reflect their interests. For example, property taxes are extremely low, below 4.2 percent, in 21 of 22 less developed countries examined in one study.[12]

Taxes can help correct for market failure in another way: They can be used to deter behaviors that have negative consequences on the general public. Activities with negative externalities, such as pollution, can be discouraged by effective implementation of targeted taxes (see our previous discussion in Chapter 2). Taxes can also be used to discourage the *tragedy of the commons* by asking people to pay for the right to do something that negatively impacts those around them, such as driving during peak hours of traffic congestion.

However, it is very important to make this point clear: While governments can correct for market failures, it is also true that governments are the source of market failures. When governments become excessively involved in markets, the bad can quickly begin to outweigh the good. In Italy—where seemingly every market activity is regulated, or requires a stamp or document produced by the government, or requires personal dealing with some public sector bureaucrat—the average Italian spends roughly 400 hours a year queuing. In fact, one of the fastest areas of growth in Italy's sclerotic labor market is jobs where people are paid to stand in line for other people (referred to as a *codista*, or queuer).[13] The only reason job growth isn't even faster in this sector is that these *codista* jobs are also regulated by the government.

Probably the most insightful economist on the dangers of government intervention in markets is the Austrian economist Friedrich Hayek.[14] In his book *The Road to Serfdom*, Hayek makes an argument for the free market system and warns of the dangers of intrusive government intervention into the economy. Hayek was particularly worried about the dangers of central planning. Hayek's critique of government planning focuses on the role of information. Information is always limited: As Adam Smith noted, no single individual knows how to make a pencil because no one could possibly learn each and every step needed to produce each and every input necessary to build a pencil. But markets—Smith's "invisible hand"—are able to make pencils because they are a means of bringing individuals together, each with specialized knowledge. Likewise, no group of people, no matter how large or intelligent, knows how to feed a city, but somehow people get fed through the actions of many people coordinated through millions of transactions with the only goal of acting in their own self-interest.

In markets, vast quantities of information are conveyed through prices. Prices reflect the cumulative knowledge of large groups of people and send signals about where resources can be used most productively. As a result, markets are always preferable to governments because a small number of government bureaucrats can never know enough by themselves to efficiently plan an economy. Centrally planned economies will always be guilty of "malinvestment" by failing to allocate resources to their best possible uses because bureaucrats are not omnipotent. Even government manipulations of markets that are not as invasive as central planning can still be harmful. Whenever governments interfere in markets so that prices do not fully reflect the full benefits and costs of a transaction, they also distort information and incentives, leading to less efficient investment decisions. As a result, according to Hayek, the best governments follow *laissez-faire* policies and intervene in markets only to provide public goods under the narrowest of definitions, or to prevent monopolistic or collusive behavior.

Hayek's observations provide powerful insight into exactly why governments in so many countries fail to establish productive institutions that encourage their citizens to invest in capital, knowledge, and technology. At the extreme, you have the failure of centrally planned economies such as the U.S.S.R., China (pre-1980), and North Korea, which perfectly illustrate what Hayek was talking about. Consider a brief history of the U.S.S.R. After the Communist revolution, private property was eliminated, agriculture was collectivized, and vast amounts of labor and capital were forcibly pushed into the manufacturing sector. Nearly six million people died of starvation between 1928 and 1933, but the dramatic increases in capital and labor within the manufacturing sector did increase macroeconomic growth for a while—the Soviet economy grew at an average of 6 percent a year between 1928 and 1960. However, this growth was completely the result of increasing inputs and occurred without any innovation or increases in efficiency. The only incentive to work hard was the fear of getting shot or sent to Siberia: Roughly one-third of the Soviet population was found guilty of shirking on the job and either murdered or sentenced to hard labor. Information used in central planning decisions was consistently biased: Stalin had a group of census officials shot because he thought their population estimates were too low. (The next group came back with higher population estimates. Surprise!) Incentives to innovate were nonexistent. For example, the only way for workers to avoid hard labor was to meet their monthly output goals. However, increasing your output beyond these arbitrary goals only led to higher goals being set in the future—goals that could get you sent to prison. Bureaucrats in Gosplan, the Soviet planning agency, worked to keep output goals low so that they, too, could report success and avoid Siberia. At the same time, malinvestment and malproduction was rampant. When Gosplan set a steel quota stated in tonnage, the heaviest, worst-quality steel was produced. When Gosplan provided resources for capital investment, it went toward purchasing whatever equipment was available up to that amount, not what was needed to do the job most efficiently. It was for this reason that the U.S.S.R. gradually accepted the use of the ultimate capitalist tool—money—and began to measure its inputs and outputs in prices denominated in rubles. Too much information was being lost without some sort of price mechanism, however distorted. The failed histories of centrally planned economies illustrate what Hayek meant when he said, in maybe the most famous quote about the profession, that "The curious task of economics is to demonstrate to men how little they really know about what they imagine they can design."

Today, there are few economies left that are completely centrally planned, but there are many economies in which the government plays an extensive role in certain sectors. State-owned enterprises in many countries often dominate natural resource industries or other sectors of the economy deemed to be "strategically important," which usually can be translated as "owned by elites." As a general rule, state-owned enterprises are inefficient, isolated from competition, and operate in domestic markets too small for them to take advantage of economies of scale. Consequently, they ultimately become large drains on the government's resources. Losses in state-owned enterprises are often as great as three percent of GDP in less developed economies.[15] State-owned enterprises also crowd out private investment and serve as a barrier to private and more innovative businesses entering many markets.

Some of the most important state-owned enterprises in many countries are state-owned banks. For example, the "Big 4" banks in China—4 of the 10 largest banks in the entire world—control 90 percent of the financial assets in the country. Reportedly, a red phone (a red cell phone today?) sits on the desk of each of the chief executives of these banks and all other state-owned enterprises, connecting them directly to a Communist party Politburo member who can help guide the CEO in the arts of political patronage and expropriation regarding who gets what, how much, and for how long. These state-owned banks also serve the interest of elites by allowing the government, including other state-owned enterprises, to borrow cheaply, usually at the expense of depositors who face interest rate ceilings on what they earn on their savings.

State-controlled banks not only distort the lending decisions of banks, but they also distort the saving and lending decisions of everyone else. There are few profitable ways to save in China because of the low returns on deposits in Chinese banks, the lack of trust in the Chinese stock market, and a nonexistent bond market that cannot develop without a reputable legal system. The most attractive way for many Chinese to save is through buying property (and, to a lesser extent, other nonfinancial assets such as gold, wine, art, etc.). The high demand for property has fueled a housing bubble in China. Housing prices in China tripled between 1992 and 2009.[16] At the same time, residential housing has grown from 2 percent of Chinese GDP in 2000 to 6 percent in 2011, while total construction stands at 13 percent of GDP, twice what it was in the early 1990s. Today it takes an average family over 50 years of disposable income to purchase an apartment in Beijing.

This housing bubble is dangerous because it is unsustainable on a number of levels. Not only can few people afford housing in many of the first-tier cities in China, but if prices drop to reflect the fundamentals of supply and demand, it will lead to a large loss of wealth for many Chinese, including banks. But the most frightening thing about this bubble is the vast amount of malinvestment that it has incentivized, just as Hayek warned. You can see this malinvestment clearly when you drive through Shanghai at night. In this huge city of more than 24 million people, there are vast residential neighborhoods where there are no lights on. These "ghost neighborhoods" have few, if any, residents living in them. They only exist because investors have built apartment complexes, which then sit empty, often for years, waiting for a profitable opportunity to be sold. Buying housing is among the most profitable ways to save (historically, not necessarily in the future), but it is certainly not a productive way to invest from the perspective of the overall Chinese economy.

The other way that many Chinese save is by lending informally to friends and family they know, particularly to private entrepreneurs who cannot get loans from the Big 4 Chinese banks because they lack political connections. Private firms account for 70 percent of employment and two-thirds of total GDP growth in China, but only 20 percent of private firms have access to formal finance through banks in China, which is roughly equivalent to countries such as India, Nigeria, and Bangladesh.[17] As a result, many informal, or "underground," lending markets have grown to fill the gap: Upwards of 80 percent of private firms use underground lending. But the problem with underground markets is that they offer little legal protection to its participants, are risky, and are still not available to everyone. Underground loans are often made based on personal relationships (the all-important word in China: *guanxi*), not the underlying value of the activity that the loan is funding. Thus, underground lending only contributes to more malinvestment. Amazingly, a large amount of the funds lent out in these underground markets are first obtained through formal banks in China by those who have *guanxi*, who then turn around and recycle these funds by lending them again through underground markets. This is known in China as "wearing a red hat" (red being the color of the Communist party) and is just another example of how convoluted, distorted, inefficient, and potentially risky most of the financial decisions made in China are because of the web of control exerted by the government.

Governments also interfere in markets when they replace the market itself. In agriculture, a common way this is done is through the creation of marketing boards, where the government becomes the sole customer for farmers. The stated rationale for marketing boards is that the government is protecting the interests of farmers by serving to provide predictable demand and stable prices. The actual rationale is usually to exploit farmers and serve the interests of the urban elite—these boards are one of the key reasons that most of the hungriest people in Africa are farmers. In Sierra Leone, the autocratic government used their marketing board to ensure that farmers got only 10 percent of the world price for the food they produced. In Zimbabwe, marketing boards are used to keep farming incomes at subsistence levels while granting the government the power to control food distribution. To enforce these agricultural marketing boards, police raids and rural roadblocks are common in Zimbabwe. With little profitability in farming, farmers have few incentives to invest in technology and other ways of increasing their productivity. This leads to the counterproductive result that policies aimed at keeping food prices low in Africa actually result in food prices being much higher than they are in countries where markets are allowed to function and the incentives to increase productivity are much higher.

One final way that governments distort markets is by setting up barriers to international trade. There is no better way to undermine the economic and political interests of elites than to broaden the perspective of your populace and force domestic monopolies to compete in global markets. As a result, protectionism is the safety blanket of dictatorships worldwide. It is no coincidence that the import substitution policies followed across Africa in the 1960s, which created barriers to foreign goods, were usually implemented by "big man" dictators who were also trying to build barriers to political and economic participation.

However, protectionism is common in democracies as well. A country that imposes tariffs on another country is imposing a penalty on its own citizens as much as on the other country. So why then do so many countries impose trade sanctions on themselves? Protectionism is the classic example of a special interest policy: The benefits of protectionism are enjoyed by a small number of people—those who see their monopolies protected and their inefficient firms allowed to remain in operation—at the costs of higher prices and lower incomes for the rest of the population. The journalist Tom Friedman has suggested that antiglobalization groups would be more accurately be referred to as "The Coalition to Keep the Poor Poor."[18] Often, democracies are not inclusive enough to allow for the voice of consumers to be heard over the voices of producers with the resources to buy political patronage.

Bad governments don't just kill growth by interfering with markets. They also kill growth through bad macroeconomic policy. The most obvious example of this is when governments spend beyond their means, accumulate debt that they can't repay, and postpone the inevitable consequences through actions that rob tomorrow in order to make it through today. Zimbabwe is an example of how corruption and patronage can lead to inefficient spending, inadequate tax collection, debt, inflation, economic stagnation, and more debt in a vicious cycle that eventually ends in collapse.

If excessive debt is the root cause of economic crises, inflation is the cure adopted by bad governments that is worse than the disease itself. Inflation is always an appealing option for governments to pay their bills because, in the words of Federal Reserve Chairman McChesney Martin, "inflation is a thief in the night."[19] The best way to understand inflation is to think of it not as rising prices, but as falling purchasing power. It eats away at the value of money and deposits in bank accounts in ways that are often not obvious to the public until it is too late. No new taxes must be levied, and no painful spending cuts must be imposed. Just turn on the printing press and your problems are solved . . . for a very short while. During the Brazilian hyperinflation in the early 1990s, the printing presses were working at such a rate that workers were taking wheelbarrows to work to hold their pay. They would get paid twice a day, first at mid-day, at which point they would fill their wheelbarrow with paper money and immediately wheel it to the market and spend it as quickly as possible because it was losing value every minute. At the end of the day, they would be paid a second time, filling the wheelbarrow even higher than it was filled earlier in the day, and repeat the same frenzied shopping trip. During the hyperinflation in Russia during the 1990s, when inflation peaked at roughly 1,000 percent a year in 1993, I was told by a nurse in Moscow that employees would throw bricks of money—their mid-day pay—out the windows of the hospital to family members waiting below (who had to be quick on their feet, because a falling brick of money is as heavy as a falling brick), who were camped out and ready to make a mad dash to spend those rubles before they lost even more value.

Inflation not only destroys financial wealth, but inflation kills finance because trading money now for money later is rarely a good deal when it's losing value so rapidly. Inevitably, high inflation rates are associated with bank failures, dysfunctional financial markets, and a lack of access to financial services for the poor. Without a means to borrow or save, the poor are made more vulnerable, even long after the inflation has diminished.

Unfortunately, there are many countries to choose from when looking for examples to illustrate the dangers of debt and inflation. However, Argentina is always a good choice when looking for a case study of how not to run macroeconomic policy. As the Nobel Prize–winning economist Simon

Kuznets said, there are four types of countries: developed, undeveloped, Japan, and Argentina. And he didn't mean that in a good way for Argentina. In the 1930s, Argentina was one of the 10 richest countries in the world. Today, the IMF ranks Argentina as having only the 54th highest level of per-capita GDP (and falling) despite remarkable endowments of energy, raw materials, agriculture, and a highly educated population.

Over the last 80 years, Argentina has suffered through five debt crises (three since 1980), numerous banking crises (four since 1980), and repeated episodes of high inflation. Between 1944 and 2013, Argentina had an average inflation rate of 205 percent a year. To put this in some perspective, a depositor with U.S. $1 billion in an Argentinean bank in 1960 who was forced to keep it in Argentinean pesos (as they were often forced to do thanks to bank account freezes imposed by rapacious politicians) would have been left with the equivalent of .0007 American dollars (one-thirteenth of one cent) by the end of 1994! It is a testament to the astonishing inefficiency of the Argentinean banking system that despite the fact that most Argentineans fled their banking system long ago, it is still common to see bank customers lined up down the block and around the corner of the branch of any Argentinean bank. Recently, it has been difficult to say what the actual inflation rate in Argentina is, as the government has been manipulating its official inflation data in an effort to reduce its debt payments to the holders of its bonds. In 2011, the government reported that inflation was 9.7 percent, while private measures of inflation based on prices reported on the Internet indicate that inflation was over 25 percent in both 2010 and 2011.[20] The government has even punished private sector economists in Argentina for releasing alternative inflation estimates, fining many economists and threatening at least one with jail time.

Why can't Argentina wean itself from debt? It has to do with the fact that good governments are inclusive and centralize power. Argentina does neither. Argentina has a long history of being ruled by a small group of elites—sometimes politicians, sometimes military officers—who steal what they can and then buy votes through a complex system of patronage that has long been accepted by the public as just the way that business is done. It is indicative of the Argentinean mindset that the most famous tourist destination in Buenos Aries is the *La Recoleta* cemetery, where the rich and powerful military and political elites throughout Argentinean history (including Eva Perón) are buried in luxurious vaults and attended to by an endless flow of adulators. Under the entrenched patronage system that rules Argentinean politics, it is very difficult to limit corruption and government spending while at the same time maintaining control of the government itself.

The second reason for Argentina's debt-loving ways is that the central government is weak and has a difficult time collecting taxes to pay for the spending demanded by political patronage. Argentineans have no faith in their government, meaning that the injunctive norm that "everyone should pay their taxes" is not the descriptive norm in the country. A big part of the reason that Argentineans have no faith in their government is that it has tried to exploit them at every turn. The World Bank reports that the effective maximum tax rate on some activities in Argentina is 108 percent![21] Because the government is weak, it is unable to enforce *de jure* tax laws so that they become the *de facto* tax laws. This is often the case in countries which have suffocating *de facto* laws: Trade only becomes possible when people break unproductive laws or pay a bribe to avoid the hassle of excessive red tape. When walking the streets of Buenos Aires' main shopping areas, retailers advertise, right out in the open, cash prices for goods (no receipt) that are 30 to 40 percent less than the credit price for these goods. Everyone knows what is going on, but no one can, or will, do anything about it, which is what prevents these excessive taxes from completely suffocating the economy.

Excessive government debt and bad macroeconomic policy are not just a third world problem, and increasingly it is rich countries that are more vulnerable to debt crises than poorer ones. In fact, low- and middle-income countries today account for less than 20 percent of all sovereign debt issued and have average debt-to-GDP ratios of less than 40 percent—these are half of what they are in developed countries. Of course, some developed countries, like the United States, have a much greater capacity to borrow given their high levels of income, relative economic stability, and political institutions that (in the past) have ensured that the government will pay its bills. But this is not true of all developed countries.

The Euro-zone debt crisis, which began in 2009, was precipitated by an election in Greece, after which the new government alerted the public that previous governments had been "cooking the books" and government borrowing was, in fact, three times what had been publicly reported. Greece's sovereign debt at the height of the crisis was more than $1.2 trillion, or roughly $250,000 for every person in the country, and interest payments on this debt accounted for one-third of total government spending. This debt was the result of a number of factors: Greece's bloated and inefficient public sector where workers were paid three times what they were paid in the private sector; unprofitable and inefficient state-owned enterprises; an unsustainably generous social safety net where men could retire at 55 years of age (women at 50) at an income greater than what most Greeks earned when they were working; little tax revenue because roughly 40 percent of all income goes unreported in Greece; and low growth suffocated by a host of other unproductive economic institutions.

The Euro-zone crisis began in Greece but immediately threatened to spread throughout Europe because it was other Europeans, particularly other European banks, who owned most of Greece's debt. Any default by Greece threatened the stability of banking systems, pensions, and individual savers across the continent. One thing that is different about this debt crisis is that Greece could not solve its debt problems using the printing press. Thanks to their membership in the European Monetary Union, Greece doesn't control its own money supply. This forced Greece to adopt difficult austerity measures, such as dramatic cuts in wages for public servants and much higher tax rates. Unlike sneaky inflation, these austerity measures took place out in the open to the detriment of Greece's political elites, but hopefully to the betterment of Greek political and economic institutions in the long run.

Here is one takeaway from our discussion of what constitutes good and bad governance, which hopefully will inform future political debates with your friends and neighbors: It is not the size of government that matters; it is the quality of government that matters. The argument about whether a big government or a small government is best is completely misplaced. For every big government (relative to the size of the economy) that fails to work such as Zimbabwe or North Korea, I can identify big governments that work well, such as those in Scandinavia. For every small government country that is rich and growing, such as Singapore or Hong Kong, I can give you a small government country that is a complete disaster, such as Somalia, South Sudan, or Haiti. Both big and small governments can foster productive institutions. The key, once again, is to build governments that are able to centralize power while also guaranteeing an inclusive role for everyone in deciding how this governmental power is to be used. There is no single recipe for building such a government. I'll have more to say on this point later.

Back in 1883, the German economist Adolf Wagner hypothesized that as countries get richer, the size of their governments would get proportionally bigger as well.[22] This is, in fact, what we have observed over the last 130 years, and has become known as "Wagner's Law." Wagner based his prediction on the fact that as economies become more complex and diverse, they would require more regulation, more extensive legal systems, and more public goods. These changes in the size of government reflect the needs of a dynamic, evolving economy. The growth we have observed in government across countries does not necessarily reflect illiberal repression of economic freedom, as some ideologues suggest, but a changing economic reality. A larger government can actually create more economic freedom than small governments that are so weak that they can't protect people's safety and property or provide needed public goods.

To further illustrate why large or small governments are not necessarily bad or good, consider the trade-off between corruption and taxation. A small, limited government is defined by many as a government that imposes the lowest level of taxation possible, even at the cost of fewer public goods. This would be the kind of government envisioned by Hayek. But some of these public goods are things like legal systems, education systems, and law enforcement that limit corruption. If lower tax rates are obtained at the cost of higher levels of corruption, this is a bad trade-off for economic growth. Corruption is always more distortionary than taxation because with taxation you get transparency; one of the biggest reasons why corruption is so costly is that its price is always uncertain and every bribe undermines confidence in the entire system of government. Why do Scandinavians continue to be productive, to work hard, and to work efficiently in the face of what many would consider to be expropriative tax rates? Because Scandinavians don't have to worry about the other ways that governments kill growth: They don't have to worry about corruption, missing public goods, or governments that will gorge on debt and then try to inflate it all away. The low tax rates in Somalia or Haiti fail to incentivize productive institutions because their governments (or lack thereof) fail people in so many other ways. So when a policy maker, politician, or expert is trying to sell you on the idea that it's size alone that matters—well, there is a crude joke that I could make here, but I had best leave it alone.

The popular press often talks about growth miracles—such as China—and growth disasters—such as Argentina or Sub-Saharan African countries—as if the things happening in these countries are somehow unexplainable. However, on closer examination, there is little about growth miracles that are truly miraculous, and growth disasters don't strike out of the blue like lightning. One definition of an economist is that an economist is someone that can tell you why something has happened after it has happened. Consistent with this, many economists and historians have documented specific institutional successes and failures that have shaped wealth and poverty across the globe.

Darin Acemoglu and James Robinson's book *Why Nations Fail* is one persuasive historical account of how political institutions interact with economic institutions to create stories of economic success and failure.[23] In brief, here is their argument: A necessary condition for economic growth is the existence of productive economic institutions, and these economic institutions are shaped by political institutions. So what determines political institutions? Acemoglu and Johnson argue that "big events" and path-dependence play a crucial role in determining whether political institutions are inclusive or exclusive. By "big event," the authors essentially mean that shit happens. Wars are fought, countries are conquered and colonized, democratic or dictatorial leaders rise or fall from power, and these sort of historical events shape political systems. While Acemoglu and Johnson are not suggesting that economic growth is random, they are suggesting that there are critical junctures in history. If things had gone differently at these junctures, history would have played out in a different way. These big events have long-lasting consequences because history and institutions are path-dependent. The important historical events of the past shape today's institutions because institutions are slow to change. In the words of William Faulkner: "The past is never dead. It's not even past."[24]

Consider the following analogy. Think about two people standing next to each other. They each flip a coin at the same time—if their coin comes up heads, the person steps to the left; if their coin comes up tails, they step to the right. After each of them complete 100 coin flips, these two people will likely be far away from each other simply by random chance. Now, repeat this experiment, but give one a loaded coin that comes up heads 60 percent of the time, and the other person a loaded coin that comes up tails 60 percent of the time. After 100 coin flips, these two people are likely to be even farther from each other, and in predictable ways: The person with the heads-loaded coin is likely to be far to the right and the person with a tails-loaded coin is likely to be far to the left. Institutions can be thought to evolve in a similar way. There is the random chance of events. But also, each country's unique history is a loaded coin in favor of moving in one direction or another. Coupled with the path-dependent nature of this process, where the last coin flip determines where you start before the next coin flip, institutions across countries will vary quite a bit and, as a result, so will income levels.

Big events are important because of path-dependence, but their importance is magnified by vicious and virtuous cycles. When countries are able to establish pluralistic governments that also centralize power, they are able to establish productive economic institutions as well. Productive economic institutions lead to general prosperity, which encourages more pluralistic politics and further enhances the power of the government, on and on, in a virtuous circle. But when countries slip into kleptocracy or anarchy, political institutions quickly get twisted toward the interests of elites, and the cynical mindset of "grab while you can" takes hold for everyone. This undermines productive economic institutions and leads to the growth-killing behaviors that we have already discussed. Lower growth means that elites are more likely to try to enrich themselves through taking, not making, and encourages them to build more barriers to political participation, which further worsens growth in a vicious circle. In essence, to return to our coin-flipping analogy, coins can become "more loaded" in one direction or another over time because of the feedback effect of past events on future events.

This process of big events, path-dependence, and virtuous/vicious cycles is analogous to Darwin's theory of biological evolution, where genetic mutations, heredity, environmental variation, and survival of the fittest lead to species differentiation over time. This idea of institutional evolution is crucial to understanding economic history across the globe. To better illustrate how institutions evolve over time, I want to examine three case studies of growth miracles and disasters in more detail: Korea, China, and Botswana.

The Korean Peninsula encompasses a clear growth miracle to the south and a growth disaster to the north. Today, per-capita GDP in South Korea is 16 times what it is in North Korea and life expectancy is 11 years higher to the south. What was one country with a homogenous culture and 1,300 years of shared history was broken into two countries along a border arbitrarily chosen on the 38th parallel. To the north, the dictatorial Kim Il-Sung established the *Juche* economic system, which rejected individual property rights, banned markets in favor of central planning, and imprisoned its population within the most isolated country on the planet. While famines are a regular fact of life throughout North Korea, the supreme leaders of North Korea had annual cognac budgets reported to be more than $800,000 a year.

To the south, the authoritarian political system that existed after the civil war adopted a market-based approach to economic development that protected individual property rights, just not individual political freedom. South Korea's post-war economic performance exemplifies two things I discussed previously. First, authoritarian political regimes can create growth, at least for a time, if they allow for inclusive economic institutions and are able to channel resources to elite-owned industries that are productive; this is exactly what South Korea did. Second, there is a virtuous circle between economic and political institutions. Growth fueled prosperity and the demand for not just more consumption goods but for greater political participation in South Korea. This was the driving force behind the gradual transition to democracy in South Korea, and was similar to the process followed in many parts of Europe over the last 300 years—only much more quickly and much less bloodily.

Politically drawn borders separating two peoples from each other such as between North and South Korea can be thought of as "natural experiments" in the importance of institutions. The borders between the United States and Mexico, East and West Germany, Israel and Syria, and many others, were subjectively drawn and arbitrarily separated one set of governmental institutions from another set of governmental institutions (a "big event"). In each case, these natural experiments attest to the importance that economic institutions play in shaping a country's quality of life. The differences in incentives on either side of the border create long-lasting disparities because of path-dependency. For example, today, 25 years after integration, regions in the former East Germany still have income levels that are one-third lower than in the former West Germany.

China is in almost every way unique, including its history of economic growth. China was a growth miracle before there was growth: the richest country in the world in the year 1000. Then it slowly fell behind Western Europe until the mid-1700s, at which point it began to fall more quickly behind Western Europe. In 1958, the Communist revolution led to a disastrous contraction in standards of living. However, a series of economic reforms begun in 1978 has generated unprecedented levels of growth over the last 35 years. China is a growth miracle, once again.

The full story of Chinese economic history is one that is too long for this book, or even a great many books. One of the reasons that I find China to be one of the most interesting places for people-watching in the world is that the history that any Chinese person older than 50 years old has experienced during their lifetime is incredible. It's almost as if you can see the stories of the Japanese occupation, the civil war, the Great Leap Forward, the Cultural Revolution, and the 1978 reforms written on the faces of older Chinese. But let's begin our abbreviated discussion with the institutional changes that were imposed by Mao Zedong when the Communists came to power in 1949 (a "big event") after a costly and prolonged civil war. The Communists banned private property, murdered landowners, collectivized farming into communes, and dramatically reduced political and personal freedom. The entire system was designed to extract the maximum amount of labor from the peasantry in an effort to increase manufacturing and pay for a military buildup. Corrupt local officials stole at will and then falsified output statistics in order to keep the central bureaucrats happy. Between 1958 and 1960, during Mao's "Great Leap Forward" and the accompanying Great Famine, grain output fell by 25 percent, but official reports said it doubled. One-third of the babies born during the famine did not survive it, and between 30 and 40 million people starved to death.

In 1976 Mao died, and in 1978 Deng Xiaoping was the unlikely winner of an internal power struggle (another "big event") to become the most influential decision maker in China. Deng was a former general and hard-line supporter of the Great Leap Forward, but lost confidence in Mao's approach during the Cultural Revolution, which began in 1966. The Cultural Revolution was predicated on destroying the "old ways" in China that were holding it back; in other words, it called for a rejection of all of the existing institutions in the country. In reality, it was an attempt by Mao to undermine all of the elites in China other than himself and further increase his own power under the pretense of increasing political inclusion. The Cultural Revolution led to the worst of all worlds: anarchy that limited centralized power, yet coalescing the power that remained in the hands of a single elite, Mao. In the words of Mao, "The more people you kill, the more revolutionary you are."[25] Millions were murdered or exiled (including Deng), particularly among the educated.

Deng was able to gradually implement a series of reforms that dramatically increased the inclusiveness and productivity of economic institutions, but also placed some constraints on extractive political institutions. The most important change in economic institutions was the household responsibility system in agriculture, where peasants could farm individual plots of land (leased, not owned) and keep whatever surplus food they produced above a government quota. Farmers were then allowed to sell this surplus food in open markets and not through marketing boards. Agricultural productivity skyrocketed, freeing up millions of rural workers to migrate to urban areas and supply the labor needed to spark the Chinese manufacturing boom. Reforms such as the household responsibility system by no means created perfect economic institutions, but they were enough to reincentivize production in a country where a spirit of entrepreneurship and hard work was still simmering after years of being stifled. Among other important changes, China also created special enterprise zones that were specifically designed to be free-market oases that would focus on export promotion. China also allowed private firms to operate and compete against favored state-owned enterprises in many industries.

Make no mistake about it: China today is no free-market panacea. In the words of Dai Bingguo, a senior Chinese foreign policy official, the Communist party's "number one core interest is to maintain its fundamental system and state security."[26] Government involvement in the economy is so extensive and convoluted that only a Chinese engineer could understand it (which is exactly the training of most of the leaders of the Chinese

Communist party). Its economic institutions, while more inclusive than in the past, favor the 10 percent of the population that is a member of the Communist party over the other 90 percent, favor elite state-owned enterprises over private firms, and favor urban residents over rural peasants. Communist party members are rewarded with plum appointments in industry and government as well as opportunities for patronage payoffs up and down the chain of *guanxi* that runs the country.

State-owned enterprises are favored by government policy in many ways. They receive the vast majority of lending from the Big 4 banks at extremely favorable rates. Bank loans of more than $500 million—an amount that can only be lent to government-owned businesses—must be directly approved by an official at the highest level of the Communist party. A 2009 study found that Chinese SOEs would lose money if they had to pay market interest rates on their loans.[27]

State-owned enterprises are also protected through the patronage they provide party members who wield inordinate influence in the Chinese legal system. While state-owned banks and corporations superficially operate under Western-like legal systems that guarantee property rights, legal protections, accounting standards, and transparency, it is generally true that political influence and organized corruption are the primary principles on which most decisions are based. State-owned enterprises that are deemed strategically important by the government do not have to worry about market pressures or social welfare as long as they meet their quotas and stay on good terms with the people in power.

Here's an anecdote to illustrate this point: I have had the opportunity to visit China's Bao Steel, the second largest steel company in the world, on three separate occasions. During the four years over which my visits spanned (between 2012 and 2015), very little changed at Bao. It still reminds me of the postapocalyptic future envisioned by many Hollywood environmental disaster movies. The air is so thick with pollution that you can taste it; the trees, the grass, a sickly looking creek, and the bitter air are all gray-toned like an old photograph. Everyone wears surgical masks—everyone, that is, but the irrepressible tour guide who gave the exact same sales pitch on each visit. For example, he claimed, using the same language almost word for word, that it was a testament to the environmental standards followed at Bao Steel that they had a "zoo" on site with two hundred *live* deer—the only firm in the country to accomplish that!! (I particularly appreciated the emphasis on the word *live* in that sentence.) The one thing that did change during his presentations, however, was the production statistics he spouted. The total tonnage of steel Bao produced goes up by 10 percent each year, as it has done for many years in the past. And this was despite the fact that global steel prices had fallen significantly, as the world market for steel was in a prolonged slump associated with the global financial crisis and then China's own economic slowdown in 2015. But that is the point: what happens at many Chinese state-owned enterprises has little to do with market conditions or making profits; it is about satisfying the demand of Communist party power brokers to always be the biggest, produce the most, and grow the fastest, regardless of the costs.

The rural poor are certainly not rewarded by Chinese institutions. The most obvious example of this is the *hukou* (household registration) system. A *hukou* is essentially an internal passport that ties your legal residence to your place of birth. If you are born in Shanghai, you have *hukou* for Shanghai, you can work freely there, and you can enjoy all of the public services provided by the government in Shanghai such as education, health care, and the ability to lease land. Under the *hukou* system, rural laborers are allowed to work in urban areas—where most of the economic growth is occurring—but their legal residences (and their families) must remain in their rural home. As a result, these people, known as "floating people" (*liudong renkou*), have a permanent status as internal migrants. They are not able to receive public services in the same place that they work; they are often forced to live in basic dormitories or share crowded apartments with other migrants; and they are separated from their families (who remain at their birth homes) for upwards of 50 weeks a year. Why does this *hukou* system exist in the first place? Because workers without *hukou* earn 40 percent less than workers with *hukou* and are forced to work 25 percent more hours.[28] In other words, the *hukou* system is a means of establishing a permanent surplus of rural labor until it is needed in urban areas, keeping wages low and preventing an urban surplus population that might lead to political unrest. The costs of this policy—if Chinese elites consider it a cost—fall on Chinese peasants who are forced to make sacrifices for their families that most of us can't even imagine.

The average Chinese household is also harmed by the government's undervalued exchange rate policy. The People's Bank of China (China's central bank) purchases huge quantities of U.S. dollar assets and sells RMB assets in an effort to depress the value of the Chinese currency relative to the dollar. The aim is to promote exports by keeping the prices of Chinese goods cheap in terms of dollars. (It is also a welcome subsidy to foreigners who travel to China. Shout-out to the exploitive Chinese government!) But the flip side of this policy is that it also keeps the price of imports expensive and reduces the standards of living of Chinese consumers. This is why shopping tourism is a favorite vacation for most mainland Chinese who travel abroad (including Chinese who travel to Hong Kong, where the Hong Kong dollar is not consistently undervalued).

Will Chinese citizens benefit from the same virtuous circle that South Koreans have benefited from, where inclusive economic institutions have encouraged more pluralistic politics and more individual freedom over time? Or is this virtuous circle blocked by the government's expropriative policies and the public's cynical attitude that the only way to get ahead is to break the rules? (An attitude that is embodied in the popular Chinese adage "The mountains are high and the emperor is far away.") In the analogy of one Communist party official, the Chinese economy is a "bird in a cage" where the party's control is the cage. The cage must be expanded over time as the bird grows so that it is not suffocated, but the cage cannot be opened lest the bird fly away.[29] But what would happen if the bird flew away? Wouldn't that make the bird better off? The fact that the government refuses to see this as an alternative suggests to me that a difficult transition in China lies ahead.

Botswana stands out as a great example of how governments can help create economic institutions that work, even under very difficult circumstances. As I mentioned before, I lived and taught in Botswana for a time. It's a great place to live, particularly for an economist. There is a reason why economists are often associated with pessimism and the phrase "the dismal science": You see how much time I have spent in this chapter talking about what doesn't work relative to what works. So time spent in Botswana was a wonderful opportunity to witness how government-created institutions can work—institutions that are much different from standard Western government institutions.

It would have taken a level of clairvoyance well beyond that of most economists to foresee how successful Botswana has been. Few countries had less going for it than Botswana did at the time of its independence in 1966. The entire country had only 12 kilometers of paved road, 22 university graduates, and 100 secondary school graduates.[30] It also had the incredible geographic disadvantage of being a landlocked country in the middle of the Kalahari Desert and surrounded on all sides by countries in political and economic turmoil. Since independence, however, Botswana has had one of the highest growth rates in the world at 9 percent a year, and today its per-capita GDP of $7,700 puts it squarely in the upper range of middle-income countries.

How did such a small, sparsely populated, and seemingly nondescript place such as Botswana achieve such success while its better-off neighbors, such as Zimbabwe and South Africa, have fallen behind? Despite the odds, Botswana was able to take its simple yet functional institutions that existed before independence and build a modern government on this foundation that has both centralized power but is also pluralistic—a rarity in Africa.

What are some of these institutions that work in Botswana? First, the traditional institutions that existed in Botswana before independence were inclusive and incentivized production over theft. Particularly important is the *kgotla*, or public meeting, in which chiefs governed in consultation with all the adult males (and today, in most cases, adult females) to determine local law, settle disputes, and agree on public works. While not quite Athenian democracy, these assemblies centralized power, encouraged inclusive participation, and limited the power of elites. An important part of the *kgotla* system is that chiefs were not strictly hereditary and, according to a local saying, "The king is king by the grace of the people." In other words, the social and cultural norms that existed in Botswana before independence established a foundation for a future democratic and pluralistic government. Also important was the fact that, historically, the vast majority of the population in Botswana consisted of cattle herders. Cattle-herding traditions remain an important part of the life of the Batswana. I know many urban professionals, some of them university professors, who still spend their weekends back in their home villages "looking at their cattle," as they would say. As a result, the elites and chiefs have always felt pressure from the public to protect and enforce property rights for everyone, including fair access to public goods such as land.

Many other countries in Africa, particularly in southern Africa, had similarly inclusive traditional institutions in place at one time. But what makes Botswana unique is that these traditional institutions were never discarded as a result of colonization. Botswana was never colonized in the same way as its neighbors. It was only a protectorate of Great Britain, meaning it was claimed by the British in an effort to keep other countries out, but then benevolently ignored. The founding story of Botswana as a country occurred in 1895 when the chiefs of the three largest tribes in what was then referred to as Bechuanaland traveled to London and successfully petitioned Queen Victoria to protect them from Cecil Rhodes and his British South African company, which had expropriated so many resources and so much labor from the rest of southern Africa. The reason the British agreed is because they saw no resources that they could exploit in Botswana, but they didn't want anyone else there either. It is a "big event" in Botswana history that likely saved it from the kinds of heavy-handed colonial policies that were followed in Zimbabwe and South Africa.

Another "big event" in Botswana history was that it has been blessed to have leaders who were committed to democracy and pluralistic participation in politics. Botswana's first president, Seretse Khama, was the chief of the largest tribe in Botswana before independence. As a young man he studied in England and eventually married a white woman there, after which he was banned from returning to Botswana for a period of time by the apartheid government in South Africa. When he was allowed to return, he was elected as president (his son, Ian Khama, is the current present of Botswana and the fourth democratically elected president in the country's history). Seretse Khama's role in Botswana is similar to that of George Washington in U.S. history: Khama was an elite who could have grabbed more power in order to enrich himself, but instead consistently worked to create pluralistic structures of government and encourage race-neutral policies that benefited the public good. His commitment to inclusive economic institutions was most evident when one of the largest treasure troves of diamonds in the world was discovered following independence on land controlled by his tribe. Instead of expropriating the revenues for himself or his tribe—what has happened too often in the rest of Africa—Botswana nationalized these resources. Diamond revenues have been used to generously provide public goods such as health care, roads, and social insurance for everyone in Botswana while helping to keep tax rates low.

Seretse Khama died in office and was succeeded by Quett Masire, who was president between 1980 and 1998. I had the honor to meet with President Masire in 2015, now 90 years old but still sharp as a tack and who remains an important elder statesman throughout Africa. When I asked him about what made Botswana successful, Masire credited the first postindependence generation that managed to centralize fiscal power in the national government while at the same time limit the influence of tribalism and encourage people to think about themselves as citizens of Botswana, not of a tribe. There is no easy answer for how to do this, other than hard work and the good fortune to be blessed with honest and skilled politicians. It says a lot about Botswana and President Masire that he mentioned to me that his primary objective as president was to leave through a peaceful transfer of power—something he was only the second African leader to achieve.

Today, Botswana is considered to be one of the most democratic countries in the world—and also the least corrupt country in Sub-Saharan Africa, on a level with South Korea.[31] But it is no economic Eden. People either farm cattle or work for the government—there is little manufacturing or diversity in the economy, making it vulnerable to economic shocks. Unemployment in Botswana is typically between 15 and 20 percent because the diamond industry (which is one-third of the economy) generates income without creating many jobs. Throughout most of the country, transaction costs are extremely high and markets are rare because of low population density and the difficulties of traveling in the Kalahari Desert. More than 40 percent of the population lacks access to formal finance. Most of the rural population still lives on tribal land that is difficult to collateralize, discouraging credit and investment. Finally, Botswana has the highest incidence of HIV/AIDS in the world, with nearly one-quarter of all adults infected with the disease.[32] HIV has reduced life expectancy in the country to only 47 years (down from 63 years in the 1980s), well below that in other countries with similar income levels.

To live in Botswana is to be consistently frustrated by the days wasted paying for bills in cash, by the hours spent filling out paperwork and getting the correct stamp (one of the few obvious legacies of the British involvement in Botswana), by the claims of "two minutes!" that quickly turn into 20 minutes, and by the endless layers of bureaucracy in any organization. When I lived there and when I return to visit, I often get sentimental feelings about my visits to the Department of Motor Vehicles back home. But in Botswana you don't have to worry about being shaken down by these bureaucrats, or being put in jail for expressing your political opinions, or about armed unrest on the streets. Botswana is much better off than anyone would have thought possible 50 years ago, thanks largely to its unique and effective institutions.

One of the important lessons that we can learn from Botswana—a lesson that is also validated by the broader global experience—is that democracy is the most conducive form of government for generating sustained economic growth. This was not obvious to many early political philosophers. Aristotle argued that democracy would only work in countries with a well-educated middle class in which voters could think broadly about the public good. Without this, democracy would degenerate into a *tyranny of the majority*, which can create extractive institutions that are every bit as damaging as those in a kleptocracy. Likewise, democracy is also vulnerable to populist policies that claim to promote "the general interest" but really promote special interests and elites. For example, many firms argue that setting up barriers that limit competition, such as protectionist trade policies or price controls, is needed to protect jobs, but these are really just examples of what economists call *rent-seeking behavior*: their principal objective is to help create payoffs for a few people by manipulating markets.

One can argue that the relationship between income and democracy works the other way: Rich countries become democracies, but only after they are already relatively rich. This is undoubtedly true to some extent. Very few countries that are rich today started off as democracies; most evolved into democracies as they developed economically, e.g., Western Europe and South Korea. But this point does not invalidate the claim that democracy promotes growth, only that there is a virtuous circle involved.

Western Europe was the first to have productive economic institutions because they were the first to have inclusive political institutions, even if these institutions fell short of what we today consider to be democratic. As these countries developed, more inclusive economic institutions also encouraged broader political participation, and more pluralistic politics encouraged more open economic institutions, and so on, in a virtuous circle.

Today, the average per-capita GDP in countries that are classified as democracies by the World Bank is $17,000—four times that of nondemocracies. The best empirical evidence suggests that this represents causation, not just correlation. Acemoglu *et al.* find that across 175 countries, those that moved toward permanent democracies—including long-lasting adoption of free elections and constraints on executive power—were 20 percent richer after 25 years, a result that holds whether the country was rich or poor to begin with.[33] The fact of the matter is that there are simply too many good reasons to think that democracy fosters economic growth. The most powerful is that democracies inherently place constraints on the power of elites by fostering broader political participation. Milton Friedman makes the most persuasive argument that economic freedom is the *meta* institution needed for economic growth, and sustainable economic freedom is not possible without the political freedom created by democratic participation.[34] For example, there is a great deal of empirical evidence that countries that are more democratic have less corruption, are better at breaking up monopolies, are more effective at protecting property rights and enforcing contracts, are better at providing public health and education, and are more stable—all important factors in creating productive institutions.[35]

During a visit to Botswana on March 19, 2015, I spent an afternoon sitting in on a session of the Botswana parliament. These were three of the important topics on the agenda during the question-and-answer session that day:

- Questions were asked about how many classes are taught under trees in the villages of Orapa, Motsumi, and Ditsweletse.
- Representatives posed questions to the Ministry of Health about conducting risk assessments to identify corruption.
- A question was posed about what to do with the horticulture market in the central business district of Francistown.

Do these topics sound boring? Of course they do, but that is the point of functioning democracies! Democracies are not always the most efficient means of technical policy making. But by fostering more inclusion and buy-in to the process of government, democracies make institutions more sustainable and stable in the long run.

There are two caveats that need to be made clear. First, democracy is best at fostering *sustainable* growth. Democracy is not necessarily best at generating the fastest growth at any one point in time. As we talked about earlier, autocracies can generate growth—for a time. They do so when they adopt some inclusive economic institutions and when they funnel capital and labor into productive industries owned by elites, taking advantage of diminishing returns to scale. But there is a limit to the growth that takes place by increasing inputs alone. Technology growth is the key to sustainable growth in the long run, and people who are not personally free are also not free to fully share ideas and maximize innovation.

Second, not all democracies are equal. Many democracies fall short of having those two prerequisites of governments that create productive institutions: centralized power and pluralistic politics. Some democracies might be "too democratic" in the sense that they do not centralize enough power in the hands of elected representatives and leave too much up to majority votes or local officials. Robert Barro conducts empirical work which suggests that past a certain point, more democracy (in the form of a more pluralistic political system) might actually reduce growth, presumably because it empowers special interests and creates a tyranny of the majority.[36] For example, one recent study showed that Kenyan districts that share the ethnicity of the president in power received twice as much spending on roads; democracy can become a game of grabbing what you can while the getting is good.[37] On the flip side, it is also possible for democracies to centralize too much power. Here, the "one-party democracies" and the kleptocracies that buy votes for patronage are not democracies in the sense that everyone has something to gain from participating in the political process.

India is often mentioned as an example of a political system that is "too democratic." Its decentralized system empowers special interests at the expense of the government's ability to efficiently provide and pay for public goods. Nearly half of the Indian population still openly defecates outside, despite the fact that public sanitation engineering has been adopted in many countries much poorer than India. Between 1973 and 2011, China built 74,000 kilometers of expressways; in India, there are 600 km of expressways in the entire country. "Why can't India be more like China?" many ask. The answer is that while autocracy is great at reallocating capital and labor in the short run (often at the expense of human rights and property rights), can it incentivize innovation in the long run as well as a democracy such as India? This is a question that I want to return to in Chapter 6 when I discuss the diffusion of technology across the globe.

I hope that we can agree that governments play an instrumental role in shaping institutions so that sustainable growth is possible that benefits everyone. But what can be done to change bad institutions into good institutions? This is a multitrillion-dollar question, and a question, quite frankly, for which economists can provide no simple answer. One thing that we do know is that institutional changes that are imposed from the outside are unlikely to work on the inside. There are too many examples—from the colonization of Latin America and Africa to the recent "liberation" of Iraq and Afghanistan—that externally imposed institutions are rarely successful regardless of the good intentions behind them. Building the right government for any specific country must reflect the social norms, culture, and history of that country. There are intricate feedback loops between these factors, political institutions, and economics institutions that will always remain largely incomprehensible to those on the outside, and, as a result, the impact of externally imposed institutional change is highly unpredictable. It is important for economists to recognize that there is a limit to both our knowledge as social scientists and our ability to implement effective change: There are some problems that experts cannot solve from the above. Creating good institutions is not some engineering project, and to treat it as such is sheer hubris.

To put this in another way, institutions result from human actions, but they not the result of human design; they evolve, they are not created. In many ways, institutions can be compared to language in that it has evolved in a bottom-up style based on people's actions, and it is constantly changing with no predetermined path. In this analogy, economists are like grammarians: we are the experts who specify rules that describe how people actually behave; we play an important role in enhancing comprehension and encouraging clear thinking, but we are not as successful prescribing, from the top down, how people should act.

Based on these same insights, many critics argue that foreign aid will never deliver on its promise to raise vast numbers of people out of poverty. According to critics such as William Easterly, the "one size fits all" approach to foreign aid often followed by governments and NGOs fails to consider the incentives that exist on the ground, so it very often fails to work within different environments.[38] For example, giving a kleptocracy money to build roads is unlikely to lead to any sustainable improvement in the lives of common people on the ground, although it will improve the lives of corrupt elites who steal the money.

Other economists are not as skeptical about foreign aid and argue that aid can be productive if it is provided in ways that are consistent with the unique institutions that exist at the local level. Banerjee and Duflo in their book *Poor Economics* argue that targeted aid projects that are specifically designed with local incentives in mind can succeed in limited ways, and over time may be able to initiate a virtuous cycle that improves institutions more broadly.[39] Acemoglu and Robinson argue that improving microinstitutions, such as encouraging more freedom of the press and increasing political participation at the local level, can improve transparency and eventually encourage more inclusive political and economic institutions.[40] But because of the path-dependent nature of institutions, their evolution is necessarily slow and can only be gently nudged, not rushed, by those on the outside.

Not everyone is so patient. A few governments, encouraged by prominent economists such as Paul Romer and George Akerlof, have begun planning "charter cities." These charter cities would be completely independent cities with new governments that would adopt open immigration policies, free-market economic institutions, and democratic political systems. The models on which charter cities are based are the free-market city states of Hong Kong and Singapore. The idea behind building these charter cities is to overcome path-dependence and to start from scratch, at least on a limited basis, in the hope that success in these charter cities would encourage these institutions adopted elsewhere. The Honduran city of Trujillo has moved furthest along toward becoming a charter city, with the Honduran government passing a constitutional amendment allowing for autonomous legal zones. While an interesting experiment, to critics such as myself, such charter cities feel like the utopian communities that were popular during the 1960s. The "clean slate" hypothesis—in which it is possible for society to start over without all of its cultural and historical baggage—is an appealing idea to many idealists. But there are too many reasons to think that there is no shortcut to creating productive institutions. People can't restart with a clean slate, so what makes us think our institutions, which reflect the shared experiences of a group of people, can return to a blank slate either? In addition, no country is truly an island, even when it is an island. Its people, its trading partners, and its neighbors will necessarily influence what goes on within any country. To think that Honduras, one of the most violent and dysfunctional countries in the world—a country in which males currently have a one in nine chance of being murdered during their lifetime—can create a sanctuary of peace and prosperity by simply changing its laws and drawing new borders seems quite naïve to the more pragmatic (cynical?) of us.[41]

So now you see how paying nothing for a farm can lead to you paying 50 billion for a bus ride. Politics and government are about power. Good governments find a workable balance between centralizing enough power so that it can enforce laws and policies that provide for the public good, while also allowing citizens to retain enough power to constrain elites from co-opting government for their own benefit. It is a difficult balance to maintain. But maybe the most important takeaway from this chapter is that the perils of government-created barriers to markets are more dangerous than the perils of the market itself. As a general rule, when a politician says that they are trying to protect you from a market, they are actually trying to protect their wallets and their power. The best governments protect markets; the bad ones protect you from markets.

CHAPTER FIVE

Nothing Needs Reform as Much as Other People: Culture and Economics

My purpose in making this wonderful journey is not to delude myself but to discover myself in the objects I see. Nothing, above all, is comparable to the new life that a reflective person experiences when he observes a new country. Though I am still always myself, I believe I have been changed to the very marrow of my bones.

—Johann Wolfgang von Goethe[1]

The tongue-in-cheek title of this chapter refers to a quote by Mark Twain, who perceptively noted that "Nothing so needs reforming as other people's habits."[2] Every foreign traveler, at some time, has agreed with his point. Even the most open-minded traveler can't help but occasionally question what these locals are thinking. Confusion regarding other people's habits is a trope of travel writing that goes back to at least the fifth century BCE and the Greek Herodotus, who remarked that Egyptians "seem to have reversed the ordinary practices of mankind."

For instance, women attend market and are employed in trade, while men stay at home and do the weaving. In weaving the normal way is to work the threads of the weft upwards, but the Egyptians work them downwards. Men in Egypt carry loads on their head, women on their shoulders; women urinate standing up, men sitting down . . . They live with their animals— unlike the rest of the world, who live apart from them. Other men live on wheat and barley, but any Egyptian who does so is blamed for it . . . In writing or calculating, instead of going, like the Greeks, from left to right, the Egyptians go from right to left—and obstinately maintain that theirs is the dexterous method, ours being left-handed and awkward.[3]

Experiencing cultural diversity is one of the most important factors that spur us to travel, and it is also one of the most consistently frustrating aspects of it. While we travel to experience difference, those differences often become dissonance when we find ourselves face-to-face with a cultural disconnect, such as waiting for the slow-moving waitperson whose pace is seemingly set according to a sundial, or interacting with people who insist on standing inside your personal space when they want to talk, or failing to understand why drivers in some places use their horn as if it were attached to their brakes. It is so very easy to blame many of the annoyances of life on the differences in other people's habits. Personally, I am routinely disappointed when I travel that people regularly fail to follow Knoop's Golden Rule: Do unto me as I would do unto me.

The shortcomings we perceive in other people are easy to chalk up to a simple failure of others to act in the ways that we think they should act. This basic human impulse explains why it is so easy to blame economic failures on culture. Culture is an easy scapegoat that we often reflexively use to explain, and damn, those who are doing less well than us.

The interplay between culture and economic behavior played a key role in the thinking of many early economists. Adam Smith and Karl Marx did not agree about much, but they did agree that culture largely reflects economic structures. Smith thought that markets promote public order while providing for greater individual liberty and fostering freedom and more moral and virtuous societies. Marx thought that culture was a reflection of the material conditions under which people live. Marxists believe that the class conflicts created by capitalism shape every aspect of culture from religious beliefs to individual psychology; as a result, if you change the economic system, you change the culture. Another influential voice on the relationship between economics and culture was Max Weber, who thought that culture impacts economics more than vice versa. Weber viewed certain religious beliefs as being better at fostering productive economic behavior than other religious beliefs (more on each of these ideas later).

However, for most of the 20th century, culture fell out of favor among economists. One of the most important reasons why economists pushed culture to the side is that economics as a discipline has generally sought to identify the *universal* characteristics of human behavior that are constant across all cultures. Economists tend to look for general tendencies that are unchanged across individuals, and operate from the principle that the similarities among us—regardless of creed, ethnicity, or upbringing—far outweigh our differences. Economists believe that we all try to do what is best for us and those we care about; that we each respond to incentives and change our behaviors when these incentives change; and that improving society does not require changing people, but requires altering the institutions that influence people's actions. To me, these beliefs make economics a noble science that seeks to bring people together, not one that focuses on the differences that drive us apart.

Recent economists have also tended to avoid culture because we are sensitive to observer bias, which is the fact that our prior beliefs influence what we observe, what we do not observe, and how we interpret these observations. In other words, our own culture biases our perception of culture. This is impossible to deny, and it is easy to find quotes from European colonizers 500 years ago—or from certain politicians today—that attest to the fact that many elites have consistently stereotyped other races and cultures as lazy, spendthrift, uneducable, and prone to crime, based on no evidence but knowledge of their own culture.

Finally, economists have sidestepped culture because, quite simply, cultural beliefs don't always seem quite rational. During a recent vacation in Quebec, everyone else in my family (who all speak French) talked about how wonderful it was to speak French and how great it felt to feel far away from home when we really weren't. On the other hand, as an "English specialist," I could not help but think about how much easier it would be for everyone if the Québécois just went over to the dark side and spoke English like the rest of their countrymen and countrywomen. Here were people surrounded by English speakers, critically linked to an English-based economy, but defiantly committed to speaking French for no obvious economic reason. I know that I was guilty of being culturally insensitive, stuck in my ivory Tower of Babel. But like many economists, my reflexive thinking about culture often is that it is something that separates people and creates economic costs without clear benefits. Language and cultural differentiation lead to divisions that increase the transaction costs associated with trade. As a result, it can be argued that cultural differentiation limits specialization, reduces trade, and discourages productivity and growth. For this reason, many economists (but certainly not all, as we will see) cheer globalization and see it as a process for homogenizing culture and increasing economic efficiency, even if it leads to a loss in cultural diversity (and devalues our traveling experiences).

However, although culture has been discounted for more than a century, today culture is once again beginning to play a more prominent role in the study of economics. Many economists have realized that culture cannot simply be ignored if we want to gain a deeper understanding of the differences in behavior across people. Economics investigates how people behave and interact, and culture sets the boundaries of just which behaviors and interactions are socially acceptable. Culture can be thought of as the "rules of the game," and when these rules are violated, societies can enforce conformity in many ways. To ignore culture is to ignore many of the incentives that influence us on a daily basis.

Or, to put this in the context of the ideas that we have already discussed in this book, culture plays an important role in shaping institutions and making them either productive or unproductive. Culture affects institutions by shaping injunctive norms and by influencing how societies enforce these norms to become descriptive norms. Culture can also play a role in explaining why *de jure* laws are different from *de facto* laws. For example, in a culture that glorifies the thief, such as the growing *narco cultura* (narcotics culture) in Mexico, it should not be surprising that many people act like a thief and many other people are accepting of it. Culture can also play a role in limiting the opportunities to get an education or for workers to specialize. Consider India, where cultural beliefs associated with the caste system have historically been used to justify prohibitions that have limited educational opportunities for certain groups of people and have also banned them from working certain jobs. Finally, there are cultural beliefs that limit pluralism and participation in the political or economic system, such as the ways that women are discriminated against in certain Muslim countries or the ways that ethnic minorities in some parts of Africa are marginalized by ethnic majorities.

Culture is also rising in importance in economics as economists loosen our death grip on the rational actor model, or the belief that people make all of their decisions by carefully balancing the known costs and benefits of any action. As new research in behavioral economics has shown (to be discussed in more detail in Chapter 7), people are often forced to make imperfect decisions when they lack fundamental information. And even when they have good information, taking the time to fully consider every alternative takes up too much time and mental energy. As a result, no one can be fully rational when making all of the many decisions that need to be made daily. Instead, humans have developed shortcuts, or rules of thumb, which allow us to make decisions quickly and cheaply, but that are often predictably biased. In other words, we are "rationally irrational."[4] Some of these shortcuts consist of adopting cultural beliefs about the way that the world works. For example, believing in a God that punishes you for failing to follow the ways of your ancestors is an easy way to reduce the complexity of many decisions. It is also a good way for society to enforce injunctive norms and make them descriptive norms, even if the requirements of such religious practices have economic costs that appear irrational to the quintessential rational economist. Such cultural beliefs shape economic behavior in ways that simple cost-benefit analysis may not be able to predict.

The purpose of this chapter is to explore the ways that culture influences economics, as well as the ways that economics influence culture. I will identify some of the ways that culture shapes behavior, but I will also argue that culture is too often and too easily blamed for social and economic failures. One of the most contentious cultural debates today relates to the impact of globalization on cultural diversity—a debate that is close to the heart of many travelers. I'll try to convince you that globalization is leading to a change in the nature of cultural diversity, but by no means is leading to the end of cultural diversity. As travelers with an economic mindset, we are in an especially advantageous position to clearly see and understand why these changes in both economics and in culture are occurring.

So what do we mean by culture? This is no easy question to answer. According to Merriam-Webster's Dictionary, culture was the word of the year in 2014 based on the frequency with which this word was looked up. So obviously, there is some confusion about exactly what culture means. There is also a great deal of confusion among academics, with hundreds of different definitions of culture depending upon the discipline— sociology, anthropology, politics, humanities, or economics—in which culture is being examined and depending on the viewpoint of the individual researcher.

This is no place for a long-winded debate over the true definition of culture. In fact, I won't even give you a single definition of culture. What I will do is to identify four characteristics of culture. Culture is:

1. *Artificial.* Culture is learned and is the result of nurture, not nature. In other words, it is created by human action.

2. *Ideas.* Culture creates "webs of significance" that provide the context in which we understand the world around us.[5]

3. *A group distinction.* Culture represents ideas that are shared by groups of people and that provide these groups with a unique identity.

4. *Socially inherited.* Culture is passed on through social norms, both injunctive and descriptive (see our discussion in Chapter 2). However, these norms are often not wholly accepted from generation to generation and can evolve over time.

To be clear, culture is not the same thing as ideology, which only encompasses the first two characteristics. Ideology refers to man-made ideas that are not necessarily inherited or differ across groups. Culture is also not the same as ethnicity or nationality because these concepts are not associated with ideas, even though they are artificial, distinguish groups, and are socially inherited. Finally, and most importantly for us, culture is not the same thing as economic institutions, a concept that we have used so frequently throughout this book. The key difference is that institutions do not necessarily create a group distinction. The same culture can operate under two different sets of institutions, such as North Korea and South Korea. Likewise, two different cultures can exist under very similar institutions, such as England and the United States. But clearly, culture can be an important influence on institutions because culture impacts the values we place on certain outcomes and the incentives each of us has to engage in behaviors that will lead to these outcomes. Culture can be thought of as the aspects of institutions that cannot easily be transferred across different groups. It's the "sticky" part of institutions that can't be copied and pasted from here to there.

Where does culture come from? Once again, this question has spawned a vast amount of debate across various disciplines. But at the risk of oversimplification, there are two big schools of thought about why cultural diversity exists. The first school of thought is that culture reflects the natural environment that a group lives within.[6] This school essentially adopts an evolutionary biology approach to studying culture. Here, culture is simply a group adaptation that helps the species survive within its distinct environment. The systems and beliefs that societies build are unique to the material conditions each society faces. Marxists are proponents of this view, which they refer to as "cultural materialism." For example, some have argued that people who live in areas where it is possible to live by foraging alone often evolve cultural practices that encourage a mentality that devalues planning for the future and encourages a "live for today" attitude. Such cultures also commonly adopt cultural practices that glorify the warrior who will help them gain control of more of those resources that can be easily taken. Agrarian societies, on the other hand, were forced to evolve cultural attitudes that encouraged hard work and a forward-looking perspective that emphasizes savings and investment.

The sacred cows of India have often been used as another example of how culture attitudes can be naturally selected for based on the natural environment. It's been argued that the belief that cows are sacred reflects the fact that herds of cows can only survive as communal property in India. This is because of the lack of high-quality grasslands in India, making it

Sacred cows going for a swim in the Ganges.

necessary for cows to graze widely to survive. However, because cows must be communal property, cows are vulnerable to free riding and the tragedy of the commons—they could be overworked or, even worse, eaten by any member of the community. So to protect cows in an effort to foster the public good, Hindu culture adopted the religious belief that cows are sacred and must be protected, to the point that they are acknowledged to have legal rights in India (including the right to freely roam and swim in public areas). This cultural belief was not purposely chosen by people, but naturally selected to help those communities who adopted it to survive and grow.

The other primary school of thought on culture is that it stems from the fact that humans are social animals. We have an inborn need to attach ourselves to other people, and we are compelled to interact and share ideas. Culture then is a set of beliefs that allows us to understand and interpret the world around us, and then share these beliefs with other people in ways that bind them to us. In other words, culture is a mindset that helps us create shared communities. This is the view of culture espoused by Adam Smith in *The Theory of Moral Sentiments*—the first book for which Smith is famous—in which Smith argues that moral and cultural beliefs come not from religion, teaching, or reason, but from social rewards and punishment—from incentives and institutions. There is an invisible hand (his original use of this phrase) of mutual sympathy that guides us toward a common morality that rewards behavior which benefits everyone. The moral principles that flow from local culture reflect specific injunctive norms already held by the group. Smith's view is that culture is bottom-up, not top-down. While there are cultural leaders who minister to us about morality and religion, they are largely "preaching to the choir" to people who have already adopted these beliefs.

This view of culture as a social phenomenon is popular in psychology, neuroscience, and linguistics, and is supported, in part, by a wealth of data that shows how differences in cultural attitudes impact how we perceive and interpret events, and can even change the physical characteristics of the brain. The author Anthony Storr said: "Whether a belief is considered to be a delusion or not depends partly upon the intensity with which it is defended, and partly upon the numbers of people subscribing to it."[7] The same can be said of culture: When a group of people hold a distinct set of ideas (regardless of the merit of these ideas) strongly enough that they are passed on from generation to generation, they share a culture.

On this question of the origin of our cultural beliefs, most economists today, if pressed, would likely favor Adam Smith's view that culture primarily serves the purpose of social bonding and group interpretation. To put it in the cost-benefit framework that most economists instinctively adopt, culture is important to social bonding, which is important in reducing transaction costs by allowing members of a group to understand, communicate, and trust one another. This allows more trade, which facilitates more individual specialization while at the same time allowing greater diversification of the overall economy. Cultural beliefs also incentivize behaviors that serve the good of the community, not just individual desires, by indoctrinating injunctive norms (societal values) and creating public pressure so that they become descriptive norms (societal practices). In other words, it can be argued that having a shared cultural perspective is an important part of what shapes productive economic institutions.

The most important aspects of culture that economists are interested in are the cultural beliefs that influence behavior. The philosopher Max Weber (more on him shortly) asked "What gives actions meaning?" Economists turn this question around and also ask "What meanings give action?" Incorporating culture into our economic analysis ensures that our focus is not just on narrow monetary payoffs, but that we recognize that values, feelings, and tradition also shape the incentives that impact human behavior.

Defining culture is only one of many problems in studying culture. Another is how we classify, or "measure," different cultures. Can we say something about the different attributes of culture and which cultures share particular behavioral traits? Cataloging cultures is yet another area of research that has a seemingly endless series of approaches that branch out across different disciplines in a myriad of ways. One of the most interesting approaches to classifying culture was developed by an IBM human resources researcher, Geert Hofstede. Collecting survey data from a wide variety of countries, Hofstede identified six primary dimensions on which cultural attitudes differ.[8] These six dimensions are widely used in international business and marketing research the world over. They are:

1. *Power distance.* A measure of how willing members of a society are to accept the unequal distribution of power and submit to top-down authority.
2. *Collectivism.* A measure of how likely people are to be organized into groups. Here, the social emphasis placed on personal achievement relative to group success is important.
3. *Uncertainty avoidance.* A measure of how open a society is to change. Is society organized in ways that reduce risk by promoting more structured and stable environments?
4. *Long-term orientation.* A measure of how much future rewards and sustainability are emphasized over immediate gratification.
5. *Masculinity.* A measure of the extent to which cultural norms favor a strict division of roles between sexes in a society. If cultural norms value competitiveness, assertiveness, and power over valuing cooperative relationships and more fluid gender roles, Hofstede would consider the culture more masculine.
6. *Indulgence.* Measures of whether people believe they should be free to pursue their individual desires versus believing that these desires should be curbed and social norms should be strictly enforced.

My purpose in discussing Hofstede's classification theory is certainly not to say that this is the only way, or even a particularly good way, of organizing and thinking about cultural attributes. What I am trying to illustrate is twofold. First, there are certain characteristics that do differ or are widely shared across cultures. The number of these characteristics might be six or 600, but the fact of the matter is that cultures are not so distinct that we cannot make any generalizations about them—we can.

The second, and more important, reason to consider classification strategies such as Hofstede's is because they illustrate the immense problems in trying to tie a specific cultural attitude to a positive or negative economic outcome. Each one of these dimensions could be consistent with institutions that encourage productive behavior or discourage it. Consider the first dimension: *power distance.* It could be argued that countries that are more accepting of unequal distributions of power and more authoritarian political systems might be less likely to experience economic growth. More authoritarian systems, as we discussed in the last chapter, allow for elites to gain inordinate power, tend to have more corruption, and often fail to protect individual property rights. But on the other hand, if there are no cultural incentives to submit to authority, anarchy will exist, and decentralized corruption, which is particularly costly, will occur.

Collectivist sentiment can increase growth by fostering cooperation, encouraging the provision of public goods, and centralizing power in the central government so that it can enforce *de jure* laws and make them *de facto* laws. On the other hand, if society completely devalues personal achievement, will it protect private property, and where will entrepreneurship and innovation come from?

A society that completely emphasizes *risk avoidance* is likely too rigid to foster much entrepreneurship and innovation. However, a society that encourages too much risk taking is one that is likely to be unstable and will discourage the long-term planning needed for investments in physical capital, human capital, and technology that are needed to grow. Likewise, savings and investment will not occur in a society that does not foster any *long-term orientation*, but a society that lives only for tomorrow might never develop markets for the consumption goods that are needed today, eliminating the potential returns on this savings and investment.

In regard to *masculinity* and *indulgence*, many of these same observations apply. A society that is strong on encouraging assertiveness but limits self-indulgence might be one in which hard work and playing by the rules are emphasized. However, this might also be a society that limits the positive roles that women play in society and reduces freedom of choice to engage in activities that both contribute to the well-being of the community. Which is it? Hofstede's classification cannot help us answer that.

In sum, while cultural characteristics do matter, cultures that create good institutions are those that find an appropriate balance between two competing dimensions of culture. Where this balance is, and how you get there, are almost impossible to identify before the fact. As a result, all we are left with is to rationalize after the fact about the ways that certain cultural norms encouraged productive behaviors or may have discouraged them. Theorizing after the fact is not a particularly scientific or persuasive way to discuss how culture impacts economics and vice versa, but it is often all that those who believe in the primacy of culture are left with.

So let's get more specific. Instead of talking about broad cultural dimensions like those identified by Hofstede, what are some specific cultural beliefs and practices that could play an important role in explaining economic behavior? I want to talk about a few ideas that some thinkers have identified, and argued about, over the years in an effort to think more concretely about exactly how culture influences economics. Particularly, I want to focus on cultural practices that most travelers have likely found themselves pondering on their journeys.

Religion

To quote from Hamlet: "There is nothing either good or bad but thinking makes it so." Religion is certainly one important reason why people believe that certain behaviors are good and others are bad. One of the first, and best-known, arguments for why culture matters for economic development was proposed by Max Weber in his theory of the Protestant work ethic. According to Weber, religious beliefs shape people's preferences for hard work, savings, and getting an education.[9] Weber was specifically interested in explaining why Protestant northern Europe has been richer than Catholic southern Europe since the 1500s. Weber's hypothesis was that the Protestant Reformation changed the course of economic history in the two regions. Catholic teachings emphasized that salvation only comes to individuals through the church, top-down, and that the church is the ultimate voice for dogma. As a result, income and labor should be devoted to the church, not necessarily to production. On the other hand, Protestant dogma emphasized individual salvation and a personal relationship with God that could be found through reading the Bible (requiring literacy) and thinking for yourself, not just through the teaching of the clergy. Protestant theology also emphasized predestination, or the belief that God has already chosen who is to be saved and who is not to be saved, and that the best evidence that someone is favored by God is to have personal success. Becoming rich—which necessitates hard work, thrift, and entrepreneurial initiative—was important under Protestant theology to publicize your selection as a chosen one. Weber also argued that religions other than Catholicism that emphasize obedience to authority and discourage individual initiative, such as Confucianism in China and the Hindu caste system in India, also failed to incentivize hard work and economic progress.

This idea of a culturally defined work ethic has been most recently promoted by the historian David Landes, who says: "If we learn anything from the history of economic development, it is that culture makes all the difference."[10] Landes argues that beliefs and attitudes toward growth are driven by culture, although he accepts the fact that multiple cultures can create individuals who are "rational, ordered, diligent, and productive." In

Landes's opinion, cultures and religious beliefs that stress education (particularly for females), emphasize precision, promote rational dissent, and do not attach a social stigma to wealth creation are those cultures that will develop economically. For example, Landes argues that South America's relative lack of economic development stems in part from the cultural attitudes of the Spanish and Portuguese. These Iberian countries adopted a "squeeze" approach to growth that focused on exploiting existing resources in Latin America, including the indigenous people there, and not on developing manufacturing and finance. In contrast to North America, few European families permanently migrated to Latin America, and, as a result, most labor there was conscripted. The institutions established in Latin America, such as limits on squatters' property rights and the exclusion of peasants from legal and financial systems, reflect the centralized power of the Catholic Church and its culture of entrenching political and economic clout in the hands of a small number of elites who continued to live in Europe.

Religious beliefs can also directly impact economic development through their impact on government policy. For example, Islamic prohibitions on usury, or the charging of interest, play a very important role in financial prohibitions (known as Islamic finance) that discourage borrowing, lending, savings, and investment in countries with large Muslim populations.

Religious beliefs are often at the core of cultural differences, and religion has been repeatedly identified by many commentators as the primary factor responsible for economic underdevelopment. Some, like Weber and Landes, see Catholicism and Confucianism as systems of beliefs that limit social mobility, discourage education, and promote a nonscientific mindset.[11] Others see Islam in a similar light: as a system of beliefs that promote submission to a religious hierarchy at the expense of individual freedom, critical thinking, and creativity.[12] Animist religious beliefs widely shared in Africa and Asia, in which outside forces and ancestors rule the world, have been blamed for promoting fatalistic outlooks, discouraging individual initiative, and emphasizing community rights at the expense of individual rights. And some see any and all religious belief as harmful for at least two reasons. First, because religious conflict is a common source of civil unrest that creates war, terrorism, special interest politics, and dysfunctional institutions. Second, because religion is just a form of central planning and subject to the dangers identified by Hayek: a small group of elites never has sufficient information to make the right decisions for everyone, and will always have their own interests in mind over that of society as a whole.

An alternative perspective on religion comes from Robert Barro and Rachel McCleary, who use international survey data to investigate whether having religious beliefs in general, regardless of the specific beliefs, impacts economic behavior.[13] They measure religiosity by asking questions such as whether people believe in heaven and hell and how often they attend religious meetings (church, synagogue, mosque, etc.) Their empirical findings suggest that countries in which more of the population believes in heaven and hell actually have higher income levels, possibly because the idea of punishment in the afterlife discourages crime and corruption, and encourages the enforcement of injunctive norms. On the other hand, countries where people more regularly attend religious services have lower income levels, possibly because more time and money are devoted to religious rites than to production. Of course, the exact way in which these religious beliefs impact growth is largely conjecture and raises all sorts of questions about how we distinguish between correlation and causation, and about what is causing what.

Linking correlation with causation is just one of the many problems associated with linking religion to culture and culture to economic behavior.[14] Another crucial difficulty is our innate observer bias. We simply can't help but theorize after the fact and view countries that are growing as having "good" religious beliefs and those that are not as having "bad" ones. Take Weber's ideas on the problems with Confucianism (and other related religious belief systems such as Shinto and Taoism). When countries like China and Japan were growing slowly for most of the last millennium, their culture was seen as holding them back. Their religious beliefs were seen as emphasizing authoritarianism and conformity, and discouraging hard work and entrepreneurship. Today, many observers speak glowingly of these Asian countries and talk about the growth benefits of "Asian values." No longer are Asian religious beliefs seen as conformist; they are now seen as promoting cooperation, harmony, and a spirit of working toward the common good. It is not the cultures or religions of these countries that have changed; it is our perspective on them.

Gender Roles

Different cultures define the socially and economically acceptable roles for men and women differently. In some cultures, gender roles are flexible, and both men and women can make their own choices about their personal and professional lives. In other cultures, gender roles are clearly demarcated, and in most of these cases they are defined for women by men.

When men limit the ability of women to work outside the home or to receive a full education, it leads to the most insidious forms of malinvestment. Likewise, as we discussed in Chapter 3, when men make the family planning decisions for women, it typically increases fertility rates and reduces the educational attainment of future generations. It is not surprising that gender equality within a society, by whatever measure you chose, universally leads to greater prosperity and a better quality of life for everyone, both men and women.[15]

Hundreds of years ago, the Middle East was the most prosperous region of the world and a center of intellectual development. The Ottoman Empire stretched from Portugal to India, and the influence of Islamic thinking extended even further because of its ability to coexist with other cultures and across many different religions. But in the 14th and 15th centuries, a conservative revolution took place in Islam that made it increasingly dogmatic. Slavery became widely accepted, and women's roles in society and in economic life were strictly curtailed. Today, women are discriminated against in many formal ways in Muslim countries: A woman cannot divorce without forfeiting her financial rights in Egypt, or drive a car in Saudi Arabia, or own land as easily as a man in Pakistan. Women are also informally discriminated against in terms of the jobs they can fill and the roles they can play in society, although the extent of this discrimination varies widely across different Muslim countries. Since this conservative evolution of Islam has taken place, Muslim countries have persistently fallen behind most of the rest of the world. The few exceptions to this rule—such as the oil-rich gulf countries or the more moderate Muslim countries of Malaysia and Indonesia—only reinforce the point that cultural beliefs that limit the contributions of women also limit economic development.

The explicit and implicit discrimination of women has many important economic implications, but let's consider one of the less obvious ones in more detail: In many countries, women cannot get access to finance. This lack of access is sometimes driven by explicit prohibitions, but primarily is the result of the fact that women often have few legal rights to assets that can be used as collateral to get a loan. As a result, they have a difficult time accumulating savings and wealth and are unable to obtain loans to start their own businesses or invest in education to further their (and their children's) future.

The growth of microfinance has been largely aimed at addressing this financial discrimination by increasing women's access to financial services. Microfinance is a term used to refer to the act of providing small loans and other financial services to those who do not have access to formal finance through traditional banks. Microfinance seeks to design lending schemes in which small entrepreneurs and households can gain access to the modest amounts of finance they need to expand the scale of their businesses or stabilize their spending. The most popular model of microfinance was first developed by the Grameen (derived from the word "rural" in Bengali) Bank in Bangladesh. Grameen Bank was founded in 1976 by Muhammad Yunus, the 2006 winner of the Nobel Peace Prize for his work there. Yunus's impetus for starting the bank was his belief that, in his words, "all human beings are born entrepreneurs." Yunus made his first loan of $27 to a group of more than 40 women who crafted bamboo.

One of the two key components of the Grameen model as it was originally formulated is group lending. Small loans are made not to individuals but to small groups of people, usually of around five people. The idea is that group lending allows for greater repayment of loans by creating incentives for individuals in these groups to screen each other as well as to use peer pressure to increase the social penalties for default. The average Grameen loan in 2010 to a group of five was $384, with loans ranging between $100 and $5,000. While this does not sound like a great deal of money, most of the recipients of these loans were living at or below $2.50 a day, meaning that these loans are large as a fraction of their annual income.

The second defining characteristic of microfinance is that it primarily goes to women. Grameen makes 98 percent of its loans to women. Women are much more likely to be denied access to formal finance, so there is a particular need for microfinance among women. There is also quite a bit of evidence that finance that is directed at women is more likely to benefit the entire household by increasing spending on food, schooling, and health care—as opposed to alcohol and other luxury goods—meaning that loans to women are also more likely to increase welfare more broadly.[16] Microfinance organizations such as Thusang Basadi ("Women's Finance House") in Botswana have made women's empowerment, as measured by increasing their female customers' range of choices over the daily conditions of their lives, the primary goal of their work. Thusang Basadi uses the group lending approach not only to administer loans, but also to provide support networks and financial training for every aspect of women's lives, both working and in the home.

Openness to New Ideas

A great deal of work on the interplay between culture and behavior has focused on the role that cultural beliefs play in limiting or promoting intellectual flexibility and the aptitude of societies to adapt new ideas over time. According to what is often referred to *modernization theory*, some cultural beliefs limit the ability of societies to evolve and grow because they empha-size birth status over meritocracy, because they are authoritarian and not pluralistic, because they are conservative in their outlook and not progres-sive, and because they emphasize religious knowledge over scientific knowledge. In the anthropology literature, these traits are often referred to as "social capability," which is evaluated based on a society's ability to orga-nize large enterprises, specialize its production, use markets, and adopt sci-entific beliefs instead of superstition.[17] According to this view, in order for more traditional cultures that rank low in social capability to thrive in a capitalist system, they must first reject many of their cultural norms, which is difficult to do.

For example, prominent economic historians have argued that the Indus-trial Revolution started in Europe and not elsewhere, thanks to the early spread of Enlightenment thinking and the general acceptance of the idea that human progress was possible and desirable.[18] Without a cultural belief in the possibility of improvement through human action, there is no imper-ative to improve institutions or promote technological progress.

Although these ideas sound plausible, it is hard to validate moderniza-tion theory because it is often subject to the same observer bias that eval-uating religious beliefs is subject to. One recent study examining data from the World Values Survey found no evidence that beliefs in the value of tech-nology over tradition played a role in explaining economic growth.[19]

Entrepreneurship and Risk Taking

There is some evidence that people's willingness to accept risk and deal with failure differs across cultures. Any global traveler has to notice that when traveling to the most difficult and remote areas of the Earth, there is likely to be a Cantonese shopkeeper there. I have seen Cantonese shop-keepers manning small retail stores in the middle of the Kalahari Desert, in the Nepalese Himalayas, and even in Iowa! On a get-away vacation to a remote beach in Belize, there were three stores in the small village that I stayed in—all of them owned by Cantonese. This led me to conclude that you can get away from work, from e-mail, and from cold weather, but you cannot get away from Cantonese shopkeepers. Surely this incredible abil-ity to take risks and live in difficult and isolating circumstances is not just coincidental among the Cantonese, and must reflect some cultural predis-position toward entrepreneurship. (The same could be said of Gujarati from India, referred to by *The Economist* as "the world's best businesspeople."[20]).

Clearly some cultures are more predisposed toward risk taking than others. Surveys suggest that Americans generally have more of a preference for self-employment, a desire for personal achievement, and are more competitive than Europeans.[21] Others have examined Hofstede's cultural dimensions index that we discussed earlier and have tried to identify the relationship between uncertainty avoidance, masculinity, indulgence, and entrepreneurship. Studies have found weak evidence that countries that are more focused on achievement, self-control, initiative, and risk taking are more entrepreneurial.[22] However, the fact of the matter is that it is difficult to measure characteristics such as "entrepreneurial," and there is likely a highly complex relationship between traits such as personal initiative and entrepreneurship. As we have talked about before, the poor tend to be highly entrepreneurial, not necessarily because they have more innate initiative but because they are forced to be self-employed due to a lack of jobs in formal labor markets. (This helps explain why the Gujarati and Cantonese are so likely to seek their fortunes as entrepreneurs abroad, where economic opportunities have historically been better than back home.) An economy in which everyone is an entrepreneur is likely to be a poor economy with lots of small and inefficient businesses. It is also likely to have a government with rampant corruption as every public worker takes their own initiative to line their own pockets.

All of this said, the claim that individual initiative and people's tolerance for risk impacts economic growth makes too much sense for it not to be true. Beliefs about how you get ahead in the world should shape people's incentives to be productive. A 2014 Pew research report surveyed 44 countries and asked people whether they agree with the question "Success in life is pretty much determined by forces outside our control."[23] Only 18 percent of Pakistanis disagreed with this statement, expressing a fatalism that discounts personal initiative as a means to achievement, while 60 percent of Americans disagreed. Americans were much more likely to attribute success to hard work and relatively little to being a man, being lucky, or who you know, while Middle East and African residents were much more likely to attribute success to these three factors. According to this survey, developed countries view hard work and education as very important. Developing countries agree, but also attach importance to giving bribes and being lucky. The poorest countries were the least optimistic and most likely to view being a man and knowing the right people as being the keys to success. Likewise, another study examining results from the World Values Survey finds that the more that a country believes that (i) individual merit determines an individual's income, and (ii) private property rights should be respected, the faster the country grows.[24]

Of course, once again there is a chicken and egg problem here. People in poor countries who believe that personal contacts are the most important factor in getting ahead might be right; in other words, their beliefs reflect their reality. People may not be poor because of their lack of faith in the value of personal initiative and hard work, but being poor has taught them that working hard does not always pay. However, the fact remains that the more that people believe that a bribe or a personal connection is needed to get ahead, the lower the benefits of individual initiative and the less productive the institutions within a country will be.

Conflict and Diversity

Culture may not matter as much as the clashes that often take place between cultures. Human history is replete with stories of cultural contact leading to conflict. The exact cultural beliefs that drive these conflicts are secondary to the fact that people from different cultures see the world differently, have different notions about how conflict should be dealt with, and respond to the actions of those from other cultures in ways that could not be anticipated by either group. To highlight just one such cultural loggerhead from the thousands in history, consider the Spanish conquest of the Inca Empire in 1532. The Incas were fearful of Spanish horses, having never seen them before, and could not understand the Spanish obsession with yellow rocks. According to Spanish legend, when the Spanish presented a Bible to the Inca emperor Atahualpa, he put his ear to it, having never having seen a book before, and said "Why doesn't it speak to me?" before throwing it aside. This action, perceived as blasphemous, sparked the slaughter of the emperor and of thousands of warriors by only 168 Spaniards.[25]

Because culture is often associated with ethnicity, many economists have focused on the role that ethnic diversity plays in creating conflict that undermines economic and social stability. Ethnicity is difficult to measure: There is far more ethnic diversity than there is genetic diversity among humans, indicating that ethnicity is largely a socially constructed concept. For example, the genocide in Rwanda in which Hutus slaughtered between 500,000 and 1 million Tutsis was based on a social distinction between groups of people preconceived as a rigid ethnic distinction by the Belgians and French. Belgian priests traveled the country in the early 1930s measuring the width of people's noses and legalizing the resulting ethnic "calculations" through the use of identity cards.

Social scientists typically measure ethnicity by looking at the degree of "ethnolinguistic fractionalization," which is a fancy way of saying how many different languages and dialects are spoken in a region. Studies have shown that countries that are more ethnically diverse have more social conflict, weaker rule of law, more corruption, and fewer public goods.[26] The common thread between these effects is that more ethnic diversity appears to lead to more special interest behavior; in other words, a focus on helping "us" as opposed to "them." This encourages discrimination and spurs majorities to ignore the rights and expropriate the property of minorities. These behaviors can increase income inequality and lead to social unrest.[27] This "us/them" mindset also reduces the incentives to invest communal resources on public goods, reduces lending, discourages education, provokes violent crime, reduces the incentives to mediate conflict using legal systems, weakens government power, and encourages the kinds of decentralized corruption that kills growth. It is easy to look to Sub-Saharan Africa and the Middle East, which are the most ethnically diverse regions of the world, and see that these regions are also the most conflict-laden. The ethnic conflict in these regions was also magnified by the fact that colonists drew borders with the explicit intent to divide ethnic groups in order to keep populations divided and weak, with the result that political violence, wars, and discrimination are all the more common among ethnicities whose homelands were divided by an arbitrarily drawn border.[28]

Ethnic diversity might also play a role in psychologically damaging people by making them feel inferior and reducing their self-confidence and individual initiative. A study of students in India found that students of lower castes performed worse on tests that involved solving mazes if they were reminded of their caste before they took the tests.[29]

The fact that ethnic diversity undermines growth helps provide an explanation for a question that came to my mind the first time I traveled to a less developed country: Why is it that the most interesting areas of the world are also some of the poorest? The fact is that many travelers, including myself, want to travel to the most culturally diverse and unique places. To the extent that cultural diversity undermines economic development, it should not be surprising that many of us who love to travel find ourselves venturing to the poorest and most challenging places to visit, not the richest and easiest.

While there is evidence that cultural diversity is a barrier to economic growth, there are also good reasons to not take this argument too far. First and foremost is the fact that higher levels of income can impact the ways that ethnic diversity influences people's behavior. In poor countries, conflict becomes endemic when people find themselves fighting over pieces of a very small pie. Poorer countries typically have more dysfunctional governments that are more likely to be governed by elites who exaggerate and exploit differences between their people for their own personal gain (think Robert Mugabe in Zimbabwe). However, richer countries with stronger governments promote unity through things such as strong educational systems, more language training, better communication and media, and broader economic opportunities that encourage people to assimilate.

Another form of diversity that can be costly is income inequality. Once again, this is because it may empower elites, lessen inclusivity, and worsen institutions. Also, poverty itself is harmful to growth because it discourages individual investments in education, capital, and technology. Studies have found that higher levels of income inequality reduce the levels of education, tax revenue, public goods, and economic growth within a country.[30] There are also psychological costs to income inequality. In America, where income inequality is much higher than Europe, 60 percent of the population believes that the poor are lazy as compared to only 26 percent of Europeans. Economists have shown that these beliefs are directly tied to the failure to adopt public policies in the United States that might help the poor rise out of poverty and raise overall economic growth, such as more spending on public goods such as education. In addition, the poor are more likely to suffer psychologically from stress, which serves to reduce IQs and discourages long-term thinking and planning.[31] These psychological costs of poverty cause the poor to be less productive and have lower qualities of life than they would otherwise have.

In summary, it's been said that there are two types of people in the world: those who think that there are two types of people in the world, and those who don't. There is good evidence that peace and prosperity are more achievable when living among those who fall into the second group.

There is one final aspect of culture that is an important factor in behavior: the role of trust. In the words of the Nobel Prize–winning economist Kenneth Arrow, "It can be plausibly argued that much of economic backwardness in the world can be explained by the lack of mutual confidence."[32] Trust encourages cooperation and minimizes the "us/them" thinking that, as we talked about above, favors expropriation over productivity. Trust reduces uncertainty by allowing us to have confidence in the predictability of other people. Trust also reduces the transaction costs associated with trade by limiting the need to verify the honesty of everyone. By reducing the costs of trade, trust encourages more specialization and facilitates the use of markets, which are at the heart of increasing productivity and income. Trust also is crucial to long-term planning and the provision of finance that encourages savings and investment. Trust gives us the confidence to build in the present in the face of an uncertain future. According to another economist: "Honesty and trust lubricate the inevitable frictions of social life."[33]

A good example of how a lack of trust discourages specialization and the use of markets is the preponderance of family companies and large conglomerates in less developed countries. Throughout southeast Asia, more than 50 percent of the top 200 companies are family-owned and not public. For example, you cannot go to India without buying goods from the Tata group of companies: They make cell phones, build cars, mine for minerals, provide financial services, develop pharmaceuticals, make fertilizer, sell watches, and generate electricity (among many other activities). How can operating across such a broad range of activities make sense given the need for specialization in order to be efficient? The reason is that family conglomerates such as Tata are able to circumvent input markets and avoid working with people outside of their company whom they cannot trust. Conglomeration also reduces the need for external finance and limits exposure to corruption. Working only with those in your inner circle makes sense when you lack trust for everyone outside the circle, so in Tata's case the idea is to make this inner circle as large as possible. For every family-owned conglomerate like Tata in India, there is a Samsung in South Korea or the Sameer Group in Kenya that face similar incentives to grow horizontally as a way of enlarging their circle of trust.

Trust plays a broader role than in just influencing interpersonal interactions. Trust is also crucial to having effective governments and productive economic institutions. Having any sort of centralized government requires a transfer of trust from individuals to the state. The same is true for political systems, legal systems, and financial systems. Causation likely goes both ways here: Trust facilitates good government, and good government also facilitates trust. Of course, the propensity to trust does not change quickly. Trust takes a long time to build, and accumulated trust can be lost very quickly. Measures of trust in the former East Germany remain well below that in the former West Germany 25 years after unification.[34]

Let's consider a concrete example of how trust can influence economic behavior using game theory. Specifically, let's reconsider the ultimatum game that we discussed in Chapter 2. If you remember, in the ultimatum game the first player is given some money and instructed to share it with the second player. If the second player accepts the offer, they divide the money accordingly and both get to keep their share; if the second player rejects the offer, then neither player gets anything. The rational way to play this game in isolation is for the first player to offer the second player only a very small amount of the total. The second player should still accept this seemingly bad deal because getting something is better than nothing. However, when this game is actually played by real people, many second players will reject any offer that is less than 50 percent of the total, punishing the first player (as well as themselves) for failing to make a "fair" offer.

So why do people punish others when they also hurt themselves in the process? We all rely on reciprocity, and if we do not punish those who violate our innate sense of fairness, then we are inviting outcomes that do not maximize everyone's welfare. In the case of the ultimatum game, when people do not play fair (as judged by the second player), then nobody gets anything. In other words, fairness and a sense of trust are injunctive social norms that are learned. In cooperative societies with productive institutions, they are often learned through punishment of those who do not play fair. In societies where this is not the case, trust and fairness never become the descriptive norm, to the detriment of society as a whole.

Not surprisingly, there are big differences across cultures in how people play the ultimatum game. Cross-country field experiments find that first players from developed or developing countries typically make offers between 40 and 50 percent of the total, and offers less than 30 percent are usually rejected by the second player. In less developed countries, the offers that are made and the likelihood of rejection are half of these amounts, suggesting that players have less of an expectation of trust and fairness when playing the game.[35]

Of course, many economic activities are not zero-sum games like the ultimatum game above where the overall size of the pie is fixed—sometimes our interactions with people are not just about fairness but also about cooperation. Consider a recast version of the game we discussed in Chapter 2 called the prisoner's dilemma, in which two prisoners are held in separate rooms and asked to confess to a crime. If one confesses and the other denies, the denier goes free and the confessor goes to jail for an extended sentence. If they both deny, they both serve a lesser amount of jail time than if the other prisoner had denied. If they both confess, then both do an even smaller amount of jail time. We can express their outcomes, or "payoffs," from this scenario in the following matrix, as shown in the table below, where the first number in each cell represents the payoff to Prisoner 1 and the second the payoff to Prisoner 2.

		Prisoner 2	
		Confess	*Deny*
Prisoner 1	*Confess*	(2,2)	(0,3)
	Deny	(3,0)	(1,1)

The outcome that maximizes the total payoffs for both prisoners is to both confess—this minimizes the total amount of time that both prisoners must spend in jail. However, the Nash equilibrium is the outcome in which everyone is doing what is best for themselves, not necessarily what is best for the group (in other words, the noncooperative equilibrium). In this case, notice that the best choice for each prisoner individually is to always deny the charge no matter what the other prisoner chooses to do. This leads to both prisoners denying the charge and to the overall payoff being lower than it could be under the cooperative outcome (confess, confess). The key insight here is that if each prisoner could trust the other prisoner, they would both confess and be made individually better off than if they both deny. But there is no trust, and there is no mechanism for building this trust or making a binding commitment to confessing. This same insight applies to many economic situations where a lack of trust reduces cooperation and eliminates the possibility of mutually beneficial transactions simply because one person cannot count on another person to hold up their end of any agreement.

Measuring trust and its impact on economic activity is a burgeoning area of economic research. How is trust measured? One approach is through field experiments, like the ultimatum game discussed above. Another is to examine survey data, such as the World Values Survey, which asks people across the globe questions related to trust and their perceptions of how honest people are. Another approach is to create opportunities in which people directly reveal the sense of trust in a society. In one such experiment, researchers left wallets full of money on public transportation and counted how many wallets were returned.[36] In Norway and Denmark, all wallets were returned; in Italy and Switzerland, less than 40 percent of wallets were returned. There is a great deal of agreement between all of these different measures of trust, and generally, studies have found that the greater the levels of measured trust, the higher the rate of economic growth across a broad range of countries.[37] Of course, the same caveats hold with trust as with other aspects of culture: While trust impacts institutions and growth, the reverse is also true because growth and productive institutions also foster greater trust.

And what fosters trust within different cultures and societies? Empirical evidence suggests that ethnic homogeneity and income equality foster trust.[38] Once again, though, this relationship is complex. It is also possible that a lack of trust is the reason for ethnic diversity. To understand why, remember that we measure ethnic diversity by examining linguistic fractionalization. One theory for why language differs as much as it does across different people is that language differentiation evolved to encourage

Jerusalem: The capital of trust and distrust.

tribalism, and tribalism was important in primitive societies because it increased the social bonds within small groups of people. These language-created social bonds encouraged cooperation and reciprocity, enhancing the chances of survival for each group in competition with other groups for scarce resources. In other words, there may be an evolutionary basis for tribalism, ethnic diversity, and language differentiation, and a lack of trust is the reason behind these social adaptations. The irony is that the things that fostered trust among small groups in the past now foster distrust more broadly today.

Clubs and volunteer organizations also appear to facilitate trust. They do this by expanding the web of contacts that individuals have with others outside of their normal groups. Countries in which their citizens identify themselves as active member of a larger number of social groups report higher measures of trust.[39] This is one reason why religion likely plays both a positive and negative role in building trust. On the positive side, religions create social groups that encourage the broader personal interactions that facilitate trust.[40] On the other hand, some religions also create hierarchical structures that foster an "us/them" mentality that entrenches conflict and discourages trust.[41] This is obvious in many places of the world, but none more so than in Jerusalem, which, more than any other area of the world, has come to symbolize the consequences of conflict and distrust. And I am not just talking about distrust between Muslims and Jews: On a visit to the Church of the Nativity in Bethlehem (where Christians believe Jesus was born), I missed by a matter of hours (but saw it later on YouTube) priests from two different Christian sects, Armenian and Greek Orthodox, sword fighting with broomsticks like some sort of medieval Jedi warriors over the crucial question of who was going to stand where in the church on Christmas Day. This fight took place near the security wall/separation wall (depending on who you ask) that separates Israel from the Palestinian territories/occupied Palestinian territories (depending on who you ask). This wall was built with the intention of disrupting travel and preventing people on one side of the wall from commuting to work or school on the other side of the wall. It is a symbol of how difficult it is to build trust in the face of constant conflict.

Finally, the lack of trust in some societies reflects the path-dependent nature of each country's historical experiences. One of the lasting legacies of colonization in many countries is not just the demolition of social and political networks, but a destruction of trust as colonizers commonly pitted one group of indigenous people against another. The Hutus and Tutsi in Rwanda are just one example of the "divide and conquer" strategy followed by many colonizers, where those identified as Tutsi were favored with jobs and higher social standing by the Belgians and French in return for their loyalty, fostering resentment among the majority Hutu population. Such strategies have left behind disastrous legacies of conflict that are still being dealt with today. The destruction of trust is one of the many ways in which colonization has left many countries trapped in unproductive economic institutions from which they cannot escape.

What if we reverse the question we have been talking about—how does culture impact economics?—and instead ask: Does economics impact culture? On this question, everyone from leftist Marxists to right-wing free-market economists agree: yes. Both the founding fathers of economics and important Enlightenment thinkers believed that both morality and culture reflect economic structures. They agreed with Adam Smith that commerce promotes peaceful, cooperative interactions over conflict and warfare. Montesquieu said, "Wherever manners are gentle there is commerce; and wherever there is commerce, manners are gentle."[42] For Alfred Marshall, one of the most important insights he gained during his travels in America in 1875 was just how people's work shaped their social interactions and their beliefs. According to Marshall, "There are no thoughts or actions, or feelings, which occupy a man and which thus have the opportunity of forming the man . . . as those thoughts and actions and feelings which make up his daily occupation."[43] Marshall was surprised by the motion and freedom of American society and just how easily its people adopted new ideas, participated in new activities, moved to new locations, and were open to new ways of living. This fluidity was a defining aspect of American culture and was a direct result, according to Marshall, of the entrepreneurial spirit that defined the American capitalist model.

The Chicago School of Economics, a well-known citadel of free-market and libertarian thinking, has long preached the doctrine that cultural attitudes directly reflect economic realities. Economists such as the Nobel Prize winner Gary Becker have examined how social arrangements, even family structure, can be understood as reflecting the underlying economic realities of life. In Becker's view, social arrangements are just a means of supporting "rational altruism," or doing what is best for other people because it is also best for you.[44] When interpersonal interactions are examined this way, economics can provide unique insights into the reasons for religion, marriage, family size, crime and punishment, tastes and fashion, the arts, and politics, among other things. Becker and his acolytes have argued that culture is economics, not a predetermined set of traditions and beliefs that exist outside of economics.

Karl Marx was greatly influenced by economists such as Smith and Marshall and also believed that culture reflects economic conditions. This is the basis for the Marxist principle of "cultural materialism," or the idea that customs, beliefs, and social structures can be traced back to an economic problem or material shortcoming that people have had to overcome (think back to our previous discussion of the sacred cows of India). Marxists who believe that cultural materialism is the only determinant of culture, however, fail to explain why some cultural beliefs don't change even as people's material conditions change, why culture varies more than environmental conditions, and also why some cultural beliefs exist that worsen, not improve, people's standards of living.

If economics influences culture, then it must also be true that economic development plays an important role in cultural evolution. Anyone who has traveled internationally would have a difficult time arguing against the fact that economic development changes how people interact in many different ways. A precondition for economic development is that people begin to network through markets, which involves widening their circle of interaction and also their ability to trust people outside of their immediate social circles. As discussed previously, the development of trust is one of the most crucial elements to building markets and fostering economic development. As a result, broader economic development builds networks of cooperation that need trust, but also fosters trust in a virtuous circle.

In one test of the role that economic development plays in facilitating trust, economists have examined exactly what factors are important in determining how people play the ultimatum game.[45] The results, not surprisingly, indicate that larger societies that have higher levels of market participation make higher first offers when playing the ultimatum game, and second players are more likely to punish first players for low offers. This suggests that cooperative behavior and the enforcement of social norms become more common with greater market development, as our previous discussion would suggest. As another piece of evidence on the relationship between trust and development, consider that the 10 most violent countries in the world—Syria, Afghanistan, South Sudan, Iraq, Somalia, Sudan, Central African Republic, Democratic Republic of the Congo, Pakistan, and North Korea—are all among the poorest and least market-oriented countries in the world. The 10 most peaceful—Iceland, Denmark, Austria, New Zealand, Switzerland, Finland, Canada, Japan, Belgium, and Norway—are all rich, market economies.[46]

There is also evidence from the World Values Survey that economic development impacts people's general beliefs in other ways. Faster economic growth is correlated with an increase in the belief that individual initiative and protecting private property are important, and away from the belief that luck and personal connections are the keys to becoming richer.[47]

Economic development also impacts cultural evolution because it coincides with urbanization and migration, mixing groups of people and cultures that were previously separate. Cities are laboratories for cultural cross-polarization and cultural assimilation. When people worry about how globalization is changing culture (about which I will have more to say shortly), they are often blaming globalization for the cultural changes caused by urbanization, which are occurring independent of globalization. Even relatively closed and isolated countries in Sub-Saharan Africa are urbanizing at very rapid rates, leading to a great deal of cultural change.

There is also a virtuous circle between economic development and building strong and pluralistic central governments that can influence culture. As mentioned before, strong governments play a crucial role in cultural assimilation by promoting social norms, encouraging language unification, and enforcing uniform educational standards. France and Turkey are just two examples of countries that today have a unified cultural identity largely because of a strong central government made possible by economic development.

Not everyone believes that the cultural changes fostered by economic development are largely for the better. There are critics on the left of the political spectrum that argue that economic development coarsens culture by making each of us more self-centered in our interactions with others. According to the philosopher Michael Sandel, economic development is harmful to culture and social bonding. In his words, "Putting a price on the good things in life can corrupt them. That's because markets don't only allocate goods; they express and promote certain attitudes toward the goods being exchanged."[48] For example, markets may encourage people to help each other only in return for a monetary reward, not because of any feelings of intrinsic satisfaction or concerns about other people's well-being. Sandel's worry is that markets turn moral responsibilities into market transactions, weakening our social bonds and subtly undermining our commitment to the welfare of society as a whole.

On the right of the political spectrum, many critics argue that the growth of the welfare state that has accompanied economic development (see Chapter 4 and Wagner's Law) has made people more dependent on handouts, less likely to work or to innovate, and less productive—i.e., to suffer from "learned helplessness."[49] In their minds, the process of modern economic development will lead to cultural deterioration and future economic stagnation.

One of the most discussed aspect of economics and culture is the impact of globalization on cultural diversity. Wings of humanities libraries (or, maybe today, acres of data storage warehouses) have been filled with articles and books examining—primarily hand-wringing about—the loss of cultural diversity caused by globalization. By globalization, most authors are talking about the increasing interconnectedness between peoples and countries across the globe that is driven by many factors, but primarily growing international trade and information technology. Many commentators use the term globalization but are primarily worried about "Americanization," or the idea that economic interconnectedness necessarily has as its end result a single homogenous culture where everyone goes on vacation to Disneyworld, goes out to eat at McDonald's, wears Levi jeans, and watches *Friends* on television before they go to bed.

Globalization is not a new phenomenon. In fact, the last 40 years can be thought of as the second wave of globalization that really began in the late 1800s but was interrupted by the Great Depression and two world wars. The first age of globalization also brought with it the age of global tourism. Before the 1900s, few people traveled beyond the borders of their home country. In England, Victorians worried that travel would encourage the adoption of foreign "vices" and would "mongrelize" the traveler. However, as people began to travel more widely, worries about the impact of travel moved to concerns not about the traveler, but about the places they traveled to. Cultural corruption was particularly obvious in small, previously isolated countries. Antiglobalizers often point to the dramatic impact of tourism on places such as Tahiti, where contact with Europeans brought higher standards of living for the indigenous population, but also colonization, missionaries, sex tourism, disease, and war. Today, citizens in many Caribbean countries are outnumbered 20 to 1 by foreigners, with enormous implications for cultural traditions in these countries.

Globalization has not just increased people-to-people contact through tourism and trade, but it has also exposed people to new ideas and ways of life through global media, particularly television. In my travels, the global reach of satellite TV has never ceased to amaze me. When I first saw a rural African woman living in the middle of the Kalahari Desert carrying wood on her head, walking toward a traditional rondavel hut with a huge satellite TV on its thatched roof, I was astonished. On a long hike in the foggy Himalayas on the India/Nepal border, I felt like I was wandering blindly over the edge of the known Earth until I boarded with a local family and abruptly found myself huddled under a Hello Kitty blanket watching Brazilian soap operas and eating custard creams.

It always strikes me as nothing short of miraculous that, in a pinch, I can enliven a conversation with just about any male across the globe by dropping a reference to English Premier League football. In my opinion, these shared global experiences help promote the kinds of interpersonal connections that are one of the best ways to enrich our lives. Of course, it is also easy to point out the costs of this inundation by global media. According to experts, half of the world's 6,000 languages, and the cultural diversity that comes with these different languages, will disappear over the next 100 years, primarily replaced by global languages such as English. Globalized media is also breaking up traditional social structures, and people are becoming more isolated from their local communities as they become more closely connected with the global community. One study of villages in Java, Indonesia, found that those villages that have worse TV reception also have more social groups and higher reported levels of trust in their neighbors.[50]

The critics of globalization point to individual cases where specific cultural practices are gradually disappearing. But the simplistic narrative that globalization leads to cultural destruction is complicated by three facts. The first is that that culture rarely develops in pristine isolation, but is almost always the result of a mix of influences, some of them local and some of them not. Six hundred years since the beginning of the age of exploration in Europe and after more than 100 years of globalization, almost every culture in the world had already been touched by global influences well before people began to be worried about it. If you go back in history far enough, few cultural practices are truly indigenous. Classical Greek culture, the basis of much Western culture, is really an amalgamation of many different Mediterranean cultures, the integration of which was facilitated by the ease of travel and trade across the sea. English is a global language, in part, because more than a dozen different languages have made important contributions to it. Most music comes from the integration of a wide variety of influences. Even the books themselves that we use to pass down cultural ideas from generation to generation are the result of the interactions between a wide variety of cultures: paper first came from China, the alphabet from Phoenicians, numbers from Arabs, printing from Germans (and the Chinese and Koreans), and libraries from the Middle East and Ireland.

The second problem with the idea that globalization leads to cultural destruction is that culture is not stagnant but always evolving, and this is a good thing. As noted by the economist Tyler Cowen, those who are concerned about preserving cultural diversity at one point in time are implicitly arguing that cultural diversity across time should not be preserved.[51] Of course, banning intertemporal cultural diversity is another way of saying that culture cannot innovate. Without cultural evolution, we never get to enjoy new forms of art, music, dance, and literature. In fact, one definition of human history is essentially just the recording of cultural evolution.

The fact of the matter is that if we examine history, we find that periods of cultural stability were not good times to be alive. Periods when trade in goods and ideas has been most restricted and culture has been static have also been periods of intellectual decline and inhumane living conditions. The Dark Ages in Europe between 422 and 1100 do not compare favorably in any respect—except in cultural stability—to the Enlightenment era when cultural developments were rapidly taking place, and intellectual growth, economic development, and the quality of life increased broadly and rapidly across the continent. This basic fact remains true today across countries: The isolation of places such as Papua New Guinea does help protect its unique cultural traditions (one-fourth of the world's languages exist on the island), but comes at the price of primitive living conditions, poverty, the repression of women, low life expectancy, and violence for its citizens. The fact is that while many people point to globalization as representing the "least common denominator," in reality it spreads more liberal and inclusive thinking. For example, one study of rural villages in India found that those with access to satellite TV had fewer incidences of domestic violence, a lower preference for sons, more female autonomy, lower fertility, and higher levels of school enrollment.[52]

Third, many critics of globalization fail to recognize that globalization leads to both homogenization and heterogenization of culture at the same time. Yes, globalization does mean that we all are familiar with—whether we want to be or not—Hollywood movies and McDonald's. But I live in Iowa and can go see a Bollywood movie anytime I want and eat at an Ethiopian restaurant before I go. Globalization increases people's freedom of choice and, in the words of Cowen, liberates people from the "tyranny of place." As a result, because of media, trade, and travel, people can self-select into communities of their choosing regardless of where they live. We now live in what George Saunders calls "fluid nations."[53] Sometimes this means that we participate in mass markets, sometimes in niche markets. Sometimes this means low-brow, least-common-denominator entertainment, and sometimes it means high-brow, artistic endeavors. Sometimes this might mean people choose to watch Disney movies and listen to Korean pop music. For others, it means spending time in a chatroom discussing Congolese music or learning the tango. The cultural traditions continue, but they are no longer only practiced locally. As a result, diversity

The "old" town of Suzhou, China.

across countries might actually diminish, but diversity within countries thrives. Who is to say that this is not increasing overall cultural diversity, particularly if people are making these choices voluntarily?

For me, food is of utmost importance, and I tend to think of the costs and benefits of globalization primarily through food. When I am traveling, I am faced with three choices for restaurants. I can go to the generic chain restaurant that is filled with other tourists and some locals. I can go to a specialty restaurant that caters to high-end "foodies" and rich locals. Or I can go to the local restaurant filled with middle- and lower-class locals. As someone who enjoys experiencing cultural diversity and who is cheap, I am most likely to go to the third type, and many might argue that this is the type of restaurant that is hurt by the existence of the first two. But the fact of the matter is that globalization helps all three types of restaurants. When people patronize the generic and specialty restaurants, they are generating jobs and incomes for locals, helping them to afford to go out to eat. This creates more customers for local restaurants and helps me as a traveler in the process. As a result, while many travelers complain about the fact that we see KFCs and Pizza Huts everywhere we go, in reality, overall restaurant diversity benefits from the existence of the chain restaurants that many of us deplore.

The most persuasive argument to be made for why globalization promotes cultural diversity is the fact that higher incomes are the best way to promote the arts and culture. One of the most effective ways to generate higher incomes, as we have talked about throughout this book, is through encouraging international trade. Artists and cultural trendsetters need to be financially supported to be able to work. Sometimes this occurs directly through commissions, such as from the Medici family in Florence. But most often this occurs indirectly through markets. As overall standards of living rise and people become more educated, they appreciate more cultural activities and can afford to spend money to do so. In the words of Walt Whitman: "To have great poets, there must be great audiences, too."[54] Globalization and economic development allows more artists to make a living by creating more market demand for their artwork and through higher levels of support from well-funded governments, educational institutions, and museums.

One of the most famous fights against globalization was Gandhi's *Swadeshi* movement aimed at burning foreign cloth in order to protect the domestic jobs of hand weavers and the cultural heritage of India. But the history of the textile industry since Gandhi's time tells a story in which the international trade and mechanization that Gandhi fought against have reduced the overall price of cloth, raised the purchasing power of the poor, and increased overall incomes. With higher incomes, the size of the market for people who can afford to purchase high-end handwoven fabrics in India and across the globe is now much larger than it has been in the past. Today, there are more people working in the handwoven cloth industry in India than during Gandhi's era.[55] This is an example of the power of globalization to actually enhance cultural traditions, but to see how it does this, we have to open our eyes and look not just at the small stitches, but at the broader tapestry.

Economists continue to disagree about how much culture matters and why it matters. But despite this lack of clarity, we can draw a few clear conclusions about the interplay between culture and economics. First, culture matters in economics, but so do many other things. Institutions are of the utmost importance, and while culture shapes institutions, institutions are about much more than just culture. The idea that culture predetermines a society's path for development is contradicted by too many examples to the contrary. We have seen countries go from growth disasters to growth miracles (and the reverse) without any change in their culture—see Japan, Korea, China, and Botswana, among many other examples. China went from a declining country in which its emperor once denied opening trade relations with England because "we possess all things" to the country that today is developing rapidly based on an economic strategy focused on international trade. This was not because of a change in culture, but in policy and incentives. There are many examples of positive and negative changes in economic institutions that have nothing to do with culture, so we should not place more blame or credit on culture than it deserves.

The fact of the matter is that culture is too easy to scapegoat for economic failure. Part of this is observer bias—our own preconceptions influence our interpretation of the impact of culture and often lead us to confuse difference with deficit. There is also another problem, which is that economists are often guilty of "overfitting," or trying to explain more than can actually be explained. It is easy to point to culture as the critical missing factor in our economic models and as the hidden reason for success and failure, when in fact some of the disparity we observe might just be unexplainable, random variation, and the accidents of history.

Second, there can be virtuous and vicious circles between economics and culture. Cultural beliefs that encourage trust and individual initiative will foster markets and economic development. At the same time, economic development encourages cooperation and wider social interactions that can help build trust and change cultural norms. Unfortunately, this can work in reverse as well with disastrous effects, leading to conflict, dysfunctional government, and economic underdevelopment.

The possibility of virtuous and vicious circles is only one reason why there is no single best culture for growth. Instead, there are multiple equilibria, and the best outcomes occur when economic institutions exist that encourage productivity within the context of the cultural environment that shapes people's beliefs and social interactions. Creating effective institutions is not like putting together a bookshelf from Ikea, with arcane directions that, if somehow followed, guarantee success. Instead, good institutions are more like good dancing, where there are no formulas or directions. Productive institutions must creatively move in synch with their partner, culture.

Finally, culture clearly plays a role in explaining why institutions that work in one place cannot just be transplanted to another place with the same results. Just as a plant may only thrive in a specific climate, economic institutions must be consistent with people's cultural norms and beliefs in order to provide the appropriate incentives to engage in productive behavior. Economic planners who thought that Chicago School free-market institutions and American economic policies would work to rebuild the economy of Iraq were ignorant of both history and economics. Similarly, critics who argued that China's land-leasing system—in which the government owns all land and leases it to its citizens—could never foster growth because it does not meet Western standards of private property protection were thinking with the wrong mindset. It is not what Western economists believe that matters in China; it is what the Chinese citizenry believes that matters.

The economist John Maynard Keynes, himself an art collector, pianist, husband of a ballerina, and member of the Bloomsbury group of English writers and painters, viewed artists as the "trustees of civilization." But he also believed that artists could not pursue their arts and make cultural contributions without economic development. As a result, economists are "the trustees, not of civilization, but of the possibility of civilization." In the same sense, economists can be thought of as the trustees of the possibility of cultural diversity. Only by facilitating high standards of living can more people be unshackled from subsistence living and free to pursue the creative endeavors and social interactions that build cultural diversity. And maybe travelers can be thought of as the historians of these changes. Travelers see cultural and economic evolution where it takes place, as it takes place. Often we are amazed by these changes because they are happening so rapidly and the juxtapositions are so stark. Sometimes we are troubled by the changes taking place because one of the primary reasons we travel is to experience difference, and a world that is trading and interacting and growing is also a world in which location matters less and less over time.

If travelers are to play their role as the record-keepers of the ongoing evolution of culture and economics, then we have to accept the good with the bad. The KFCs and Starbucks that now litter every important travel location are one consequence of having more open doors and greater integration. The freedom that has expanded economic opportunity within these countries and which allows us as travelers to gain broader access to more of the world is the same freedom that allows more people across the globe to eat bad fast food. Freedom is not free and development is not always pretty. But if the places we go are less distinctive because they are more free and prosperous, then that seems like a reasonable price to pay, more reasonable than the price paid for a coffee at the Starbucks near the Parthenon in Athens.

CHAPTER SIX

What's a Landline? Technological Diffusion around the World

The world has become more complex as technology and easy travel mixes cultures without homogenizing them.

—Norman Spinrad[1]

Creating a new theory is not like destroying an old barn and erecting a skyscraper in its place. It is rather like climbing a mountain, gaining new and wider views, discovering unexpected connections between our starting point and its rich environment . . .

—Albert Einstein and Leopold Infeld[2]

One of the great things about being a college professor is that the foundation of your position of authority in the classroom is always a little wobbly, and students often ask questions that force you to rethink something you thought you were the expert on. In this sense, a good student is like a good trip in that they both challenge your preconceptions about what you think you know. One example of this comes to my mind. In 2009, I was lecturing to a group of students at the University of Botswana about technological development. I was trying to impress upon them the cumulative nature of technology—that knowledge is complementary and that one technological invention builds on another, like moving up rungs on a ladder. To illustrate, I referred to the incredible advances in the speed with which information travels. In 1805, it took 62 days for news about the Battle of the Nile to cover the 2,073 miles to London (at a speed of 1.4 miles an hour).[3] The invention of the telegraph in the mid-1800s allowed information to travel more than 100 times faster than it could previously. Land-line telephone service in the 1900s once again doubled the speed with which information traveled. And today, with the Internet and mobile phones, the speed with which information travels is primarily limited by our mental abilities to process it, not by our ability to gain access to it. As I was speaking, I noticed a few puzzled looks among the students' faces (not an uncommon experience for me). One tentative hand rose, and the student attached to that hand asked a simple question: "What is a land-line telephone?"

This student almost certainly had a mobile phone in her pocket—in fact, most likely it was a smart phone that was many times more powerful than the computers I messed around with when I was her age. Almost certainly she was doing things with her phone—banking, shopping, social networking—that I had no idea how, nor any inclination, to do. Yet she had never seen an old-fashioned telephone (probably had no idea what a telegraph was either). Her question caused me to pause and rethink this idea of a technology ladder. She certainly has not experienced technology moving on any constant trajectory over her life—she was born in a country where the most common mode of travel was by donkey cart and where 60 percent of the population lived in poverty, but today is one of the fastest-growing countries in the world and solidly middle-income by world standards. Her country and its level of technological development took a gigantic, discontinuous leap forward. This student didn't see technology as a process of steady, stepwise advancement, so why was I telling her it was so?

It is not surprising that traveling has opened my eyes to many new ideas—travel has always played a crucial role in the creation of new ideas that form the basis of new technology. (I will use the word "ideas" here to denote new thinking that leads to changes in technology.) In the second quote at the beginning of this chapter, Einstein directly compares creating new ideas to the process of travel where one eventually obtains new and unobstructed views of the world. The seed for the creation of one of the most famous ideas in human history—Charles Darwin's theory of evolution—was sown during his voyage on the HMS *Beagle* to the Galápagos. Viewing the vastly different species that lived in the isolated environments he visited not only spurred new thinking about the role of natural selection, but also about the geological processes that create ocean atolls. (Darwin was the first to correctly hypothesize that atolls were decaying volcanos that are gradually replaced by the growth of coral reefs.)

The global economy of today is one in which some countries are catching up while others are falling behind. Some countries have made leaps in their standards of living because they have been able to adopt technologies first created in the developed world; in many cases, they have actually improved on first-world technologies. But in other countries technology transfer is not occurring, and, in fact, it is often actively discouraged by governments or by societal norms. This lack of technological development gives a certain timelessness to some of the poorest places on Earth. In his memoir *Dreams from My Father*, Barack Obama recounts his visit as a young man to his father's ancestral home in Kogelo, a small village in Western Kenya.[4] About life there, he wrote: "I began to imagine an unchanging rhythm of days, lived on firm soil where you could wake up each morning and know that all was as it had been yesterday, where you saw how the things that you used had been made and could recite the lives of those who had made them." This changelessness was part of this small village's appeal, but also explains why its low living standards, short life expectancy, and limited literacy were unchanging as well.

In this chapter, I want to discuss the incentives and barriers that impact technology diffusion across countries. Understanding technology transfer first requires an examination of how new ideas are produced in the first place (hint: producing ideas is different than producing hamburgers) and how ideas "leak" and "match" with other ideas. The fact that ideas are clumpy (it's a technical term) explains a number of facts about inequality and the geographical distribution of income across the globe. If technology is so important to growth, then why do so many countries create barriers to technology transfer? I will discuss five reasons: special interest politics, the fallacy that technology eliminates jobs, protectionist instincts, a lack of access to finance, and risky economic environments that encourage diversification over specialization. By the end of this chapter, I hope to convince you that a lot of what you think you know about technological transfer across the globe is both right and wrong. In other words, I am going to ask you, once again, to think like an economist.

Technology is one of those concepts that is hard to put into words—we know it when we see it. Economists typically define technology as the way that inputs (labor and capital) are combined to produce output. This is a very broad definition, and it should be. Our concept of technology should include a wide variety of activities that include the invention of new products, new processes, new markets, new inputs, and even new methods of organization (Henry Ford's assembly line was a new technology). Technology also incorporates innovation, meaning the use of existing ideas in a new way; for example, using the GPS system built to track nuclear missiles to direct you to the nearest Thai restaurant using your mobile phone.

Beginning with Adam Smith, many economists have realized that economic growth is a dynamic process, driven by businesses that are constantly implementing new technologies to increase productivity in order to stay ahead of their competition. But as discussed in the first chapter, it wasn't until Robert Solow's work in the 1950s that economists were first able to quantify the importance of technology growth in explaining economic growth. According to Solow, growth in inputs only explains about one-third of economic growth, meaning the other two-thirds is caused by increases in productivity driven by technological change.

Why does technology play such an outsized role in driving economic growth? Previously (Chapter 3), we introduced the important economic concept of diminishing marginal returns to labor and capital: as you add more and more capital to a fixed amount of labor (or vice versa), the new inputs become less productive than the existing inputs, reducing their contribution to overall growth. What is so powerful about technology is that it does not suffer from the same physical limitations. Technology does not experience the drag of diminishing marginal returns and, a result, constant improvements in technology can lead to constant improvements in income. This is the primary reason why improving technology is so important to economic development and sustaining growth.

Technology doesn't suffer from diminishing marginal returns because it is different from capital and labor in a fundamental way: Technology is primarily about ideas that have no physical dimension. Physical goods like capital and labor are uniformly *rival*: When I am using a piece of machinery, someone else can't use the same piece of machinery. When I am working at one task, I am precluded from working at another task (contrary to what dedicated multitaskers seem to believe). But because ideas are not tangible, technology is nonrival and can be shared and used in ways that labor, capital, or a hamburger cannot. Thomas Jefferson, writing to a petitioner regarding a patent dispute, beautifully expresses (despite the excess of commas) the essence of technology when he said: "He who receives an idea from me, receives instruction himself without lessening mine; as he who lights his taper at mine, receives light without darkening me. That ideas should freely spread from one to another over the globe, for the moral and mutual instruction of man, and improvement of his condition, seems to have been peculiarly and benevolently designed by nature . . . and like the air in which we breathe, move, and have our physical being, incapable of confinement or exclusive appropriation."[5]

Technology growth is the most powerful lever of economic development because it allows us all to have our cake and eat it too. And then eat it again, and again, and again. Technological improvements not only allow us to produce more output with fewer inputs, but technology can be endlessly borrowed and adopted by those who had no hand in creating it or, many times, even understanding it. Technology is the classic example of a public good: Technology provides a positive externality and benefits everyone, regardless of whether you developed it or are even directly using it. It is the tide that raises all ships—assuming you have a ship to float on.

Because of the intangibility of technology, the production of ideas is inherently different from the production of other goods in three important ways. First, the costs of producing technologies are mostly paid upfront, and they are often very large. In other words, there are large fixed costs associated with the research and development of certain technologies. But once the technology exists, it can be shared easily and often at very low cost, or even for free. This creates a free-rider problem, which always exists with public goods (as discussed when we talked about roads and traffic in Chapter 2). Why should anyone want to invest in the research and development of ideas if others will just come along and then take these ideas for free? As a result, if left to the market alone, fewer ideas will be produced than is good for society. This is particularly true for basic research in the sciences that has no direct commercial application. This, of course, is the rationale for the government subsidization of ideas through public education research, as well as for providing patent protection for the creation of new ideas (although patents create another set of problems, which I will discuss shortly).

Second, the production of ideas creates monopolies. Ideas only need to be produced once by a single firm, creating a monopolist. In fact, monopolies are good for society in this case because we don't want multiple firms wasting huge amounts on research and development to produce the same ideas over and over again. However, the free-rider problem remains. Other firms will freely use the idea if they can, reducing the profitability of creating new ideas and reducing the likelihood that firms will invest in the research and development needed to produce them. The rationale behind granting patents is that patents turn ideas into intellectual property that can be owned. Once ideas are owned, the possibility of future monopoly profits from any ideas they produce will incentivize firms to spend more on research and development, leading to more ideas overall. Because of the necessity of monopolies in creating ideas, you can't think about the production of technology as the result of efficient and perfectly competitive markets. All of the big technology-producing companies—from Google, to Samsung, to Pfizer Pharmaceuticals, to Toyota—are, to a greater or lesser extent, monopolists. And what do monopolists do? Monopolists increase price and restrict quantity in order to increase profits. As a result, given the inherent nature of technology, ideas are always likely to be more expensive and scarcer than they would be if they could be produced in a perfectly competitive market—which they can't.

Third, ideas "leak" and ideas "match."[6] Let me explain. Ideas leak because they are intangible. As Thomas Jefferson noted, ideas can freely spread across the globe. However, this does not mean that the same idea is equally productive everywhere. In many cases, you need to have an existing stock of knowledge and complementary technology to be able to maximize the benefits of an idea. This might be a group of people with the appropriate educational background, an already existing technology that the new idea relies on, a certain skill set, a particular machine, or specific experiences. In order to leak, ideas also require institutional structures, such as a legal system and open markets, in order to spread. When these environments aren't present, they become "zombie ideas"—ideas that exist, but they are not living, and they are not enhancing productivity.

Ideas also match because when two ideas come together, they often add up to something much greater than just two separate ideas. Good ideas augment and amplify one another. A single idea is most likely to create a powerful new technology when it can be matched with the ideas of other people because the positive spillovers from one idea can magnify the benefits of another idea, and vice versa. For example, consider the development of the Internet, which required the simultaneous development of computers, communications, software, and protocol technologies. According to the technology writer Steven Johnson, "Like many of the bedrock technologies that have come to define the digital age, the internet was created by—and continues to be shaped by—decentralized groups of scientists and programmers and hobbyists (and more than a few entrepreneurs) freely sharing the fruits of their intellectual labor with the entire world."[7]

One of the most widely known concepts in modern innovation is Moore's Law. In 1965, computer expert Gordon Moore recognized that computing power appeared to double every 18 months, and what was true in 1965 has continued, leading to the exponential increase in information technology that we are enjoying today. In fact, Moore's Law might have been in effect well before modern computers were invented, all the way back to 1900 if you incorporate other forms of electric communication.[8] Why is there such incredible regularity in Moore's Law? While the ideas of one creative individual might grow linearly, the ideas created by a group of complementary individuals can grow exponentially because they compound upon one another. Because each new idea builds on another, every idea is a necessary step in creating the next idea and leads to a predictability in the rate, if not the exact form, of technology. To use a concept from evolutionary biology, change today is a function of the "adjacent possible." Technology growth, as exemplified by Moore's Law, is another example of the path-dependence of history we have talked about throughout this book.

Moore's Law points to a fundamental fact—and a major misperception— about how ideas and new technologies are produced. The popular conception of invention is that ideas are the product of lone, heroic geniuses struck with great ideas like lightning bolts out of the sky. In popular culture, we glorify the individual technology guru: Thomas Edison, Bill Gates, and Steve Jobs. But as Steven Johnson has noted, in reality, the modern history of technology is not the story of the solo genius.[9] It is the story of networking, leaks, and matches. The vast majority of the great ideas and inventions of the 20th century—germ theory, penicillin, radar, the personal computer, the Internet—were not the result of a single individual, but of groups of people working together, one idea feeding off another idea in unexpected ways, with existing ideas being subtly improved upon iteration after iteration, creating linkages toward the development of new technologies that no single mind could have developed in isolation. Even the prototypical genius inventor Thomas Edison didn't build his light bulb by himself, but as part of an extensive team of people with diverse skills and backgrounds, and in an environment that encouraged experimentation and sharing.[10] To take this one step further, history is filled with examples of concurrent invention—the creation of new ideas simultaneously at different places by different people. Many people credit Joseph Swan (not Thomas Edison) for inventing the light bulb, Alfred Russell Wallace for the theory of evolution, and Henri Poincaré for the theory of relativity. There were, in fact, multiple independent inventors of the phone, light bulb, thermometer, vaccinations, decimal fractions, the electric telegraph, logarithms, the steamboat, photography, and the electric railroad—even though each of these inventions today are often associated with the name of a single inventor.

This leads to another important observation: Not only are most modern technologies the result of networks and not individuals, but a large number of ideas were not created by markets but through nonmarket activities. All of the networked ideas mentioned in the last paragraph were not directly driven by the profit motive. Instead they were developed through nonmarket interactions between people in academia, government, and even by hobbyists. This contradicts the commonly held fallacy that technological progress is purely profit-driven. The fact that a great deal of technology is created outside of markets makes sense, though, given what we have already learned about the market failures inherent in the production of technology. Markets will never produce efficient levels of technology by themselves because technology is a public good. But other incentives outside of the profit motive—government subsidies, social recognition, altruism, philanthropy, our desire to interact with like-minded people, and just plain curiosity—play a crucial role in explaining the origins of invention and innovation.

Where do these networks that facilitate leaks and matches exist? First, where there are lots of people. More people lead to more leaks and matches: This is an important fact that explains why most of the world has escaped the Malthusian trap that we examined in Chapter 3. Contrary to the predictions of Malthus, the world has gotten richer on a per-capita basis as its population has risen. More people have created larger networks, fueling the technology growth that is the principal driver of economic development.

Today, most people live in cities, which is also where most technology is created and diffuses. Stepping back to consider the breadth of human history, technology never substantially advanced until large cities came into existence. Cities were not only a place for people to congregate and take advantage of leaks and matches; cities were also closely associated with the development of ways to record and store information (before the Internet). All of the great libraries and other repositories of knowledge—from Alexandria to Timbuktu to Rome to Dublin to London—have been inexorably linked to the growth of the cities they were located in.

Cities are essentially gigantic labs for developing new ideas and for diffusing technology, which in part explains the massive move toward urbanization that has been occurring across the world, and particularly in developing countries, over the last 50 years. Today, roughly half of the world's population lives in an urban area, and by 2050 this number will be nearly 70 percent. Increasingly, people are not just moving to cities, but to megacities of more than 10 million people. While there were 5 of these megacities in 1970, in 2015 there are 23. People are pulled to cities and particularly to megacities because of the higher wages that jobs in urban areas provide. And why are wages higher? In large part because people are more productive in cities where they have better access to technology and the leaks and matches associated with it. One of the strongest results from the research studying the creation of ideas is that innovation is closely linked to cities.[11] In the United States, 63 percent of patents are developed by the populations of just 20 cities.[12] Innovation in any city increases exponentially with its size. A city that is 10 times larger than another city is 17 times more innovative—a city 50 times bigger is 130 times more innovative.[13] These astonishing findings stem from the fact that cities are filled with networks where the individual skills of each person spill over and complement other people's skills. Some of these networks are created by firms, but others occur in the coffeehouses, reading groups, neighborhood parks, restaurants, etc., that exist in thriving, growing cities. The cities of today are not characterized by one unique culture, but by hundreds and thousands of unique subcultures—the development of which is aided by globalization and information technology (see the discussion in the previous chapter on cultural diversity)—that create avenues for people to mix and for ideas to leak and match. A city is not a place; it is hundreds of thousands of connected places.

Cities also have another quality that make them innovative, and that is that they are inherently experimental: People often move to cities to enjoy the social and economic fluidity of urban areas where they can experiment with different personalities and different ways of living. Another study on innovation finds that people with diverse backgrounds, diverse experiences, and diverse social groups are three times more innovative than those who are not.[14] These same factors explain, as discussed earlier, why travel has played such a significant role in helping to creating new ideas. By creating the opportunities for people to mix and match, traveling allows for the happy possibilities of chance and for ideas to mingle within new networks of people. As the quote by Norman Spinrad at the beginning of this chapter asserts, travel and technology generate complexity, and it is this ability to combine people and ideas in novel groupings that creates new ideas.

We are all familiar with the cultural diversity of cities, but many of us ignore the economic diversity of cities. Cities often have very different economic institutions than the areas that surround them. Because cities have traditionally emerged as places where people can come together specifically to trade, they typically develop information networks, informal legal systems, and more trust than can be found outside of cities. As discussed in the first chapter of this book when talking about the economics of slums, some of the poorest areas of the world are actually economic empowerment zones. Slums can become safe zones from the dysfunctional laws, public corruption, choking bureaucracy, and stifling social norms that strangle growth in the formal economy. The microeconomies that thrive within cities do so because cities are where the economically disadvantaged can find relative freedom. The mixing bowls of urban environments ensure that the different ingredients that go into creating technology have a chance to connect and create new and interesting combinations.

The same economic forces that drive urbanization also drive cross-country migration. People not only want to move to cities for higher wages, but they also want to move to cities in richer countries for even higher wages. More than 230 million people migrate across international borders each year—more than three percent of the world's population. A sizeable majority of these migrants move from poor to rich countries despite the many barriers, legal and otherwise, to doing so. This doesn't seem surprising—until you think about it a little. We observe both unskilled and skilled workers—the educated and uneducated—trying to migrate to rich countries. But simple supply and demand analysis would suggest that skilled workers should get higher wages in those countries where there are fewer skilled workers because there is a lower supply of them. However, what we actually observe is that skilled workers migrate to areas where there are more skilled workers, not fewer. The only explanation for this must be that migration is not driven by the supply of skilled workers, but by the demand for skilled workers. The most skilled and best educated workers are in higher demand in rich countries despite the fact that there are many more of these kinds of workers there. Why? Because skilled workers are more productive in rich countries where they can take advantage of idea networks and better institutions. The benefits of complementary knowledge held by the people migrants work with far outweigh any wage benefits created by the scarcity of their skills in their home countries. In fact, the hidden secret about "brain drain" from the underdeveloped to the developed world is that many of these best and brightest workers would be no more productive (and have no different wages) than an unskilled worker if they stayed home and no longer had access to other educated people, productive institutions, and educational facilities. Many skilled workers can only become more productive away from home, and would become unskilled again if they returned home.

This is the essence of a poverty trap, and it explains one of the basic facts about the distribution of world income: both wealth and poverty are highly concentrated geographically. More than 50 percent of world GDP is produced on 10 percent of the world's land (in the United States, 50 percent of GDP is produced on only 2 percent of its land). Wealth and poverty are also highly concentrated among certain cultural and social groups. In the United States, we all know that poverty is closely correlated with ethnicity, but did you also know that it is correlated with religion?

Protestants are wealthier than Mormons, who are wealthier than those who are unaffiliated with a church, who are wealthier than Catholics.[15] In the previous chapter, we discussed the theories of why culture may or may not matter in economics. Here is a fact that makes it appear that culture matters a great deal. However, it may not be culture itself, but the people that we network with that really matters. If those in your culture are educated and rich for reasons that have nothing to do with their specific cultural beliefs or practices, then any other member of that cultural group is more likely to be richer as well because they will naturally benefit from the leaks and matches that come from the people they socialize with. Likewise, those cultural groups that are poorer for whatever reason can become trapped in poverty because they get few of the positive spillovers of idea transfer. In other words, the poor are trapped in poverty because they interact with those who are poor; the rich are rich because they interact with those who are rich. It is a depressing conclusion, but one that is consistent with the facts of income and technology distribution across the globe. In fact, according to one economic study, the technology levels of today across different regions of the world are path-dependent on the technology levels of these regions going all the way back to 0 BCE.[16]

Because of the persistence of technological backwardness, one of the best avenues for escaping from poverty traps is migration. The simple fact of the matter is that a person who migrates from a less developed, less educated, less technologically advanced country becomes more productive the second they set foot on the soil of a developed country. This is one of the big reasons why economists are generally fans of more open immigration policies. To think of immigration as something that always depresses wages in the destination country misses a big part of the story: New immigrants also create new leaks and matches that raise the wages of current residents. Even the countries from which people are leaving may benefit from migration if it encourages more people to get an education and invest in the skills that might help them migrate in the future. Some of these people will migrate, but not all. If enough of these people stay behind, and over time are supplemented by immigrants who return home and become instruments of technological diffusion, then it is possible to reach a tipping point where enough ideas are leaking and matching in domestic networks to turn a poverty trap into a virtuous circle. Once again, immigration can be a tide that raises all ships, but you first have to have a ship.

Creating an environment conducive to technological development and diffusion is like many challenges in economics: It is much more complex than following a simple recipe. In fact, there are important trade-offs that exist in building technology enclaves, and finding the right mix of incentives is a very difficult balancing act. The most difficult challenge is that different technologies are created and shared in different ways. Some new technologies are the result of the market process: They are driven by corporate research and development, often involving large fixed costs, and are aimed at making a profit. For these kinds of ideas, it is crucial that economic institutions protect the intellectual property rights of the inventor. Foremost among these is a patent system, whereby a firm that produces a new idea can make monopoly profits from it in order to recoup its fixed costs and make a profit. Essentially, a patent allows a firm to keep some of the social benefits from their inventions for themselves and not be forced to give them away to free-riders.

According to the economic historian Douglas North, the protection of intellectual property rights was a key step in triggering the Industrial Revolution because it created an incentive for entrepreneurs to take their ideas and turn them into productive technologies.[17] A close look at the history of technological development reveals that many of the technologies that we associate with the Industrial Revolution, such as the steam engine, actually existed well before the mid-1700s. The Romans had steam engines, but they used them to open and close doors, not for transportation and making profits, because there were no incentives, economic or social, to do so. They were, to use the phrase I used before, "zombie ideas" that existed but were not used in productive ways. The Romans also had glass. According to historians, glass was invented by a slave. When it was shown to the emperor Tiberius, he immediately had the slave beheaded because "if once the secret became known, we should think no more of gold than of so much dirt."[18] Similarly, when modern governments fail to protect intellectual property, they give entrepreneurs little incentive to create new technologies even when they have the knowledge to do so.

Having said this, however, there is a big problem with turning ideas into a legal good through patents: Doing so blocks the ability of patented ideas to leak and match as fluidly as when ideas are free to flow. In other words, protecting the ability to profit from an idea can also prevent the networking that creates future ideas. In the IT community, the move toward open-source software, which is software created by networks of independent software developers who freely share their programs with others in the network, is a recognition that trying to make ideas proprietary by turning them into intellectual property can lead to less innovation for everyone. By increasing the price of using a technology, patent monopolies prevent the diffusion of technology, particularly in poorer countries or among startup firms that cannot afford licensing rights.

One example of the costs and benefits of patents is the development of new pharmaceutical products for deadly diseases, such as antiviral drugs that suppress the HIV virus. On one hand, the manufacturers of these drugs have developed a product that has saved millions of lives, and they deserve to profit from their amazing innovations, lest future pharmaceutical companies be discouraged from undertaking the huge research and development costs needed to find a cure for the next epidemic. On the other hand, patenting these treatments prevents other pharmaceutical manufacturers from tweaking these drugs in order to develop more effective variations. Also, patents have allowed pharmaceutical companies to charge high monopoly prices. The costs of a month's worth of treatment for the average antiviral drug is more than the yearly per-capita GDP of many less developed countries. To many, it is immoral to doom millions of poor people to death by pricing them out of the market for these drugs in order to protect the intellectual property rights of large pharmaceutical companies.

In an effort to close this gap, many governments have begun to view HIV treatment as a public good and heavily subsidize the distribution of these drugs. The funds to do this have come from many international public health and humanitarian organizations, including the World Health Organization and the Clinton Foundation. However, it remains the case that more than half of those who need HIV treatment across the globe are not receiving it, and price is a large part of the reason why. Even with subsidization, a year's worth of antiviral drugs typically costs about $100, or a third of total income for those living in extreme poverty.

The most counterinnovative use of patents is the growing popularity of "patent trolling." Here, companies acquire patents with the intention of suing innovative competitors, essentially trying to create barriers to new technologies that will help dominant companies protect market share at the expense of the customer. There are two problems here. First, patents make the concurrent inventions of the past illegal—whoever files the patent first owns it, even if someone else develops it independently. The second, and even larger, problem revolves around the question of what merits a patent. According to U.S. law, for an idea to be patentable it must be novel, nonobvious, and have a commercial use. These, of course, are subjective concepts. When companies engage in patent trolling, they file patents for ideas that are close to being obvious and non-novel in order to sue competitors who independently come up with a similar idea. Forty percent or more of U.S. patents are never licensed out by their owners, suggesting that many of these are speculative patents whose primary value is their potential value in a potential lawsuit, not necessarily in the market.[19] Patent trolling has traditionally existed in older and competitive industries in which established firms have tried to protect their monopolies by blocking new technologies. But today, patent trolling has become big business in some industries known for innovation—the constant series of lawsuits amongst the big mobile phone companies such as Apple and Samsung being the best example.[20]

Having laid the foundation for how economists think about the production of ideas and technology, let's now return to the question that is of interest to travelers: Why do technology levels differ so widely across countries? Why is it that people can travel to places that some technologies can't? From my own travels, I can think of many technology paradoxes that left me puzzled. For example, a woman in South Africa with a stack of wood for cooking and heating balanced on her head walking toward a simple wooden rondoval (round house) . . . with a satellite dish on its roof. Or a Chinese peasant farming on her knees with a hand shovel . . . only a few miles from the state-of-the-art Foxconn factory where iPhones are assembled. Or an elementary schoolboy in Argentina talking on his own iPhone . . . while doing his school work on a desktop computer a decade older than him (and almost as big as him) with no access to the Internet. Why is it that some technologies diffuse, and some do not? Why is it that technology flows to some places and activities, but not to others?

The most obvious answer to this question would be the poverty trap idea just discussed: Those who are poor and who have low levels of technology are trapped because they do not have the complementary inputs—educations, information systems, institutions—needed to facilitate the leaking and matching of ideas. But it is too simplistic to blame technological backwardness only on the path-dependence of history. For one, we have seen many countries break out of technology traps and take great, discontinuous leaps up the technology ladder—think about my mobile-savvy Botswana student who didn't know what a landline phone was. The other problem with this idea of historical determinism is that many countries go right to the frontier of technology in some areas, but lag far behind in others. Africa is actually pushing the boundaries of mobile phone technology, particularly in the ways that mobile phones can be used in daily life in order to conduct banking, make purchases, share price information, and network ideas. Yet most of these same countries lag far behind in health, transportation, and industrial technology.

I would like to discuss five sources of technology blocking; five barriers that governments (driven by societal norms and political interests) create that prevent technology from diffusing and which stop ideas from leaking and matching. Each of these five barriers play a crucial role in explaining why some countries continue to lag behind the technology curve and their citizens fail to enjoy the full fruits of modernization.

First, within any country there are vested interests that are potentially harmed by new technologies and economic growth. New technologies do not universally benefit everyone in a society. One of the first to recognize this was the Austrian economist Joseph Schumpeter.[21] Schumpeter viewed capitalism as an evolutionary process driven by competition between entrepreneurs. The primary way that entrepreneurs outcompete their rivals is through technological innovation. According to Schumpeter, "The fundamental impulse that sets and keeps the capitalist engine in motion comes from the new consumers, goods, the new methods of production or transportation, the new markets, the new forms of industrial organization that capitalist enterprise creates."

Like biological evolution, technological development generated by this competition does not take place at a constant rate. Instead, innovation is the result of big ideas that are developed sporadically (mutated, to use a biological term) within different industries. Initially, these new technologies are not unambiguously good for economic growth because new technologies replace old technologies, leading to obsolescence and requiring resources to be reallocated, retrained, and replaced. This is the basis of Schumpeter's theory of creative destruction, where new technologies eventually lead to growth, but are initially chaotic and require costly retrenchment. For every Google, there is a print newspaper, and for every MP3 player, there is a cassette player. Technology builds on itself, but it also relegates some of what has been built before to the trash bins of history.

The key for this process to work well, according to Schumpeter, is that failure must be allowed to occur. The death of firms and industries is essentially the way that the dead brush of capitalism is cleared to allow new growth to occur. Without failure, resources will continue to be allocated to less productive businesses, leaving fewer resources available for the entrepreneurs that will potentially drive the next great wave of technological innovation. Without failure, capitalism cannot thrive. For this reason, Schumpeter worried about the dangers of socialism in democratic nations. Because state-owned firms that are nationalized are not allowed to fail, they are a threat to entrepreneurship and economic growth. Likewise, Schumpeter believed that the safety net provided by the modern welfare state discourages risk-taking and fails to incentivize the entrepreneurial spirit that is at the root of capitalist success.

Regardless of what you think about Schumpeter's theory (and there is certainly more than a little Ayn Rand in its escalation of the solo entrepreneur as the savior of the entire social system), it is true that barriers have often been built to block "the perennial gale of creative destruction" (Schumpeter's phrasing), stunting innovation in the process. There are many examples of this occurring throughout history, in rich and poor countries alike. We have talked about one example in this chapter: the Roman emperor Tiberius and his banning of glass because he thought it threatened the value of gold and his existing wealth. In Chapter 3, we talked about Queen Elizabeth I banning knitting machines in 1589 and the Luddites smashing sewing machines in 1793. In each of these cases, powerful interests tried to protect existing jobs at the expense of future jobs, and were able to do so because workers in jobs not yet filled do not have a voice in the public debate.

Today, technology blocking is often less egregious, but no less harmful, than these well-known historical examples. The "tyranny of the status quo" can often block necessary, but difficult, restructuring from taking place.[22] Any regulation aimed at "protecting jobs" has the potential to block new technologies, whether these regulations make it prohibitively expensive to fire unproductive workers, or difficult to close businesses that are losing money, or too easy to gain patent protection for patent trolling. These kinds of regulations, as we talked about extensively in Chapter 3, are most common in less developed economies where the government often places the heavy hand of regulation on businesses as a way to gain leverage for more political influence and corruption. Excessive regulation also encourages technology blocking because it encourages unwarranted litigation, such as patent trolling. Regulation is often sold under the guise of "protection," but in many cases, what they are protecting is an existing stream of profits that is under threat by market competition and newer, better technologies.

Sometimes, technology blocking occurs because of populist politics and the inherent messiness of the democratic process. Here, the difficulty of adopting technologies that are also public goods comes to mind. One extreme example is the problem of public sanitation in India, a country that is a global leader in IT, but has largely failed to adopt sanitation technologies that are hundreds of years old. It can be argued that the discovery of germ theory and the implementation of public sanitation in the early 1900s are the most beneficial technological developments of the last two centuries in terms of increasing the quality of life and worker productivity. Between 1900 and 1930, the chlorination of water and other water filtration techniques are estimated to have reduced total mortality in American cities by 43 percent on average, and infant mortality by more than 70 percent.[23] Yet these technologies are not widely adopted in India. On a trip to the holy city of Varanasi along the Ganges River, I had the opportunity to be appalled, firsthand, at the terrible quality of the water in the river. When most people think about water quality and Varanasi, they think about the traditional practice of burning bodies alongside the river and pushing the remains into the river. But that is one of the smallest problems with the water quality. The biggest is that the river sits below the city and all of the unprocessed sewage from Varanasi runs down the banks of the river upon which steps have been built (referred to as *Ghats*) and right into the river where people bathe and drink. This is in addition to the industrial sewage that is dumped into the Ganges upriver. As a result, the crowds of people who take ritual baths in Varanasi are exposing themselves to water that is polluted with chemicals and fecal coliform bacteria levels that are thousands of times greater than what is regarded as safe by public health professionals.

According to experts, the solution to this polluted water is relatively straightforward: Make sure that sewage from the city is treated before it is returned to the river, and make sure that rainwater from the city does not directly run down the Ghats and into the river from city streets. To accomplish these changes, it would mean making modest changes to the Ghats—which have remained largely unchanged for hundreds of years—and building public sanitation systems that would require the use of *eminent domain* to purchase property and force property owners to make costly changes to their properties. It would also require the government to enforce practices regarding sanitation—for example, banning outdoor defecation—so that it remains neither *de jure* nor *de facto* behavior. But in the chaotic world of Indian politics, it is almost impossible to get a majority of the population to agree to anything. Hence, coordination failure and special interest politics prevent the adoption of modern sanitation practices and technology. It is another example of the failure of some governments to provide much needed public goods and enforce socially beneficial behaviors.

The implications of such public health failures across India are shocking: Nearly one-third of all Indian children (both in poor and rich families) are malnourished—much higher levels than in other much poorer countries. This is not a result of too little food but too little public sanitation, making children vulnerable to malnourishment even when they have plenty to eat.[24] Nearly half of all Indians defecate outdoors, which is directly related to the spread of disease, digestive illness, and malnutrition.[25] As a result, malnourishment in India has only slowly diminished despite a rapid increase in income. Public sanitation became a major issue during the national elections in India in 2014, but questions remain about whether special interest politics and a lack of policy coordination will continue to prevent the country from adopting sanitation technologies that have existed for a hundred years and are widely adopted across most of the rest of the world.

Sometimes the special interests that block technology are part of the government itself. The importance of state-owned enterprises (SOEs) in many countries creates important incentives to block competition from new firms using new technologies, and as a result also protects government coffers and the power of bureaucrats. SOEs serve to technology-block even in countries in which technology growth is fairly rapid—China is an example of this. While SOEs produce only one-third of Chinese GDP, they receive two-thirds of total credit and total investment in the country.[26] These SOEs—just like the large state-owned banks that lend to them— are run by political appointees of the Communist party and are unprofitable despite their high levels of investment. One study estimates that profits in Chinese SOEs would be negative if they had to pay market interest rates (in other words, if they were not subsidized by the state).[27] By soaking up public investment money and formal credit (only 20 percent of private Chinese firms get credit through banks), Chinese SOEs strangle the private sector of the economy where 70 percent of employment, two-thirds of GDP growth in China, and almost all of the innovation is occurring.

Of course, entrepreneurs are entrepreneurial. While the Chinese private sector finds itself blocked by state-owned banks, private firms also find themselves free to ignore patent and copyright laws in ways that are not possible in other countries. China is famous for its innovative knock-off products that actually improve on the originals (but with no royalties paid). This includes: the NKIE sandals with heels (to make me look taller) that I once found in my Shanghai hotel room; an iPad tablet I found in a mall in Yiwu that ran Windows; and the Obama phones produced in China but which quickly found their way to the street vendors of Africa days after his winning the election (these phones included an FM radio, a flashlight, and a "Yes We Can!" logo on the back). The Chinese word for these goods is *Shanzhai*, which literally means "mountain stronghold," a reference to the ability of these goods to operate beyond the law. *Shanzhai* goods are not just fake knock-offs, like the "Stars and Bucks" coffee shop I saw in Bethlehem, Palestine. *Shanzhai* goods are cheap, but they are also innovative. For example, some *Shanzhai* mobile phones run both Apple and Google-based applications. Hence, *Shanzhai* goods are popular not only in China but across the world.

Shanzhai goods perfectly illustrate the trade-off with proprietary technology: They involve a blatant theft of intellectual property that costs innovative companies profits, but they also represent the possibilities of an

Portraits of revered technology entrepreneurs on the streets of Shanghai.

open-sourced world in which hackers can populate and spread new ideas freely. *Shanzhai* goods also capture another trade-off with technology: the conflict between the entrepreneur and authority (as captured nicely in these portraits of the icons Steve Jobs, Che Guevara, and Deng Xiaoping).

Shanzhai goods illustrate one final interesting fact about technological diffusion: It is possible that there are certain advantages to technological backwardness, in the sense that many barriers to technological development don't exist in poor countries. In countries without certain industries, there are no existing firms to block new firms entering that industry, or to stop the creative destruction that would prevent firms from leap-frogging older technologies and moving to the forefront of the technology curve. Japan's steel industry leads the world in efficiency today in part because its old steel industry was destroyed during World War II, allowing it to freely invest in new micro-mill technology. This has not happened in places such as the United States, where Rust Belt technology and organized labor have routinely blocked change in a declining industry. In China, there were no intellectual property rights enforced on the first *Shanzhai* mobile phones because there were, for a long time, no formal mobile phone makers in China.

Mobile phone use is spreading rapidly throughout Africa in part because there were few entrenched interests in the landline phone market to build barriers to entry (hence the question from my student that I shared at the beginning of this chapter). Nigeria has more than 60 million mobile phone subscriptions today, compared to only 400,000 landlines in the entire country in 2000. Mobile phones allow people to cross the vast expanses of Africa in ways that they could never do before. This is much different than in India, where the government's extensive public landline monopoly (which had more than 25 million subscribers in the early 2000s) has, until recently, attempted to block the expansion of mobile phone service at every turn and is the principal reason why India lags behind Africa in mobile phone adoption.

In Africa, the easy expansion of mobile access has led to incredible innovation that has improved incomes and the lives of many. In places like Kenya, it has led to new technologies such as iCow, a mobile phone app to help farmers take better care of their cows and sell dairy products where prices are most favorable. Even more importantly, it has sparked the development of the M-Pesa mobile transactions (M for mobile, *Pesa* meaning money in Swahili), which allow for mobile transfers of money across the country and the world via text messages. Today, two-thirds of Kenyans use it, with nearly 25 percent of GDP flowing through the system.[28] M-Pesa has allowed a network of 40,000 small retailers, many of whom also sell mobile phone minutes and food as street vendors, to become mobile bank managers as well, facilitating savings and lending accounts. Any subscriber to the M-Pesa program (which is available to anyone with a mobile phone) can go to one of these money managers and make a deposit or a withdrawal of currency. These transactions are recorded in each customer's e-account electronically via texting, and a return text serves as a receipt to verify the transaction. Mobile banking has thrived in Kenya because formal banking is so underdeveloped: There are only 1.38 branch banks and .56 ATMs per 100,000 residents.[29] Kenyans and many people throughout Africa are now able to make purchases directly through their cell phones, and they do not find this strange or unusual. I think of them whenever I go to the store in the United States and get stuck behind someone writing a check— sometimes it is hard to tell if you are in the developed or less developed world when it comes to the speed with which new technologies are adopted, and this is a good thing for the less developed world.

Second, technology blocking is also motivated by the persistent belief in the fallacy that new technologies eliminate the need for labor and reduce the total number of jobs. Technology does eliminate the need for specific jobs; there are few people today who are employed as cotton spinners, wheat threshers, ice cutters, and switchboard operators. Job obsolescence in specific industries can lead to the special interest policies that we discussed previously. But some people believe that technology also leads to a reduction in the *total* number of jobs; in other words, technology eliminates the overall need for labor and, possibly in the future, will make work obsolete. This is the thinking behind many recent articles asking questions such as "Will robots take our jobs?"[30] The future envisioned by believers in the impending "jobs apocalypse" is a future similar to the Disney movie *Wall-E* where intelligent robots work and humans are left with nothing to do but meaninglessly consume. The only way to prevent such a future is to build barriers to new technologies: bans, taxes, regulations, and other market manipulations. It is interesting to note that no one ever discusses banning *existing* technology—it is always the new technologies that we fear. We fear future robots, but don't touch my mobile phone!

This belief in the job-destroying power of technology has a long history in economics. Marxist economic theory (see Chapter 3) is predicated on a belief that long-term economic and technological progress will make workers superfluous, triggering a social and economic revolution. Even one of the founding fathers of classical economics, David Ricardo, worried that "substitution of machinery for human labour is often very injurious to the interests of the class of labourers . . . [It] may render the population redundant and deteriorate the condition of the labourer."[31]

However, history has constantly proven such doomsayers wrong: Technology and new forms of capital create jobs; they do not destroy jobs. The main point of Chapter 3 of this book was to show how capital and technology are not substitutes for labor, as is assumed under the erroneous Malthusian mindset. Instead, technology is a complement to labor. By making labor more productive, technology not only increases wages, but it actually increases the overall demand for labor. As we discussed earlier, the positive impact of technology will be most pronounced when workers have the skills, education, and proper institutions to use this technology effectively. Technology will contribute little to the demand for labor and higher wages when the labor force is raw, unskilled, and unproductive. It is for this reason that technology might, in the short run, contribute to income inequality by raising the wages of skilled relative to unskilled employees.[32]

Despite the lessons of history, many continue to predict the end of labor, in large part because it is a simplistic and enticing fallacy. In the words of the economic historian Joel Mokyr and his coauthors: "If someone as brilliant as David Ricardo could be so terribly wrong in how machinery would reduce the overall demand for labor, modern economists should be cautious in making pronouncements about the end of work."[33] The persistence of this fallacy is also due to the fact that we tend to more clearly remember recent examples of jobs lost to new technology, but fail to recognize the jobs created by technological innovation over the longer term. It is an example of what some people call Amara's Law (named after Roy Amara, president of the think tank Institute for the Future): "We tend to over-estimate the effect of a technology in the short run and underestimate the effect in the long run."[34]

Third, governments block technological diffusion by building barriers to international trade and travel. Trade is possibly the greatest technological innovation of all time. Trade creates the possibility of turning carrots into computers, or anything else that can be produced anywhere else in the world at any time. When you think of it this way, international trade is a magical way of turning what you have into what you want. Yet many countries deny themselves the benefits of international trade because of a different form of magical thinking: that somehow, if I don't buy a good from somewhere else, a business will appear out of nowhere to make it domestically. Many countries have set their trade policies according to the premise that by blocking imports, a domestic industry will have to grow.

There is no better (or worse) example of this magical thinking than the import substitution policies followed by African countries after they became independent in the 1960s. African countries set up extensive systems of trade barriers and tariffs aimed at protecting domestic industries, even those that did not yet exist, at the expense of foreign competition. While the goals of import substitution are understandable given the ugly history of colonization in Africa, the results of closed borders have been disastrous. The residents of the 53 relatively small countries that make up Africa have often found themselves without access to global markets, foreign direct investment, and new technologies. Because existing domestic industry was nonexistent in many of these countries and there was no possibility of attracting foreign firms that could bring foreign investment and technology, governments typically stepped in to create SOEs in a "big push" to industrialization. Run by greedy and incompetent political appointees, these SOEs usually saw their primary purpose as contributing to a political patronage system, not to become profitable. They faced little domestic competition and, as a result, had little incentive to increase the productivity of labor by adopting new technology from outside of the country. In a review of one African country's economic policy, an economist wrote: "To set up a cannery without products to can, a textile factory that lacked cotton supplies, a cigarette factory without sufficient locally grown tobacco and to develop . . . a forest region that had no roads and trucks to carry its output—all of these were gambles taken by utopian idealists and ignoramuses."[35]

The fact of the matter is that import substitution regimes such as those set up in Africa don't serve only to block imports; they also serve to change the mix of imports away from goods that are productive and enhance technology, and toward those goods that are prized by elites. Consider the fact that immediately after the independence movement in the year 1964, fourteen African Francophone countries combined to spend six times as much on imported alcoholic drinks (which somehow slipped through trade barriers) than fertilizer, and five times as much on imported high-end cars than on agricultural equipment.[36]

Trade barriers in rich countries can also block the diffusion of technology to the rest of the world. The developed world has consistently impeded technological diffusion by imposing targeted tariffs aimed at privileging their own domestic industries. Developed countries have also used their political power to influence international trade agreements in order to grant themselves unreasonably strict intellectual property rights protections in ways that many critics have called "neo-mercantilist."[37]

Nowhere do the trade policies of developed countries do more to block technological diffusion than in agriculture, where special interests in developed countries have built trade barriers that close their markets to products from the rest of the world. Consider the cotton market, an agricultural market that the United States has dominated for more than 200 years. It did this at first because it produced the cheapest cotton (in part because of slavery), but today the United States maintains its dominance through the use of government subsidies that effectively price foreign cotton manufacturers out of international markets. U.S. cotton farmers receive 30 percent of their income (over $140,000 on average) from government-funded price subsidies, 5 to 10 times what corn or soybean farmers receive in America. These U.S. subsidies reduce world cotton prices by roughly 12 percent on average, but by as much as 30 percent in some years.[38]

U.S. taxpayers pay for this program to the tune of nearly $3.5 billion a year, which is greater than the yearly GDP of 13 African countries. This subsidy is actually larger than the value of all of the cotton produced in the United States! While 25,000 American cotton farmers benefit, the 18 million African farmers that grow cotton (75 percent of the population in some countries) are devastated. Cotton accounts for more than 25 percent of exports in 11 West African countries. Cotton is a major industry there because, absent cotton subsidies, West Africa produces the cheapest cotton in the world. However, because world prices are kept so low (and U.S. farmers are kept in business) by American cotton subsidies, African farmers have seen prices and their incomes fall, keeping them in poverty and providing few resources to invest in new technologies and capital. As a result, American subsidies reduce the incomes of poor farmers in places like West Africa by between 8 to 20 percent a year.[39] This estimate does not include the costs of the myriad of other trade barriers that the United States imposes on imported textiles and apparel, which also reduce the demand for foreign cotton, nor the myriad of subsidies provided by other countries in agricultural goods other than cotton. The total costs of these trade barriers far outweigh any foreign aid that these African countries receive from America, suggesting that a great (and politically utopian) trade that would benefit both American taxpayers and African farmers would be to eliminate aid to both African and American farmers.

International barriers that make it difficult for people to travel also prevent the diffusion of technology. As travelers, we know the importance of broadening our experiences through travel. We innately understand the role that travel plays in exposing us to new ideas, in widening our perspectives so that we are more receptive to these ideas, and in creating possible leaks and matches for these ideas. And this is exactly why repressive, totalitarian governments create as many barriers to the movement of people and the diffusion of technology as they can. It is not surprising that when comparing North Korea to South Korea, it is South Korea that allows for the free movement of its people. However, it is not just totalitarian regimes that make travel difficult. In 2013, two-thirds of the world's population required a costly and time-consuming visa approval prior to their arrival at the airport.[40] Facilitating more international trade in ideas requires reducing visa fees and easing onerous visa applications through the better sharing of information across countries and the adoption of new technologies such as international electronic visas. Plus, these changes would reduce corruption opportunities at border crossings, reduce time spent waiting for sleepy-eyed officials to browse our passports, and dramatically reduce the blood pressure of travelers across the globe.

Fourth, financial repression also represses technological development. Finance is the process of trading money today for money tomorrow, with conditions such as interest payments attached. Technological development also involves this process of trading production of goods that could be consumed today for the creation of ideas that will improve our lives tomorrow. As a result, the ability to get credit is crucial to bridging the gap between the costs incurred today and the benefits gained tomorrow from investing in technology. In the words of historian Niall Ferguson: "The evolution of credit and debt was as important as any technological innovation in the rise of civilization, from ancient Babylon to present-day Hong Kong."[41] According to Joseph Schumpeter, finance plays a crucial role in funneling resources to entrepreneurs who are creating the new technologies that are the engines of growth.[42] Entrepreneurship is impossible without the "bankers and other financial middlemen who mobilize savings, evaluate projects, manage risk, monitor managers, acquire facilities and otherwise redirected resources from old to new channels." Schumpeter identified England's strong and efficient financial system as a primary reason why the Industrial Revolution began there and not elsewhere.

The simple fact of the matter is that there is no guarantee that those who have money are also those with the best ideas. A key role of a well-functioning financial system is to funnel money from those with wealth to those who innovate. In the words of Frederic Mishkin, "the financial system [is] the brain of the economy . . . It acts as a coordinating mechanism that allocates capital, the lifeblood of economic activity, to its most productive uses by businesses and households."[43] And money's most productive use is to facilitate the creation of new technology.

However, many countries view their financial sector not as a tool to empower their people and foster technological development, but as a way to leverage government power and enrich elites. This is the source of financial repression policies such as interest rate controls, barriers to foreign bank entry, barriers to foreign investment, high inflation, government-directed lending, and exchange rate controls. These policies often direct resources and power to the government, to SOEs, or to the borrowers that politicians favor. These policies increase the costs and reduce the access that most individuals have to financial services, limiting their ability to innovate.

Between 40 to 80 percent of all individuals in emerging and less developed economies lack access to formal banking services.[44] The lack of financial access is particularly acute for the entrepreneurial poor: Across 18 less developed countries, less than 5 percent of the rural poor and less than 10 percent of the urban poor have access to formal lending.[45] In China, only 20 percent of private firms have access to formal finance through banks because of financial repression aimed at supporting SOEs. Instead, most innovators across the world must rely on informal loans from individuals, their suppliers, or their customers—not from banks or from financial markets. These informal loans are usually small in size and short in length of time. They are also expensive: across less developed countries, interest rates for the poor are consistently between 40 and 200 percent a year.[46]

To help put these costs in perspective, the ladies selling phone minutes at street shops in Botswana reported to me that they regularly paid 5 percent a day for credit—an amount that didn't strike them as thievery. But if you borrow $1 for a year at a compounded rate of 5 percent a day, you would owe $20 million at the end of the year! Such is the power of compounding, and it's a powerful example of the way that expensive finance stealthily eats away at the incomes of the poor. Given the difficulty and cost of obtaining formal finance, coupled with the fact that informal borrowing is inappropriate for the long-term credit needed to finance research and development, financial underdevelopment and technological backwardness are inexorably linked.

Fifth, risky economic environments discourage investment in technology. Once again, we return to the importance of institutions. Having stable and low-risk economic environments is crucial to creating the productive institutions that encourage research and development. Investing in technology is by itself extremely risky. It requires devoting many years to education, years spent acquiring specific experience in a narrow field, extensive resources needed to purchase new equipment and information systems, and time spent experimenting with new methods of production and organization, among many other costs. Because technological development is innately so risky, it is very sensitive to a change in the overall riskiness of the economic environment. Essentially, innovation is the first thing to stop when confidence begins to wane and fear rises.

Increased risk also discourages technological diffusion because it discourages specialization. To be close to the cutting edge of any technology in any field requires years of specialized education and training. This is the reason, as first highlighted by Adam Smith, that specialization and trade are the two most important factors to growth: Specialization is needed to acquire the specific skills, experiences, and capital needed to become highly productive at one activity, and markets are needed to coordinate these activities. But when people live and work in risky environments, the incentives they face on a day-to-day basis discourage specialization. Specialization only increases risk because it prevents diversification: When you can only do one thing well, you are vulnerable if that skill or the equipment you invested in is no longer needed. In an environment where daily life is already too risky, most people cannot afford to take the chance and specialize.

As discussed previously, one of the most difficult things about living in poverty is not just the lack of income; it is the variability of income. Those who are living on $2.50 a day cannot count on receiving $2.50 each and every day. Because income is irregular and most poor have limited access to a social safety net in the form of health, unemployment, retirement, and

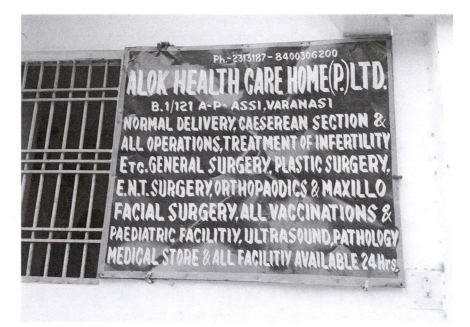

A small business that largely does everything.

disability insurance, the poor cannot afford to put all of their few eggs in one basket. They must attempt to diversity their income by doing multiple jobs. This is one of the primary reasons why the poor are so entrepreneurial: In an attempt to reduce their risk from volatile incomes, the poor work at many different jobs. But when you work at multiple jobs, you are likely to be doing none of them particularly well, and you certainly don't have the time or resources to improve the technology that you are working with in order to improve your productivity. This is why the millions of new, small, entrepreneurial, and undercapitalized businesses throughout most of the world use outdated technology, leaving these businesses unable to significantly raise their owners out of poverty.

This photo perfectly captures the problem that small businesses face across most of the world. The picture is of a sign advertising a health care practice in Varanasi, India (where health care is frequently needed given the quality of their water). This small practice of one doctor (I didn't check for a diploma) offers most every medical service I could think of, in addition to a medical store. Does this mean that the doctor is a modern Renaissance man with the natural capabilities to thrive in all of these fields at once? Or does it mean that the doctor provides low-quality service in any of these fields but is trying to cover as many bases as he can in order to make ends meet? All I can say with absolute certainty is that if I needed both infertility treatments and plastic surgery, I would look for a specialist in each of these fields.

What are the factors that contribute to risky economic environments and, by doing so, discourage specialization and technological development? They are the factors that create the unproductive institutions that we have talked about throughout this book: failing to protect property rights, periodic economic crises, excessive government debt, high and variable inflation, extractive regulation, corruption, excessive taxation, etc. A lack of access to finance also increases the risk of investment, particularly in new technologies, because having reliable finance in the form of loans, credit cards, savings accounts, and life insurance creates an important safety net—a safety net that those of us living in the developed world take for granted. Without finance, the technology investment of the poor must be kept at a very small scale in order to reduce risk, which also reduces potential returns.

The power of human ingenuity across the globe is impossible to deny. To travel is to see the ways that different people have found resourceful ways to use whatever is at hand to accomplish what they need to get by. Innovation is everywhere: in the donkey cart made from the bed of an old pickup, in the motor from a first-world clothes dryer being used to run a

Diversification, not specialization.

third-world fan or a motorized bicycle, or in the making of infant incubators out of used car parts. Maybe the most ubiquitous example of this is the fact that across the world—from Mexico, to Western Africa, to Burma, to Australia—the poor have independently figured out ways to refashion used tire treads into durable, effective footwear.

However, all too often this ingenuity, like much of the hard work of the poor, is wasted. The same ideas must be created again and again because of the lack of networks that allow ideas to leak and match. Technologies cannot be adopted from the rich world because poor world businesses are too small, people seek to avoid risky specialization, and the education needed to implement new technologies is simply unavailable. Even when new ideas and innovative technology are available, people are blocked from using it because they cannot gain access to international markets or are barred by the excessive regulation of self-interested government bureaucrats. The lack of technological diffusion across the world says little about the ability of different groups of people to innovate; it says much more about their inability to foster productive institutions that facilitate innovation.

All of this said, it is very difficult to engineer innovative environments that generate ideas and increase growth. There is a reason why there is so much discussion, from Silicon Valley to Shanghai, focusing on how to create environments that are conducive to the building and sharing of ideas. There is no simple recipe for how to do this. Maybe the best expression of the ephemeral nature of what creates the best conditions for innovation can be found in the Orson Welles movie *The Third Man* (written by Graham Greene) in which Welles' character says: "In Italy for thirty years under the Borgias they had warfare, terror, murder, bloodshed—they produced Michelangelo, Leonardo da Vinci, and the Renaissance. In Switzerland they had brotherly love, five hundred years of democracy, and peace, and what did they produce? The cuckoo clock."

Innovative environments are a mix of contradictions. One of the biggest contradictions is that adopting new technologies requires the creative destruction of old ideas as well as "standing on the shoulders of giants" (in the words of Isaac Newton) and building on old ideas. It is crucial to have an existing stock of knowledge, but there also may be an "advantage of backwardness" and starting with a clean slate. Likewise, it is important for people who create ideas to have specialized knowledge, but not so specialized that their perspective becomes too narrow to think broadly.

Another important contradiction is that on the one hand, you need flexible social structures that allow ideas to leak and match in unstructured ways. But on the other hand, you also need robust legal systems and markets that protect intellectual property so that those who innovate can cover their fixed costs and profit from it. In the words of Steven Johnson, you need a "liquid network": something between being too solid and too ethereal, between too much structure and chaos.[47] Too much structure—where every idea becomes patented into intellectual property—kills innovation, but too much chaos infringes on the intellectual property rights of truly innovative ideas that are costly to produce. An innovative environment must balance the development of both markets and networks, and find reasonable ways for ideas to be both patented and open-sourced.

So the bad news is that there is no simple formula for how countries can produce and adopt more ideas. The good news is that many of the tools needed to create liquid networks are more widely available and cheaper today than they have ever been in human history. Today there are more than two billion mobile phone users, but there will be nearly four billion by the end of the decade (80 percent of all adults worldwide). Over 500 million mobile phones will be sold in China *this year*.[48] Most of this growth in mobile phones is taking place in the less developed, and less technologically advanced, world. It is also occurring more rapidly among the young, who have grown up with the Internet and social media and will increasingly use their cell phones as a second brain, completely integrating IT into both their personal and professional lives. This will make idea networks much larger, more diverse, and more liquid than an old fogey like me imagines. The fact of the matter is that ideas are increasingly free to cross all sorts of borders and connect with those on the other side. In other words, ideas want to go on journeys, and today they can, more than ever before. The most innovative countries will let these ideas, and the people who create them, travel.

CHAPTER SEVEN

Best Price for You!
The Economics of Haggling

Money can't buy love, but it improves your bargaining position.
　　　　　　　　　　　　　　　　　　　　　　　—Anonymous

What then is a travelling mind-set? Receptivity might be said to be its chief characteristic. Receptive, we approach new places with humility. We carry with us no rigid ideas about what is or is not interesting . . . We find a supermarket or a hairdresser's shop unusually fascinating. We dwell at length on the layout of a menu or the clothes of the presenters on the evening news. We are alive to the layers of history beneath the present and take notes and photographs.
　　　　　　　　　　　　　　　　　　　　—Alain de Botton[1]

Just like any other traveler, I carry my own emotional baggage with me. (The airlines can't charge me extra for this kind of baggage, although they would if they could—just think of the heavy bag fee!) And one of my strongest personal biases is against haggling. I dread it as much as anything associated with traveling. Few things are more frustrating to me than endlessly haggling over every single purchase. While I am generally outgoing in my interactions with people, the thought of a protracted, difficult, and cantankerous negotiation can cause me to put my chin down and my collar up like a turtle in its shell. Haggling, even with the most hospitable merchants, leaves me exhausted in a way that hours of physical effort does not. I usually end the haggling process feeling as if I have either gotten ripped off or I have taken advantage of someone. I suspect that these feelings hold for many travelers. It is all the more disappointing to me, however, because I am supposed to be the intrepid economist, looking to put economics into action by personally engaging in local commerce. Instead, I avoid haggling when I can and overpay when I can't.

There is a movie scene that continually runs through my head while I am haggling in local markets: It's from Monty Python's slapstick comedy *The Life of Brian*. In this scene, set in Jerusalem in the time of Jesus of Nazareth, Brian is chased by the Roman army into a typical Middle Eastern street market. Looking to hide, he tries to purchase a fake beard from a local street vendor. Panicked, Brian asks: "How much? Quick!" Recognizing that Brian is in a hurry, the beard merchant names a price of 20. Brian quickly says yes, to which the seller responds loudly, so that everyone can hear, "We're supposed to haggle! This bloke won't haggle!" In an effort to speed up the process, Brian counter-offers 10, and the seller loudly responds "10! Do you want to ruin me!" A painful back-and-forth negotiation ensues. Eventually, the merchant makes a final offer: "17. My last word. I won't take a penny less or strike me dead!" Brian replies with a counter-offer of 16, and the seller happily exclaims "Done!"

This scene captures much about what I perceive to be unpleasant about haggling. The buyer is always in a rush, with many things to do, while the seller seemingly has all the time in the world. For both the buyer and seller, it appears that a price can't be the best price unless there is a bitter fight to establish it. And in the end, both parties feel bad about the transaction, the buyer because of the time and stress incurred, the seller because he or she knows that in the end the buyer lords the ultimate power because they can (and usually do) walk away.

Because haggling is such an important part of commerce and traveling in most of the world, it is worth taking a closer look at haggling. While haggling does not take place in markets (it is a one-on-one negotiation), thinking carefully about haggling helps us better understand how markets work and how the benefits of trade are distributed. In this chapter I will discuss why haggling is so common in some parts of the world, but rare elsewhere. What strategies can a traveler use to "win" when haggling? And what does haggling tell us about broader issues such as the connection between trust and trade? In order to think about these questions more deeply, I will rely upon insights initially made by the Nobel Prize–winning economist George Akerlof on the market for lemons (as in poor-quality used cars). I will also briefly discuss behavioral economics, which has broadened the perspective of economists by examining how neurology and psychology impact the economic decisions that people make. Finally, talking about haggling provides an opportunity to discuss why we use money in trade, particularly paper currency without any inherent value.

We will see that haggling is a lot more complicated than it first appears; in fact, it is a complex performance art in which we as actors are often playing roles that we don't consciously realize we are performing. A deeper understanding of the economics behind prices and negotiation allows us to peek behind the curtain, and it might possibly allow us as travelers to play our own parts more thoughtfully, reduce our performance anxiety, and avoid turning the entire act into a farce.

What is haggling? Haggling is a specific type of bargaining that takes place on a one-on-one basis. Now, interpersonal bargaining is everywhere—from dating to figuring out who does the dishes. But haggling specifically involves bargaining toward a settlement price that must be mutually beneficial. Haggling typically begins when the merchant grabs the shopper's attention and offers an opening price. If interested, the shopper then makes a counteroffer, followed by a counteroffer by the merchant, etc., until either the process converges on a settlement price or the shopper walks away and no deal is made. Haggling takes place in lieu of posted, or stated, prices. Posted prices are common in more formal commerce, such as menu prices in restaurants or price tags and signs in retail stores.

In order to understand the reasons behind haggling and not simply posting prices, we first have to think a little more deeply about what prices really represent and how they are determined. In any trade, the buyer has a maximum price they are willing to pay based on what they estimate that the good is worth to them, which is based on what they know about the good. The seller has a minimum price that they are willing to sell the good for, which covers their costs, including their opportunity costs such as time. Every trade has to take place between the seller's minimum price and the buyer's maximum price. When a transaction takes place where the price is greater than the buyer's maximum price or less than the seller's minimum price, it is not trade—it is thievery.

When a mutually beneficial trade does take place, the difference between the maximum and the minimum prices is referred to by economists as the "total surplus" created by the trade. How much of this total surplus goes to the buyer and how much to the seller depends upon the settlement price that is haggled for. The closer the settlement price is to the maximum price, the more surplus the seller gets; the closer the settlement price is to the minimum price, the more surplus the buyer gets. So haggling over the settlement price is really a negotiation over how the surplus from trade is shared. Haggling does not result in a winner and loser because both the buyer and the seller win in the sense that they both gain some surplus if the trade takes place. Instead, haggling over a settlement price is really about determining who "wins the most" and who "wins the least."

Once again, we can turn to game theory for a simple illustration of the role that haggling plays in trade. Consider a simple game in which there are two players, a seller and a buyer. We can express their outcomes, or the surplus they receive, from negotiating a high or low price as a simple numerical payoff. In the matrix shown in the table below, the first number in each cell represents the payoff to the buyer and the second the payoff to the seller.

		Seller	
		Low price	*High price*
Buyer	*Low price*	(3,1)	(0,0)
	High price	(0,0)	(1,3)

The payoffs in this game reflect the fact that if the buyer and seller can't agree on a settlement price, then no trade takes place. A seller is better off making a trade even at a low price, and a buyer is better off making a trade even at a high price, as opposed to having no trade at all. The problem here is that the potential exists for coordination failure. Somehow, the buyer and seller must agree on a single price, either high or low, or they will both lose out. But exactly how this settlement price is to be determined remains unclear. So this is the role of haggling: to overcome coordination failure by giving both parties the opportunity to coordinate on a settlement price that allows trade to take place when it might otherwise fail to occur.

When haggling, both the buyer and the seller use bargaining strategies (which we will discuss later) to divide up the surplus from a trade and convince each other that their offered settlement price is the "best" one from the perspective that it overcomes coordination failure and allocates a "fair" amount of the surplus to each of them. The biggest problem with haggling, however, is that it takes time, and it requires an expenditure of energy; effective hagglers must engage in acting, rhetoric, and clever thinking to be successful. Often, buyers and sellers don't want to incur these costs for every transaction; I don't want to haggle over every gallon of gasoline I purchase or my morning coffee. As a result, many transactions simply take place according to posted prices, where the seller chooses a single price for all buyers that attempts to balance the additional surplus gained from setting a higher price against the surplus that is potentially lost if the posted price is above the maximum price of some buyers. In effect, posted prices reflect the inflection point where the gains from haggling for a higher price begin to be outweighed by the higher transaction costs associated with haggling. As you would expect, posted prices are most common in larger markets where there is a greater volume of trade taking place and where the opportunity costs of haggling become prohibitive.

Consider the Chinese menu pictured here. By advertising a posted price, everyone who enters this restaurant knows exactly

No haggling over "Irritable Squid Volume."

how much "slides the stomach piece" and "yan explodes the shredded meat" cost, even if they don't know exactly what those dishes are (and may not really want to know). Freed from having to haggle over a price, the potential surplus lost by the restaurant or its customers from possibly getting a better price is more than offset by the fact that they now have more time to cook and savor these intriguing entrees (and their curious English translations).

Keeping in mind this balance between the surplus from trade versus the opportunity cost of time, it becomes clear that there are economic factors that explain why haggling is more common in some places than other places. First, haggling is more common when the opportunity cost of haggling—the value of people's time—is lower. This is most likely to be true in poorer countries where wages are lower and the prospects for work in formal markets are fewer. As a result, any surplus that can be gained by haggling is more likely to be worth the time of buyers and sellers in poorer countries. This, of course, is a fundamental reason why travelers (who tend to be wealthier) are at a distinct disadvantage when haggling in the less developed world: we are more impatient for economic reasons, and sellers know this and can take advantage of it to get us to pay higher prices.

Second, haggling is more common when markets are less developed and information about the good being traded is harder to obtain. Haggling is about bargaining, but it is also about trying to convince the other party that the good is worth more or less than they initially think it is. Buyers try to convince sellers to lower their minimum price by, for instance, pointing out defects in the good, while sellers try to persuade buyers to increase their maximum price by pointing out indicators of a good's quality, among other things. But when both parties have more information, minimum and maximum prices are likely to be more accurate and less flexible, reducing the potential gains even master hagglers can gain by going through the process.

Let me illustrate by using an example. If you asked me what my maximum price is for a gold-plated toilet seat, I would have no idea where to begin, and my answer might vary widely depending on the mood I am in or how frustrated I am at the moment with my old, boring toilet seats. It would be relatively easy for any haggler to persuade me to raise my maximum price during any negotiation. But luckily, I can go online and find information about how much other people are paying for gold-plated toilet seats (for Kanye West and Kim Kardashian, about $200,000 each).[2] That then gives me a much clearer idea of what my maximum price should be when I go to visit my local plumbing supply shop, making prolonged and costly haggling less likely. Of course, the ridiculousness of this example unnecessarily obfuscates the simple point I am trying to make: Having more information on market prices means that buyers and sellers should be able to identify acceptable settlement prices more quickly and easily, often making haggling unnecessary. On the other hand, when information is hard to come by, haggling will become more common.

Third, haggling should be more common when fewer trades are taking place in the formal, market-based economy. In subsistence economies where most people are producing their own consumption goods, haggling is common. But in a world where workers are increasingly specialized and consumption much more diverse, we rely on markets to obtain almost everything that we use. The transaction costs associated with haggling over each and every one of these goods would become overwhelming. As a result, more specialization, more trade, and more markets mean less haggling.

These three market-wide factors—the opportunity cost of time, the existence of market information, and the number of trades taking place— explain why haggling has become less common over time across most countries. Worldwide markets and information technology have increased both the amount of information that is available and also the number of trades taking place for many goods, reducing the benefits and increasing the costs of haggling. This is a process that economists call "commodification," which involves turning goods that are sold individually because their attributes are variable and uncertain into goods that are standardized and can be sold in batches on markets. Modern agriculture is defined by commodification. Take, for example, the history of the market for wheat. Before commodity markets were established, bags of wheat had to be sold by sample, which was costly and time-consuming because it required each buyer to individually verify the quality of every batch of wheat sold, and then individual buyers would have to agree on trades with specific sellers via haggling. The Chicago Board of Trade, founded in 1948, solved these problems by having certified inspectors classify and verify wheat crops, creating a standardized product with a known quality. Once wheat was homogenized, wheat of similar quality from different sellers could be mixed and matched. Now, buyers could buy large quantities of wheat without any regard for who exactly was selling it to them. The commodification of wheat meant that the only factor that was now uncertain to a buyer of wheat was its price, which was no longer negotiated individually but set by the market. The result was vast increases in the efficiency and size of wheat markets, as well as an end to the need for haggling. The same thing has happened in many markets, agricultural and otherwise, across the world.

Where commodification hasn't happened (as in this photo of a traditional spice market in Mumbai), the quality of the goods in every trade has to be verified and the price haggled over in a time-consuming way.

Haggling has also become costlier because the value of our time has risen with our standards of living. Today, almost any good that traditionally has been haggled for, whether street crafts or new automobiles, can now be purchased somewhere from merchants who advertise posted prices and market themselves as "no-hassle"

Let's get ready to haggle.

retailers. While eBay is not a haggling site but an auction site where multiple buyers and sellers compete for the same good at one time, changes in their business model illustrate how behavior has changed as shoppers become more savvy and prosperous. Today, only 20 percent of eBay sales are via auction, down from 80 percent when it began. One study finds evidence that the "hassle cost," which is the discount that an eBay shopper can expect to receive by purchasing a good through an auction as opposed to the "buy it now" price, has doubled between 2003 and 2009 as shoppers demand a higher return for their time.[3]

In fact, across most of the developed world, the decline of haggling, which started as a consequence of economic development, has begun to move toward something of a social norm. The default injunctive social norm in many places is now that bargaining over prices is impolite, even tactless, and is unacceptable even when it can be economically justified. Haggling is increasingly seen as arbitrary and unjust—it is seen as violating common social norms such as fairness and transparency. For example, recently there was outrage in the online community over the perception that Amazon.com was posting different prices for different customers (Amazon has denied this). Many customers viewed these individually based prices as both arbitrary and exploitive because Amazon was allegedly using the private shopping history of each buyer against them. Essentially, as we have moved to a market-based society in which haggling is increasingly rare, both buyers and sellers increasingly demand posted prices that must be perceived as fair and transparent.

Here is one example of how haggling can lead to unfair outcomes—unfair in the sense that haggling can lead to different people consistently paying different prices for the same good. Two economists ran an experiment involving car shopping.[4] College graduates of different races and genders, but similar across other demographic characteristics, were given careful instructions on how to solicit an initial price offer from various car salespeople. The authors found that white women were given a quote roughly $250 higher than white men, black women nearly $800 more than white men, and black men roughly $2,000 more than white men. Because final deals often depend heavily upon initial offers (we will explain why later when we talk about "anchoring bias"), the implication is that black men and women are likely to get worse deals than white men. However, we cannot definitively say that this is because of explicit gender and racial discrimination because black and female salespeople quoted similar high prices to their black and female customers. Instead, the salespeople may just be doing what any haggler does: basing their high initial offers on their perceptions that some people are less likely to walk away from a bad deal than other people—possibly because they have less leisure time to shop or fewer dealers to choose from in their neighborhood. In other words, salespeople are basing their initial offers on stereotypes about people's socioeconomic backgrounds. Because of the ways that haggling encourages sellers to take a harder negotiating line with some customers than others, car salespeople report that they make 50 percent of their profits from 10 percent of their customers.[5] While discriminating between buyers might be good business for each salesperson in isolation because it maximizes the return from each individual sale, it is troubling from the standpoint of society as a whole because certain people are consistently asked to pay higher prices based on stereotypes. As a result, one of the good things about the disappearance of haggling is that posted prices may actually foster more productive institutions by promoting a greater sense of fairness and transparency.

How can buyers enforce the social norms of fairness and transparency when it comes to pricing? Think back to the ultimatum game (Chapter 2). When fairness in trade becomes an injunctive norm, meaning that it becomes a common belief that one side should not take an inordinate amount of the surplus available to them in any trade, customers can enforce fairness and create a *de facto* norm by refusing to buy a good, even if it is below their maximum price, in an effort to punish an offending seller. This is the reason for Amazon's fear of customers punishing them for haggling and their aggressive public relations response to these claims.

To be clear: the increasing prejudice against haggling in many parts of the world does not mean that everyone always has to pay the same posted price for the same good. Businesses regularly participate in what economists call "price discrimination," meaning that they will charge different groups of customers different prices. Senior citizen discounts, family discounts, frequent shopper discounts, volume discounts, and weekend discounts are all aimed at trying to find customers who might have a higher or lower maximum price and charge them a different posted price accordingly. But price discrimination is conducted according to public and preset rules for groups of people, not on a one-to-one basis for individuals. As a result, they do not violate commonly held social norms demanding fairness and transparency.

Haggling seems unlikely to completely disappear, however, even where it has become rare. The growth of e-commerce has reduced the time and the effort needed to haggle when buyers and sellers want to do so. Amazon.com now offers a "Make an Offer" option for some merchants and some goods, primarily collectables and other unique goods. Here, sellers and buyers can accept, reject, or counteroffer quickly and easily through e-mails. Other haggling sites like Greentoe and Priceline also remain popular.

As just mentioned, haggling is not always only about the economics of maximum and minimum prices. There is also a social aspect to it. While in many Western developed countries there is an increasingly prevalent social norm that disdains haggling, in other societies haggling remains a way of life. In these countries, haggling is an important form of social bonding. If you remember our discussion of the importance of trust in Chapter 5, haggling can be a way of building trust through talking, trade, and establishing a reputation as someone who can be relied on. In this context, haggling is likely to be most common in societies where the overall level of trust is low. Haggling is a common workaround that some societies have developed to overcome a general trust shortage that poses an important barrier to trade, which can trap people in poverty.

The frequency with which merchants appeal to behavioral norms indicate just how important social bonding is in haggling. Think back to the Monty Python skit I talked about earlier. "We're supposed to haggle! This bloke won't haggle!" is an appeal made by the beard merchant to his fellow merchants—and also to Brian—that is aimed at convincing everyone that the local injunctive norm should be the *de facto* norm for everyone, even for Brian as a visitor. "Do you want to ruin me!" is an appeal by the merchant to Brian's sense of fairness. I have commonly heard "Why won't you answer me?" from merchants after they shout out opening prices as I walk by their stalls in an effort to get haggling started by appealing to the social norms of transparency and communication. And in many places, haggling has not officially begun until a seller says "Why do you insult me with that price?", appealing to our shared sense of decency and common good.

The noneconomic motivations behind haggling may also lie deeper in people's psyches. Using surveys of locals, one study finds that haggling fulfills three inherent psychological desires.[6] First, as we talked about before, people haggle to affiliate with people and gain personal acceptance, not just to facilitate trade but also because these interactions between sellers and buyers are desirable in and of themselves. Second, people haggle for achievement, which is gained by overcoming obstacles and performing difficult tasks well (i.e., "winning" by getting more of the surplus from the trade). Finally, people haggle to gain dominance and wield power over people. Haggling might have some of the same psychological impacts as war, but with less dire consequences. (If this analogy holds, it might explain my angst over haggling as some very mild form of post-traumatic stress disorder.) These psychological aspects of haggling do help explain the seriousness with which locals often take their haggling and why some people treat it (as wonderfully illustrated in the Monty Python skit) as something that is as important in the trading process as the good itself.

While there are "big picture" factors that influence how common haggling is in any country, there are also individual, good-specific factors that determine whether particular goods are haggled for. First, haggling is most common for goods that are more expensive and sold at lower volume. For these goods, haggling is not only less costly because it is less frequent, but also because gaining even a small additional share of the surplus can lead to larger absolute gains. This is the reason haggling for automobiles is still common everywhere (but less so than it used to be).

Haggling is common for goods where formal markets are banned. In countries with exchange rate controls, it is common for street vendors to create black market exchange opportunities (often allowed, and even taxed through bribes by the local police) that involve haggling. Probably the single easiest—and most accurate—measure of a country's commitment to a market-based economy is the number of people standing on the other side of any border crossing looking to sell you some local currency before you are taken advantage of by the official exchange rate at the *bureau de change*.

The most important factor influencing how likely specific goods are to be haggled for has to do with differences in information: more specifically, the fact that in any transaction, buyers and sellers rarely have the same knowledge. The implications of these informational differences between buyers and sellers were not fully appreciated until the Nobel Prize–winning economist George Akerlof got to thinking while he was in graduate school about the market for used cars.[7] (He was discouraged by his professors and the editors of major journals from pursuing such a "trivial" subject.) Prior to the 1970s, economists often assumed that market participants had perfect information about the goods they bought and sold, and almost always had the *same* information about the trade in question. But Akerlof recognized that this was typically not the case. As he saw it, any used car on a dealer's lot is much more likely to be a lemon than the average car on the street. Why? Because the seller of the car knows a lot more about that car and its unique history—whether it has been in an accident, was well maintained, was driven hard, etc. If the car is a high-quality car—in other words, worth more than other cars with similar observable characteristics—then the owner of the car would be unlikely to sell it. The simple fact that the current owner wants to sell it should be an indication to the buyer that this car is much more likely to be a lemon than similar cars on the road. This is the reason why new cars typically lose 20 percent of their value the second they are driven off a lot. As a result, Akerlof argued that people often buy new cars, and pay a premium for them, simply because they can't trust used car sellers and know that there is an increased chance that any used car they purchase is a lemon.

At the heart of the matter here is the phenomenon of "asymmetric information": The seller has private information about the automobile that the buyer does not have and cannot easily observe. As a result, the buyer is at a distinct disadvantage in this transaction—there is information about the good being traded that is hidden, but only to one side of the deal. The implication of asymmetric information is what Akerlof identified as "adverse selection": In this case, the market for used cars will be dominated by lemons, not by average cars and fair deals. In Akerlof's words, "The bad cars tend to drive out the good."

Asymmetric information and adverse selection aren't just important in the market for used cars; they are crucial to understanding the behavior of a vast variety of markets. They are essential to understanding financial markets, where a borrower always has better information about their creditworthiness than the lender. As a result, riskier borrowers are more likely to apply for loans, meaning all parties involved—both low- and high-risk borrowers—are less likely to receive a loan as a result (economists call this "credit rationing"). Adverse selection is crucial to understanding sports free agency markets, as any player who leaves their current team is more likely to underperform because a player's current team likely has better information about that player than other teams.[8] Adverse selection is crucial to explaining long-term unemployment: Those who have not had a job for an extended period of time carry with them the stigma that, for some reason a prospective employer doesn't know about, these workers are lemons. Adverse selection even gives us insight into dating markets and might explain why you may be more attractive to others when you already are in a relationship, or why you want to stay away from online dating where information can be easily hidden.[9]

Now, you might be thinking: George Akerlof won a Nobel Prize for arguing that markets for used cars shouldn't exist? Not quite—don't call up your used car local dealer and tell them that economists say they don't actually exist. Akerlof said it was difficult to make mutually beneficial trades in markets with asymmetric information, but not impossible. For these markets to work well, buyers and sellers must find ways to overcome the asymmetric information problems in order to prevent adverse selection from suffocating trade. So how can they do this? In a few ways. First, by figuring out ways to share information. For example, in many developed countries, any accidents a car has been involved in can be found in public records attached to the legal title of the car. Likewise, most car repair agencies keep the maintenance records of the cars they work on, and they can be shared with future owners of the car. Sellers also share information by offering warranties and money-back guarantees, essentially saying to the buyer that you know what I know, and if you find out something different, then you can invalidate the trade later.

The importance of finding ways to share information in order to foster greater economic development is a recurring theme of this book. One key to having productive institutions that encourage economic growth is having inclusive political participation that shares information and allows for the building of enough trust that people will allow power to be centralized in the government. In this sense, trade and the institutions that support trade are built upon the same stuff: information sharing and building trust.

However, sharing information alone is not always enough to solve the adverse selection problem. While buyers have a lot to lose because they have information disadvantages, merchants also suffer from what can be thought of as a "seller's curse." This curse comes from the fact that the seller is not always in the best position to persuade buyers to make trades that could be mutually beneficial. For instance, sellers are inherently seen as untrustworthy—not because they are, but because they have known incentives to be untrustworthy because of the private information that they have. Used car dealers are notorious for being deceitful. I don't think that this is because selling used cars attracts people who are more dishonest; it is more about the opportunities afforded in this job to leverage dishonesty and the skepticism it raises.

The other problem sellers have is that when they are highly informed about their product, they may not be able to see things from the perspective of the uninformed buyer. While a seller might know a great deal about the quality and craftsmanship of their product, they find it difficult to adopt the point of view of a buyer with little idea of how to assess the good's quality. The opening salvo of many street merchants—"good quality!"—is an attempt to address this problem, but it is counterproductive because it reminds the buyer that not only does the seller know more about the good they are selling, but that the seller is unable to succinctly explain exactly why his good is so desirable. Because of the seller's curse, many merchants fail to convince buyers that their maximum price should be above the seller's minimum price, and potentially beneficial trades are not made. In essence, there is a "curse of knowledge" that results from skepticism and from the fact that it is hard to see things from the perspective of the uninformed. (In academia, we usually don't refer to this phenomenon as the "curse of knowledge." We refer to it as "teaching.") Bridging this gap between the information differences on either side of a transaction is crucial to making sure that both buyers and sellers benefit as much as they can from any trade, but it is very often a bridge too far.

Reputation is also crucial to overcoming asymmetric information problems. Can you trust the seller to share all relevant information with the buyer? Reputation can only be built up over repeated transactions, either through personal interactions or by receiving recommendations from other people that you trust. This is the reason why used cars are typically sold in one of two ways. First, they are sold informally between people who know and trust each other. Second, they are sold through auto dealers who have a reputation to uphold and who can be threatened with the loss of future business if a buyer ends up purchasing a lemon. In essence, the common retail practice of branding is as much as about building a reputation and convincing buyers of the trustworthiness of a good as it is about actually marketing a good to buyers. Reputation is essentially a way to ensure that the seller has something to lose if the buyer is not satisfied. The equivalent to reputation in financial transactions is collateral—it is a cost that must be paid so that both sides of the transaction have some "skin in the game."

Unfortunately, not all markets and not all goods have mechanisms for information sharing and reputation building. Adverse selection worsens as it becomes more difficult for buyers to determine the true value of the good. This happens when the good is unique, idiosyncratic, or the buyer is inexperienced in the market, which is true for collectibles, art, and other highly speculative assets. Adverse selection is also worsened by the overall lack of formal markets, which makes it difficult to obtain information about prices of similar goods. It is exacerbated by a lack of publicly collected information, such as title registration and credit rating agencies. Adverse selection is worsened by the absence of middlemen—such as car dealers, retailers, auction houses, commodity exchanges, and banks—who can use their size and power to gain better information and have a reputation to protect. And finally, adverse selection is also most likely to occur when a trade is a one-time transaction—such as is common for big-ticket items such as cars and housing—so that reputation cannot be used as collateral.

Given this, we can see how haggling can make the trading process much more efficient—for locals, at least. Haggling can be used to level the playing field. Savvy buyers with lots of local knowledge have more power to pick and choose among multiple sellers, and they can develop a relationship with sellers who deal fairly with them and punish the sellers who don't. Local buyers also have experience that makes unique goods less unique. Finally, local buyers have a psychological advantage over sellers in that they are aware of how the haggling game is played locally and can use their power to walk away in order to leverage this knowledge to its maximum advantage. All of this said, haggling can also be good for sellers dealing with local buyers. In regard to the curse of knowledge, having an interpersonal connection and an opportunity to discuss the quality of the good through negotiation will facilitate trades that would not have happened at posted prices. And when haggling with experienced locals, the process is much more efficient and less costly to everyone in terms of time and energy.

The visiting traveler doesn't have the same advantages of locals, however, and so asymmetric information is particularly acute for us. We are not savvy, we have not shopped around very much, and we have little experience in evaluating the merits of most local goods. In addition, goods bought while traveling are mostly one-time transactions, and as a result we do not know which sellers are trustworthy and, even more importantly, sellers do not care because they are unlikely to see us again. As a result, travelers are very likely to be the victim of adverse selection in two ways: Either we buy overpriced and shoddy goods and gain little surplus from trade, or we fail to make any trade at all because we know that we are likely to be taken advantage of. This is why, for me as well as for many other people, haggling abroad is unpleasant and always feels like a missed opportunity.

I have daydreamed about doing the following. While traveling, I identify a good that I want to purchase. But instead of haggling for it, I take out an amount of currency equal to the price that I think is fair for both of us and near my maximum price, folding it up so that the seller cannot clearly see how much money I am holding. I then make a take-it-or-leave-it offer to the seller for the amount of money that I am holding in my hand, and see if he or she accepts. While I have never done this for fear of violating some unknown social norm and insulting someone unintentionally, I suspect that I know what would happen. The seller would reject my offer. Why? Because they don't know anything about me and they can't accurately judge the value of what I am offering. In other words, I have flipped the haggling situation around on them and now I have the information advantages. Yet this is only the reverse of the trade that hagglers are asking shopping travelers to say yes to all of the time. I don't know exactly what point I would be making to some random, unfortunate merchant if I ever actually do this, but I think it would—however briefly—grant me a sense of vindication regarding my harsh attitude toward haggling.

Uncertainty, beliefs, trust, perceptions, interpersonal interactions: these are all important factors in haggling. While there is an economic basis for each of these things, sometimes our perceptions of the world and our inter-actions with the people in it are driven by not just by cost-benefit analysis but by our psychological needs and desires. As I pointed out earlier, there may be psychological justifications for haggling. Likewise, psychology likely plays an important role in influencing our beliefs, trust, uncertainty, and the ways that different people approach the bargaining process. A burgeoning new field of economics, known as behavioral economics, has somewhat belatedly attempted to study the psychological underpinnings of humans in an attempt to better understand how our perceptions of the world influence our decision making. The goal of behavioral economics is to rebalance the study of economics away from overreliance on the dispas-sionate rational actor model of decision making. In rational actor models, people always balance costs and benefits in order to determine their every action and people deal with uncertainty using only probability theory and statistics. Behavioral economics, on the other hand, attempts to explain why people may not always behave rationally given our psychological biases and neurological makeup.

To be clear, all economists have not universally claimed that people are always and everywhere rational and respond only to economic incentives based strictly on cost-benefit analysis. Throughout history, many econo-mists have rejected the dogma that people are unerringly mechanical in their thinking. The most famous characterization of irrational behavior was made by the British economist John Maynard Keynes, who was the founder of modern macroeconomic theory as well as, according to one of his Cam-bridge contemporaries, "a don, a civil servant, a speculator, a businessman, a journalist, a writer, a farmer, a picture-dealer, a statesman, a theatrical manager, a book collector, and half a dozen other things"[10] (one of them being an economist). In his spare time, Keynes speculated in highly volatile foreign exchange markets and became a self-made millionaire (although in the process of making his fortune, he nearly went bankrupt twice). Based on his experiences in watching markets at work and in bargaining with other people, Keynes coined the phrase "the animal spirits of the market-place" to describe human behavior. In using this phrase, Keynes was trying to convey his observation that many people are fundamentally uninformed about the way that trade and markets work, and also that psychology and emotion often influence the behavior of buyers and sellers. While rational-ity might be ideal in the long run, in the short run our decision making is often distorted by passions, prejudices, and shortcuts.

The problem with Keynes's idea of animal spirits is that while it was intuitively appealing, it was not easily tested. However, over the last decade, psychologists, neurologists, and economists have gotten more interested in trying to deconstruct the decision-making process that goes on within our minds in order to identify just how closely we behave like the mythical "rational economic actor" in everyday life, particularly when we are bargaining. The goal of this research has been to identify the conditions under which we exhibit biased decision making and the impact that these biases have on economic outcomes.

Two of the leaders in this movement are the psychologists Amos Tversky and Daniel Kahneman. Kahneman has identified two different forms of decision processing: "intuitive," which is fast and automatic decision making that relies on rules of thumb (called heuristics), and "reasoning," which is slower and more deliberative decision making.[11] Kahneman argues that intuitive decisions have the advantages of being quick and less costly in terms of energy spent, but they are also subject to many systematic biases. While economists typically assume people use reasoning processing, they actually use intuitive processing for most day-to-day decisions because of its speed and ease. Experimental subject research has identified many different cognitive biases that run contrary to rational decision making but are commonly observed when people are making decisions based on intuitive processing. According to Kahneman and others, here are just a few of the predictable psychological traps that people fall into that are particularly relevant to haggling:

1. *Loss aversion bias:* People weigh losses more heavily than gains of equal amounts. In fact, based on experimental evidence, people act as if losses are about twice as painful as gains are satisfying.[12] As a result, people are more likely to fixate on avoiding bad deals than on obtaining good ones, and tend to bargain from a perspective of avoiding being ripped off. They are also more concerned about paying more than other people paid than they are about maximizing their own surplus. This helps explain my own persistent unhappiness with haggling—a trade that I should remember positively because I paid much less than my maximum price is likely to be remembered by me as a negative experience if I think that I paid more than other people.

2. *Risk aversion bias:* People prefer certain outcomes to uncertain ones, even when the returns are significantly lower. This is one important reason why people often prefer posted prices even when they can do better by haggling.

3. *Ownership bias:* We tend to overvalue goods once we own them. Studies have shown that once people own a good, they often place a higher sale price on it than they would be willing to pay themselves if they had to repurchase it.[13] In other words, as with loss bias and risk aversion, initial conditions and reference points matter. This creates a "status quo bias" in trade that makes it difficult for buyers and sellers to overcome their initial conditions of no-trade, even when they could both benefit.[14]

4. *Availability bias:* We tend to overgeneralize from small amounts of information that is easily available. Hence, the influence of first impressions in our decision making. Why did I choose that merchant? Because I liked his face. Why do I like that vase? Because it was the first one I saw. These initial observations create a path-dependency in our future decision making that plays an inordinately large role in determining eventual outcomes.

5. *Confirmation bias:* The tendency to look for evidence that confirms an initial hypothesis and ignore evidence that would invalidate it. When we see something that we initially like and then take the time to look at it more closely, we are more likely to focus on the good that we learn than the bad, meaning, once again, that our first impressions play a larger role than they should play in determining the maximum amount we are willing to pay for a good.

6. *Attribution bias:* We are much more likely to attach untoward motives to other people and accuse them of unfair dealings than we are to identify similar motives in ourselves.

7. *Contamination bias:* Irrelevant but contemporaneous events and experiences often influence decision making. I once paid an extravagant amount for a Mao pen (Mao raised his hand when you turned the pen upside down), and in hindsight I can see that I mainly did this because I was eating ice cream at the time and feeling in a good mood.

8. *Present bias:* People want to accomplish difficult things (such as not overspending) but often break these plans because of the lure of immediate gratification. This is the reason why some people impose arbitrary rules on themselves, such as a budget, in order to promote their own self-control.

9. *Overconfidence bias:* We tend to overstate the accuracy of our estimates of the value of goods and minimize the uncertainty associated with how much goods are worth. As a result, both buyers and sellers are less willing to change their offers and counteroffers as much as they should while haggling, leading to mutually beneficial trades remaining uncompleted.

10. *Framing bias:* Context matters, even when it shouldn't. Merchants have long known that you can push a specific product by showcasing it between a more expensive and less expensive version of the same product. Likewise, some items are always on "sale" (particularly goods that are bought infrequently and which buyers have less information about, i.e., mattresses and other home furnishings) because the use of the term sale frames our starting point for whether we are getting a good deal or not.

11. *Anchoring bias:* Arbitrary numbers influence the path of bargaining and price setting. For example, in one experiment, researchers fixed a roulette wheel to land on either 10 or 65. They then spun this wheel before asking the subjects of the experiments what percentage of member nations in the United Nations were from Africa. The average guess after a spin of 10 was 25 percent; after a spin of 65, it was 45 percent.[15] Anchoring bias is an important reason

why sellers like to throw out outrageous first offers, even if they immediately back off these prices by 50 percent or more—they know that by planting a high initial price in your mind, it makes you a little less sane than you were a few moments ago. As a result, offering a high initial price and discounting liberally during the haggling process is more likely to lead to a higher settlement price than a low initial price but little discount offered by the seller. Anchoring bias also creates a great deal of path-dependency in any bargaining process because the initial bid plays an inordinately large role in the price that is eventually agreed upon. This is why the high initial prices offered to black and women customers by car salesmen in the study discussed earlier were likely to end in higher final negotiated prices as well.

The point of listing all of these psychological biases is not to make you feel that you are preprogrammed to inevitably make bad decisions; in fact, just the opposite. To be forewarned is to be forearmed. The more we recognize these predictable biases in our behaviors, the more confident we can be that we will act more rationally when it comes to haggling. There is a rational basis for each of these irrational biases. Biases are shortcuts; they allow people to make quicker decisions based on less information and expend less mental energy doing it. Given the innumerable decisions that each of us are forced to quickly make each and every day, intuition is absolutely crucial to our survival as a species. However, if we are familiar with the shortcuts that our minds want to make all of the time, we can purposely discipline our minds and choose to think rationally when we really need to. We can recognize when we might be undervaluing something simply because we are not completely sure of its true value, or are being tricked by context into thinking that something is worth more than it is, or are refusing to change our bargaining stance because of overconfidence in our own knowledge. Recognizing these fallacies is not the same thing as avoiding them, but it is a first step. Good hagglers are already avoiding these biases in themselves and looking to take advantage of these biases in others. The more both buyers and sellers can overcome their behavioral biases, the more mutually advantageous trades can be made, and the better off everyone will be.

When we haggle, we haggle over money. So this seems like a good time to talk about a topic that has been surprisingly ignored in this book about economics: money. When an economist talks about money, we are not talking about income, wealth, borrowing, or lending. To an economist, money refers to an asset that is generally accepted in payment for goods, services, or in the repayment of debts. As a result, money could be almost any object of value, from money with intrinsic value such as gold, silver, or cigarettes, to fiat money, or paper money that has value only because people accept it in exchange.

Money makes trade more efficient for a number of reasons. First, it serves as a medium of exchange that makes trade easier. In barter economies, or economies without money, one good has to be bargained for in terms of another good. If you think haggling using money is difficult, consider haggling over a trade of goats for rice! The difficulties of haggling for either goats or rice alone are essentially doubled. Barter is tedious and time-consuming because it involves a double coincidence of wants—the other party has to have what you want, and you have to want what they have. Money, on the other hand, allows individuals to break transactions into separate parts. I can trade my goats for money, then take this money to buy rice, making trade much easier.

Just as importantly, money is a unit of account in which to measure the relative value of things. Money is essentially the language of trade—it is a tool that can be used to succinctly communicate a large amount of information. A barter economy requires people to be familiar with many more prices: in an economy with only 1,000 goods, barter would require traders to be familiar with nearly half a million exchange rates! Another big reason why haggling over an exchange of rice for a goat is difficult is that while everyone has some idea of the value of money, many fewer people have a good grasp of the value of goats or of rice. If someone tells you that her car is worth four goats, that probably will not mean much to you. If someone tells you that her car is worth $1,000, it quickly and clearly communicates something important: she needs a new car.

Finally, money is also a store of value that allows people to easily postpone trades until a later date without losing purchasing power (absent inflation); hence, the reason why fish has never been widely used as money. This is an important service because people prefer to spread their consumption evenly over time, but their incomes often fluctuate greatly from one day to the next. Recognizing the importance of having a store of value, the biologist Richard Dawkins has argued that there is an evolutionary imperative to money because "money is a formal token of delayed reciprocal altruism"[16]—it's a way of returning favors at any point of time.

Because money is so important in conducting economic transactions, money is itself the object of many economic transactions. Finance is essentially the trading of money across time, or the trading of money today for money tomorrow, with conditions attached. Usually, financial intermediation is accompanied by a *financial instrument*, or a legal contract that specifies the responsibilities of the person who is giving up money now for money later (the lender) and the person who is giving up money later for money now (the borrower). When you make a purchase with a credit card, you are actually not using money—you are postponing the need for money until you pay your bill. While credit cards are a valuable form of finance for most people, they also create a disconnect between the immediate satisfaction we get through purchases and the need to actually forego money. In this way, credit card finance can lead to overspending—it's an example of the *present bias* identified by behavioral economics. For example, studies have shown that tips left by those paying with a credit card are 10 percent higher than left by those paying in cash.[17] Other studies have found that those who shop with credit cards spend more at department stores than those who use cash.[18]

Today, fiat money is common across the world, but this has only been true for roughly the last 70 years. Before this, premodern economies used basic commodity monies like gold, cowrie shells, or ivory. As economic development occurred, many countries moved to the gold standard, where paper currency issued by the government represented a claim to a set amount of gold held by the central bank. In the 1960s and 1970s, governments gradually broke this link between gold and paper money, allowing fiat money to become the standard type of money.

How did this evolution from commodity money to the gold standard to fiat money take place? First, it is important to realize that fiat money has important advantages over commodity money. The big drawback of commodity money is that it is vulnerable to adverse selection: people keep the good quality items for themselves and use the poorest quality in trade. History is replete with commodity monies that have been devalued, from gold coins being reminted with cheaper metals, to the poorest quality cigarettes (with cheaper or less tobacco) being circulated as money while good quality cigarettes are smoked. The problem with commodity money is that its quality matters, and the holders of commodity money know more about the quality of the money than the next person to receive it in a trade. As a result of this asymmetric information, the quality of money declines over time as the result of adverse selection, meaning the value of commodity money will also decline and reduce its usefulness in trade. Bad money drives out good.

So where does fiat money get its value from? While fiat money has the backing of the government, this backing alone is not enough to get people to use paper currency in voluntary trade. Instead, fiat money gets its real value from the extent to which it is generally accepted as having value. Any fiat money can be effective as money as long as enough people will accept it in trade because they think that others will accept it in trade. In essence, fiat money is built around a cooperative equilibrium in which we all accept these pieces of paper as having value, and as a result they have value. When stated this way, this seems like a shaky belief system on which to base trade and our economy as a whole. But it really isn't, for two reasons. First, the fact that people's beliefs play an important role in the value of fiat money is true about most goods that people trade for. Why do people believe that gold is valuable when it is really just yellow rocks? People believe gold is valuable because they believe other people believe the same thing—gold is based on a group belief system that is really no different from that of fiat money. This is why it was relatively easy for governments to break the link between gold and paper money in the 1960s and 1970s, as most people had already come to view the paper, not the gold, as the true store of value well before then. Second, fiat money is just another example of how trust is important to trade in general. The use of fiat money allows us to reduce transaction costs by trading paper "IOUs" to the benefit of everyone. Here, the trust extends not just to the other buyers and sellers that we rely on to accept the currency that we hold. We must also trust the government to not abuse its power over the supply of fiat money by printing too much and undermining its value. In the words of historian Yuval Harari: "Money is the only trust system created by humans that can bridge almost any cultural gap, and that does not discriminate on the basis of religion, gender, race, age or sexual orientation."[19]

While fiat money can be very effective at reducing the transaction costs associated with trade because it is easy to transport, easily created, easy to account for, and uniform in quality, fiat money is not a perfect money that always and everywhere guarantees frictionless trade. Because governments control the supply of currency, they have asymmetric information about how quickly they are increasing its supply and its true value. They can take advantage of this hidden information to print up currency to pay their bills and leave the public as victims of adverse selection, holding currency that is less valuable than they thought it was. This is the nature of the inflation tax that we talked about in Chapter 4. Governments that do this are the ones that typically fail to promote productive institutions—including public trust—in many other ways that we discussed in that chapter.

The inflation that governments create by expanding the supply of fiat money can discourage trade, ruin the cooperative equilibrium for fiat money based on trust, and complicate haggling in two distinct ways. First, while the stated value of a unit of fiat money does not change, inflation eats away at the purchasing power of currency that is being held. For example, suppose that the government doubles the money supply so that twice the amount of fiat money is chasing a fixed number of goods. Merchants such as Taco Bell should now charge double for a given good in order to receive identical value in terms of purchasing power—their dollar menu will become a two-dollar menu—and each dollar will only buy half as much as it did before. This inflation has reduced the ability of fiat money to serve one of its primary functions—to be a store of value. This makes trades involving money costlier.

The other way that inflation discourages trade is by making money less useful as a unit of account because inflation serves as noise in the system, causing prices to be constantly changing in uncertain ways that reduce the information that is conveyed by using money prices. Without accurate, timely information, trade and haggling become much harder. In fact, behavioral economics research has found that people often suffer from "money illusion," meaning they are often fooled by the higher prices and larger currency denominations caused by inflation when real values based on purchasing power have not changed. These mistakes in assessing value create significant barriers to trade. Mark Twain, in his travel book *The Innocents Abroad*, provides an amusing example of how a traveler can be tricked by money illusion into thinking that goods are much more expensive than they actually are simply because the stated units on the currency are different than back home. According to Twain's account, a traveling companion bought dinner for a group of people in a restaurant in Portugal without first checking the exchange rate. When he received the bill he exclaimed "Ten dinners, at 600 reis, 6,000 reis! Ruin and Desolation! . . . Landlord, this is a low, mean swindle, and I'll never, never stand it. Here's a hundred and fifty dollars, sir, and it's all you'll get—I'll swim in blood before I'll pay a penny more."[20] When he then found out that the bill actually converted to $21, the spirts of the dinner party rose enough to purchase more spirits.

Not every government uses their information advantages and control over the supply of currency to exploit the holders of their fiat money. However, enough people fear that governments will do this that there is a continuous search for other types of money that have limited supplies and, as a result, have an anchored real value in terms of purchasing power. Gold has long served as an alternative to fiat money. Another alternative money that has been in the news recently is Bitcoin, an electronic currency that is traded online. While the technical aspects of Bitcoin—such as block chains and public ledgers—are well beyond this discussion, for our purposes there are two key aspects of Bitcoin that make it potentially attractive as money: It claims to have certain scarcity and absolute privacy. First, the growth rate of Bitcoin is based on a predetermined algorithm that, in theory, limits growth in its supply and which is known to all Bitcoin holders. By making Bitcoin scarce and eliminating the asymmetric information problem that exists for traditional currencies, Bitcoin should, in theory, eliminate the problem of adverse selection in money and be both a better store of value and a better unit of account. The second important characteristic of Bitcoin is that it is a crypto-currency, meaning that Bitcoin ownership and trades cannot be easily tracked because its supply is not controlled by a government and Bitcoin trades do not rely upon formal financial systems. This makes Bitcoin a perfect money for illegal activities or tax evasion.

In practice, however, Bitcoin is lousy money. It is not widely accepted in trade, making it a very poor medium of exchange. Just as importantly, the price of Bitcoin has been extremely volatile. Bitcoin has experienced huge booms followed by large busts (Bitcoin fell in value by roughly 70 percent in 2014, and in early 2016 is priced at only one-third of its high price in 2013). This makes Bitcoin a very poor store of value and unit of account. This volatility has been driven by a lack of trust in Bitcoin: security concerns, worries about market manipulation, an inability to correct mistaken transactions once made, and fears that Bitcoin is not as untraceable as previously thought. The volatility of Bitcoin suggests that markets fear there is a significant asymmetric information problem—they just don't know exactly what it is that they don't know.

The media attention received by Bitcoin has outpaced its real impact. Growth in Bitcoin has only been about 5 percent of the total growth in another financial product we have talked about that has had a real impact on people's lives: M-Pesa, the Kenyan mobile payment system.[21] However, Bitcoin cannot be ignored either, with more than $50 million of Bitcoin traded each day.[22] Why do people continue to hold Bitcoin? According to economists Vigna and Casey, "At its core, crypto-currency is not about the ups and downs of the digital currency market, . . . (but) about freeing people from the tyranny of centralized trust."[23] The tyranny of centralized trust? This is a shocking statement coming from economists who generally view centralized trust as key to functioning markets and economic prosperity. However, Bitcoin is not about efficient markets and productive institutions. It is about filling niches where markets are not functioning because of legal prohibitions, a lack of information, a lack of trust, and poor institutions. Bitcoin is trying to solve a human problem with a technical solution by creating a form of crypto-trust. In this sense, Bitcoin is much like haggling: when traditional markets and fiat money don't work well, people derive workarounds and figure out ways to trade even in the face of significant transaction costs.

So how do you "win" at haggling? Remember that any trade has to be mutually beneficial, so both parties must win in every trade, and there are many negotiated prices that ensure that this is the case. What we are really talking about is: how do you get more of the surplus from any trade that involves haggling? First, figure out ways to deal with the problem of asymmetric information. Watch other merchants and particularly local buyers and observe their behaviors. What prices are they paying for similar goods? How much are goods discounted from initial offers? Can you ask a trusted local for advice about the most reliable merchants before you begin to haggle? All of these things will help you bridge the gap between the merchant's knowledge and yours, making it quicker and easier to find a price that fairly distributes the surplus.

Second, bargain as if you know something about the good that you want to purchase. If you make lots of counteroffers that start ridiculously low and then vary widely from your initial offer, it only sends the signal that you don't really know what you are doing and can be taken advantage of. Instead, win by making fewer counteroffers. Counter only a little below a price you would say yes to. And always be prepared to use the only real leverage you have: walk away quickly (not saunter) after a few moments.

Third, be aware of your own biases; a little knowledge of behavioral economics should help. Remember that we are vulnerable to lazy thinking and too often overrely on our existing beliefs, on recent information, on avoiding losses rather than gains, on irrelevant context, on avoiding uncertainty, on our ability to generalize from small amounts of information, on initial offers, and on our own confidence. Being aware of our own fallacious thinking creates a degree of humility and flexibility in haggling that can lead to less conflict and more constructive interactions between buyers and sellers.

Fourth, your haggling experience is not likely to be a repeated game, so reputation is not an issue for either you or the seller. As a result, view everything that the merchant says with skepticism, and do not be afraid to bend the truth slightly yourself in an effort to fight fire with fire. "I saw it cheaper from another seller" can be a very effective haggling strategy as long as it cannot be easily refuted. And "I don't know if I really like this" always works, but only use this ploy if you are actually willing to walk away. Be careful with bending the truth, however, because merchants talk, and if you become known as someone who cannot be trusted and bargained with, your local haggling experience will be at an end.

Finally, remember that it is local social norms that matter, not your own norms. Haggling is not tacky, it is not rude, and it is not exploitive in many areas of the world. It is often an integral part of the social scene, and as with other local manners and traditions, you should assimilate haggling into your everyday life whenever possible while you are traveling. Haggling is a way for a tourist to become a traveler and experience life as it is lived by locals. Locals do not feel shame for bargaining hard, so why should you? The injunctive norm of fairness can vary greatly in practice across different societies, but the *de facto* norm of gaining more surplus when you can is the one you should focus on. However, don't try to gain surplus in a way that violates other social norms, such as getting too personal or haggling in a confrontational manner that might make the merchant feel that they are losing face. But also keep in mind that while we travel in part to have social interactions with new people, smart merchants know this and will try to build a personal connection with you in order to gain leverage in the haggle. Be careful about becoming too friendly unless you are willing to pay for your new friendship.

Let me conclude with a personal story about haggling in which I followed some of my own advice—maybe too well. During a trip in China, I was walking through the old city of Shanghai with a group of friends on our way to lunch. There were many local hawkers in the area selling knockoff luggage, purses, electronics, and watches to tourists. On the spur of the moment, I thought it might be fun to have a "Rolex" watch. So when a hawker came up to me and made me an exorbitant offer for a "high-quality Rolex watch." I immediately countered with a price about one-third of the initial offer, but kept on walking with my friends toward our restaurant. As the hawker followed us across the old city, she kept on making new offers, but given that I was not all that interested in the watch, I only made a couple small improvements in my offer. She used every ploy in the book: pleas to my humanity, appeals to the Swiss quality of the watch (!), and accusations of rudeness on my part. But I kept close to my offered price and kept on walking. As I was about to enter the restaurant, she accepted my low price, gave me the watch with a "humpf!", and walked away while I celebrated with my friends (possibly she saw this and perceived a loss of face, which was a mistake on my part). Over lunch, I regaled my party with tales of my haggling acumen and glorious success.

After lunch, we left the restaurant only to find that same hawker waiting for us. Politely, she asked to see my watch because she thought there was something wrong with it. Naïvely—probably because I was drunk with my own haggling success—I proudly produced my prize for all to see, at which point the hawker quickly grabbed it from my hand, stuck the bills I had given her in their place, and disappeared into the crowd before I could comprehend what had happened. Obviously, in retrospect, I had somehow managed to pay less than her (or her boss's) minimum price, and she could not let my temporary victory stand. My personal loss was more than offset by the joy my companions received in seeing the trophy of my short-lived victory slip from my grasp.

There are many possible morals that one could choose to draw from this story. Here is the one I have chosen. Contrary to the findings of behavioral economics that we suffer from loss bias and weigh losing more than winning, I choose to remember this event as a splendid triumph, not a heinous defeat, because this is an excellent reminder to me that trade is never about who wins and who loses, but about both parties always winning, just winning more or winning less. To view trade as a competition instead of a process by which we help each other is a certain way to ensure that you are always the loser in any transaction. Through my haggling, I ended up without a watch but with a story that memorably illustrates this point to me, and hopefully to you as well.

I Think That I Shall Never See Any Economics as Lovely as a Tree: Nature and Economics

At the gates of the forest, the surprised man of the world is forced to leave his city estimates of great and small, wise and foolish. The knapsack of custom falls off his back with the first step he takes into these precincts. Here is sanctity which shames our religions, and reality which discredits our heroes. Here we find Nature to be the circumstance which dwarfs every other circumstance, and judges like a god all men that come to her.

—Ralph Waldo Emerson[1]

To my mind, the greatest reward and luxury of travel is to be able to experience everyday things as if for the first time, to be in a position in which almost nothing is so familiar it is taken for granted.

—Bill Bryson[2]

Many people—particularly, it seems, those with more of an artistic bent—think that the study of economics and the enjoyment of nature are so completely opposed that their only real connection is that enjoying one requires the abnegation of the other. The poet William Wordsworth writes that one of the principal joys of taking a nature walk is to escape "the dreary intercourse of daily life," by which he means the need to make financial ends meet.[3] Poets like Wordsworth and Emerson (see the quote at the beginning of this chapter) talk about nature as if it is something that is much closer to the true human spirit than the coldly rational, incentive-responding environment that we are forced to live in by modern society. These poets use artistic license to ignore the fact that throughout most of human history, there has been no distinction between our everyday economic lives and nature—nature was our marketplace for most of our existence. Such poets repeatedly express the belief that nature offers humankind a respite from the bounds of economically motivated living, as if nature is the absence of economics.

Of course, this is not the case. There are many ways in which nature and economics are intrinsically linked. Among the most obvious similarities, both nature and economics are driven by the same phenomena: specialization and competition. Charles Darwin's theory that evolution is the product of natural selection propelled by competition and the survival of the fittest was inspired by Darwin's reading of Thomas Malthus's *Principle of Population*. As we have discussed before, Malthus's theory of population rested on the belief that labor productivity in the future would collapse because a growing population would be forced to rely on a fixed amount of natural resources. This process would eventually end in economic calamity. Darwin's insight—he was not only a better biologist than Malthus, but also a better economist—was to see that a larger and more diverse population of animals could be maintained in any ecosystem if each species competed more efficiently and specialized in ways that allowed them to use the resources at their disposal more productively. This is exactly how humans have escaped the Malthusian trap.

Nature's ability to compete and specialize is something that humans have inherited as part of our biological birthright. It manifests itself in our economic and social arrangements in a myriad of ways that we observe in our travels. Throughout this book we have talked about how people's behaviors and actions can be better understood by analytically examining the deeper incentives and constraints that shape our decision making. From explaining income inequality, to elucidating technological diffusion, to understanding why different societies have adopted different driving behaviors when behind the wheels of their automobiles, the economics of incentives and the biology of natural selection are powerful—and similar—ways of looking at the world that allow us to more clearly see the determinative factors that underlie the complicated natural and human worlds in which we live.

With apologies to Joyce Kilmer—whose poem "Trees" is alluded to in the title of this chapter—I think that both economics and nature, both markets and trees, are beautiful.[4] Like any successful bird-watcher or champion gardener, the insightful economist is a naturalist who carefully notices the beauty around them and uses it as motivation to more clearly see things as they actually are, not how they assume, intuit, or accept them to be out of habit. Careful observation is contingent on an ability to appreciate the beauty and uniqueness of what exists around us. To the true observer—and the good economist—nothing is mundane. We can't understand what we can't see, we can't truly see what we can't learn to appreciate, and we can't appreciate that which we don't find interesting and in some sense beautiful. A sense of wonder, regardless of whether it is conjured by a tree, a trip, or a transaction, is maybe the most important and valuable sense that our experiences, our studies, and our travels can stimulate.

In this chapter, I discuss the insights that economics can provide into why we enjoy nature travel and also why "back to nature" movements are so appealing to many of us, even those of us who appreciate most of what modern economic development affords. Nature offers us many things that we inherently desire as humans but that we cannot easily find in modern life, such as opportunities to engage in physical labor, to escape from technology, to despecialize in our work, and to enjoy risk. However, economic development poses challenges for the enjoyment of nature—particularly in terms of environmental degradation. This relationship between economic growth and the environment will be examined. Of course, nature also poses important challenges to economic development, particularly in terms of geography and climate, which we will also discuss. Most importantly, the goal of this chapter is to gain a deeper awareness of the ways in which nature and economics are related and how our appreciation of one during our travels can be enhanced by gaining more of an appreciation of the other.

So what can economics tell us about the appeal of nature and why so many of us make exploring nature, in all of its forms, the centerpiece of our traveling? As I see it, there are four primary motivations behind nature travel, and economics can help us understand these inherent impulses within each of us.

First, we explore nature in an attempt to experience beauty. So talking about beauty in a book that is primarily about economics seems more than a little weird. But I am not going to present a long-winded digression about what beauty is and what defines it. Instead, let me simply say that for myself, one of the most important aspects of beauty is that something is beautiful when it is distinctive, either aesthetically or even intellectually. Given that beauty is beautiful in part because it is different, or out of the ordinary, it then becomes obvious why spending time in nature and travel go together.

Beauty: Same as it ever was.

We enjoy both because both nature and travel are about experiencing the beauty of difference. In other words, nature travel allows us to experience the exotic.

For me, the thrill of seeing something of natural beauty, something that has always existed but has been freshly discovered by me, is difficult to beat. The jolt of beauty that can be found when setting out in the early morning mist on a Jeep safari, or reaching a lookout point at the end of a long hike, or listening to the loud whisper of a rolling river, feels as if it satisfies a physical need, like an itch that needed to be scratched. It is the contrast between these ageless scenes and our hectic daily lives that makes our experiences in nature so beautiful. In the midst of each day's challenges and upheavals, it is always comforting to me to spend a few moments thinking about that giraffe who is still quietly reaching for leaves at the top of that acacia tree, the river that continues to run downhill the same as ever, or the vista that assuredly looks the same right now as it did on the day when I stood there.

Difference, and the beauty it creates, is also an important aspect of our economic lives. For example, we like diversity in our consumption. We prefer some change in our spending simply for change's sake. For those of us living middle-class lives in developed countries, we take it for granted that we can enjoy crepes with a breakfast burrito in the morning and eat bananas with our sushi at night, or any of thousands of other combinations, if we so choose. In fact, today we have so much diversity in our consumption thanks to higher standards of living, larger markets, and improved international trade that it is almost impossible for us not to take all of this variety for granted. We have lost the ability to notice the wealth of options and conveniences that we have nowadays, and we don't appreciate how much better (for the most part) our lives are as a result. Modern market economies envelop us in such a panoply of choice that that we have become inured to the luxury in all of the variety that it affords.

To this end, I think that the only way to truly appreciate the beauty of markets and specialization—to see economic development as the blessing that it generally is—is to spend time in nonmarket environments. A great way to go "Robinson Crusoe" is to take a backpacking trip in the wilderness. Strictly in my role as an economist trying to understand nonmarket economics, I typically go once every year on a week-long backpacking trip into the backcountry of Montana with a rotating group of friends. For those of you who are not familiar with a backcountry backpacking trip, let me briefly describe one to you. You begin by spending the day before you leave filling an enormous backpack with everything that you think you will need in order to survive on your own for a week, including many different forms of densely nutritious food that tastes like some variety of tree bark (which is ironic given that tree bark is one of the few things that is widely available in the Montana backcountry). Loaded with 60 plus pounds of stuff in your backpack, you drive to the trailhead and start walking. Roughly 15 minutes into this beautiful walk, you begin to question whether you can keep carrying this land anchor on your back for another 15 minutes more without your shoulders snapping off. You then keep this same thought in your head continuously for the next week during your roughly 10 hours a day of hiking, except for the days when you get lost (if you are with me, this is a fairly common occurrence), in which case you will hike for more than 10 hours a day. When you do stop at the end of each day's hike, you then get to spend a few hours making camp and doing the things that would only take you minutes to do with the modern conveniences of home at your disposal. As you make your way from camp to camp each day, you discover that most of the 60 pounds of stuff you brought is not the 60 pounds of stuff that you needed or now want, but you can't just throw this junk off the side of the trail, so you have to continue carrying it around like an angry chimpanzee that has jumped on your back. It's a lot of work to have fun!

And why do people do this to themselves, you might ask? Because it is beautiful. The backcountry of Montana affords people, at the cost of a few

days hiking, the opportunity to be lost in wilderness as pristine as anywhere you can find in the 48 contiguous states of the United States. All of
the wonders of nature, from its quiet austereness to its vast immutability,
are on full display, and those who are adventurous enough to make the
effort to visit nature on its own terms get to enjoy it all by themselves.

But there are other reasons to go backpacking: to get back home and
enjoy that first shower, the first full meal, and the first opportunity to slip
into clean sheets on a soft bed. Having done without for so long, it feels
exquisite to do with. On the return home from backpacking, I always bring
with me a hard-gained receptivity to the luxuries of modern life from my
new experiences living in the old ways. As Bill Bryson says in the quote at
the beginning of this chapter, I can now see old things again as new (at
least for a while). The modern, hectic, evolving, specialized, impersonal,
and market-based ways of daily living take on a fresh coat of paint after
taking some time away from them.

According to the art critic John Ruskin, people have an innate desire not
only to appreciate beauty but to possess it. But how can you possess the
beauty of nature or the beauty of our complex modern economy? According to Ruskin, the best way to possess such things is to understand them.
We can understand beauty both by spending more time around it, but also
by spending time away from it. Time spent moving back and forth between
modern markets and nature contributes to seeing both more clearly,
which is the first step to a better understanding of each, which in turn
maximizes the impact we receive from their beauty. It makes us happier,
more satisfied people.

Second, we explore nature to reward our inner Luddite. While past generations were able to share stories of the hardships they experienced in the
old days without indoor plumbing and antibiotics, the best I could do to
convince my daughters of the privations I have lived through was to buy
an old Atari console and have them play Space Invaders and Asteroids.
However, despite the relative comfort that modern technology affords, I
think that all of us—whether you are Bill Gates, a teacher, or an assembly
line worker—harbor some lingering suspicions about all of this ease that
technology has created. Even the ancient Greeks told the story of Icarus
whose new invention tempted him to fly too close to the sun. I love my
computer, my cell phone, and modern medicine, like most people, but I also
feel a sense of unease about many of these new and disruptive technologies. I am not saying that I want to go back to typewriters and outhouses,
but I—and I think most people—also feel some nostalgia for the time when
employment usually meant lifetime employment and when job training

was something that you did when you began a job, not something you were constantly engaged in. The speed of our psychological adjustment to change has lagged behind the speed of technological advancement. While there are billions of times more information coming at us at much faster speeds than ever before, we process and understand this information in most of the same ways that our ancestors did when scanning the sky for smoke signals and listening for drumbeats. It is another example of diminishing marginal returns in action: adding more and more information to minds that are limited in their capacity to expand has not necessarily left us much more informed than we have been in the past.

New technologies and the continuous changes that they bring about are disconcerting. Each of us has an evolutionary predisposition toward being self-sufficient and providing for our own survival; this desire for self-reliance, of course, is balanced by our innate desires as social creatures to be part of a group. It is this conflict between self-reliance and sociability—among other contradictions—that makes humans complex, conflicted, and interesting. But one of the challenges with modern, market-based economies built on technological development is that each of us—as labor inputs—are required to become even smaller cogs in an increasingly complex machine. The power of markets is that we are asked to specialize narrowly to gain expertise and then trade our services for the variety in consumption that we desire. New technologies have only increased the incentives created by markets to specialize in even narrower ways as time goes on. In some ways this specialization and the interaction it demands works well with the social aspects of our human nature, but it runs contrary to our desires to be self-sufficient. This increasing dependency is frustrating to many of us. The division of labor, in a very real sense, runs contrary to aspects of our human nature. How many people today can claim the satisfaction of full ownership of a project from their work, from beginning to end? This loss of personal autonomy is one of the costs of market-based economic development.

These are not new concerns about market economics.[5] John Ruskin was not just an art critic, but also a critic of economic specialization for the reason discussed above: The division of labor runs contrary to man's inherent desire to be self-sufficient and well-rounded. "We have studied and much perfected, of late, the great civilized invention of the division of labour; only we give it a false name. It is not, truly speaking, the labour that is divided; but the men—divided into mere segments of men—broken into small fragments and crumbs of life; so that all the little piece of intelligence that is left in a man is not enough to make a pin, or a nail, but exhausts itself in making the point of a pin or the head of a nail."[6] Even the most famous proponent of markets—Adam Smith—worried about the dehumanizing impact of specialization: "The man whose whole life is spent in performing a few simple operations, of which the effects are perhaps always the same, or very nearly the same, has no occasion to exert his understanding or to exercise his invention in finding out expedients for removing difficulties which never occur."[7]

This loss of personal autonomy, however, is compensated for by the fact that specialization is an incredibly powerful technique—THE most powerful technique—for improving productivity and our quality of life. We have gotten to the point where throughout most of the world, not only does Adam Smith's observation still hold that no one knows how to build a pencil, but today few of us could get a glass of water, cook a standard family meal, or even light a fire for warmth if left to only our own devices without help from anything but what nature provides. The fact that we cannot provide these things for ourselves any more is a testament to the luxury of our modern lives: We can't do many of these things because specialization and markets have made it so that we don't have to.

While it is true that our physical activities have become extremely specialized, to an even greater extent our knowledge has become specialized. Today, information is the primary input into the creation of most goods, particularly services (which now account for more than 50 percent of GDP in most developed and even emerging market economies). As the Austrian economist Friedrich Hayek recognized, the biggest danger of eschewing markets is that our individual ability to process information is limited and restricts our ability to create complex goods and services by ourselves. However, markets are able to synthesize the specialized knowledge of many individuals and aggregate this into goods and services that are incomprehensible to any single person. The coordinating mechanism markets use is prices. Prices reflect the cumulative knowledge of large groups of people and send signals about where labor, knowledge, capital, and technology can be used most productively. As a result, a group of individuals working through markets is more than just the sum of its members—it is something much greater because of the immense power that comes from synthesizing specialized information.

So yes, specialization and markets are very powerful and they make our lives better. The fact that millions of people across the world have moved away from farms—the job most people identify with personal autonomy—and into urban areas where they work in more specialized jobs in the manufacturing and services industries is strong evidence that the exchange of specialization for autonomy is one that many people happily make. But like many things that we like, that doesn't mean we have to like it all of the time. Sometimes we can psychologically benefit from getting away from the prosperity but narrowness of our professional lives and getting back to a more primitive way of living, at least for a while. This is another reason why many of us find opportunities to travel and escape into nature so appealing. Nature appeals to our inner Luddite: It provides us an outlet to reject technology for a while. In this day and age when most of us work for other people, nature provides a feeling of independence. It provides opportunities for us to experience, even in somewhat artificial ways, opportunities for self-sufficiency, personal initiative, physical endurance, and asceticism. These are the things that modern economics has allowed us to give up. Most people would happily sacrifice some self-sufficiency for comfort, but maybe not all of the time. While most of the time I want to sleep in a house with indoor heating, Wi-Fi, and a comfortable bed, sometimes—just to reconnect with that other simpler part of my nature—I want to carry everything I need on my back and sleep on the ground next to some fading embers. In this day and age when most of us are employed by other people, work as part of teams, spend more time typing than standing, and contribute to only small parts of the whole, nature provides a wonderful feeling of autonomy with an expiration date of our choosing.

Third, we explore nature to enjoy our occasional love for risk. When I was young, the uncertainty in my life made me miserable. Now that I am old, it's the certainty that makes me unhappy. When I was younger and unsure about what I wanted to do, how I was going to do it, and—most importantly—how I was going to pay for it, I was desperate to have the stability of a permanent job and one place to live in for more than a nine-month interval. I wanted some sort of routine in which I didn't have to fret about every penny spent and using every minute more productively. Now that I have an established job, career, and home, the routine that I once longed for often seems like a prison, and I love to spend my free time planning travel during which I can leave the class schedules, chauffeuring to swimming practices, and endless runs to the grocery store far behind.

The thing is, I greatly enjoy my daily life. My days are filled with people I love and work that is fulfilling and, I feel, is important. But at the same time, the pull of the exotic—which daily life has very little of—often gnaws at me and has motivated much of my love for travel. In the words of Emerson at the beginning of this chapter, nature travel allows us to take off the weighty "knapsack of custom"—we travel a little more lightly when we explore nature than we do in our daily lives under the burdens we all must carry. No matter how good the usual is, what is routine can quickly become banal. And, in the words of Henry David Thoreau, "The mind can be permanently profaned by the habit of attending to trivial things, so that all our thoughts shall be tinged with triviality."[8] We can begin to lose the single trees of our blessings in a forest of minutiae.

This is another contradiction in human nature: We are risk-averse most of the time, but risk-loving some of the time. As we discussed in the previous chapter, research in behavioral economics has found that people generally have a risk aversion bias. People prefer certainty over uncertainty even when the expected returns from the certain outcomes are far lower. The standard economic theory of behavior assumes that everyone is a rational actor, and predicts that we estimate the probability of different costs and benefits that could occur from each possible action and then choose the action that maximizes the expected net benefit. In reality, we tend to place too much weight on unlikely outcomes in our decision making relative to likely outcomes. The result is that we often take too few chances and fail to choose alternatives with higher expected returns. For example, if offered a choice between a sure $500 and a bet that offers a 60 percent chance to win $1,000 and a 40 percent chance to win nothing, many people will choose the sure thing even though it has a lower expected payoff. This choice makes sense when we consider that many people abhor risk and seek to avoid it even at substantial cost. It is the same psychology that causes people to believe that rare events—terrorist events, shark attacks—are much more likely to occur than they actually are. It is the extraordinary uncommonness of these events that shock our risk-averse psyches and imprint themselves on our memories and beliefs.

But while we are generally risk averse, we also have a tendency to seek out risk under certain circumstances. While many people claim that gambling is irrational and the lottery is a tax on people who don't understand expected returns, these activities can also be seen as the prices people are willing to pay for the entertainment value of experiencing the occasional exotic thrill of risk. (When this thrill is no longer exotic, and the stakes are no longer proportional to your wealth, it becomes a gambling addiction.)

Another source of risk seeking is loss aversion bias (see Chapter 7), which refers to the phenomena that we typically act as if losses are about twice as painful as gains are satisfying. As a result, when offered a choice between LOSING $500 for sure and a bet that offers a 60 percent chance to lose $1,000 and a 40 percent chance to lose nothing, many people will accept the risky bet in the hope that they lose nothing. This seeming inconsistency in human behavior is consistent with people weighing the psychological costs of losses more heavily in their decision making than their dislike of risk.

For those who have taken too many probability and statistics courses to enjoy gambling, spending time in nature or engaging in extreme sports are also ways of scratching the itch of experiencing the exotic thrill of risk. One rarely sees people living in war zones or struggling in extreme poverty use their free time to base jump or freestyle rock climb. They already have too much risk in their daily lives. But for those of us who are now faced with the historical anomaly of having lives that are devoid of worries about predators, marauders, and starvation, the thrill of outdoor activities is appealing. While I have never bungee-jumped or paraglided, every time I go backpacking I am met with questions about why I would want to risk the bears, the wolves, the raging rivers, the falling rocks, the lightning, and the lack of cell phone contact (apparently being offline is inching toward becoming an adventure sport nowadays). For the people asking these questions, hiking and enjoying nature seem as irrational as playing craps. To me, it seems like a small-stake risk taken to break my routine and enjoy some natural beauty.

Having said this, there are real dangers associated with spending time in nature; many people have forgotten about these risks as we have become more divorced from the natural world. Every year an average of roughly 150 people die in America's natural parks as they try to get closer to bears for better pictures, traverse slippery rocks near waterfalls in order to cool off, peek out over the edge of cliffs, drive while sightseeing, and go for summit hikes with only the t-shirts on their backs.[9] Having seen some of these behaviors in person, I attribute these to the fact that when it comes to safety in nature, people have failed to make the important distinction between an injunctive norm and a descriptive norm, which we discussed in Chapter 2. Our modern lives have become largely sanitized of risk—in part because of the potential litigation associated with accidental injury, regardless of how minor. Many people have confused the now widely accepted injunctive norm that all reasonable (and some unreasonable) action should be taken to protect public safety, with a descriptive norm that does not hold true: that national parks should be safe because they are public places. Unfortunately, too many people's last thoughts have been something along these lines: How dangerous could the edge of that waterfall be if no one bothered to put up some obstructions to protect me from doing damage to myself?

Nature and outdoor activities provide us an opportunity to seek out some risk commensurate with our need to break out of the routine that is an inherent part of our daily lives. Nature, once again, plays an important economic role in helping us enjoy diversity in our experiences and get just enough risk into our lives so that we get back to avoiding risk when we go back home.

Fourth, we explore nature to get back in touch with the land. One of the biggest events in human history has been the massive migration of people from rural to urban areas over the last 200 years. This migration has had huge consequences for society in general, and economics in particular. As discussed in Chapter 2, increases in agricultural productivity driven by technological advances from the Neolithic Revolution to the modern Green Revolution have dramatically increased the food production of farm workers. By reducing the number of people living as subsistence farmers, the economic link between the land and most of the population has been broken across most of the world. As a result, people are now free to move to urban areas where there are opportunities for more productive jobs in manufacturing and services that pay higher wages, and also where there are more opportunities for leaks and matches to occur that allow ideas to fruitfully multiply. The massive economics-driven migrations of people today—such as the one that has been occurring in China with over 300 million people moving from rural to urban areas since 1980—have led to a world population that is much more urban and also much wealthier.

However, this migration off the farm has left most of us isolated from the land as outside work has moved inside. In the United States, the percentage of workers in agriculture has dropped from roughly 75 percent in the late 1800s to less than 2 percent today.[10] In the process, modern economies have evolved from being physically intensive to knowledge-intensive. Our jobs have become more challenging mentally, but physically sedentary. The lack of physicality in so many jobs today can actually be stressful given that humans have evolved to engage in physical work. In the words of one labor economist, "evolution presumably imbued us with a work ethic for our survival and not a Garden of Eden existence."[11] In fact, according to anthropologists, our physical evolution to standing upright was in part driven by the evolutionary survival strategy of being able to run for longer periods of time than four-legged animals could sustain, essentially wearing down our prey. Few modern jobs replicate these same physical demands that were required to survive on the savannahs of Africa. This is a good thing, but modern health challenges such as obesity, diabetes, depression, and heart disease are directly attributable to the fact that the physical realities of modern labor are so much different from what our bodies evolved to do.

In many ways, it is not the physical changes but the psychological adjustments to our unnatural work environments that are proving to be most difficult for us to make. According to the World Health Organization, mental health disorders increase with urbanization. Urban migration has weakened the family and other social ties that exist more strongly in rural areas. Urbanization has also separated more people from the psychologically restorative power of nature. At the same time, mental illness also appears to grow with income, as people live longer, are more likely to be diagnosed with mental disorders, and—at least according to Sigmund Freud—suffer from the faster pace of life that accompanies economic progress.[12] As a result, while mental health issues today account for 12 percent of the global disease burden, by 2020 it is expected that 20 percent of the DALYs (disability-adjusted life-years) lost to illness will be attributable to mental health problems.[13]

Human societies are evolving to help cope with the physical consequences of these changes in our ways of living. The growth of the exercise industry and the importance of fitness services in developed economies attest to this. Spending on personal trainers, gym memberships, and high-tech training equipment is outpacing growth in overall consumption growth across the world. Likewise, the growth in nature travel—particularly things such as environmental tourism—suggest that people are increasingly using their travel resources to reconnect with nature. But it is worrisome that the increase in mental health disorders is particularly pronounced among the young—the social media generation that spends less time outdoors and spends less time traveling in nature.

So this is another link between nature and economics. Our economic lives have evolved in ways that are inconsistent with our natural ones. In order for our urbanized, knowledge-intensive jobs to be sustainable for many of us, we also need to occasionally refresh our instinctive selves by spending time in nature, engaging in physical activity, enjoying some quiet, and breathing fresh air. Economic thinking that treats humans like automatons—whether it does this in the form of always assuming people are perfectly rational and ignoring our behavioral biases, or whether it does this by assuming that humans are some sort of machinery that is completely divorced from its natural environment—is economic thinking that sees human behavior as it would like it to be, not the way that it actually is. To ignore the impact that the natural world has on our economic behavior is as foolish as believing that our economic behavior has had no impact on nature.

What is the impact of economic development on nature? There is no doubt that economic development has had a devastating impact on the natural environment and ecological diversity. The impact of industrialization and population growth on water quality, air quality, biological diversity, and woodlands have been dramatic. But returning to the time before the Neolithic Revolution—when man's negative impacts on the environment began—is impossible. The question is whether economic development today necessarily has to lead to a continuing deterioration of our natural environment. The answer is no. Let me explain why.

Pollution is the quintessential example of what economists call a negative externality—it creates costs for society that are felt by more than just the producer and consumers of the good that creates the pollution. As we have talked about before (see Chapter 2), the solution to eliminating negative externalities is to first stop subsidizing the activities that create them. There are many examples of governments prioritizing the maximization of GDP to the exclusion of any other measure of social welfare, and, as a result, actively encouraging pollution. Policies that have paid farmers to conduct deforestation in an effort to boost agricultural output, or energy subsidies aimed at keeping dirty hydrocarbon fuels cheap, are just two common examples of this. Second, governments can "internalize" the negative externalities by charging producers (and consumers, as a consequence) taxes that are equivalent to the social costs of the pollution they create, forcing them to take into consideration—and pay for—the full impact of their actions.

The fact of the matter is that as countries get richer, they generally work to improve the quality of their environments. As evidence of this, the Environmental Performance Index reported by Yale University shows a strong correlation between per-capita GDP and the quality of the environment in a country.[14] There is empirical evidence that the point past which economic development begins to significantly improve the environment occurs somewhere between $6,000 and $13,000 of per-capita GDP—in other words, as countries become middle-income.[15]

There are many specific examples of the connection between better environmental quality and economic growth. Consider air pollution as one example. In the United States, automobile pollution has fallen by 50 percent from its peak in the 1970s.[16] While many people associate economic development with the deadly smog that fills the skies in China today, it is important to remember that the air in London in the 1850s and the air in Tokyo in the 1960s was just as bad. Today, thanks to their much higher standards of living, airborne particulates in both cities have fallen dramatically to less than 1 percent of these highs. There is evidence that similar reductions in pollution are beginning to happen in China today as its income rises.[17] Investment in renewable energy in China has increased by 73 percent between 2010 and 2014 and is now greater than in Japan and America combined.[18]

No need for sun block in many cities in China.

Richer countries have cleaner environments for at least two reasons. First, because clean air, clean water, healthy forests, and natural resource protection are normal goods—they are things that people want more of as their income rises. As countries become richer, they have more resources to pay for the technologies that can prevent future pollution and the costs of cleaning up the consequences of past pollution. The simple fact of the matter is that it is hard for governments or people to care about a clean environment when a sizeable proportion of the population does not know where their next meal is going to come from.

Second, richer countries are better able to protect the environment because they have better institutions with the strong, high-quality governments needed to impose pollution taxes, monitor environmental standards, and enforce environmental regulations. Many of the most polluted areas of the world are poor, in large part because pollution and poverty often have the same source: failing institutions that incentivize unproductive behavior and that provide people few incentives to consider their wider social responsibilities.

However, there are two huge caveats here. The first is that some forms of pollution are not national in scope; they are global and beyond the ability of a single government to deal with. This is at the core of the problem with carbon pollution and its role in global warming, which I will talk about in greater detail in the next chapter (Chapter 9). With no international government having the power to enforce an international carbon tax, there is a great deal of coordination failure across countries when it comes to enacting policies to deal with global warming. Individual countries have incentives to free-ride off the carbon reduction efforts of other countries.

The second caveat is that even with quality institutions and a lot of financial resources, it is ultimately the responsibility of citizens to value a clean environment and to be well informed about the costs of maintaining it. Economic possibilities are often trumped by political realities. When the public and elites cannot muster the political will to implement the policies needed to deal with environmental degradation (usually because of special interest politics aimed at thwarting such policies and spreading disinformation), then all of our carefully constructed economic theories about how economic development can help protect the environment go right into the swelling intellectual landfill filled with good economic ideas ruined by political realities. As the world has grown richer, environmental disasters are less about the consequences of economic development than the realities of political underdevelopment.

Now, let's turn around the question from the previous section, and instead of asking how economic development impacts the natural environment, let's ask this: Does the natural environment contribute to some countries being poor and others being rich? This idea is at the root of Malthusian economics (Chapter 3), which is based on the belief that economic development is strictly constrained by our natural environment, specifically the population density in any specific area. A more modern proponent of natural determinism is Jared Diamond, the author of *Guns, Germs, and Steel* (first discussed in Chapter 2). Diamond's argument is that Europe and Asia colonized the Americas and Africa, and not vice versa, because of Eurasia's inherent ecological advantages: a more temperate climate that allowed for higher agricultural productivity, more native domesticable animals, and native plants that are easier to cultivate, among other reasons. These ecological advantages led to an earlier Neolithic transition in Eurasia, creating more surplus labor and also supporting a greater population that facilitated technological development. The jump-start that Eurasia had on the rest of the world gave them economic, military, and disease immunity advantages that eventually allowed them to dominate Africa and the Americas when these regions came into sustained contact with each other. But at the heart of this argument is the primacy of natural advantages in the gaining of economic advantage.

There has recently been a great deal of economic research on the role of nature—specifically the role of geography—in explaining differences in income across countries. We tend to think of the most rugged, unusual, and challenging landscapes as being the most beautiful and travel-worthy. However, these areas of challenging geography are also some of the poorest regions of the world, and that may not be a coincidence.

There are a number of hypotheses about how geography contributes to income disparities and poverty. One is that geography impacts the transaction costs associated with trade, limiting the ability of some countries to develop economically. One of the most important factors here is access to ocean ports and navigable rivers, as water transportation is typically cheaper and faster than overland or air transportation. Access to water transportation also facilitates technology transfer, trade in raw materials, and cultural integration. Only 17 percent of the world's land is within 60 miles of an ocean or a navigable river connected to the ocean, but this small area produces nearly 70 percent of world GDP and has 50 percent of the world's population.[19] However, access to the cheap transportation that water affords is not shared equally across the globe. Compare the geography of Europe and Africa. Africa is about eight times the size of Europe, but it has half the amount of coastline, few deepwater ports, and a very limited number of navigable rivers. In addition, most of Africa's population lives in the interior, away from the coast, which is typically very arid given oceanic weather patterns. The drawing of postcolonial borders in Africa also hasn't helped: half of the world's landlocked countries are on the continent.

Geography also plays an important role in climate. As we have discussed before, the most important geographical fact in economics is that as you move away from the equator, average incomes increase. Per-capita GDP in tropical countries is roughly $4,000 compared to about $17,000 on average in temperate countries north and south of the tropics. The fact that income increases with distance from the equator is generally true even within regions (e.g., Europe and Africa) and within countries (e.g., Italy, the United States, Mexico, and Brazil).

There are a few reasons why a tropical climate might harm economic development. The most obvious is that the warmer temperatures in the tropics reduce agricultural productivity by an estimated 30 to 40 percent, which is a huge problem given that half of all employment in the tropics is in agriculture.[20] The reasons for this are complex, but result from a combination of factors that come along with warmer temperatures: more drought, poorer soils, more monsoon flooding, and the absence of frost that kills plant parasites.

Without seasonal frost, warmer tropical climates are also associated with increases in parasitic diseases such as malaria, sleeping sickness, dengue fever, river blindness, and hookworm. As discussed in Chapter 1, such diseases lead to lost workdays, missed schooling, higher health care costs, and reduced productivity that contributes to poverty. According to one study by the World Health Organization, adults in malaria-free Latin America earn 50 percent more than adults living in malaria zones.[21] Historically, disease has also discouraged development by reducing population densities, slowing the beginning of the Neolithic transition while also increasing the costs of trade and serving as significant barriers to technology and knowledge transfer.

One final way that warmer climates frustrate economic development is by making it harder to work hard. Three-fourths of the energy released by muscles when they are working comes in the form of heat, and it takes more effort to dissipate this heat in warmer climates. This contributes to lower labor productivity and reduced standards of living.

However, significant objections can be raised against these arguments of natural and geographical determinism when it comes to economic development. The biggest is that while there is a correlation between the natural environment and economic development, the actual causation may be reversed: It is poverty that makes environmental factors such as geography and climate critical, not the environment that is creating the poverty. More specifically, it is the poor economic institutions and distorted incentives that exist in many countries that perpetuate poverty and prevent an escape from the geography trap. For example, in many countries, the high incidence of disease is attributable as much to inadequate public health as to the natural environment. To pick just one example, Spain and India have roughly the same malarial ecology according to scientists, based on their climates and geography. But Spain has no malaria because of effective implementation of parasite eradication programs, while 66 percent of India's population is at daily risk for malaria.[22]

Likewise, government-created barriers to trade are at least as costly as the transaction costs created by geography. Bad governments also create bad institutions that reduce agricultural productivity in ways that are as damaging as any climate challenges, particularly given new technologies that allow arid land to be much more intensively farmed than before but which are not adopted everywhere because of numerous institutional barriers to technology transfer. Even the role that a warmer climate plays in discouraging hard work can be seen today as a failure of economic development, not the cause of it. In developed countries with the institutions to build reliable power grids and the incomes to pay for them, air conditioning has contributed to a great migration of people and businesses to hotter climates (e.g., the U.S. Sun Belt, Dubai, and Singapore) without a loss in labor effort or productivity.

The fact of the matter is that there is a lot more variability in incomes than there is variation in geography and climate. Countries with constant geography have experienced growth miracles and disasters, such as China, Korea, and Botswana, which were discussed in Chapter 4. Today, we are seeing more growth in the tropics than we have ever seen before. While the natural environment may be a contributing factor in economic development, it is not the determining factor. Institutions and incentives—are you sick of hearing this yet?—continue to be the deepest rivers and highest mountains that block economic progress.

Given that economic institutions are preeminent, could nature shape institutions in ways that make it indirectly important in economic development? Some historians and geographers have argued that the more inclusive and decentralized institutions that exist in Europe are a direct result of Europe's geography.[23] Because Europe was naturally fragmented by multiple mountain ranges and numerous rivers, seas, and channels, it encouraged more localized power, competition between various states, and more trade in goods and ideas. This fragmentation led to better protection of individual property rights and more productive institutions, in general. Compare this to China, whose 3,000 years of unified history have typically been dominated by a powerful centralized government controlled by a very small number of elites. China's relatively cohesive geography—at least along the coasts and moving west toward the Tibetan plateau—facilitated the excessive centralization of power in ways that may have

The mountains are high and the emperor is far away.

worsened the productivity of its institutions.[24] In spite of the common Chinese adage discounting the influence of centralized power—"the mountains are high and the emperor is far away"—typically the mountains have not been high enough and powerful elites not far enough away to protect local institutions throughout much of China's historical geographic core.

These and other such arguments about the role of geography in shaping institutions—whether you completely buy them or not—only reinforce the conclusion that the potential links between the economic and natural worlds are too numerous and interesting to ignore.

While many view economics as man-made and nature as that which is not, in this chapter we have talked about a number of ways in which the two are inescapably linked. Economic activities undoubtedly impact nature, while the natural world influences economic decisions and their human impact on each of us. We are all part of the natural world we shape for better or worse, and to treat our deep connections to nature as something separate from our economics is to really be engaged in unnaturally bad economics.

Studying economics and studying nature are not so different: Economists have shaped our understanding of the natural world, beginning with Malthus, while evolutionary biologists such as Darwin have, in turn, influenced how economists think about economic development (for example, Schumpeter's theory of creative destruction and technology waves discussed in Chapter 6). The fact is that the best economists are economic naturalists—striving to more clearly see the deeper mechanics of the world around us, and always attempting to better explain why we observe what we observe.

It is in this sense that studying economics has been at times for me as satisfying and as comforting as going for a beautiful walk in the wild. The wonders and complexity of the natural world are almost matched by the wonders of markets and of the complexity of modern economies. I agree with John Ruskin's idea that the best way to appreciate the beauty of anything, the natural and unnatural, is to understand it better. Traveling to different places, spending time in nature, or thinking about economics affords us the opportunity to gain a new perspective on the world around us and allows us to appreciate both the natural and the man-made with fresh eyes.

CHAPTER NINE

Who Owns the Space Behind My Seat? Traveling Economics

Travel far enough, you meet yourself.

—David Mitchell[1]

It ain't what you don't know that gets you into trouble.
It's what you know for sure that just ain't so.
—Anonymous (often attributed to Mark Twain)

In a book that examines the ways in which economics can inform our travels, it is about time that we got around to discussing the economics of travel itself. While economics plays an obvious role in many aspects of travel—such as determining airplane ticket prices or hotel room rates—there are many other less obvious ways in which economics impacts the costs, benefits, and experiences that we have when we travel. In this chapter I want to examine how economics can help us understand a few of the less obvious but very meaningful aspects of travel.

At the crux of the economics of travel is a basic fact: In many different ways, tourism creates public goods. Remember that a public good is one that benefits many, not just those who use it or paid for it. In economics-speak, public goods create "positive externalities." If you remember our discussions in Chapters 2 and 6, public goods such as roads or new technologies are different from typical goods, such as hamburgers. Many public goods are *nonexcludable*, meaning that it is not easy to prevent everyone from enjoying the benefits of a public good, and they are *nonrivalrous*, meaning that when one person receives benefits from a public good, it does not necessarily impinge upon other people benefiting as well at the same time.

The act of travel creates public goods. The transportation infrastructures that we use to get from here to there—roads, airplanes, trains, buses, subways—are public goods because they provide positive benefits for everyone, not just those travelers who are using it at the time. A tourism industry also creates a wide variety of economic activities in many different industries within an economy—hospitality, food, and retail particularly— that can spur the wider public good of economic development by creating a diverse set of employment opportunities. Tourism can also improve a country's tax base and create revenue that can be used to pay for more public goods for the local population. Even the people that we meet while traveling help us to create new networks that allow ideas and experiences to mix and match, creating technologies that can benefit everyone. In fact, the main reason we travel is because travel is a public good and not a private one. We travel to certain places because we want to enjoy the benefits that naturally diffuse from the public goods that exist in specific locales—public goods such as nature, historical sites, tourist attractions, climate, and local culture.

However, it is not the case that tourism is always and everywhere a positive thing; in fact, public goods can contribute to the creation of public bads. For example, growing tourism in a country can contribute to activities that have significant negative externalities, including things we have discussed in earlier chapters of this book: traffic congestion, pollution, and reduced cultural diversity across countries.

The challenge of the public goods associated with travel is that they are inherently complex. Because their benefits and costs flow to everyone, if left to markets alone, too few public goods will be produced and too many public bads. When it comes to public goods, people have many incentives to free-ride and are reluctant to spend their own resources on goods they can enjoy for free. The solution to the underprovision of public goods is for the government to subsidize or directly provide public goods, collecting taxes to pay for this. This creates a whole new set of complications involving special interest politics and public decision making. Public goods are also challenging to manage because everyone can use them, so it is often the case that everyone does so without regard to their impact on others. This is the tragedy of the commons problem, where public goods that can be freely enjoyed by everyone are often exploited in unsustainable ways that serve no one's interest in the long run.

The purpose of this chapter is to examine the hidden benefits and costs of the travel industry more clearly by examining the public goods aspects of travel and tourism, and the macroeconomic impacts of tourism, including the sizeable foreign aid industry in many countries. The most important new economic concept introduced here is the Coase theorem, which explains why public goods exist when property rights are not fully assigned. The Coase theorem can help us understand why people feel excessively squeezed during air travel, why you should generously tip your travel guides, and why some of the most beautiful and interesting travel destinations in the world are also the most dysfunctional and poor.

The well-worn adage that "the true joy in travel is found in the journey, not the destination" sounds nice, but is rarely experienced in the real world. The act of travel has always been difficult, and while today we no longer have to rely on months-long ship rides or ox-drawn Conestoga wagons to get to the places we want to go, getting from here to there remains mostly unpleasant. I am not aware of anyone who flies coach or regularly rides trains in Mumbai for fun. In part, travel is unpleasant because it is time-consuming and inherently monotonous. Just as importantly, travel is difficult because of the economics involved. The costs of travel largely reflect space and time. The faster you want to get somewhere, the more you have to pay for either a more personal mode of transportation (private jets and cars over commercial airlines and buses) or a more technologically intensive mode of transportation (airplanes over cars). Saving time costs money.

Getting more space when traveling is also very expensive. When flying first class internationally, travelers typically pay between 5 and 10 times more to receive roughly twice the traveling space as coach. For the more price-sensitive travelers who fly coach, many airlines have attempted to increase the number of passengers on each flight by pushing seats closer together and having more narrow rows. In essence, the airlines are trying to convert a public good on an airplane (the aisles and leg space) into more private goods (seats) that they can sell and make a profit from.

But it is not just the airlines that are competing with passengers for the public space on a plane—it is also passengers in close quarters competing among themselves for space. Consider the reclining airplane seat back: Most coach airline seats are able to recline backward by approximately four inches (10 centimeters). As a result, the front passenger gains four inches of space at the cost of the back passenger's four inches of space when they recline their seat. Jousting for airplane space is a zero-sum game in which the recliner gains at the expense of the passenger in back of them, but then that passenger can steal space from the passenger in back of them. Here is the question that I want to consider: Should passengers have the right to recline their seats? Is reclining a personal freedom that should not be impinged upon? Or should reclining be banned in the interest of avoiding a tragedy of the commons, where everyone is stealing everyone else's space to the detriment of all?

The Nobel Prize–winning economist Ronald Coase developed a unique perspective that changed the way economists think about the nature of goods that have both negative and positive externalities. In his paper "The Problem of Social Cost," Coase did not see problems such as pollution, the overgrazing of public lands, or reclining seatbacks as the inevitable result of the nature of the good itself or of people being inherently selfish.[2] Coase saw the crucial problem as one of a lack of ownership. The problem with reclining seatbacks from Coase's perspective is that no one owns the space in back of a seat. Both the person sitting in the front and the back seats have a competing claim to those four inches of space that they cannot both use at the same time. As a result, they will compete over this space in ways that will not be beneficial for everyone involved. For example, maybe I will recline my seat, not because I want to, but because I am forced to because the person in front of me is reclining their seat. Likewise, maybe I value the space in front of me much more than the person ahead of me values their ability to recline; in this case, they should be able to trade me that space— for compensation—and make both of us better off. But you can't trade things that you don't own—that is the crux of the problem according to Coase.

Coase's fundamental insight was to see that for goods with positive and negative externalities, markets cannot work efficiently because there is a failure to properly assign rights and responsibilities. In other words, positive and negative externalities exist when the proper institutions—of which property rights are a big part—are not in place. If the property rights for the space in back of the airplane seat were explicitly owned by either the person in the front or the back, then this space would become a private good because it would now be excludable. Once the space is privately owned, people would then have incentives to explore whether there are mutually advantageous trades that could make both the back and front passengers better off. According to what is known as the Coase theorem, assets will flow to their highest-valued uses as long as people can make such trades. But trading is contingent on someone owning the property right to the resource being traded. Without property rights, it is impossible for markets to work because no one owns these goods that could be traded to everyone's benefit.

Let's leave airplane seats for a moment and talk about another real-world application of the Coase theorem: efforts to reduce carbon emissions through "cap and trade" programs (which have been adopted in Europe and California). Airborne carbon, like many other forms of pollution, is a classic example of a negative externality associated with a public good. In this case, the public good is the atmosphere. Because everyone owns the atmosphere, no one owns the atmosphere, so people and firms have been free to pump carbon into it, greatly contributing to global warming. This includes tourists who can freely produce carbon with impunity while traveling. Applying the Coase theorem, a solution to this problem is to create a carbon emission permit program that explicitly requires firms to own the carbon they produce and purchase permits to emit this carbon into the atmosphere. Once the property rights for carbon have been established, mutually beneficial trades can take place. Under a cap and trade program, governments put a cap on the overall amount of carbon it is going to allow firms to release in the atmosphere by limiting the total supply of permits. These permits can now be bought and sold, creating a market for them. The firms that are most likely to purchase these permits are those that find it costliest to avoid emitting carbon. (Some of these firms are likely to be transportation firms, such as airlines, who will then pass these higher costs along to passengers, forcing passengers to also incorporate the costs of the carbon we produce in our decision making.) On the other hand, firms that find it relatively inexpensive to avoid emitting carbon are incentivized to do so in order to avoid having to purchase permits.

The beauty of a cap and trade system is that it provides market incentives for firms that can most cheaply reduce emissions to play the largest role in reducing emissions. This lowers the total costs of reducing carbon emissions for society as a whole. The problem is that global warming is not just a local but a global problem, meaning that unless all countries can be forced to take ownership of the carbon they produce, then individual countries have the incentive to free-ride off the carbon reductions made by other countries. But the key, as identified by Coase, is making sure someone owns the carbon problem, and then using the power of markets to minimize the costs of solving the problem.

This same thinking can be applied to airplane seatbacks, although the problem here is much simpler because it involves only two people—not everyone on the planet as in the case of carbon emissions. The problem with airplane seats is that no one really owns the space in back of any seat. While airplane seats are capable of reclining without the permission of the backseat passenger, backseat passengers can purchase devices (such as the "Knee Defender") that can be can hooked to their tray table that prevent the seat in front of them from reclining, allowing them to recapture (or steal, depending upon your perspective) that space. When passengers have used such devices on their flights, the resulting disputes have not only made everyone more uncomfortable, but have actually resulted in planes making unscheduled stops to discharge unruly passengers.[3] Coase's solution to dealing with these potential disputes is to assign property rights to this space and then explore the possibility that mutually beneficial trades between the front and back passengers can be negotiated. The key insight of the Coase theorem, however, is that it doesn't matter who actually is given the property rights to this space from the perspective of society as a whole. The person who values the space the most will get it. The only difference is who pays and who receives a payment for the space.

For example, consider a situation in which the back passenger values this space more than the front passenger. In this case, if the back passenger is granted the property right to the space, then no transfer of money will take place, but if the property right is granted to the front passenger, money will then change hands because the back passenger should be willing to pay the front passenger enough to allow a mutually beneficial trade of the space to take place. Regardless of who owned the space in the first place, the front passenger will not be reclining and the back passenger (who values it the most) gets to enjoy the space. On the other hand, if the front passenger values this space more, then money will change hands if the property right is granted to the front passenger, and no exchange will occur if granted to the back passenger. But in either scenario, the front passenger (who values the space the most) will be reclining. Because the person who values the space the most is always able to use it, the total gains from trade are maximized.

Now, you might be thinking: Coase won a Nobel Prize for thinking that the world would be better off if people bargained over reclining seatbacks prior to the departure of the airplane? Isn't boarding an airplane already chaotic enough, what with everyone trying to get on and off first and attempting to jam obscene amounts of carry-on luggage into the overhead luggage space? (By the way, carry-on luggage is another example of a failure to properly assign property rights to airplane space. I recently witnessed an example of this at the end of a 16-hour flight when a slap fight in the aisle next to me occurred as passengers were attempting to get off a plane. A woman somehow managed to bring two steamer trunks as her single carry-on, and then she and her husband tried to push their way to the front of the plane to be the first off, despite the fact that they were seated in row 52. One older gentleman didn't like this and assigned the husband the "property right" of his right hand across the queue jumper's face. I don't think he was thinking about the Coase theorem as he did this, however.)

Well, Coase actually agreed that applying his theorem in many real-world situations would often be difficult. The Coase theorem is an interesting idea in theory, but in practice there are two problems that must be overcome for it to actually work. First, there can't be any barriers to negotiation, such as legal prohibitions or social norms. The airlines would likely have sound legal grounds, given current law in most places, to prohibit passengers from reselling the space in back of their seats in secondary markets. The social norm against haggling in many developed countries, discussed in Chapter 7, would also be a significant barrier to negotiation between passengers. In addition, there is also an issue with social norms regarding what is perceived as fair when it comes to making trades. If you remember the ultimatum game from Chapters 2 and 5, people often punish other people, at a cost to themselves, by not making mutually advantageous trades if they think that some part of the trade violates their idea of fairness. As we discussed before, punishment is one important way in which injunctive social norms become *de facto* social norms within any community. If airplane passengers consider it unfair to pay another passenger for space that they do not believe is theirs, then they may walk away from all trades, even trades that would benefit everyone. Our social norms of fairness can be a significant barrier to applying the Coase theorem in practice. If you don't believe this, think about what your initial reaction might be if the next time you get on a plane, someone turns around as says "Give me 50 bucks or I am going to push my seat all the way back as soon as I can."

The second friction that throws a monkey wrench into the Coase theorem is the transaction costs associated with bargaining. When it is difficult to bargain because of the time involved, there is pressure to complete the negotiation swiftly, or if people lack information about the other party that they are dealing with—in other words, all of the things we discussed in Chapter 7 that make haggling and bargaining difficult—then the benefits from assigning property rights and making trades can quickly be swamped by the transaction costs involved. When transaction costs are relatively large, as they would be in negotiating seatback space during the boarding process, the default position is that no trade takes place and the party that is assigned the property right always keeps it.

When transaction costs are high or there are barriers to negotiation, Coase argued that the best outcome for society is that the rights to the resource should be assigned to the party who typically values it the most. In the case of seatback space, it is unclear who actually does value this space the most, the front or the back passenger. However, the fact that airlines discourage the use of the Knee Defender and have adopted the default position that the front passenger ultimately gets to decide whether or not to recline their seat suggests that the airlines believe that the passengers value their own reclining more than they are harmed by other passengers reclining.

In an interesting trial of how Coase-style pricing for seat reclining might work, two law professors conducted an online experiment attempting to identify the value that front and back passengers place on the space in back of their seats.[4] Their results suggested that front passengers in the experiment demanded an average of at least $41 to give up the right to recline, while back passengers were only willing to pay up to an average of $18 to prevent reclining. These numbers suggest that few mutually beneficial trades would take place given that front passengers appear to value the space the most and are the *de facto* owners of it.

In order to test the Coase theorem, the professors reran the experiment, but this time assigned the property right to the back passenger. The previous results would suggest that if the Coase theorem is correct, many trades would now take place because the front passengers who valued the space more would have to pay for it. But, in fact, now that back passengers owned the space, they demanded an average of at least $39 to give it up, while front passengers were only willing to pay a maximum of $12 to recline. These results run counter to the Coase theorem, which predicts that prices should remain the same regardless of who owns the good.

How do we explain why the price that this space is valued at changes simply because of who holds the property right? The answer likely lies in behavioral economics, which we discussed in Chapter 7. Specifically, ownership bias (the price to give something up once we own it is greater than the price we are willing to pay to buy it back if we don't) and loss aversion bias (paying feels bad more than receiving feels good) may explain why passengers overvalue what they have and are reluctant to pay for what they don't have. Together, these behaviors create a status quo bias that prevents trades. There may also be framing bias going on, in that the participants of the survey might have had difficulty in actually setting a monetary value on the space in the absence of other relative prices to compare it with. When the authors offered participants $8 in cash or airplane snacks in order to sell their rights to the seatback space, roughly two-thirds of the front and one-third of the back passengers accepted, despite the fact that this compensation was significantly less than their previous demands. It appears that once a concrete value was placed in people's minds that was less abstract than "four inches of room," people were much more likely to make a trade. Taken together, these results suggest that behavioral economics may have more to say about how we as passengers actually think about our cramped travel spaces than the Coase theorem.

However, despite its limitations, understanding the Coase theorem remains very important to understanding many aspects of the economics of travel. Let me briefly offer some other examples. The management of wildlife in Africa has always been extremely challenging because of the huge amount of space that its large animals need. The problem with government-managed game parks is that the tragedy of the commons threatens the wildlife in these parks in two ways: first, through excessive tourism and overcrowding, and second, through the poaching of wildlife by locals. One solution adopted throughout Southern Africa is to instead create privately managed game parks: local populations are given property rights to the wildlife and the land that comprises the park, and also play a role in running the game park. By attracting outside capital and expertise in managing these parks, the local populations can gain employment opportunities and share the profits created by local tourism. Through granting the local population property rights, private game parks help ensure that local populations are invested in sustainably managing their

An Indian rickshaw where the seatbacks do not recline.

natural resources and are making trades that allow everyone to share in the benefits of their public good. In some sense, what these game parks have done is make lions and elephants more like cows—animals that grant their owners recurring benefits over long periods of time. Cows are not on any endangered species lists for just this reason.

The Coase theorem can also help us understand why people's conception of personal space differs so much across countries. As illustrated in this picture, or in pictures of the incredible overcrowding on Indian trains, the average Indian has a much more limited requirement when it comes to the amount of personal space they expect when traveling, and they certainly don't demand that their seat backs recline in their rickshaws or their trains. One way to think about these differences in *de facto* social norms regarding personal space is that in the presence of so many people in a limited amount of space, the transaction costs and complexity of negotiating for a little bit of elbow room are prohibitively large in India. As a result, social norms have had to adjust to these realities in order to avoid endless conflict. The conception of a generous amount of personal space as a social property right has never been established in India as it is in other areas of the world where space is at less of a premium. From a Western perspective, this leads to suboptimal outcomes when it comes to sharing public space (I still have a crimp in my neck years later from the cramped nights I spent folded into Indian trains).

The Coase theorem argues that if property rights can be assigned appropriately, we can maximize the social benefits associated with goods that have externalities. However, the Coase theorem has nothing to tell us about the biggest difficulty in actually assigning these property rights, which is that this must be done as part of both a legal and political process. Setting property rights is almost always contentious because of the special interest politics involved. We have previously talked about a number of instances in which special interests prohibit the optimal assignation of property rights in regard to traffic (Chapter 2), taxes and public infrastructure (Chapter 4), and patent trolling (Chapter 6).

One advantage of having a stronger central government (at the expense of less inclusive politics) is that it becomes easier to avoid the messy politics that accompany assigning property rights to public goods, which keeps the transaction costs associated with negotiating compensation low. For example, in China it is a lot easier for the government to gain access to land for public infrastructure projects through the use of *eminent domain* than it is in India. Stories of the years spent negotiating with farmers in India over the sale of both formally and informally held land are easy to contrast with the situation in China, in which the government owns all the land and can break leases and force people to move with impunity.

What is gained in efficiency in China, however, is paid for in the unfairness of the process. While certainly not inclusive and often exploitive, China's ability to clearly define property rights and reduce the transaction costs involved, in contrast with India, has contributed to its higher growth rate over the last generation.

Recreational travel was rare prior to the 1800s. Before this, travel was mainly for trade, pilgrimages, medical treatments, and education. Tourism as an industry really began in the mid-1800s with the growing popularity of the "Grand European Tour" among the upper class and educated, such as the one undertaken (and lampooned) by Mark Twain in *The Innocents Abroad*. In the 20th century, mass tourism grew in conjunction with the development of the necessary transportation infrastructure and factors that increased the demand for travel: higher incomes, more leisure time, immigration (and return travel to visit home), and higher educational levels. Today, tourism (both business and recreational) accounts for 9.8 percent of global GDP and more than 280 million formal sector jobs.[5] These jobs exist across many sectors of the economy, including transportation, accommodation, tourist attractions, restaurants, shopping, and public sector support (roads, safety). In some countries, tourism plays an even larger role. Tourism directly accounts for between 20 and 30 percent of GDP in many Caribbean countries and up to nearly 50 percent of GDP in the island gambling destination of Macau.

The tourism sector is also growing faster than most other segments of the global economy and will play an increasingly large role in future economic development. Projections are that the number of people residing in the middle class will double across the globe by 2030, and one of the first things they want to do with this newly earned income is travel. One of the most interesting aspects of traveling in a country with a fast-growing middle class is that you find yourself in the middle of their domestic tourism booms, allowing you to directly observe many people of all ages on their first real trip. In China, this is particularly striking. I have walked to the top of three of the five great mountains in China, each of which is regarded as holy and has been an important pilgrimage for emperors and other royalty for thousands of years. For me, much more fascinating than the scenery and the history was the opportunity to watch large groups of the vast new Chinese middle class scramble upward—the symbolism is perfect—in their high heels, flip-flops, and "Adidass" shoes along paths that not long ago were reserved only for only the privileged elite, but now are lined by souvenir shops and tea stands serving Coca-Cola. These mountain hikes perfectly encapsulate the incredible changes and contradictions that are at the heart of tourism and development.

The overall macroeconomic impact of tourism depends on the extent to which tourism spending creates a multiplier effect on GDP. The idea of spending multipliers has a long history in economics but is most closely identified with the great economist John Maynard Keynes. Keynes realized that any change in spending does not just stop there. New increases in spending create new income for others who then, in turn, spend some of this new income, and on and on. The end result is that the eventual change in aggregate spending and aggregate income (GDP) can be much bigger than the initial increase in spending.

Spending multipliers are at the heart of Keynesian theories of business cycles. Keynes believed that recessions are triggered by declines in spending spurred by pessimism and "animal spirits" that would then be magnified by the multiplier effect into large declines in GDP. To escape a recession, Keynes believed that it was the government's responsibility to spur spending during downturns and reverse the multiplier effect. Governments could attempt to do this through cutting taxes or increasing the money supply, but the problem with these approaches is that in order to have large multipliers, both of these solutions require people to spend in the midst of an economic downturn, just when people are most reluctant to do so. A better alternative, in the Keynesian view, is to have the government directly increase its spending in order to maximize the amount of new spending that takes place in the economy and the size of the positive multiplier. Exactly what the government spends its money on is less important than the fact that it spends it on something, kick-starting the positive multiplier and also sparking a rebound in economic optimism. According to one historian's description of Keynes, "The motive force of his life was that, if only human stupidity could be overcome, and pessimism eradicated, most of the world's evils were remediable."[6] Keynes's theory provided the economic rationale behind the New Deal public works projects in the United States during the Great Depression and also modern-day stimulus packages commonly adopted by countries during economic recessions.

Tourism spending has these same multipliers associated with it, although the net aggregate effect is complicated by the fact that tourism creates both positive and negative multipliers in any economy. To the extent that tourism creates an inflow of spending from those outside of the community or new spending by those within the community, it will create a positive multiplier that increases income. But when those in the community travel and spend outside of it, tourism can decrease spending and reduce local income. The net impact of tourism, then, is the balance between tourism inflows and outflows. In practice, the net impact of tourism inflows and outflows is difficult to identify and will obviously differ widely across countries based on the ability of people to get into and out of a country, as well as the local characteristics that attract or repel tourists. For example, cruiseship-based tourism is much less likely to have a large multiplier than immersion tourism, which relies on local goods and services. However, we can generally say that larger, more diversified economies are more likely to enjoy net inflows from tourism because they have more varied goods and services, a wider variety of attractions, and are able to offer more domestic travel experiences for their citizens. That said, the countries with the largest levels of net inflows tend to be small, island nations that have almost completely specialized in attracting foreign tourists (such as the Caribbean Islands or Macau).

There is a crucial trade-off at the heart of tourism-led development. Because tourism is a public good, it is vulnerable to the tragedy of the commons. If the only objective is to maximize the macroeconomic impact of tourism, then too much tourism will take place, ruining the experience for most tourists and, even more importantly, the tourist destinations themselves. This is an especially large concern in countries where tourism is crucial to the economy but limited to a small number of attractions. Everyone who visits Peru wants to visit Machu Picchu, leading to thousands of visitors a day, crumbling trails, and deforestation that threatens its future existence. The same holds in Tanzania, where every visitor wants to hike to the top of Mt. Kilimanjaro despite the fact that it is already overcongested and is becoming the world's highest street market.

How can we balance the needs of economic development versus the protection of these valuable natural resources? Once again, the Coase theorem can help. Visitors need to be held economically responsible for their impact on the destinations that they visit by assigning them property rights—in this case, property responsibilities. One way to do this is to require visitors to pay taxes and fees that correspond to the costs that they create in terms of congestion and deterioration of the site. Another solution is cap and trade: limit the number of permits granted to visit a site, sell these permits to travel companies, and then allow Coase-style bargaining to take place so that those who value a visit the most can purchase one of the limited number of slots available. Either of these solutions—taxes or cap and trade—will reduce the number of tourists in the short run, but hopefully lead to more tourists in the long run by creating resources to preserve the site that will allow it to become more sustainably visited. By applying one of these Coase solutions, countries can balance the needs of locals to have more economic opportunity today versus the necessity of preserving these sites for both current and future travelers. (Of course, in order to apply these policies properly, countries also have to have responsible governments with quality institutions so that these taxes or permits are not turned into just another opportunity to leverage greater corruption or divert resources to other wasteful spending.)

Having talked about the spending impacts of tourism, the largest economic impacts of travel are likely to be more indirect and more interpersonal. Travel not only improves the quality of our lives and makes us better people, but it also improves the productivity of our economic interactions. Travel contributes to greater leaks and matches of ideas and helps create networks of people that spur technological development and economic growth (Chapter 6). Travel encourages cultural diversity within countries, making us more educated about those around us and broadening our perspective so that we each can become more insightful and productive (Chapter 5). Travel can contribute to better institutions by encouraging the sharing of examples of what works and what does not work in government, and also by promoting more social and political stability (Chapters 3 and 4). And in every chapter of this book, I have argued that travel is a great way to learn about economics, and learning about economics is the first step in applying its lessons to improving every aspect of our lives, economic and otherwise.

What about the impact of tourism on local employment? Tourism has the potential to create jobs and raise wages in every sector of the economy, and here's why. Tourism tends to be more service-based, more labor-intensive, and more reliant on specialized labor with marketable skills than most other industries. For example, many hospitality workers need English language skills, specialized business education, guide training, etc., in order to perform their jobs. This is true up and down the employment ladder, from the manager of a high-end game lodge to cabbies and hawkers interacting with tourists on the street. As a result, wages in tourism jobs tend to be higher than average wages, particularly so in poorer countries. But these effects are not limited only to the tourism sector. The demand for skilled workers in tourism tends to put upward pressure on wages in other sectors of the economy, particularly for skilled labor. As we have talked about repeatedly, rising wages are an important spur to economic growth, and vice versa. The Catch-22 of development is that low wages lead to using lots of labor and too little capital, which keeps the productivity of labor and wages low (see Chapter 3). To the extent that the growth of tourism within a country can increase wages and incentivize investment in capital, developing a tourism industry can be an important first step for less developed countries in escaping from the poverty trap associated with labor-intensive, low-wage, undercapitalized economies.

Is it possible to make a clear distinction between tourism jobs that provide needed employment at reasonable wages and jobs that exploit local labor? Consider the much publicized case of the Himalayan Sherpa, who are paid roughly $400 a month to haul gear at great personal risk (more than 12 times the fatality rates of U.S. soldiers in Iraq) for foreign climbers who pay more than $60,000 for the opportunity to reach the top of mountains such as Mt. Everest.[7] On one extreme, market fundamentalists argue that these Sherpa are acting in their own self-interest and voluntarily choose this work, meaning that it must be beneficial for them relative to their other employment options. Guide jobs provide these Sherpa with much needed opportunities to gain valuable experience and develop important skills that they can eventually use when they move to other safer and more lucrative jobs. On the other hand, there is a good argument to be made that the labor markets in these countries, particularly for dangerous jobs such as mountain guiding, are in no way competitive, efficient, or fair. The limited number of guiding businesses act like monopolists in the market, using their power to depress wages. Also, workers often have incomplete information about what will be expected of them and how dangerous the work is that they will be required to do. Finally, we know from behavioral economics that people have many biases—including an overconfidence bias in which we overstate our own abilities, and a present bias in which we discount the future too heavily—that employers can exploit to convince workers to accept wages that don't fully compensate guides for the value of their work and the risks that they take.

There is no simple and consistent answer about what is a fair wage because fairness is a socially constructed notion based on local injunctive and *de facto* norms. However, there are two crucial practices that every traveler who worries about the treatment of tourism workers should follow. The first is to find out everything about the businesses that you will be working with on your travels before you leave and ask them about the ways workers are treated and the wages they receive. Travel guidebooks are increasingly investigating the employment practices and environmental impact of the travel businesses they recommend, and they are a good place to start.

The other option is simpler: tip generously! Many people argue that the purpose of tipping is to create an incentive for workers to provide better service. In practice, it doesn't work this way. Tipping is usually given after the service is provided, and workers have no idea about how they will be compensated for their hard work before they actually provide it, making it a very weak incentive. Instead, I think that there are two better economic justifications for tipping. The first is that tipping is an opportunity for you to pursue your definition of fairness and share some of the surplus that you gain from your tourism trades. If you feel that you got a good deal, meaning you think that the price you paid was significantly greater that the benefits of experiences you gained, share some of this windfall with the local workers you come in contact with. Generous tipping is a great way of ensuring that your travel is always a mutually beneficial experience for everyone.

The second economic justification for tipping is that if we care about the well-being of the people we meet on our travels, then the better off they are, the more this creates a positive externality for us. In other words, the welfare of the people we meet while traveling can itself become a public good. And as such, like any public good, we should subsidize the well-being of local workers through our tipping. We travelers should listen to Coase and assign some of the property rights for the welfare of local workers to ourselves, and with these rights comes the responsibility to make sure that they are adequately compensated through our tipping.

Is it possible that being a tourist destination is less of a blessing than it first appears and could even become a curse? The destinations that people want to visit can be thought of as a natural resource, and economists have long recognized that there is the possibility of a resource curse. A resource curse exists when having abundant amounts of scarce natural resources—such as minerals, energy, and even tourist attractions—actually hinders economic development instead of encouraging it, as simple intuition would suggest.

Why would the gift of abundance be bad for economic growth? There are a number of possible reasons. One is the problem of excessive specialization at the cost of diversification. In many countries where income can be easily generated by drilling in the ground or selling visitor permits, there are few incentives to diversify and make the investments needed to broadly increase productivity and become more competitive across a wide variety of industries. This often leaves resource-intensive economies vulnerable to shocks in the particular industry they specialize in. For example, most energy-intensive economies in the Middle East are vulnerable to fluctuations in highly volatile energy markets because they have never made the investments needed to compete in other industries. The same holds for mineral-dependent Sub-Saharan African countries, where 42 percent of gold reserves, 50 percent of diamonds, and 80 percent of platinum reserves are located—and this is only what has been discovered, as Africa contains the world's least explored regions.[8] Likewise, countries that are tourism-centric, such as in the Caribbean, are vulnerable to economic downturns in the countries from which their visitors originate, such as what occurred in 2009 when the Global Financial Crisis in the United States led to debilitating recessions across the Caribbean.

The resource curse can also result from a phenomena known as *Dutch disease*. The moniker "Dutch disease" refers to the discovery of a huge natural gas field in the Netherlands in 1959. The ensuing boom in natural gas exports that resulted from this newfound abundance led to a huge appreciation of the Danish krone, making other Danish exports too expensive to compete on international markets, while also making imports much cheaper. Over time, the increasing specialization of the economy in energy occurred at great cost to its export economy, particularly its more labor-intensive manufacturing sector, and led to long-lasting unemployment in the country. Tourism booms can create similar exchange rate appreciations that reduce the international competitiveness of other domestic industries.

One final source of a resource curse is that having resources which are easily controlled by centralized authorities and elites can eventually do harm to economic institutions. As discussed in Chapter 4, institutions are most likely to be productive and encourage economic growth when they effectively balance two competing objectives: (i) centralize power in the hands of government so that it can enforce laws and policies that provide for the public good, but also (ii) allow citizens to retain enough power to constrain elites from co-opting government for their own individual benefit. It is a difficult balance to maintain, and having abundant resources that can be leveraged by elites with either military or economic power to gain more power often skews this balance in favor of autocrats and dictators. Hence, oil-rich countries in the Gulf are led by sheiks, mineral-rich central African countries are often ruled by military dictators, and banana-republic autocrats were common until recently in Central America. In these cases, the benefits from the natural resources that the country owns only flows to a small number of elites, making them stronger and creating a vicious circle of power that limits overall economic opportunity.

The resource curse is not an iron law. There are countries with abundant natural resources in energy, minerals, and tourism—such as Norway or Botswana—who have been able to put their natural wealth to good use toward building better institutions that have fostered wider economic development. But these exceptions illustrate the primacy of institutions in creating economic success, and not the necessity of resources. Botswana and Norway each had productive institutions before their natural resources were discovered, and as a result they were able to avoid the power grabs that often occur with easy wealth, and have managed the problems of diversification and Dutch disease through prudent macroeconomic management.

Macau: The tourism capital of the world (in terms of percent of GDP).

Many other countries have not been so lucky and have seen weak institutions leading to the wasting of resources and the worsening of institutions. For example, the tiny island of Macau is the most tourism-dependent country in the world because of its unique history and geography. A one-time colony of Portugal (today it is a special administrative region of China, similar to Hong Kong), Macau became, and remains, a tourist haven because of its legalized gambling and proximity to mainland China and Hong Kong. Today's Macau looks as if it was assembled from the pieces of completely different puzzles. The street signs are in Chinese, English, and Portuguese. Once-grand Christian cathedrals crumble next to makeshift Buddhist temples. Glitzy, million-dollar hotels and casinos rub against decrepit, European-style row houses on brick-lined, narrow lanes.

Macau is the richest city in the world in terms of per-capita income and has a gambling industry that is seven times that of Las Vegas. However, Macau also has one of the highest levels of income inequality in the world, with nearly one-fifth of its population living in poverty, and has an extraordinary level of corruption associated with organized crime and money laundering. Its tourist resources have been almost completely co-opted by elites, who have rigged the game so that they always win big pots, but have left most Macau residents bust.

While it may often be true that being blessed with tourism resources can harm economic institutions, in some cases it has also been true that poor institutions have created our most well-known tourist destinations. Dysfunctional institutions throughout history have turned some cities that were once economic power-houses into places so deserted that they were not to be rediscovered for hundreds and even thousands of years, such as the ruined Mayan cities in jungles throughout Central America, or the "lost city" of Petra in Jordan. Cities such as Venice, Alexandria, Damascus, Timbuktu, Baghdad, St. Petersburg, and Buenos Aires were once thriving economic centers, but after deterioration in their institutions for a variety of reasons, these cities have largely been left frozen in time and are now more attractive to travelers than to businesses.

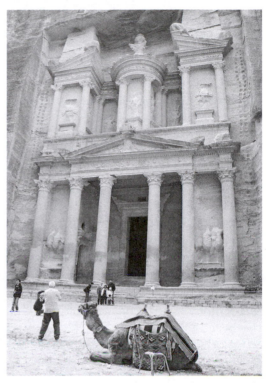

Petra: Former economic powerhouse made modern tourist attraction.

Another potential example of the tourism resource curse is foreign aid. The growth of foreign aid and the travel associated with it is a major proportion of the travel industry in some countries. In Afghanistan, where billions of foreign dollars have been spent to build public infrastructure over the last decade, the most significant lasting accomplishment has been the building of new airports, airlines, roads, armored automobiles, and chaperones designed not to serve most Afghanis, but to shuttle international aid workers and foreign officials around to "see the country." And while less egregious, the ubiquitous white Land Rovers with tinted windows favored by foreign aid agencies that you see throughout Africa (there are 600,000 foreign aid workers in Africa alone) are a constant reminder that a great deal of foreign aid goes to aid foreigners traveling in their countries.

In 2013, nearly $135 billion was spent on foreign aid in the form of grants, loans, technical advice, and debt forgiveness across the globe. This amount is more than the combined output of Africa's 20 poorest economies.[9] Foreign aid averages out to roughly $112 a year per person for the 1.2 billion living on $1.25 or less a day on the continent, or about 25 percent of the income of those living in extreme poverty. This $112 should seemingly make an important dent in reducing poverty if all of this money were directly given to the poor. However, Angus Deaton refers to this idea as the "aid illusion": the belief that we could get rid of global poverty if the rich were to just give a little more money to the poor.[10] The fallacy of the aid illusion is that aid does not magically end up in the pockets of the poor, and that the poor then have ready access to all of the things they need to improve their standards of living. In fact, most aid doesn't get to the poor, and even when aid does trickle down to them, the poor often don't have access to what they would like to buy with it, which is reliable health care, quality education, etc. It is similar to a fallacy that we have talked about throughout this book, which is the idea that getting richer is simply a matter of acquiring more capital. In fact, most aid is wasted or unproductive because many poor countries lack the complementary inputs needed to make aid truly effective: technology, skilled labor, public capital, and— by far the most important—institutions that provide people with the right incentives to use aid productively.

In reality, alleviating poverty is not the primary aim of most aid. Among the biggest recipients of U.S. foreign aid are Israel and Columbia, for reasons that have little to do with the poverty in these countries and much more to do with U.S. domestic interests. Afghanistan, Egypt, Turkey, Jordan, and Syria each get more foreign aid than the considerably poorer Bangladesh. Less than 50 percent of all foreign aid goes to the poorest 65 countries, while roughly 10 percent of foreign aid goes to developed countries.[11]

Most of the foreign aid that is targeted at poverty reduction is wasted because of the corrupt practices of local elites and government officials (see our previous discussion in Chapter 4). Foreign aid agencies do not give aid directly to people, but they work through elites in government and the private sector who often use this aid to centralize their power and worsen institutions. Foreign aid can become part of a vicious circle: the poorest, most corrupt countries need aid, but granting further aid only further weakens economic institutions and fosters a greater reliance on aid, keeping people in poverty and sustaining the need for more aid, etc., etc. Or, in the words of the economist Peter Bauer, "The argument that aid is indispensable for development runs into an inescapable dilemma. If the conditions for development other than capital are present, the capital required will either be generated locally or be available commercially from abroad to governments or to businesses. If the required conditions are not present, then aid will be ineffective and wasted."[12]

To connect this back to a previous discussion (from Chapter 7), one way to think about the problems with foreign aid is that donors face the problem of adverse selection: recipient countries always know more than donors about how any aid is going to be used, and as a result, the countries most likely to misuse aid are the countries that are most likely to request it. As a result, foreign aid does less good than it should, and less foreign aid is then provided.

Economists have been unable to consistently identify an empirical relationship between receiving more foreign aid and growing faster or reducing poverty—in fact, the best evidence suggests that receiving more foreign aid actually lowers economic growth.[13] Likewise, not receiving aid seems to be no major barrier to economic development. The countries that have been most successful at reducing poverty—China and India—have received very little foreign aid relative to the size of their populations.

Foreign aid providers have recently attempted to make future aid conditional on hitting targets and being sufficiently democratic, transparent, and market-oriented. But in practice, it is very hard to make aid conditional because it is hard for donors to say no. This is because of the legitimate empathy they feel for the poor, because they care about protecting their own bureaucratic influence, and because of the domestic political pressures that aid agencies face to "do something" about poverty. Even when certain aid agencies manage to say no to those countries that waste aid, some other donor agency often steps in to fill the gap, leaving many recipient governments and their elites unaccountable for their actions.

This is not to say that aid should never be given. Aid can help at the margin in countries with some semblance of productive institutions. The empirical evidence suggests that aid works best when it is a reward for having already adopted good policy, not as a carrot that fails to entice good policy.[14] Aid is often necessary during humanitarian emergencies, even if a huge proportion of the donations are wasted through corruption or ineffectiveness. And aid has been effective in one area: public health research directed toward single-disease programs (HIV, tuberculosis, smallpox, and malaria vaccination programs, for example). These programs have been effective for two reasons. First, because the challenges here are primarily scientific, not political (science is easy in comparison). And second, because much of the actual spending and research is done within rich countries with quality institutions. But aid for general health care outside of these big diseases often gets bogged down by local institutions like other forms of foreign aid.

As discussed before, a much more effective way to help the poor than foreign aid is to trade more fairly with less developed nations. The total costs of trade barriers set up to protect certain industries in developed countries, particularly in agricultural products such as cotton (see Chapter 6), far outweigh any foreign aid that these countries receive. Not only do these trade barriers price the products of less developed countries out of markets and reduce their income in the short run, but they also prevent the diffusion of technology and bar foreign capital flows that can contribute to sustainable growth in the long run.

Can a country build a tourism industry that can serve as a source of income growth and employment, and which maximizes the positive externalities created by the public goods tourism provides? Doing this requires the existence of productive economic institutions and efficient governments. It's no coincidence that the stable and effective democracy of Costa Rica was able to set aside 25 percent of its land for national parks and build a top-flight tourism industry that accounts for roughly 12 percent of its GDP.[15] In general, the productivity-enhancing policies that good governments follow in their pursuit of higher growth will also directly foster more tourism. Let me focus on two areas in which this is particularly true: public transportation and free trade.

In regard to public transportation, governments in most countries have been highly involved in developing rail, air, and road networks. Railroads and airlines in many countries are operated as state-owned enterprises (SOEs). Today there are nearly 150 government-owned (in part) national airlines. In many countries, private railroads and airlines are public monopolies protected through government-created barriers that block the entry of new firms or foreign competition. The argument for SOEs and public monopolies in transportation is that these are public goods that must be subsidized and protected in order to develop in a sustainable way given the free-rider problem. The problem with SOEs and public monopolies in practice, however, is that they are typically inefficient because they face no competition, leading to higher prices and lower-quality service. In smaller, isolated, and poorer countries, SOE transportation is probably unavoidable, and also why no one wants to fly Turkmenistan Airlines or Air Koryo in North Korea.

However, in countries with larger domestic markets where more competition is possible, deregulation and privatization have been very effective in increasing competition and productivity in the transportation industry. In the United States, regulations that allowed airlines to act like monopolies and coordinate prices were eliminated in 1978, setting the stage for the entry of new airlines, significantly lower prices for travelers, and, surprising to some people, more profitable airlines. Today, this same deregulation is occurring largely without government approval in the taxi industry thanks to Uber and similar applications that use information technology to gain entry into the previously government-controlled market for ground transportation. The booming popularity of Uber says a lot more than any economic study could say about the benefits of private competition in public transportation.

Governments can also play an important role in promoting tourism by adopting polices that free up both the movement of goods and the movements of people across borders. Tourism and economic development are most likely to thrive as countries adopt freer trade policies: ending controls on exchange rates and foreign capital, eliminating travel restrictions, improving the efficiency of visa issuances, minimizing licensing (for cabbies, travel guides, and travel agents), promoting social stability and safety, limiting corruption, and imposing only moderate taxation (particularly avoiding excessive arrival/departure taxes, visa fees, and bed taxes). In other words, get the incentives correct, and tourism development will occur along with overall economic development.

It is for these reasons that by any ranking of the most desired travel destinations, developed countries such as America, France, Britain, and Japan continue to dominate. I don't think that this is simply because people like to visit wealth—it's because people respond to incentives and want to visit places with quality institutions, just as they want to live in these same places. While we travel to experience difference, we also care about the quality of our experiences. This does not mean that every traveler demands complete comfort—in fact, many of us travel explicitly to be forced out of our comfort zone. But few of us will travel to places where we cannot walk the streets because of the danger involved, or we are likely to be extorted by a visa-granting bureaucrat, or we cannot count on the train running long enough to get us to where we want to go, or the departure tax makes us question why we ever arrived in the first place.

Looking to the future of tourism, we can assume that traditional tourist destinations such as Caribbean beaches, the Egyptian pyramids, Parisian museums, and the Italian countryside will all remain popular. But what are the new tourist destinations, and what do they tell us about the economics of travel? The best example of a modern travel destination that jumps to my mind is Dubai in the United Arab Emirates (UAE). The UAE is now the seventh richest economy in the world with a per-capital GDP of roughly $63,000 in 2014. It has become rich in large part because it has 10 percent of the world's oil reserves (sixth largest in the world) and 4 percent of the world's natural gas reserves; all of this for a small country of five million people, four million of whom are expatriates. But the UAE has also developed thanks to its free-market institutions that emphasize *laissez-faire* capitalism and offshore banking services for the rich and those looking to avoid government scrutiny.

In an effort to diversify its economy away from just oil and finance—and desperate to find some way to productively invest their oil revenues and the abundant credit in their booming banking system—Dubai pursed a seemingly unrealistic dream of becoming the playground of the Middle East. Despite being little more than a collection of Bedouin tents and mud shacks 50 years ago, Dubai has become home to the iconic *Burj Al Arab*, the world's second tallest hotel with the world's most expensive rooms (averaging $25,000 a night, with the cheapest room at $1,000 a night); *Burj Khalifa*, the world's tallest building; the Palm Island and The World projects, which consist of a vast network of man-made islands in the shape of a giant palm tree and the Earth; and also world-renowned airlines, shopping malls, and even indoor skiing. Despite a real estate bust during the 2009 Global Financial Crisis, Dubai has bounced back and remains one of the fastest-growing cities in the world with plans for new underwater hotels and a Disneyland-style theme park known as "Dubailand." In 2014, Dubai attracted more than 10 million visitors, making it the fifth most visited city in the world.[16]

The most dazzling aspect of Dubai is how new everything is—even the things that should be old. Every Arabian-themed village, oasis, palm tree, and souk market is new. Even the people are largely new, given that 80 percent of the population are expatriates. Dubai is not fake and it is not ironic—it is just more purposely designed than any other place in the world.

The biggest attraction of Dubai for most is the shopping: Its souks are full of hagglers and Chinese goods, and its luxury malls are full of designer blue jeans and perfume. Dubai has become the ground zero of global consumerism; it is the world's largest duty-free shop. The world-famous Dubai Mall feels like something that future archeologists might mistake for a temple.

Dubai's incredible inequality is largely hidden behind its lavishness. For tourists, UAE nationals, and a small number of elite expatriates, Dubai is one large luxury hotel. For the vast majority of Dubai's population that has migrated from all across South Asia—these are the workers who have done the construction and provide the housecleaning—Dubai offers employment and significantly higher wages than can be found at home. However, living in Dubai as a lower-level migrant extends few additional benefits and no protection. Most of these migrant workers have gotten to Dubai by signing up for what amounts to indentured servitude, receiving transportation and a stipend for their families back home in return for turning over their passports to their employers and working without recourse in Dubai for a prolonged period of time. So while Dubai has become a playground for tourists, it is also a vast, modern-day Dickensian poorhouse that requires its laborers to live in congested labor camps outside the city—camps that are not open to tourists. Dubai is a dream for local elites and lucky travelers, but also a harsh reality for the vast majority of the people who make Dubai a reality.

The fact of the matter is that Dubai represents a moral quandary at the heart of economics and the Coase theorem that we introduced in this chapter. By assigning property rights with brutal efficiency—only a small majority have them, but those who do can exercise them in a *laissez-faire* environment—Dubai has been able to build the remarkable public good of "Dubai"; it has achieved remarkable economic growth, and it has improved the welfare of its people. The problem is that many of the people who live in Dubai are not "its people." Maximizing total welfare is not the same as ensuring that it is equitably distributed. While economists have a lot to say about how to enlarge the size of the pie, we struggle in providing clear answers regarding how to divide it up fairly, because fair means very different things to different people and societies.

Regardless, Dubai appears to exemplify what many of our future travel destinations will be like; if so, the future looks more like Disneyland than Paris. South Korea is already planning on spending nearly $300 billion to build a new tourist city called "8city" that focuses on shopping, luxury, predictability, and replicability. Many people find Dubai-style tourism to be tasteless or exploitive, and see it as the result of a belief that homogeneity and development is preferable to humanity and sustainability. I find this tourist capital of modern capitalism to be a fascinating mix of contradictions and trade-offs, like many things in economics. Dubai is deeply traditional, culturally restrictive, economically open, yet highly planned. While Dubai seems different, it really is just like any other not-to-be-missed destination and another fascinating example of the many things that we love about travel wherever we go. It is a place to experience difference and the paradoxes that often accompany them; to observe firsthand people at both their best and their worst; and to enjoy pleasure-seeking while we gain some context that allows us to better appreciate the simpler comforts we enjoy when we return back home.

CHAPTER TEN

Coming Home

The real voyage of discovery consists not in seeking new landscapes, but in having new eyes.

—Marcel Proust[1]

We shall not cease from exploration, and the end of all our exploring will be to arrive where we started and know the place for the first time.

—T. S. Eliot[2]

There is a certain momentum to traveling that can make it difficult to stop. There is always another town to visit just down the road, a different vista just over this next ridge, one more border that could be crossed. In the movie *Vacation*, Chevy Chase captures the essence of this "quest for fun" by rhetorically asking "You don't want to see the second largest ball of twine on the face of the earth, which is only four short hours away?" There is always the potential for experiencing something life-changing if we can make it just a little bit further. Traveling can easily become the ultimate carrot on a stick, the lure of complete fulfillment always almost attainable. In the words of Susan Sontag, "I haven't been everywhere, but it is on my list."[3]

One of the contradictions at the heart of travel is that travel lures us away from home, but home is also something we spend a great deal of time and money trying to recapture while we are traveling. When we take a trip, we give up domestic comforts and go off to strange places with mysterious food, unusual people, and days spent in modes of uncomfortable transportation. How many hours of our travels are spent thinking about the coziness of our own bed, the particular brand of coffee we can only find at home, or what is going on in our favorite television shows? In fact, one of the newest trends in high-end luxury travel is for the super-rich to take their own beds, IT systems, and espresso machines along with them when they travel. I guess that home can be the biggest luxury of all. The fact that the allure of home shapes our travels to such an extent might make us question whether travel really changes us.

The writer Karen Blixen said about Africa that it "gives itself to you when you are about to leave."[4] This can be true of any travel destination. Often, we only gain knowledge from our travels once we have had a chance to get back to our comfortable surroundings and process our experiences. However, there is no guarantee that, along with an inflated credit card bill, you will receive "deeper understanding" at the end of a trip. Unlike most travel souvenirs, knowledge has to be worked for. So how can we make the most of what we have learned during our travels once we have come back? How can we make sure that leaving and coming back enriches our lives and makes us different from those that never left?

Maximizing the value of any trip requires travelers to create a structure to think about their experiences so that they can learn from them and then put this new insight to use at home. In this chapter, I would like to share the thoughts of other learned travelers on this subject and discuss why having a theory about the way that the world works—an economic theory or otherwise—allows one not just to see but to appreciate everything more deeply. Without a structure for seeing, there can be no critical thinking, no real observation, and thus no deeper understanding of what we observe during our travels or even the things that happen to us during our day-to-day lives.

As Proust says in the quote at the beginning of this chapter, one of the principal reasons for travel is to see the world with new eyes. Upon my return to Iowa after living abroad, I wondered "Why does everyone smile at me as they walk by?"; "Why aren't people driving faster when there is so much space that needs to be covered?"; and "Why is everyone always talking about the weather?" These things had not struck me as particularly unusual before I left, but they certainly did once I returned.

More importantly, traveling gives you a new perspective on yourself. Mark Twain—always the sharpest observer of human foibles—said that through travel "We see ourselves in a different light and can gain a new appreciation (or disgust) for ourselves. The gentle reader will never, never know what a consummate ass he can become until he goes abroad."[5] The self-reflection that accompanies thoughtful travel can spur self-improvement by broadening our perspective, showing us other ways of living, and—most importantly—developing empathy. Only by seeing our small place in this large and diverse world can we take the true measure of our own individuality and see how we can make a more meaningful contribution to those around us. Once again, Twain: "It liberates the vandal to travel—you never saw a bigoted, opinionated, stubborn, narrow-minded, self-conceited, almighty mean man in your life but he had stuck in one place since he was born and thought God made the world and dyspepsia and bile for his especial comfort and satisfaction."[6]

The simple act of traveling alone won't provide these new eyes and make you a better person. Some people move around but never open themselves to new experiences: There are reasons that there are McDonald's on the Champs-Èlysèes in Paris and Holiday Inns in Rome. Even for those of us hungry for local experiences, our journeys to new and much different places can amount to nothing more than baffling dissonance. We need a way to process and comprehend what we see on our travels in order to develop our intuition, lest our travels become just a random series of experiences and facts that we cannot connect in any sort of comprehensible way. Experiencing is not the same as understanding.

Your senses can provide you with facts, but these facts are only small glimpses of the wider picture of any place. To see the deeper reality and to gain wider understanding, you must first have a theory as to why these things are happening. What do I mean by a theory? I mean a set of preconceived propositions, assumptions, and ideas about the way the world works that serve as a lens through which you can bring into focus the fuzzy facts and bewildering experiences that you have while traveling. Having a theory allows you to interconnect information and interpret it in a systematic way. Having a theory requires you to do some thinking before you start looking, and it also requires you to think about what you have seen in order to actively evaluate whether what you have seen is consistent with your expectations. Having a theory about the way the world works is crucial to thinking more deeply and analytically about your experiences; it forces you to be a more active observer before, during, and after your travels. Having a theory is the way that you manage your experiences into a form in which you can grasp the fundamental forces at play and actually see what you might only notice.

The facts that Darwin learned during his travels on the HMS *Beagle* about the diversity of life and the regular shape of many Pacific coral reefs were only facts. They would have made no real contribution to the study of science or even to Darwin's own life if these observations had been left as jottings in a journal and samples in a museum. It was only when these facts were animated and invigorated with Darwin's theories about how to explain this diversity in life or the circular patterns of coral reefs that deeper understanding and real value came from Darwin's travels. On our own travels, using theory to filter our experiences can serve the same purpose.

Without the deeper thinking that comes with having and applying theories, we don't know what to look for or what to focus on as important and unimportant. A 1:1 map of the world would be useless in our travels—we need a wider perspective that allows us to focus on the most relevant factors. This is exactly what theory can provide: a version of reality that is scaled to our ability to comprehend reality. In physics, the universe in the absence of theory is too complicated and too enormous for us to distinguish between what is important from what is not, and observation alone fails to identify what specific information is crucial versus what is ancillary. It was only through the work of theoretical physicists such as Einstein that we have theories, such as relativity theory, that simplify reality and delineate exactly what is most important to look for in understanding the universe. In the words of the physicist Werner Heisenberg: "It is quite wrong to try founding a theory on observable magnitudes alone. . . . It is the theory which decides what we can observe."[7]

This doesn't mean that facts are less important than theory, just that facts are weak and lifeless in isolation. Facts need to be animated by theory if they are to become powerful. On the other hand, theory without facts—hypothesizing without testing—is at best foolish, and at worst can be outright dangerous. Ad-hoc theorizing without ever attempting to validate your beliefs has been behind the worst failed social experiments in human history.

Once again, Darwin provides a perfect example of why we need facts to inform our theory and theory to understand facts. From his journals, we know that Darwin didn't begin to contemplate his famously diverse finches until five months after his visit to the Galápagos. It then took him an additional five months to contextualize the facts that he gained from his travels using the lens of his evolutionary theory to see why what he observed in his finches was important. And all of this took place five years after he had read Malthus, which was the impetus that initially got him thinking about his theory of survival of the fittest. It's an excellent example of how theory leads to observation, which in turn leads to better theory. This is the process of building knowledge; it is also integral to developing a love of travel and benefiting from it.

One common misunderstanding is that theory only narrows a person's worldview and prohibits "outside the box" thinking. But how do you know what is outside the box if you don't first understand what the box is? Theory gives clarity to our thinking and defines its limits. When we observe facts that our theory cannot encompass, it is up to us to change the boundaries of our theories and make our boxes larger and more inclusive. This is how science advances.

Testing hypotheses under controlled environments is at the heart of the scientific method. In some disciplines, such as chemistry, controlled experiments are easier to run. In other sciences, such as astrophysics and economics, this is often hard to do, either because it is impossible to control for everything that needs to be controlled for or because it is impossible to re-create experiments once done. This is one of the big reasons why the study of economics, in particular, is so fraught with disagreement at its best, and outright idiocy its at worst. In the words of John Maynard Keynes, "It is astonishing what foolish things one can temporarily believe if one thinks too long alone, particularly in economics . . . where it is often impossible to bring one's ideas to a conclusive test either formal or experimental."[8]

As Keynes says, because economics is not an experimental science, it makes it all the more important that economists actively engage the world around them and use observation to inform their theory. All of the great economists that we have talked about in this book shared one great skill in common—they were careful observers who not only meticulously collected facts on their journeys, but actively attempted to integrate these facts in ways that they could use to directly test their theories. In the cases where the facts and theories diverged, theory was adjusted in order to strengthen its power of explanation and prediction. When asked about his tendency to change his economic theories over time, Keynes succinctly and powerfully (as usual) summed up the proper response: "When my information changes, I alter my conclusions. What do you do, sir?"[9]

In summary, travel is at the heart of good economics, and understanding economic theory can make us all better travelers who get more out of our experiences while improving our own lives, and the lives of others around us, for the better. Theories from other disciplines such as political science, anthropology, sociology, history, and the natural sciences can also achieve this, but I hope that I have convinced you that economic theory can do this particularly well. Having and using a theory is what separates the critical thinker from the passive spectator, the traveler from the simple tourist.

So what are the key aspects of economic theory that, once understood, will enhance your journeys and allow you to gain more knowledge from your experiences—knowledge that you can use at home or on the next trip? In this book, I have identified a few of the core economic concepts that can make you a more perceptive traveler and can turn you from a tourist (someone who sees what they know is there) into an explorer (someone who learns anew each and every day from what they see). Let me very briefly recap a few of these ideas here. I also want to connect these ideas to a few of the contentious public debates that are being held in my home of the United States in an effort to illustrate the insights that economic thinking can provide to everyday life even when you are not traveling.

Incentives

Economics is the study of how people respond to incentives, both financial and also social incentives. *It is the diversity in incentives that people face across cultures and countries that motivate the diversity in behavior across people, societies, and even in the same person over time.*

The most effective public policies are those that focus first and foremost on the incentives that exist at the individual level, not just the desired result policymakers would like to achieve. Most bad economic policy throughout history—in the United States and elsewhere—has tried to impose outcomes using a top-down approach, instead of incentivizing solutions from the bottom up. Unfortunately, both the right and the left have been guilty of ignoring incentives, whether it is the left trying to regulate full employment by imposing barriers to capital investment and innovation (ignoring the fact that this only makes labor less productive and incentivizes hiring less of it), or the right trying to impose social policies that are inconsistent with social norms.

Wealth and Poverty

Enormous disparities in standards of living, health, and the riskiness of people's lives can be attributed to differences in three factors: the quantity of labor, the quantity of capital, and the level of technology. *But of these three, it is the enormous power of small, sustained improvements in technology that are compounded over time—and the corresponding lack of sustained improvements in technology in poor countries—that explain most of the vast differences in incomes across countries.* In other words, our ability to satisfy our economic needs is not always a matter of having more resources; it is a primarily a matter of generating more ideas that allow us to use these resources more efficiently and produce more with less.

Many have bought into the fallacy that having more output is only a matter of having more inputs—this is the mistake of development policies (on the right and left) that have emphasized eliminating the investment gap as the best way of reducing poverty, but have ignored the costs to innovation of imposing trade barriers, or the costs of special interest politics that block new technologies.

Institutions

Labor, capital, and technology differ across countries because of the variety of institutions created by markets, societies, and governments that shape incentives and influence individual behavior in different ways. Productive institutions create incentives to engage in productive behaviors such as investing in education, physical capital, and particularly technology. *The incredible varieties of human behavior that we observe in the world are not created by our inherent dissimilarities but are the result of the diversity of our social environments, government policies, and the institutions that they create.*

Beware of any policy that is predicated on the belief that people are innately different, or that people lack the capacity to change their behavior when faced with a different set of rewards and punishments. Such policies—whether they are bans on the immigration of certain ethnic groups "who can never change" or laws aimed at regulating finance because bankers are "particularly greedy"—are not just discriminatory, they are uneconomical.

Descriptive and Injunctive Norms

Institutions and the different behaviors that they favor can create environments in many countries in which injunctive norms (how people should behave) are quite different from descriptive norms (how people actually behave), and it becomes socially acceptable for *de facto* behavior to significantly differ from *de jure* law. *Institutions will not be productive when societies do not promote cooperative behavior by failing to punish (socially or economically) those who engage in descriptive norms that differ from injunctive norms.* This often occurs in countries with historical legacies of conflict, rampant corruption, and political dysfunction that have created institutions that favor a few elites over the many.

Failing to understand the importance of social norms lies at the heart of the problem with pure libertarian policies supported by those on the far right (in terms of economic policy) and the far left (in terms of social policy). The fact of the matter is that true freedom is impossible. Not only do our actions directly impact each other, but together we influence the environment we live in by shaping social norms and institutions.

Labor Productivity

Countries are not poor and do not suffer from high unemployment because they have too many people. When the demand for labor is low relative to its supply, it is because the productivity of labor is too low to incentivize hiring more of it. *As a result, whenever labor is kept unproductive and cheap, it discourages businesses and governments from investing in the capital and technology needed to make labor more productive so that unemployment falls and wages can rise.* Unemployment is not caused by a surplus of people but by a shortage of capital, technology, and education created by unproductive institutions.

Both the left and the right have been guilty of thinking too much about labor supply and not enough about labor demand. Those who argue for banning immigration in the United States assume that immigration must reduce wages because it increases labor supply, but ignore the fact that these immigrants bring many forms of human capital, physical capital, and ideas that increase labor demand and increase wages. This is the same mistake made by population control proponents who focus on eliminating the surplus population by forcibly reducing its supply, not by incentivizing more employment and having fewer children by increasing labor demand.

Market Failure

It is not the size of government that matters; it is the quality of government that matters. Quality governments foster productive economic institutions when they correct for market failures, such as providing public goods or taxing and regulating behaviors that have negative consequences for the general public. While governments can correct market failures, it is also true that they are the source of many market failures through excessive regulation and promoting policies that favor the interests of a small number of elites. *The best governments build and protect competitive markets; the bad ones protect you from markets.*

This last sentence outlines the boundaries between which those on the political right and the left compete. A huge proportion of the political disagreements in the United States and elsewhere take place between those who think that taxes, regulation, and other market interventions are needed to make markets more competitive and prevent those with monopoly power or other forms of market power from exploiting everyone else (this is the "more government" position most likely taken by those on the left), and those who see these interventions as disrupting the functioning of otherwise well-functioning markets (this is the "less government" position taken by those on the right). The best economists serve as the referees of this contest, attempting to identify the crucial distinctions and make unbiased judgements with a subtlety that is sometimes misconstrued, often purposefully, by those firmly on one team or another.

Centralized Power and Pluralism

Quality governments are also able to maintain the difficult balance of building and maintaining centralized power, but then sharing this power by allowing a broad range of voices to be included in the decision-making process. Strong centralized governments are needed to build institutions that can deal with market failure and create social stability. But when strong governments are not pluralistic, it inevitably leads to extractive institutions: Elites that have few restrictions placed on their power consistently rig the rules of the game so that they always come out the winner. Because they are best at balancing these two objectives, democratic republics are the most conducive form of government for generating sustained economic growth.

As we see in the United States, however, democracy does not always guarantee a balance between centralized power and pluralism; in fact, as society changes, we are forced to continually recalibrate the scales in order to—hopefully—keep centralization and pluralism in balance. The resulting political debates are messy, and there is often no simple solution. In the United States, one of the important public policy debates is over whether there should be limits on the amount of money people can contribute to political campaigns. Those on the left argue that unlimited contributions are a megaphone for the voices of moneyed elites and tip the balance too far in the favor of centralized power. On the other hand, those on the right can argue that money is speech, and limits on speech are never pluralistic and might end up granting too much power to entrenched government elites.

Cultural Norms

Culture matters in economics because culture shapes institutions by molding injunctive norms and by influencing how societies enforce these norms to become descriptive norms. However, the idea that culture predetermines a society's path for development is contradicted by many examples to the contrary. *Good institutions that work in one country cannot simply be transplanted elsewhere, but instead institutions must evolve in unique ways that are consistent with local cultural norms if they are to be productive.*

A virtuous circle exists between culture and development: Cultural beliefs that encourage trust and individual initiative foster markets and economic development, while economic development encourages cooperation and wider social interactions that can help build trust and change cultural norms.

Public policy debates tend to emphasize the extreme positions that either culture defines economics (usually on the right) or that economics determines culture (usually on the left). As with most debates, the insistence of seeing things as a dichotomy only leads to simplistic thinking. Instead we should think of these as both true; that culture and economics are interdependent, and that productive cultures and productive economies can be self-reinforcing or self-defeating.

Technology

Sustained, compounded improvements in technology are the key to increasing productivity and economic growth. The production of new technology is inherently different than most goods because ideas are intangible, they are public goods, and they leak and match such that they do not experience the same drag of diminishing marginal returns as labor or capital. *The lack of technological diffusion in many poor countries says little about the ability of different groups of people to innovate; it says much more about their unproductive institutions that block the networking of ideas, and also their failure to provide legal systems that provide reasonable protections for intellectual property so that those who innovate can cover their fixed costs and profit from it.* The biggest barriers to economic development are the factors that make "liquid" information networks difficult to build: risky economic environments that keep businesses small and unspecialized, dysfunctional education systems, limited access to international markets, and excessive regulation by self-interested political elites.

Once again, both the right and the left in the United States tend to get this wrong. By thinking about innovation as only driven by the profit motive, the right ignores the costs of strict patent laws in blocking the networking of ideas as well as the importance of the government in developing and networking ideas through public goods such as basic research. On the other hand, granting monopolies via patent can be an important incentive to innovation, particularly when the private costs of research and development are large, and those on the left are mistaken if they think that we will always have more ideas if every idea—from new pharmaceutical drugs to new music—must be free.

Asymmetric Information and Adverse Selection

Specialization and trade are at the heart of economics, but many barriers to trade exist, such as the time it takes to negotiate trades or the lack of functional markets for some goods. *One of the most important barriers to trade is asymmetric information: the fact that sellers typically have better information than buyers, which leads to adverse selection, or the fact that bad goods (and unfair trades) can drive better goods out of any market. As a result, efficient trade is dependent on information sharing, gaining trust, and building a reputation.* Modern markets accomplish these things in many different ways, while traditional markets accomplish these things through haggling. Because of imperfect information, trade is also influenced by many physiological biases identified by behavioral economics that lead otherwise rational people to act "predictably irrational" and overemphasize the following: preexisting beliefs, recent information, avoiding losses rather than gains, irrelevant context, avoiding uncertainty, generalizing from small amounts of information, and their own self-confidence.

Trade is not a zero-sum game—except in our policy debates. Take, for example, the debate over free trade. Too many people on both sides of the ideological divide view trade as the equivalent to sharing the back seat of the car with your sibling—if I get more, you have to get less; I win only if you lose. Trade is not a nationalistic competition; it is a wonderful technology for turning what we have into what we want with the potential to make everyone better off.

Public Goods and the Coase Theorem

Public goods are integral to modern economies. The act of travel itself creates public goods. Like all public goods, travel destinations and tourism suffer from the tragedy of the commons and are often overused. Public goods related to tourism also suffer from the free-rider problem and are often underprovided. *Markets alone cannot adequately provide for public goods; the problem identified by the Coase theorem is that no one owns public goods because of a lack of property rights, and as a result people are not incentivized to consider the positive or negative externalities of their actions and how they impact others.* Good governments create productive institutions when they mitigate these externalities by properly assigning property rights through the law, by taxing and regulating activities with negative externalities, and by subsidizing (or directly providing) goods with positive externalities.

Here is another flashpoint for public policy debates. Those on the right say that governments too often try to turn private goods into public goods.

Health care insurance would be an example of a good that many conserva-
tives think would best be provided directly through markets, and argue
that by making health insurance a public good, the government has only
served to make it unnecessarily complex, inefficient, and expensive. Those
on the left would argue that thinking of health care as a strictly private
good ignores the many negative externalities (e.g., that the public inevitably
ends up paying for the uninsured in one way or another) and positive externalities (e.g., that public health programs such as vaccinations benefit the
community as a whole) that are associated with our health care system.

Natural Environment

Nature offers us many things that we inherently desire as humans but
that we have purposely abandoned as we increasingly rely on markets. This
includes the opportunities nature offers us to unspecialize in our work, to
engage in physical labor, to vacation from technology, and to enjoy risk.
Nature also poses economic challenges, particularly in terms of geography and climate, that can become important barriers to development in
poor countries with unproductive institutions and stagnant technology.
*Economics is not unnatural, and our deep connections to the natural world can-
not be treated as something separate from our economic thinking.*
Public policy debates surrounding the environment can be as brutal as
nature itself. Take global warming, for example. Those on the right clearly
see the costs of policies aimed at combating global warming, such as imposing carbon taxes, but less clearly see the costs of not doing anything about
it. For those on the left, the opposite is true. Because there is real uncertainty associated with the costs and the benefits of a global carbon tax, our
public debates over environmental policy quickly degenerate into an illustration of how quickly people can fall into the traps of confirmation bias,
overconfidence bias, loss aversion bias, risk aversion bias, availability bias,
attribution bias, contamination bias, and present bias. Unfortunately, the
loudest voices in these debates are also the best examples of how our
thinking about complex issues can be distorted by our preconceived biases
and are often not based on a careful weighing of the evidence.

Theory and Observation

*Becoming a real traveler, as well as a real economist, means that we must
sharpen our awareness by applying theory, not just by relying on intuition, because
theory is crucial to knowing what to look for as well as to understanding what
you see.* A grasp of economics—particularly in becoming aware of all of

the ways that incentives shape our behavior that we have talked about in this book—fosters and grounds our intuition. It allows us to more carefully weigh evidence and do what F. Scott Fitzgerald considers the true test of a first-rate intellect: "to hold two opposing ideas in mind at the same time and still retain the ability to function."[10] This is exactly the trait that is lacking from most of our ideologically driven political debates in the United States, or political diatribes as they might more accurately be called. Economic theory not only makes us more perceptive about public policy debates, but it also deepens our insight and appreciation of the differences we observe while traveling. Having an understanding of economic theory gives travelers a way to interpret and process what they experience, and allows a tourist to become an explorer.

These 13 takeaways may be too many to remember for long after you have finished this book, but all of these fundamental ideas from economic theory have one insight in common: *people respond to incentives, and careful observation coupled with a healthy dose of critical thinking about how people might possibly respond to these incentives allow us to better understand—if not always predict—human behavior.*

Consider the following quote from the Nobel Prize–winning economist George Stigler (1962): "A logician is a wondrous creature, but he cannot distinguish between the two simple errors: If A = B, and B = C, then (1) A = 1.01C and (2) A = 10^{65}C. An *economist* can."

Stigler is getting at the heart of what this book is about. Economists cannot simply be mathematicians because people do not behave according to algorithms. Economics will never be the predictive science that mechanical physics is. But those of us who have learned how to think like an economist can provide generalized but important insights into human behavior. More importantly, as Stigler emphasizes, we can separate statements that are approximately correct from those that are outright false. We can distinguish simplification and generalization from BS. We can recognize that there are concrete things that can be done to change incentives and improve the quality of life for those who live in poverty, and reject the idea that people are poor because they are different or that they deserve it. We can rebuff arguments based on the nature of those who are different from us and critically think about the ways that different incentives nurture diversity. Most importantly, we can observe more and we can critically analyze what we see so that we can gain a deeper understanding and a richer appreciation of the real beauty of the wonderfully complicated world we live in.

The knowledge that can be gained through a basic understanding of economics is useful during your travels, but as I hope I have illustrated with my brief survey of U.S. political debates, can also be applied at home to other journeys of the mind. Just looking around your own room and out your own window can be enough of an adventure for a dedicated observer. In *Voyage around My Room*, the Frenchman Xavier de Maistre became an explorer of the most accessible type when he was placed under house arrest after taking part in a duel in 1790.[11] Stirred by his love of adventure and travel, de Maistre attempted to accomplish what he could in a pair of pajamas. He saw himself as a pioneer for those too poor, too indolent, too sick, or too frightened to leave home. Less than humbly, he declared: "Thousands of people who, before I came along, had never dared to travel, and others who had not been able to, and yet others who had never even dreamed of travelling, will be emboldened to do so by my example. Would even the most indolent of men hesitate to set off with me in search of a pleasure that will cost him neither effort nor money?" Filling his book with observations about his sofa, his feet, his bed, and the sunsets he watched through his window, de Maistre illustrates how through careful observation and a theory of life—that everything is potentially interesting and nothing is too insignificant to ignore—even the mundane can become informative. He brought the most important thing needed for any trip—a mindset of receptiveness and curiosity—home.

As I mentioned before, having lived abroad for a period of time, I observed a number of things that struck me as odd once I returned home to Iowa that I had never noticed before. Luckily, I had some economics at hand to help me understand, or at least think, about these phenomena. Why are people so friendly in Iowa? Maybe all of the smiles are our way of building trust and overcoming the transaction costs created by a lack of information and the challenges of adverse selection; these smiles might be indicative of one of the reasons Iowa generally works well and has productive institutions. Maybe people are so polite in Iowa for the same reason that Iowans drive so slowly: because Iowa is a more cohesive society where deviations from the injunctive norms of politeness and following the rules are more likely to be punished, making descriptive norms closer to injunctive norms. It is also possible that Iowans drive slowly because there are so many million-dollar tractors clogging the road, a testament to the high productivity of agricultural labor in the state.

Why do people talk about the weather so much in Iowa? Possibly because, as behavioral economics would suggest, people overreact to uncertainty (and if there is anything in this world that is truly uncertain, it is the weather in Iowa). Iowans might also talk about the weather as a way to affirm their connection to nature, which is important in an agricultural state that is also very much a part of the global economy. Talking about

Iowa: Where we talk about the weather a lot.

the weather is also a way for Iowans to connect with each other, and the conversations we have on sidewalks and grocery stores are just a few of the myriad of formal and informal networks through which people interact, allowing ideas to better leak and match. Our Iowan obsession with the weather is also a reminder of the importance of geography and the role it plays in shaping economics and society in general. Finally, these observations about Iowa also illustrate to me how local cultural norms still exist, and globalization does not mean the end of cultural diversity. As Eliot says in the quote at the beginning of this chapter, it was only at the end of my exploring that I knew the place I call home for the first time.

In thinking about these questions of what makes Iowans different, I may not have the right answers, but I have a way to think about them that makes me appreciate home and maybe understand it a little better. This is exactly the point of learning to use economic theory.

I hope that after reading this book from the comfort of your living room (or wherever you are reading this), you too can now see the world around you with new eyes. I believe that even a rough understanding of the simple economic concepts that we have discussed here can help you to better understand the differences between the people and places you witness during your journeys, near or far. You can appreciate why being poor is not a function of innate nature and ability, but much more about the incentives that surround us. You can understand why 10 men are needed to move a ladder in Nepal. You can explain why autocracy leads to more dangerous driving. You recognize how paying nothing for a farm is linked to paying $50 billion for a bus ride. You see why a culture that creates trust is more important than trusting explanations that always appeal to cultural differences. You comprehend why poverty is both a trap that prevents technology transfer but can also be a springboard to technology adoption. You will look forward to your next haggling experience as an opportunity to use your newfound understanding of asymmetric information to avoid the winner's curse and take advantage of the curse of knowledge. You will stop to smell the roses the next time you visit your garden and appreciate these roses for what they are: a labor-intensive, non-technology-based, premodern, but beautiful outcome of a production process that involves little specialization, few market interactions, and is risky. And finally, you can be happy to be at home where some airline cannot charge you for pushing back your chair, and you can take a nice, long nap in preparation for traveling to your next destination, either physical or mental, wherever that may be.

Notes

Preface

1. Annie Dillard, *The Abundance: Narrative Essays New and Old* (New York: Ecco Press, 2016).
2. Adam Smith, *An Inquiry into the Nature and the Causes of the Wealth of Nations* (London: W. Strahan and T. Cadell, 1776).
3. Samuel Johnson, *The Letters of Samuel Johnson, Volume II: 1773–1776*, ed. Bruce Redford (Oxford: Oxford University Press, 1991).
4. Friedrich Nietzsche, *Human, All Too Human: A Book for Free Spirits* (Cambridge: Cambridge University Press, 1996).

Chapter 1

1. Albert Einstein, "Physics and Reality," in *Ideas and Opinions of Albert Einstein*, ed. Carl Seelig (New York: Crown Publishers, 1954).
2. George Orwell, *Keep the Aspidistra Flying* (London: Victor Gollancz Ltd, 1936).
3. ABC News Staff, "100 Million Dieters, $20 Billion: The Weight-Loss Industry by the Numbers," ABCNews.com, May 8, 2012, accessed September 16, 2016, http://abcnews.go.com/Health/100-million-dieters-20-billion-weight-loss-industry/story?id=16297197#.UeHccW3YFoU.
4. Paul Theroux, *The Last Train to Zona Verde* (Boston: Mariner Books, 2014).
5. Benjamin Marx, Thomas Stoker, and Tavneet Suri, "The Economics of Slums in the Developing World," *Journal of Economic Perspectives* 27 (2013): 187–210.
6. Camillo Boano, Melissa Garcia Lamarca, and William Hunter, "The Frontlines of Contested Urbanism: Mega-Projects and Mega-Resistances in Dharavi," *Journal of Developing Societies* 27 (2011): 295–326.

7. Abhijit Banerjee and Ester Duflo, *Poor Economics: A Radical Rethinking of the Way to Fight Global Poverty* (New York: PublicAffairs, 2012).

8. Gardiner Harris, "Poor Sanitation in India May Afflict Well-Fed Children with Malnutrition," *New York Times*, July 13, 2014, accessed September 16, 2015, http://www.nytimes.com/2014/07/15/world/asia/poor-sanitation-in-india-may-afflict-well-fed-children-with-malnutrition.html?_r=0.

9. Charles Dickens, *Bleak House* (London: Bradbury & Evans, 1852).

10. Marx, Stoker, and Suri, "Slums."

11. Edward Glaeser, *Triumph of the City: How Our Greatest Invention Makes Us Richer, Smarter, Greener, Healthier, and Happier* (London: Penguin Books, 2012).

12. World Bank, "Report Finds 400 Million Children Living in Extreme Poverty," Press Release, October 10, 2013, accessed September 16, 2016, http://www.worldbank.org/en/news/press-release/2013/10/10/report-finds-400-million-children-living-extreme-poverty.

13. Thorsten Beck, Asli Demirgüç-Kunt, and Maria Soledad Martinez Peria, "Reaching Out: Access to and Use of Banking Services Across Countries," *Journal of Financial Economics* 85 (2008): 234–66.

14. For detailed case studies examining the impact of the lack of formal finance on the poor, see Todd Knoop, *Global Finance in Emerging Market Economies* (London: Routledge, 2013).

15. The Maddison-Project, 2013 edition, accessed March 17, 2016, http://www.ggdc.net/maddison/maddison-project/home.htm.

16. World Bank Open Data, accessed January 16, 2016, http://data.worldbank.org/indicator/SI.POV.GINI.

17. Pooja Thakur and Ailing Tan, "Mumbai Is the World's Least Affordable Home Market," Bloomberg.com, accessed June 16, 2015, http://www.bloomberg.com/news/2012-04-10/mumbai-is-world-s-least-affordable-home-market-chart-of-the-day.html.

18. Thomas Piketty, *Capital in the Twenty-First Century* (Cambridge, MA: Harvard University Press, 2014).

19. Carmen DeNavas-Walt and Bernadette D. Proctor, "Income and Poverty in the United States: 2014," United States Census Bureau, accessed September 9, 2016, http://www.census.gov/content/dam/Census/library/publications/2015/demo/p60-252.pdf.

20. Bureau of Economic Analysis, "Measuring the Economy: A Primer on GDP and National Product and Income Accounts," U.S. Department of Commerce (2015), accessed September 16, 2016, http://www.bea.gov/national/pdf/nipa_primer.pdf.

21. Nadim Ahmad and Seung-Hee Koh, "Incorporating Estimates of Household Production of Non-Market Services into International Comparisons of Material Well-Being," OECD Statistics Directorate Working Paper No. 42, 2011.

22. Mark Twain, "Chapters from my Autobiography," *North American Review* vol. 598 (1906).

23. Amartya Sen, *Development as Freedom* (New York: Anchor, 2000).

24. Angus Deaton, *The Great Escape: Health, Wealth, and the Origins of Inequality* (Princeton, NJ: Princeton University Press, 2013).

25. Rafael Di Tella and Robert MacCulloch, "Some Uses of Happiness Data in Economics," *Journal of Economic Perspectives* 20 (2006): 25–46.

26. Charles Dickens, *David Copperfield* (London: Bradbury & Evans, 1850).

27. David Dollar and Aart Kraay, "Growth Is Good for the Poor," *Journal of Economic Growth* 7 (2002):195–225.

28. World Bank, "Pro-Poor Growth in the 1990s. Lessons and Insights from 14 Countries," Discussion Paper (2005), accessed June 10, 2016, http://siteresources .worldbank.org/INTPGI/Resources/342674-1119450037681/Pro-poor_growth _in_the_1990s.pdf.

29. Martin Ravallion, "How Long Will It Take to Lift One Billion People Out of Poverty?" *World Bank Research Observer* 28 (2013): 139–58.

30. Angus Deaton, *The Great Escape.*

31. Samuel H. Preston, "The Changing Relation between Mortality and Level of Economic Development," *Population Studies* 29 (1975): 231–48.

32. Angus Deaton, *The Great Escape.*

33. Bernard de Mandeville, "An Essay on Charity and Charity Schools," in *The Fable of the Bees: Or, Private Vices, Publick Benefits* (Oxford: Oxford University Press., 1732).

34. Sylvia Nasar, *Grand Pursuit: The Story of Economic Genius* (New York: Simon & Schuster, 2011).

35. Alfred Marshall, *Principles of Economics* (London: MacMillan & Co., 1890).

36. Alfred Marshall, *The Correspondence of Alfred Marshall, Economist*, ed. John K. Whitaker (Cambridge: Cambridge University Press, 1996).

37. Alfred Marshall, *Correspondence.*

38. A nifty rule of thumb in thinking about growth rates is the Rule of 70, which says that something that is growing at x percent a year doubles in size every $70/x$ years. This simple rule illustrates why growing only marginally faster but over a long period of time leads to income doubling more often, creating large income gaps.

39. Robert Solow, "A Contribution to the Theory of Economic Growth," *Quarterly Journal of Economics* 70 (1965): 65–94.

40. Lant Pritchett, *The Rebirth of Education: Schooling Ain't Learning* (Washington, DC: Brookings Institution Press, 2013). Also see Jonathan R.W. Temple, "Generalizations that Aren't? Evidence on Education and Growth," *European Economic Review* 45 (2001): 901–18.

41. Paul Romer, "Economic Growth," *The Concise Encyclopedia of Economics, Library of Economics and Liberty*, accessed January 7, 2016, http://www.econlib .org/library/Enc/EconomicGrowth.html.

42. Deirdre N. McCloskey, *The Bourgeois Virtues: Ethics for an Age of Commerce* (Chicago: University of Chicago Press, 2006).

43. Steven Pinker, *The Blank Slate: The Modern Denial of Human Nature* (New York: Viking Press, 2002).

Chapter 2

1. George Saunders, *The Braindead Microphone* (New York: Riverhead Books, 2007).

2. Jack Kerouac, *On the Road* (New York: Viking Press, 1957).

3. United National Economic Council for Europe, "Aggressive Driving Behavior," accessed September 16, 2016, http://www.unece.org/trans/roadsafe /rs4aggr.html.

4. Türker Özkan, Timo Lajunen, Joannes El. Chliaoutakis, Dianne Parker, and Heikki Summala, "Cross-Cultural Differences in Driving Behaviours: A Comparison of Six Countries," *Transportation Research* 9 (2006): 227–42.

5. World Health Organization, "Road Traffic Injuries," accessed September 16, 2016, http://www.who.int/mediacentre/factsheets/fs358/en.

6. World Health Organization, "Global Status Report on Road Safety 2015," accessed September 16, 2016, http://www.who.int/violence_injury_prevention /road_safety_status/2015/en.

7. Rund Elvik and Astrid Amundsen, "Improving Road Safety in Sweden: An Analysis of the Potential for Improving Safety, the Cost-Effectiveness and Cost-Benefit Ratios of Road Safety Measures," *TOI Report* 490/2000 (Oslo: Institute of Transport Economics, 2000).

8. Experimental evidence in support of the claim that people are conditional cooperators can be found in Urs Fischbacher, Simon Gachter, and Ernst Fehr, "Are People Conditionally Cooperative? Evidence from a Public Goods Experiment," *Economic Letters* 71 (2001): 397–404.

9. Özkan *et al.*, "Driving Behavior."

10. *The Economist*, "Dropping the Scales," May 21, 2016, accessed September 16, 2016, http://www.economist.com/news/asia/21699156-overburdened -yet-overactive-indias-courts-are-failing-do-justice-dropping-scales.

11. Franklin Allen, *et al.*, "Law, Institutions, and Finance in India and China," in *Emerging Giants: China and India in the World Economy*, eds. Barry Eichengreen, Poonam Gupta, and Rajiv Kumar (New York: Oxford University Press, 2009).

12. Thomas Vanderbilt, *Traffic: Why We Drive the Way We Do (And What it Says About Us)* (New York: Knopf, 2008).

13. World Health Organization, "Global Health Observatory Data: Road Traffic Deaths," accessed September 16, 2016, http://www.who.int/gho/road_safety /mortality/en.

14. Transparency International, "Perceptions of Corruption, 2015 edition," accessed September 16, 2016. http://www.transparency.org/cpi2015/.

15. Raymond Fisman and Edward Migual, "Corruption, Norms, and Legal Enforcement: Evidence from Diplomatic Parking Tickets," *Journal of Political Economy* 115 (2007): 1020–48.

16. Nejat Anbarci, Monica Escaleras, and Charles Register, "Traffic Fatalities and Public Sector Corruption," *Kyklos* 59 (2006): 327–44.

17. Marianne Bertrand, *et al.*, "Obtaining a Drivers License in India: An Experimental Approach to Studying Corruption," *Quarterly Journal of Economics* 122 (2006): 1639–76.

18. Kenneth Tynan, *The Diaries of Kenneth Tynan*, ed. John Lahr (New York: Bloomsbury, 2003).

19. Jakob Svensson, "Eight Questions about Corruption," *Journal of Economic Perspectives* 19 (2005): 18–42.

20. Jakob Svensson, "Corruption."

21. William Faulkner, *Requiem for a Nun* (New York: Random House, 1951).

22. Darin Acemoglu, Simon Johnson, and James A. Robinson, "The Colonial Origins of Comparative Development: An Empirical Investigation," *American Economic Review* 91 (2001): 1369–401.

23. An excellent example of this is the Belgian Congo, grippingly portrayed in *King Leopold's Ghost* (New York: Mariner Books, 1998) by Adam Hochschild.

24. Jared Diamond, *Guns, Germs, and Steel: The Fates of Human Societies* (New York: W.W. Norton & Co, 1997).

25. Elizabeth Kopits and Maureen Cropper, "Traffic Fatalities and Economic Growth," *Accident Analysis & Prevention* 37 (2005): 169–78.

26. China People's Daily, "Car Drivers in China Exceeds 200 Million," January 31, 2013, accessed September 16, 2016, http://english.peopledaily.com.cn /90882/8115465.html.

27. Geoffrey Sant, "Driven to Kill," *Slate*, September 4, 2015, accessed September 16, 2016, http://www.slate.com/articles/news_and_politics/foreigners/2015 /09/why_drivers_in_china_intentionally_kill_the_pedestrians_they_hit_china _s.html?wpsrc=sh_all_mob_em_ru.

28. *The Economist*, "Driving to an Early Grave," January 23, 2014, accessed September 16, 2016, http://www.economist.com/news/international/21595031-rich -countries-have-cut-deaths-and-injuries-caused-crashes-toll-growing.

29. Peter Hessler, *Country Driving: A Journey Through China from Farm to Factory* (New York: HarperCollins, 2010).

30. Michael Collins, "Welcome to the Traffic Capital of the World," *The New Republic*, July 2, 2014, accessed September 16, 2016, https://newrepublic.com /article/118416/what-dhaka-bangladesh-traffic-capital-world-can-teach-us.

31. Thomas Vanderbilt, *Traffic*.

32. Xu Wei, "Beijing Cuts Number of New Cars," *China Daily USA*, November 29, 2013, accessed September 16, 2016, http://usa.chinadaily.com.cn/china /2013-11/29/content_17138933.htm.

33. Sam Peltzman, "The Effects of Automobile Safety Regulations," *Journal of Political Economy* 83 (1975): 677–726.

Chapter 3

1. Arthur Waley, *Three Ways of Thought in Ancient China* (Palo Alto: Stanford University Press, 1939).

2. Franz Kafka, *The Trial* (Berlin: Verlag Die Schmiede, 1925).

3. Thomas Robert Malthus, *An Essay on the Principle of Population* (London: J. Johnson, 1798).

4. Gary Clark, *A Farewell to Alms: A Brief Economic History of the World* (Princeton, NJ: Princeton University Press, 2007).

5. Matthew Connelly, *Fatal Misconception: The Struggle to Control World Population* (Cambridge, MA: Belknap Press, 2008).

6. Lant H. Pritchett, "Desired Fertility and the Impact of Population Policies," *Population and Development Review* 20 (1994): 1–55.

7. World Health Organization, "Obesity and Overweight," June 2016, accessed February 24, 2016, http://www.who.int/mediacentre/factsheets/fs311/en.

8. Mark Overton, *Agricultural Revolution in England: The Transformation of the Agrarian Economy 1500–1850* (Cambridge: Cambridge University Press, 1996).

9. David H. Autor, "Why Are There Still So Many Jobs? The History and Future of Workplace Automation," *Journal of Economic Perspectives* 29 (2015): 3–30.

10. World Bank Open Data, accessed June 11, 2016, http://data.worldbank.org/indicator/SP.DYN.TFRT.IN.

11. Russel Shorto, "No Babies?", *New York Times*, June 29, 2009, accessed March 11, 2015, http://www.nytimes.com/2008/06/29/magazine/29Birth-t.html?pagewanted=all&_r=0.

12. United Nations Economic and Social Affairs, "World Population to 2300," United Nations (2004), accessed on March 26, 2015, http://www.un.org/esa/population/publications/longrange2/WorldPop2300final.pdf.

13. Amartya Sen, *Poverty and Famines* (Oxford: Oxford University Press, 1999).

14. The Great Chinese Famine is documented in detail in the book by Yang Jisheng entitled *Tombstone: The Great Chinese Famine, 1958–1962* (New York: Farrar, Straus and Giroux, 2012).

15. William Easterly, *White Man's Burden: Why the West's Efforts to Aid the Rest Have Done So Much Ill and So Little Good* (New York: Penguin Books, 2006).

16. David H. Autor, "Workplace Automation."

17. Sven Beckert, *Empire of Cotton: A Global History* (New York: Alfred A. Knopf, 2014).

18. James Bessen, "Toil and Technology," *Finance and Development* 52 (2015): 16–19.

19. Jared Diamond, *Guns, Germs, and Steel*.

20. Darin Acemoglu, Simon Johnson, and James A. Robinson, "The Colonial Origins."

21. World Bank, "Doing Business 2015," October 29, 2014, accessed July 5, 2016, http://www.doingbusiness.org/reports/global-reports/doing-business-2015.

22. Banerjee and Duflo, *Poor Economics*.

23. Banerjee and Duflo, *Poor Economics*.

24. Organization for Economic Cooperation and Development, "Benefits and Wages: Tax-Benefit Calculator," accessed November 23, 2015, http://www.oecd.org/social/soc/benefitsandwagestax-benefitcalculator.htm.

25. Thorsten Beck, Asli Demirgüç-Kunt, and Maria Soledad Martinez Peria, "Reaching Out."

26. Abhijit Banerjee and Ester Duflo, *Poor Economics*.

27. See Abhijit Banerjee and Ester Duflo, *Poor Economics*, for a more detailed discussion of controlled studies aimed at identifying exactly how public education can be improved in both poor and rich countries.

28. *U.S. News and World Report*, "Best Global Universities Rankings," accessed May 25, 2016, http://www.usnews.com/education/best-global-universities/rankings?int=a27a09.

29. Michael S. Christian, "Human Capital Accounting in the United States: Context, Measurement, and Application," in *Measuring Economic Sustainability and Progress*, eds. Dale W. Jorgenson, J. Steven Landefeld, and Paul Schreyer (Chicago: University of Chicago Press, 2014): 461–91.

30. Robert J. Barro and Jong-Wha Lee, "A New Data Set of Educational Attainment in the World, 1950–2010," *Journal of Development Economics* 104 (2013): 184–98.

31. Paul T. Schultz, "School Subsidies for the Poor: Evaluating the Mexican Progresa Poverty Program," *Journal of Development Economics* 74 (2004): 199–250.

32. Douglas North, *Institutions, Institutional Change and Economic Performance* (Cambridge: Cambridge University Press, 1990).

33. Hernando de Soto, *The Mystery of Capital: Why Capitalism Triumphs in the West and Fails Everywhere Else* (New York: Basic Books, 2000).

34. *The Economist*, "Title to Come," July 14, 2016, accessed July 23, 2016, http://www.economist.com/news/middle-east-and-africa/21702175-property-rights-are-still-wretchedly-insecure-africa-title-come.

35. Romain Wacziarg and Karen Horn Welch, "Trade Liberalization and Growth: New Evidence," *World Bank Economic Review* 22 (2008): 187–231.

36. See, for example, the Population Connection at http://www.populationconnection.org.

37. For an excellent discussion of how the productivity of agriculture has increased over time, see Rivoli Pietra, *The Travels of a T-Shirt in the Global Economy: An Economist Examines the Markets, Power, and Politics of World Trade* (Hoboken: Wiley Publishers, 2009). Also, for examinations of the history of cotton farming in the United States and across the globe, see Sven Beckert, *Empire of Cotton*.

38. Martin Meredith, *The Fortunes of Africa: A 5,000-Year History of Wealth, Greed, and Endeavor* (New York: PublicAffairs, 2014).

39. A. Ganesh-Kumar, Ashtok Gulati, and Ralph Cummings, Jr., *Food Grains Policy and Management in India: Responding to Today's Challenges and Opportunities* (Mumbai and Washington, DC: Indira Gandhi Institute of Development Research and IFPRI, 2007).

40. Organization of Economic Cooperation and Development, *The Cost of Air Pollution: Health Impacts of Road Transportation* (Paris: OECD Publishing, 2014).

41. World Bank, *Cost of Pollution in China: Economic Estimates of Physical Damages* (Washington, DC: World Bank, 2007).

42. U.S. Energy Information Administration, Annual Energy Outlook 2015 (Washington, DC: U.S. Department of Energy, 2015).

43. Arik Levinson, "Technology, International Trade, and Pollution from US Manufacturing," *American Economic Review* 99 (2009): 2177–92.

44. *The Economist*, "Peak Toil," January 24, 2013, accessed on October 23, 2016, http://www.economist.com/news/china/21570750-first-two-articles-about -impact-chinas-one-child-policy-we-look-shrinking.

Chapter 4

1. *Lynch v Household Finance Co.*, 405 U.S. 538, 552 (1972).

2. John Maynard Keynes, *Essays in Persuasion* (London: Macmillan, 1931).

3. "Mugabe 'Zimbabwe is Mine'," last modified May 29, 2014, https://www .youtube.com/watch?v=zXX_G14tJ-A.

4. *The Economist*, "Who Wants to be a Trillionaire?" May 12, 2016, accessed May 20, 2016, http://www.economist.com/news/middle-east-and-africa/21698658 -lock-up-your-dollars-right-now-mugabenomics-back-who-wants-be.

5. Max Weber, "The Three Types of Legitimate Rule," *Berkeley Publications in Society and Institutions* 4 (1958): 1–11.

6. Jonathan Swift, *Gulliver's Travels* (London: Benjamin Motte, 1726).

7. Edward Miguel, Shanker Satyanath, and Ernest Sergenti, "Economic Shocks and Civil Conflict: An Instrumental Variables Approach," *Journal of Political Economy* 112 (2004): 725–53.

8. Pearl Buck, *The Good Earth* (New York: John Day, 1931).

9. David Landes, *The Wealth and Poverty of Nations* (New York: W. W. Norton & Company, 1998).

10. Michelle Wrong, *In the Footsteps of Mr. Kurtz: Living on the Brink of Disaster in Mobutu's Congo* (New York: HarperCollins, 2001).

11. Vito Tanzi and Howell H. Zee, "Tax Policy for Emerging Markets: Developing Countries," *National Tax Journal* 53 (2000): 299–322.

12. Vito Tanzi, "Quantitative Characteristics of the Tax Systems of Developing Countries," in *The Theory of Taxation for Developing Countries,* eds. David Newbery and Nicholas Stern (New York: Oxford University Press, 1987): 205–41.

13. *The Economist*, "Worth Their Wait in Gold," March 17, 2016, accessed March 25, 2016, http://www.economist.com/news/europe/21695055-italian-red -tape-means-jobs-those-who-stand-line-worth-their-wait-gold.

14. Friedrich Hayek, *The Road to Serfdom* (Chicago: University of Chicago Press, 1944).

15. William L. Megginson, *The Financial Economics of Privatization* (Cambridge: Cambridge University Press, 2005).

16. *The Economist*, "Global House Prices," March 31, 2016, accessed April 3, 2016, http://www.economist.com/blogs/dailychart/2011/11/global-house-prices.

17. Meghanna Ayyagari, Asli Demirgüç-Kunt, and Vogislav Maksimovic, "Small vs. Young Firms Across The World—Contribution to Employment, Job Creation, and Growth," World Bank Policy Research Working Paper No. 5631, 2011.

18. Friedman, Thomas, "Foreign Affairs; Parsing the Protests," *New York Times*, April 14, 2000, accessed March 27, 2015, http://www.nytimes.com/2000/04/14 /opinion/foreign-affairs-parsing-the-protests.html.

19. Board of Governors of the Federal Reserve System, "Minutes of the Federal Open Market Committee," August 2, 1955, accessed June 23, 2015, https:// fraser.stlouisfed.org/scribd/?item_id=22678&filepath=/docs/historical/FOMC /meetingdocuments/fomcropa19550802.pdf.

20. Alberto Cavallo, "Online and Official Price Indexes: Measuring Argentina's Inflation," *Journal of Monetary Economics* 60 (2012): 152–65.

21. World Bank, "Doing Business 2011," November 4, 2010, accessed July 5, 2016, http://www.doingbusiness.org/reports/global-reports/doing-business-2011.

22. Adolf Wagner, "Extracts on Public Finance," in *Classics in the Theory of Public Finance*, eds. Richard A. Musgrave and Alan T. Peacock (London: Macmillan, 1958).

23. Darin Acemoglu and James Robinson, *Why Nations Fail: The Origins of Power, Prosperity, and Poverty* (New York: Crown Publishing Group, 2012).

24. William Faulkner, *Requiem for a Nun*.

25. Darin Acemoglu and James Robinson, *Why Nations Fail*.

26. Robert McGregor, *The Party: The Secret World of China's Communist Rulers* (New York: Harper Perennial, 2010).

27. Giovanni Ferri and Li-Gang Liu, "Honor Thy Creditors Before Thy Shareholders: Are the Profits of Chinese State-Owned Enterprises Real?" *Asian Economic Papers* 9 (2010): 50–71.

28. Feng Wang and Xuejin Zuo, "Inside China's Cities: Institutional Barriers and Opportunities for Urban Migrants," *American Economic Review* 89 (1999): 276–80.

29. Robert McGregor, *The Party*.

30. Darin Acemoglu, Simon Johnson, and James A. Robinson, "Colonial Origins."

31. Transparency International, "Perceptions of Corruption, 2015 edition," accessed September 16, 2016. http://www.transparency.org/cpi2015/.

32. UNICEF, "Botswana Statistics," accessed August 12, 2015, http://www .unicef.org/infobycountry/botswana_statistics.html.

33. Darin Acemoglu, *et al.*, "Democracy Does Cause Growth," NBER Working Paper No. 20004, 2014.

34. Milton Friedman, *Capitalism and Freedom* (Chicago: University of Chicago, 1962).

35. See the following: Daniel Treisman, "The Causes of Corruption: A Cross-National Study," *Journal of Public Economics* 76 (2000): 399–457; David A. Leblang, "Property Rights, Democracy and Economic Growth," *Political Research Quarterly* 49 (1996): 5–26; Christopher Clague, Philip Keefer, Stephen Knack, and

Mancur Olson, "Property and Contract Rights in Autocracies and Democracies," *MPRA Paper* 25720, University Library of Munich, Germany (1996); and Acemoglu *et al.*, "*Democracy.*"

36. Robert J. Barro, *Determinants of Economic Growth: A Cross-Country Empirical Study* (Cambridge, MA: MIT Press, 1997).

37. Robin Burgess, *et al.*, "The Value of Democracy: Evidence from Road Building in Kenya," *American Economic Review* 105 (2015): 1817–51.

38. William Easterly, *White Man's Burden: Why the West's Efforts to Aid the Rest Have Done So Much Ill and So Little Good* (New York: Penguin Books, 2006).

39. Abhijit Banerjee and Ester Duflo, *Poor Economics.*

40. Darin Acemoglu and James Robinson, *Why Nations Fail.*

41. *The Economist*, "Dicing with Death," April 12, 2014, accessed April 28, 2014, http://www.economist.com/news/international/21600713-un-offers-some-hints -how-avoid-being-bumped-dicing-death.

Chapter 5

1. Johann Wolfgang von Goethe, *Italian Journey* (New York: Penguin Publishing, 1816 [1992]).

2. Mark Twain, *Pudd'nhead Wilson* (New York: Charles L. Webster & Company, 1894).

3. Lásló Török, *Herodotus in Nubia* (Boston: Brill Academic Publishers, 2014).

4. This phrase was first used by Bryan Caplan, "Rational Ignorance versus Rational Irrationality," *Kyklos* 54 (2001): 3–26.

5. This phrase was first used by Clifford Geertz, *The Interpretation of Cultures: Selected Essays* (New York: Basic Books, 1973).

6. The primary proponent of this theory is Roger Keesing, "Theories of Culture," *Annual Review of Anthropology* 3 (1974): 73–97.

7. Anthony Storr, *Feet of Clay: Saints, Sinners, and Madmen: A Study of Gurus* (New York: Free Press, 1996).

8. Geert Hofstede, *Culture's Consequences: International Differences in Work-Related Values* (Beverly Hills: Sage Publications, 1984).

9. Max Weber, *The Protestant Ethic and the Spirit of Capitalism* (New York: Scribner, 1930).

10. David Landes, *The Wealth and Poverty of Nations.*

11. For a study that has found that countries that have higher levels of religiosity have lower levels of innovation, see Roland Bénabou, Davide Ticchi, and Andrea Vindigni, "Forbidden Fruits: The Political Economy of Science, Religion, and Growth," National Bureau of Economic Research Working Paper No. 21105 (2015).

12. Timur Kuran, "Why the Middle East Is Economically Underdeveloped: Historical Mechanisms of Institutional Stagnation," *Journal of Economic Perspectives* 18 (2004): 71–90.

13. Robert Barro and Rachel M. McCleary, "Religion and Economic Growth Across Countries," *American Sociological Review* 68 (2003): 760–81.

14. For a complete review of empirical research linking religion to economics, see Syria Iyer, "The New Economics of Religion," *Journal of Economic Literature* 54 (2016): 395–441.

15. Andrew Morrison, Dhushyanth Raju, and Nistha Sinha, "Gender Equality, Poverty, and Economic Growth," Policy Research Working Paper No. 4349 (Washington, DC: World Bank, 2007).

16. Shahidur R. Khandker, "Microfinance and Poverty: Evidence Using Panel Data from Bangladesh," *World Bank Economic Review* 19 (2004): 263–86.

17. Moses Abramovitz, "Catching Up, Forging Ahead, and Falling Behind," *Journal of Economic History* 46 (1986): 385–406.

18. Joel Mokyr, Chris Vickers, and Nicolas L. Ziebarth, "The History of Technological Anxiety and the Future of Economic Growth: Is This Time Different?" *Journal of Economic Perspectives* 29 (2015): 31–50.

19. Rafael Di Tella and Robert MacCulloch, "Culture, Beliefs and Economic Performance," Motu Economic and Public Policy Research Working Papers 14–06, 2014.

20. *The Economist*, "Going Global," December 15, 2015, accessed December 20, 2015, http://www.economist.com/news/christmas-specials/21683983-secrets -worlds-best-businesspeople-going-global.

21. European Commission, "Entrepreneurship in the EU and Beyond," Flash Eurobarometer 343 Report, August, 2012, accessed January 30, 2015, http://ec .europa.eu/public_opinion/flash/fl_354_en.pdf.

22. Kashifa Suddle, Sjoerd Beugelsdijk, and Sander Wennekers, "Entrepreneurial Culture and its Effect on the Rate of Nascent Entrepreneurship," in *Entrepreneurship and Culture*, eds. Anreas Freitag and Roy Thurik (New York: Springer, 2010): 227–44.

23. Pew Research Center, "Emerging and Developing Economies Much More Optimistic than Rich Countries about the Future," October 9, 2014, accessed November 5, 2016, http://www.pewglobal.org/2014/10/09/emerging -and-developing-economies-much-more-optimistic-than-rich-countries-about -the-future.

24. Rafael Di Tella and Robert MacCulloch, "Culture, Beliefs and Economic Performance."

25. Jared Diamond, *Guns, Germs, and Steel*.

26. William Easterly and Ross Levine, "Africa's Growth Tragedy: Policies and Ethnic Divisions," *Quarterly Journal of Economics* 112 (1997): 1203–50.

27. Alberto Alesina, Stelios Michalopoulos, and Elias Papaioannou, "Ethnic Inequality," *CEPR Discussion Papers* 9225, 2012.

28. Stelios Michalopoulos and Elias Papaioannou, "The Long-Run Effects of the Scramble for Africa," *American Economic Review* 106 (2016): 1802–48.

29. Karla Hoff and Priyanka Pandey, "Belief Systems and Durable Inequalities: An Experimental Investigation of Indian Caste," World Bank Policy Research Working Papers, 2004.

30. Fedrico Cingano, "Trends in Income Inequality and Its Impact on Economic Growth," OECD SEM Working Paper No. 163, 2014.

31. Sendhil Mullainathan and Eldar Shafir, *Scarcity: Why Having Too Little Means So Much* (New York: Times Books, 2013).

32. Kenneth Arrow, "Gifts and Exchanges," *Philosophy and Public Affairs* 1 (1972): 343–62.

33. Robert D. Putnam, *Bowling Alone: The Collapse and Revival of American Community* (New York: Simon & Schuster, 2000).

34. Helmut Rainer and Thomas Siedler, "The Role of Social Networks in Determining Migration and Labour Market Outcomes: Evidence from German Reunification," *Munich Reprints in Economics* 19783, University of Munich, Department of Economics, 2009.

35. Frank W. Marlowe, J. Colette Berbesque, Abigail Barr, Clark Barrett, Alexander Bolyanatz, Juan Camilo Cardenas, Jean Ensminger, Michael Gurven, Edwins Gwako, Joseph Henrich, Natalie Henrich, Carolyn Lesorogol, Richard McElreath, and David Tracer, "Costly Punishment Across Human Societies," *Science* 312 (2006): 1767–70.

36. Paul J. Zak and Stephen Knack, "Trust and Growth," *Economic Journal* 111 (2001): 295–321.

37. Sjoerd Beugelsdijk, Henri L.F. De Groot, and Anton B.T.M. Van Schaik, "Trust and Economic Growth: A Robustness Analysis," *Oxford Economic Papers* 56 (2004): 118–34.

38. See Paul J. Zak and Stephen Knack, "Trust and Growth," and Stephen Knack and Philip Keefer, "Does Social Capital Have an Economic Payoff? A Cross-Country Investigation," *Quarterly Journal of Economics* 112 (2007): 1251–88.

39. Stephan Knack, "Groups, Growth and Trust: Cross-Country Evidence on the Olson and Putnam Hypotheses," *Public Choice* 117 (2003): 341–55.

40. Empirical evidence that religious belief is associated with more trust in the government, markets, and each other, but is also less tolerant on social and gender issues, can be found in Luigi Guiso, Paola Sapienza, and Luigi Zingales, "People's Opium? Religion and Economic Attitudes," *Journal of Monetary Economics* 50 (2003): 225–82. Other experiments find that people play games, such as the ultimatum game, in more prosocial ways once cued to religious thoughts. See Ara Norenzayan and Azim F. Shariff, "The Origin and Evolution of Religious Prosociality," *Science* 322 (2008): 58–62.

41. Rafael La Porta, Florencio Lopez-de-Silane, Andrei Shleifer, and Robert W. Vishny, "Trust in Large Organizations," *American Economic Review* 87 (1997): 333–38.

42. Montesquieu, *The Spirit of Laws* (Anonymous, 1748).

43. Alfred Marshall, *Correspondence*.

44. Gary S. Becker, "Altruism, Egoism, and Genetic Fitness: Economics and Sociobiology," *American Economic Review* 17 (1976): 817–26.

45. Marlow *et al.*, "Costly Punishment."

46. This observation was first made by Matthew Ridley, *The Evolution of Everything: How New Ideas Emerge* (New York: Harper, 2015).

47. Rafael Di Tella and Robert MacCulloch, "Culture, Beliefs and Economic Performance."

48. Michael Sandel, *What Money Can't Buy: The Moral Limits of Markets* (New York: Farrar, Strauss and Giroux, 2012).

49. Assar Lindbeck, "Hazardous Welfare-State Dynamics," *American Economic Review* 85 (1995): 9–15.

50. Benjamin Olken, "Do TV and Radio Destroy Social Capital? Evidence from Indonesian Villages," *American Economic Journal: Applied Economics* 1 (2009): 1–35.

51. Tyler Cowen, *Creative Destruction: How Globalization Is Changing the World's Cultures* (Princeton, NJ: Princeton University Press, 2004).

52. Robert Jensen and Emily Oster, "The Power of TV: Cable Television and Women's Status in India," *Quarterly Journal of Economics* 124 (2009): 1057–94.

53. George Saunders, *The Braindead Microphone*.

54. Walt Whitman, *Specimen Days and Collect* (Philadelphia: Rees, Welsh & Co., 1882).

55. Linda Lynton, *The Sari* (New York: Harry N. Abrams, Incorporated, 1995).

Chapter 6

1. Norman Spinrad, *The Druid King* (New York: Knopf, 2003).

2. Albert Einstein and Leopold Infeld, *The Evolution of Physics* (New York: Touchstone Books, 1967).

3. James Gleick, *The Information: A History, A Theory, A Flood* (New York: Pantheon Books, 2011).

4. Barack Obama, *Dreams from My Father* (New York: Times Books, 1995).

5. Thomas Jefferson, *The Writings of Thomas Jefferson*, eds. Andrew A. Lipscomb and Albert Ellery Bergh (Washington: Thomas Jefferson Memorial Association, 1905).

6. This language was first used by William Easterly, *The Elusive Quest for Growth*.

7. Steven Johnson, *Future Perfect: The Case for Progress in a Networked Age* (New York: Penguin Press, 2012).

8. Ray Kurzweil, *The Singularity Is Near* (New York: Penguin Books, 2006).

9. Steven Johnson, *Where Good Ideas Come From: The Natural History of Innovation* (New York: Riverhead Books, 2010).

10. Steven Johnson, *How We Got to Now: Six Innovations That Made the Modern World* (New York: Riverhead Books, 2014).

11. Diego Comin, William Easterly, and Erick Gong, "Was the Wealth of Nations Determined in 1000 BC?" *American Economic Journal: Macroeconomics* 2 (2010): 65–97.

12. Jonathan Rothwell, *et al.*, "Patenting Prosperity: Invention and Economic Performance in the United States and its Metropolitan Areas," *Brookings Institution* (2013): 1–49.

13. Luis M. A. Bettencourt, *et al.*, "Growth, Innovation, Scaling, and the Pace of Life in Cities," *Proceedings of the National Academies of Science* 104 (2007): 7301–06.

14. Martin Ruef, "Strong Ties, Weak Ties and Islands: Structural and Cultural Predictors of Organizational Innovation," *Industrial and Corporate Change* 11 (2002): 427–49.

15. Pew Research Center, "Religious Landscape Survey," 2009, accessed April 23, 2016, http://religions.pewforum.org.

16. Diego Comin, William Easterly, and Erick Gong, "Was the Wealth of Nations Determined in 1000 BC?"

17. Douglas North, *Institutions, Institutional Change and Economic Performance.*

18. J.P. Sullivan, *The Satyricon* (New York: Penguin Classics, 1984).

19. Michele Boldrin, and David K. Levine, "The Case against Patents," *Journal of Economic Perspectives* 27 (2013): 3–22.

20. See Michele Boldrin and David K. Levine, "The Case Against Patents," for an argument for the justifications for changing patent protection in the United States. Their prescription would limit patents to situations where (1) companies would have to "use it or lose it" after patenting an idea, (2) only consequential ideas could be patented, (3) patents would last for shorter periods of time depending upon the extent of the fixed costs that went into developing the patent.

21. Joseph Schumpeter, *Business Cycles* (New York: McGraw Hill Book Co., 1939) and *Capitalism, Socialism, and Democracy* (New York: Harper & Brothers, 1942).

22. Charles Wheelan, *Naked Economics: Undressing the Dismal Science* (New York: W.W. Norton & Co., 2010).

23. David M. Cutler and Grant Miller, "The Role of Public Health Improvements in Health Advances: The Twentieth-Century United States," *Demography* 42 (2005): 1–22.

24. Gardiner Harris, "Poor Sanitation in India May Afflict Well-Fed Children with Malnutrition," *New York Times*, July 13, 2014, accessed September 16, 2015, http://www.nytimes.com/2014/07/15/world/asia/poor-sanitation-in-india -may-afflict-well-fed-children-with-malnutrition.html?_r=0.

25. *The Economist*, "Of Secrecy and Stunting," July 2, 2015, accessed July 30, 2016, http://www.economist.com/news/asia/21656709-government-withholds -report-nutrition-contains-valuable-lessons-secrecy-and.

26. James A. Dorn, "Ending Financial Repression in China," *Global Economic Review* 35 (2006): 231–38.

27. Giovanni Ferri and Li-Gang Liu, "Honor Thy Creditors Before Thy Share-holders: Are the Profits of Chinese State-Owned Enterprises Real?" *Asian Economic Papers* 9 (2010): 50–71.

28. *The Economist*, "Why Does Kenya Lead the World in Mobile Money?" May 27, 2013, accessed June 10, 2015, http://www.economist.com/blogs/economist -explains/2013/05/economist-explains-18.

29. Thorsten Beck, Asli Demirgüç-Kunt, and Maria Soledad Martinez Peria, "Reaching Out."

30. For example, this article in *The Atlantic Monthly*, "A World Without Work," July/August 2015, accessed August 21, 2015, http://www.theatlantic.com/magazine /archive/2015/07/world-without-work/395294.

31. David Ricardo, *On the Principles of Political Economy and Taxation* (London: John Murray, 1817).

32. David Rotman, "Technology and Inequality," *MIT Technology Review* October 21, 2014, accessed November 20, 2015, https://www.technologyreview.com /s/531726/technology-and-inequality.

33. Joel Mokyr, Chris Vickers, and Nicolas L. Ziebarth, "The History of Technological Anxiety."

34. *Computer Desktop Encyclopedia*, "Amara's law," accessed February 14 2016, http://encyclopedia2.thefreedictionary.com/Amara%27s+law.

35. Martin Meredith, *The Fortunes of Africa*.

36. Martin Meredith, *The Fortunes of Africa*.

37. The Trade-Related Aspects of International Property Rights (TRIPS) agreement, which is part of the World Trade Organization, governs many aspects of technology transfer for patented ideas. For a more detailed discussion and critique, see Michele Boldrin and David K. Levine, "The Case Against Patents," who refer to this agreement as neo-mercantilist.

38. Julian M. Alston, Daniel A. Sumner, and Henrich Brunke, *Impacts of Reductions in U.S. Cotton Subsidies on West African Cotton Producers* (Boston: Oxfam, 2007).

39. Julian M. Alston, Daniel A. Sumner, and Henrich Brunke, "U.S. Cotton Subsidies."

40. World Economic Forum, "Smart Travel: Unlocking Economic Growth and Development through Travel Facilitation," June, 2014, accessed May 21, 2015, http://www3.weforum.org/docs/GAC/2014/WEF_GAC_TravelTourism_Smart Travel_WhitePaper_2014.pdf.

41. Niall Ferguson, *The Ascent of Money: A Financial History of the World* (New York: Penguin Press, 2008).

42. Joseph Schumpeter, "The Communist Manifesto in Sociology and Economics," *Journal of Political Economy* 57 (1949): 199–212.

43. Frederic S. Mishkin, "Globalization: A Force for Good?", speech given for Weissman Center Distinguished Lecture Series, New York, October 12, 2006, accessed February 13, 2016, http://www.federalreserve.gov/newsevents/speech /Mishkin20061012a.htm.

44. Thorsten Beck, Asli Demirgüç-Kunt, and Maria Soledad Martinez Peria, "Reaching Out."

45. Abhijit Banerjee and Ester Duflo, *Poor Economics*.

46. Abhijit Banerjee and Ester Duflo, *Poor Economics*.

47. Steven Johnson, *Where Good Ideas Come From*.

48. Charles Arthur, "Smartphone Sales Pass 1 Billion in 2013 as China Booms," The Guardian, January 29, 2014, accessed May 21, 2016, http://www.theguardian .com/technology/2014/jan/29/smartphone-sales-billion-2013-samsung-apple -china.

Chapter 7

1. Alain de Botton, *The Art of Travel* (New York: Pantheon, 2002).

2. Jade Watkins, "Gild The Throne! Kanye West and Kim Kardashian flush nearly $1 million on gold plated toilets for their new Bel Air mansion," Daily Mail, July 24, 2013, accesses September 3, 2015, http://www.dailymail.co.uk/tvshowbiz /article-2376311/Kanye-West-Kim-Kardashian-flush-nearly-1-million-gold-plated -toilets-new-Bel-Air-mansion.html#ixzz4KvFuxFjp.

3. Liran Einav, Chiara Farronato, and Jonathan Levin, "Peer-to-Peer Markets," NBER Working Papers No. 21496, 2015.

4. Ian Ayres and Peter Siegelman, "Race and Gender Discrimination in Bargaining for a New Car," *American Economic Review* 85 (1995): 304–21.

5. Ian Ayres, "Fair Driving: Gender and Race Discrimination in Retail Car Negotiations," *Harvard Law Review* 104 (1991): 854.

6. Michael A. Jones, Philip J. Trocchia, and David L. Mothersbaugh, "Non-economic Motivations For Price Haggling: An Exploratory Study," *Advances in Consumer Research* 24 (1997): 388–91.

7. George Akerlof, "The Market for 'Lemons': Quality Uncertainty and the Market Mechanism," *Quarterly Journal of Economics* 84 (1970): 353–74.

8. Kenneth Lehn, "Information Asymmetries in Baseball's Free Agency Market," *Economic Inquiry* 22 (1984): 37–44.

9. Roughly 70 percent of all participants of an online dating service report that they are above-average looking, and only 1 percent say they are below-average. See Gunter J. Hitsch, Ali Hortaçsu, and Dan Ariely, "Matching and Sorting in Online Dating," *American Economic Review* 100 (2010): 130–63.

10. Richard Davenport-Hines, *The Universal Man: The Seven Lives of John Maynard Keynes* (Glasgow: William Collins, 2015).

11. Daniel Kahneman, *Thinking, Fast and Slow* (New York: Farrar, Straus, and Giroux, 2011).

12. Richard Thaler, *Misbehaving: The Making of Behavioural Economics* (London: Allen Lane, 2015).

13. The vast majority of fans who bought Super Bowl tickets at face value were unwilling to either buy or sell their tickets at the scalp (market) price. See Alan B. Krueger, "Economic Scene: Seven Lessons About Super Bowl Ticket Prices." *New York Times*, February 1, 2001, accessed September 17, 2015, http://www.nytimes .com/2001/02/01/business/economic-scene-seven-lessons-about-super-bowl-ticket -prices.html?scp=1&sq=Economic%20Scene:%20Seven%20Lessons%20 About%20Super%20Bowl%20Ticket%20Prices&st=cse.

14. This status quo bias in trade was first identified by William Samuelson and Richard Zeckhauser, "Status Quo Bias in Decision Making," *Journal of Risk and Uncertainty* 1 (1988): 7–59.

15. Amos Tversky and Daniel Kahneman, "Judgment under Uncertainty: Heuristics and Biases," *Science* 185 (1974): 1124–31.

16. Richard Dawkins, *The Selfish Gene* (Oxford: Oxford University Press, 1976).

17. Richard A. Feinberg, "Credit Cards as Spending Facilitating Stimuli: A Conditioning Interpretation," *Journal of Consumer Research* 13 (1986): 348–56.

18. Elizabeth C. Hirschman, "Differences in Consumer Purchase Behavior by Credit Card Payment System," *Journal of Consumer Research* 6 (1986): 58–66.

19. Yuval Noah Harari, *Sapiens: A Brief History of Humankind* (New York: Harper, 2015).

20. Mark Twain, *The Innocents Abroad* (Hartford: American Publishing Company, 1869).

21. David S. Evans, "Economic Aspects of Bitcoin and Other Decentralized Public-Ledger Currency Platforms," University of Chicago Coase-Sandor Institute for Law & Economics Research Paper No. 685, 2014.

22. Rainer Böhme, Nicolas Christin, Benjamin Edelman, and Tyler Moore, "Bitcoin: Economics, Technology, and Governance," *Journal of Economic Perspectives* 29 (2015): 213–38.

23. Paul Vigna and Michael J. Casey, *The Age of Cryptocurrency: How Bitcoin and Digital Money Are Challenging the Global Economic Order* (New York: St. Martin's Press, 2015).

Chapter 8

1. Ralph Waldo Emerson, *Essays: Second Series* (Boston: James Monroe and Company, 1844).

2. Bill Bryson, *Best American Travel Writing 2000* (New York: Mariner Books, 2000).

3. William Wordsworth, *Lyrical Ballads* (London: J. & A. Arch, 1798).

4. Joyce Kilmer, *Trees and Other Poems* (New York: George H. Doran Company, 1914).

5. For references to other historical arguments that industrialization leads to the alienation of labor, see Joel Moykr, Chris Vickers, and Nicolas L. Ziebarth, "The History of Technological Anxiety and the Future of Economic Growth: Is This Time Different?" *Journal of Economic Perspectives* 29 (2015): 31–50.

6. John Ruskin, *Unto This Last and Other Writings*, ed. Clive Wilmer (New York: Penguin Classics, 1986).

7. Adam Smith, *Wealth of Nations*.

8. Henry David Thoreau, "Life Without Principle," *Atlantic Monthly* 12 (1863): 484–95.

9. Marisol Bello, "So Far in 2011, Fewer Deaths in National Parks," *USA Today*, August 8, 2011, accessed July 10, 2015, http://usatoday30.usatoday.com /news/nation/2011-08-07-national-parks-accidental-deaths_n.htm.

10. U.S. Bureau of Labor Statistics, "Employment by Major Industry Sector," accessed July 14, 2015, http://www.bls.gov/emp/ep_table_201.htm.

11. Richard B. Freeman, "Why Do We Work More than Keynes Expected?" in *Revisiting Keynes: Economic Possibilities for Our Grandchildren*, eds. Lorenzo Pecchi and Gustavo Piga (Cambridge, MA: MIT Press, 2008).

12. Sigmund Freud, *Civilization and Its Discontents* (Vienna: Internationaler Psychoanalytischer Verlag Wien, 1930).

13. World Health Organization, *Comprehensive mental health action plan 2013–2020* (Geneva: World Health Organization, 2013).

14. Yale University, "Environmental Performance Index: 2016," accessed June 10, 2016, http://epi.yale.edu.

15. Bruce Yandle, Maya Vijayaraghavan, and Madhusudan Bhattarai, "The Environmental Kuznets Curve: A Primer," *PERC Research Study* 02–1 (2002), accessed June 17, 2016, http://www.macalester.edu/~wests/econ231/yandleetal.pdf.

16. Matthew Ridley, *The Evolution of Everything: How New Ideas Emerge* (New York: Harper, 2015).

17. *The Economist*, "The East Is Grey," April 8, 2013, accessed May 12, 2015, http://www.economist.com/news/briefing/21583245-china-worlds-worst-polluter-largest-investor-green-energy-its-rise-will-have.

18. *The Economist*, "Aiming Low," March 10, 2016, accessed March 14, 2015, http://www.economist.com/news/china/21694577-research-shows-chinas-dirtiest-days-could-be-over-sooner-officials-say-aiming-low.

19. John Luke Gallup, Jeffrey D. Sachs, and Andrew D. Mellinger, "Geography and Economic Development," *International Regional Science Review* 22 (1999): 179–232.

20. John Luke Gallup and Jeffrey D. Sachs, "Agriculture, Climate, and Technology: Why Are the Tropics Falling Behind?" *American Journal of Agricultural Economics* 82 (2000): 731–37.

21. World Health Organization, *World Malaria Report 2010* (Geneva: World Health Organization, 2010).

22. Anthony Kiszewski, Andrew Mellinger, Andrew Spielman, Pia Malaney, Sonia Ehrlich Sachs, and Jeffrey Sachs, "A Global Index Representing the Stability of Malaria Transmission," *American Journal of Tropical Medicine and Hygiene* 70 (2004): 486–98.

23. See Eric Jones, *The European Miracle: Environments, Economies and Geopolitics in the History of Europe and Asia* (Cambridge: Cambridge University Press, 1981). See also Norman J. G. Pounds and Sue Simons Ball, "Core-Areas and the Development of the European States System," *Annals of the Association of American Geographers* 54 (1964): 24–40.

24. Leon E. Stover, *The Cultural Ecology of Chinese Civilization* (New York: Mentor Books, 1974).

Chapter 9

1. David Mitchell, *Cloud Atlas* (London: Sceptre, 2004).

2. Ronald Coase, "The Problem of Social Cost," *Journal of Law and Economics* 3 (1960): 1–44.

3. Associated Press, "Plane diverted as passengers fight over seat reclining," *The Guardian*, August 25, 2014, accessed December 10, 2015, http://www

.theguardian.com/business/2014/aug/26/plane-diverted-as-passengers-fight
-over-seat-reclining.

4. Christopher Buccafusco and Christopher Jon Sprigman, "Who Deserves
Those 4 Inches of Airplane Seat Space?" *Slate*, September 23, 2014, accessed
May 25, 2015, available at: http://www.slate.com/articles/health_and_science
/science/2014/09/airplane_seat_reclining_can_economics_reveal_who_deserves
_the_space.html.

5. World Travel and Tourism Council, "Global Travel & Tourism Economic
Impact Update," August 2016, accessed September 16, 2016, http://www.wttc.org
/-/media/files/reports/economic-impact-research/wttc-global-travel—tourism
-economic-impact-update_july-2016_encrypted.pdf.

6. Richard Davenport-Hines, *The Universal Man*.

7. Jonah Ogles, "Everest Deaths: How Many Sherpas Have Been Killed?"
April 18, 2014, accessed October 28, 2015, http://www.outsideonline.com
/1922431/everest-deaths-how-many-sherpas-have-been-killed.

8. Alex Perry, *The Rift* (New York: Little, Brown, and Company, 2015).

9. Alex Perry, *The Rift*.

10. Angus Deaton, *The Great Escape*.

11. Carol Lancaster, *Foreign Aid* (Chicago: University of Chicago Press, 2007).

12. Peter T. Bauer, "Creating the Third World: Foreign Aid and Its Offspring,"
Journal of Economic Growth 2 (1981): 3–9.

13. Raghuram G. Rajan and Arvind Subramanian, "Aid and Growth: What
Does the Cross-Country Evidence Really Show?" *Review of Economics and Statistics* 90 (2008): 643–65.

14. Craig Burnside and David Dollar, "Aid, Policies, and Growth," *American
Economic Review* 90 (2000): 847–68.

15. World Travel and Tourism Council, "Travel & Tourism: Economic Impact
2016 Costa Rica," March 2016, accessed September 16, 2016, http://www.wttc.org
/-/media/files/reports/economic-impact-research/countries-2016/costarica2016
.pdf.

16. Deborah L. Jacobs, "The 20 Most Popular Cities in the World to Visit 2014,"
Forbes, July 31, 2014, accessed February 15, 2016, http://www.forbes.com/sites
/deborahljacobs/2014/07/31/the-20-most-popular-cities-in-the-world-to-visit-in
-2014.

Chapter 10

1. Marcel Proust, *In Search of Lost Time: The Prisoner Vol. 5* (Paris: Grasset and
Gallimard, 1923).

2. T. S. Eliot, *The Waste Land* (New York: Horace Liveright, 1922).

3. Susan Sontag, *Susan Sontag: Essays of the 1960s & 70s*, ed. David Reiff (New
York: Library of America, 2013).

4. Karen Blixen, *Out of Africa* (London: Putnam, 1937).

5. Mark Twain, *The Innocents Abroad* (Hartford: American Publishing Company, 1869).

6. Mark Twain, *The Innocents Abroad*.

7. Werner Heisenberg, *Physics and Beyond* (London: George Allen & Unwin Ltd, 1971).

8. John Maynard Keynes, *The General Theory*.

9. Paul Samuelson, "The Keynes Centenary," *The Economist* 25 (1983): 19–21.

10. F. Scott Fitzgerald, *The Crack-up* (New York: New Directions Publishing, 1936).

11. Xavier de Maistre, *Voyage around My Room* (New York: Hurd and Houghton, 1794).

Bibliography

Abramovitz, Moses. "Catching Up, Forging Ahead, and Falling Behind." *Journal of Economic History* 46 (1986): 385–406.

Acemoglu, Darin, and James Robinson. *Why Nations Fail: The Origins of Power, Prosperity, and Poverty.* New York: Crown Publishing Group, 2012.

Acemoglu, Darin, Simon Johnson, and James A. Robinson. "The Colonial Origins of Comparative Development: An Empirical Investigation." *American Economic Review* 91 (2001): 1369–1401.

Acemoglu, Darin, Suresh Naidu, Pascual Restrepo, and James A. Robinson. "Democracy Does Cause Growth." NBER Working Paper No. 20004, March 2014.

Ahmad, Nadim, and Seung-Hee Koh. "Incorporating Estimates of Household Production of Non-Market Services into International Comparisons of Material Well-Being." OECD Statistics Directorate Working Paper No. 42, 2011.

Akerlof, George. "The Market for 'Lemons': Quality Uncertainty and the Market Mechanism." *Quarterly Journal of Economics* 84 (1970): 353–374.

Alesina, Alberto, Stelios Michalopoulos, and Elias Papaioannou. "Ethnic Inequality." *CEPR Discussion Papers* 9225, 2012.

Allen, Franklin, Rajesh Chakrabarti, Sankar De, Jun Qian, and Meijun Qian. "Law, Institutions, and Finance in India and China." In *Emerging Giants: China and India in the World Economy*, edited by Barry Eichengreen, Poonam Gupta, and Rajiv Kumar. New York: Oxford University Press, 2009.

Alston, Julian M., Daniel A. Sumner, and Henrich Brunke. "Impacts of Reductions in U.S. Cotton Subsidies on West African Cotton Producers." Boston: Oxfam, 2007.

Anbarci, Nejat, Monica Escaleras, and Charles Register. "Traffic Fatalities and Public Sector Corruption." *Kyklos* 59 (2006): 327–44.

Arrow, Kenneth. "Gifts and Exchanges." *Philosophy and Public Affairs* 1 (1972): 343–62.

Autor, David H. "Why Are There Still So Many Jobs? The History and Future of Workplace Automation." *Journal of Economic Perspectives* 29 (2015): 3–30.

Ayres, Ian. "Fair Driving: Gender and Race Discrimination in Retail Car Negotiations." *Harvard Law Review* 104 (1991): 854.

Ayres, Ian, and Peter Siegelman. "Race and Gender Discrimination in Bargaining
for a New Car." *American Economic Review* 85 (1995): 304–21.

Ayyagari, Meghanna, Asli Demirgüç-Kunt, and Vogislav Maksimovic. "Small
vs. Young Firms Across the World—Contribution to Employment, Job
Creation, and Growth." The World Bank Policy Research Working Paper
No. 5631, 2011.

Banerjee, Abhijit, and Ester Duflo. *Poor Economics: A Radical Rethinking of the Way
to Fight Global Poverty.* New York: PublicAffairs, 2012.

Barro, Robert J. *Determinants of Economic Growth: A Cross-Country Empirical Study.*
Cambridge, MA: MIT Press, 1997.

Barro, Robert J., and Jong-Wha Lee. "A New Data Set of Educational Attainment
in the World, 1950–2010." *Journal of Development Economics* 104 (2013):
184–98.

Barro, Robert J., and Rachel M. McCleary. "Religion and Economic Growth Across
Countries." *American Sociological Review* 68 (2003): 760–81.

Bauer, Peter T. "Creating the Third World: Foreign Aid and Its Offspring." *Journal of Economic Growth* 2 (1981): 3–9.

Beck, Thorsten, Asli Demirgüç-Kunt, and Maria Soledad Martinez Peria. "Reaching Out: Access to and Use of Banking Services Across Countries." *Journal of Financial Economics* 85 (2008): 234–66.

Becker, Gary S. "Altruism, Egoism, and Genetic Fitness: Economics and Sociobiology." *American Economic Review* 17 (1976): 817–26.

Beckert, Sven. *Empire of Cotton: A Global History.* New York: Alfred A. Knopf, 2014.

Bénabou, Roland, Davide Ticchi, and Andrea Vindigni. "Forbidden Fruits: The
Political Economy of Science, Religion, and Growth." National Bureau of
Economic Research Working Paper No. 21105, 2015.

Bertrand, Marianne, Simeon Djankov, Rema Hanna, and Sendhil Mullainathan.
"Obtaining a Drivers License in India: An Experimental Approach to
Studying Corruption." *Quarterly Journal of Economics* 122 (2006): 1639–76.

Bessen, James. "Toil and Technology." *Finance and Development* 52 (2015): 16–19.

Bettencourt, Luis M. A., José Lobo, Dirk Helbing, Christian Kühnert, and Geoffrey B. West. "Growth, Innovation, Scaling, and the Pace of Life in Cities." *Proceedings of the National Academy of Sciences* 104 (2007), 7301–06.

Beugelsdijk, Sjoerd, Henri L.F. De Groot, and Anton B.T.M. Van Schaik. "Trust
and Economic Growth: A Robustness Analysis." *Oxford Economic Papers*
56 (2004): 118–34.

Blixen, Karen. *Out of Africa.* London: Putnam, 1937.

Boano, Camillo, Melissa Garcia Lamarca, and William Hunter. "The Frontlines
of Contested Urbanism: Mega-Projects and Mega-Resistances in Dharavi."
Journal of Developing Societies 27 (2011): 295–326.

Böhme, Rainer, Nicolas Christin, Benjamin Edelman, and Tyler Moore. "Bitcoin:
Economics, Technology, and Governance." *Journal of Economic Perspectives*
29 (2015): 213–38.

Boldrin, Michele, and David K. Levine. "The Case Against Patents." *Journal of Economic Perspectives* 27 (2013): 3–22.

Bryson, Bill. *Best American Travel Writing 2000.* New York: Mariner Books, 2000.

Buck, Pearl. *The Good Earth.* New York: John Day, 1931.

Burgess, Robin, Remi Jedwab, Edward Miguel, Ameet Morjaria, and Gerard Padró i Miquel. "The Value of Democracy: Evidence from Road Building in Kenya." *American Economic Review* 105 (2015): 1817–51.

Burnside, Craig, and David Dollar. "Aid, Policies, and Growth." *American Economic Review* 90 (2000): 847–68.

Caplan, Bryan. "Rational Ignorance versus Rational Irrationality." *Kyklos* 54 (2001): 3–26.

Cavallo, Alberto. "Online and Official Price Indexes: Measuring Argentina's Inflation." *Journal of Monetary Economics* 60 (2012): 152–65.

Christian, Michael S. "Human Capital Accounting in the United States: Context, Measurement, and Application." In *Measuring Economic Sustainability and Progress,* edited by Dale W. Jorgenson, J. Steven Landefeld, and Paul Schreyer: 461–91. Chicago: University of Chicago Press, 2014.

Cingano, Federico. "Trends in Income Inequality and Its Impact on Economic Growth." OECD SEM Working Paper No. 163, 2014.

Clague, Christopher, Philip Keefer, Stephen Knack, and Mancur Olson. "Property and Contract Rights in Autocracies and Democracies." *MPRA Paper* 25720, University Library of Munich, Germany, 1996.

Clark, Gary. *A Farewell to Alms: A Brief Economic History of the World.* Princeton, NJ: Princeton University Press, 2007.

Coase, Ronald H. "The Problem of Social Cost." *Journal of Law and Economics* 3 (1960): 1–44.

Comin, Diego, William Easterly, and Erick Gong. "Was the Wealth of Nations Determined in 1000 BC?" *American Economic Journal: Macroeconomics* 2 (2010): 65–97.

Connelly, Matthew. *Fatal Misconception: The Struggle to Control World Population.* Cambridge, MA: Belknap Press, 2008.

Cowen, Tyler. *Creative Destruction: How Globalization Is Changing the World's Cultures.* Princeton, NJ: Princeton University Press, 2004.

Cutler, David M., and Grant Miller. "The Role of Public Health Improvements in Health Advances: The Twentieth-Century United States." *Demography* 42 (2005): 1–22.

Davenport-Hines, Richard. *The Universal Man: The Seven Lives of John Maynard Keynes.* Glasgow: William Collins, 2015.

Dawkins, Richard. *The Selfish Gene.* Oxford: Oxford University Press, 1976.

Deaton, Angus. *The Great Escape: Health, Wealth, and the Origins of Inequality.* Princeton, NJ: Princeton University Press, 2013.

de Botton, Alain. *The Art of Travel.* New York: Pantheon, 2002.

Defoe, Daniel. *Robinson Crusoe.* London: W. Taylor, 1719.

de Maistre, Xavier. *Voyage around My Room.* New York: Hurd and Houghton, 1794.

de Mandeville, Bernard. "An Essay on Charity and Charity Schools." In *The Fable of the Bees: Or, Private Vices, Publick Benefits*. Oxford: Oxford University Press, 1732.

de Soto, Hernando. *The Mystery of Capital: Why Capitalism Triumphs in the West and Fails Everywhere Else*. New York: Basic Books, 2000.

Dickens, Charles. *Bleak House*. London: Bradbury & Evans, 1852.

Dickens, Charles. *David Copperfield*. London: Bradbury & Evans, 1850.

Diamond, Jared. *Guns, Germs, and Steel: The Fates of Human Societies*. New York: W.W. Norton & Co, 1997.

Dillard, Annie. *The Abundance: Narrative Essays New and Old*. New York: Ecco Press, 2016.

Di Tella, Rafael, and Robert MacCulloch. "Some Uses of Happiness Data in Economics." *Journal of Economic Perspectives* 20 (2006): 25–46.

Di Tella, Rafael, and Robert MacCulloch. "Culture, Beliefs and Economic Performance." Motu Economic and Public Policy Research Working Papers 14–06, 2014.

Dollar, David, and Aart Kraay. "Growth Is Good for the Poor." *Journal of Economic Growth* 7 (2002):195–225.

Dorn, James A. "Ending Financial Repression in China." *Global Economic Review* 35 (2006): 231–38.

Easterly, William. *The Elusive Quest for Growth: Economists' Adventures and Misadventures in the Tropics*. Cambridge, MA: MIT Press, 2001.

Easterly, William. *White Man's Burden: Why the West's Efforts to Aid the Rest Have Done So Much Ill and So Little Good*. New York: Penguin Books, 2006.

Easterly, William, and Ross Levine. "Africa's Growth Tragedy: Policies and Ethnic Divisions." *Quarterly Journal of Economics* 112 (1997): 1203–50.

Einav, Liran, Chiara Farronato, and Jonathan Levin. "Peer-to-Peer Markets." NBER Working Papers No. 21496, 2015.

Einstein, Albert. "Physics and Reality." In *Ideas and Opinions of Albert Einstein*, edited by Carl Seelig. New York: Crown Publishers, 1954.

Einstein, Albert, and Leopold Infeld. *The Evolution of Physics*. New York: Touchstone Books, 1967.

Eliot, T. S. *The Waste Land*. New York: Horace Liverlight, 1922.

Elvik, Rund, and Astrid Amundsen. "Improving Road Safety in Sweden: An Analysis of the Potential for Improving Safety, the Cost-Effectiveness and Cost-Benefit Ratios of Road Safety Measures." TOI Report 490/2000. Institute of Transport Economics, Oslo, 2000.

Emerson, Ralph Waldo. *Essays: Second Series*. Boston: James Monroe and Company, 1844.

Evans, David S. "Economic Aspects of Bitcoin and Other Decentralized Public-Ledger Currency Platforms." University of Chicago Coase-Sandor Institute for Law & Economics Research Paper No. 685, 2014.

Faulkner, William. *Requiem for a Nun*. New York: Random House, 1951.

Feinberg, Richard A. "Credit Cards as Spending Facilitating Stimuli: A Conditioning Interpretation." *Journal of Consumer Research* 13 (1986): 348–56.

Ferguson, Niall. *The Ascent of Money: A Financial History of the World.* New York: Penguin Press, 2008.

Ferri, Giovanni, and Li-Gang Liu. "Honor Thy Creditors Before Thy Shareholders: Are the Profits of Chinese State-Owned Enterprises Real?" *Asian Economic Papers* 9 (2010): 50–71.

Fischbacher, Urs, Simon Gachter, and Ernst Fehr. "Are People Conditionally Cooperative? Evidence from a Public Goods Experiment." *Economic Letters* 71 (2001): 397–404.

Fisman, Raymond, and Edward Migual. "Corruption, Norms, and Legal Enforcement: Evidence from Diplomatic Parking Tickets." *Journal of Political Economy* 115 (2007): 1020–48.

Fitzgerald, F. Scott. *The Crack-up.* New York: New Directions Publishing, 1936.

Freeman, Richard B. "Why Do We Work More than Keynes Expected?" In *Revisiting Keynes: Economic Possibilities for our Grandchildren*, edited by Lorenzo Pecchi and Gustavo Piga. Cambridge, MA: MIT Press, 2008.

Freud, Sigmund. *Civilization and its Discontents.* Vienna: Internationaler Psycho-analytischer Verlag Wien, 1930.

Friedman, Milton. *Capitalism and Freedom.* Chicago: University of Chicago, 1962.

Gallup, John Luke, Jeffrey D. Sachs, and Andrew D. Mellinger. "Geography and Economic Development." *International Regional Science Review* 22 (1999): 179–232.

Gallup, John Luke, and Jeffrey D. Sachs. "Agriculture, Climate, and Technology: Why Are the Tropics Falling behind?" *American Journal of Agricultural Economics* 82 (2000): 731–37.

Ganesh-Kumar, Anand, Ashtok Gulati, and Ralph Cummings, Jr. *Food Grains Policy and Management in India: Responding to Today's Challenges and Opportunities.* Mumbai and Washington, DC. Indira Gandhi Institute of Development Research and IFPRI, 2007.

Geertz, Clifford. *The Interpretation of Cultures: Selected Essays.* New York: Basic Books, 1973.

Glaeser, Edward. *Triumph of the City: How Our Greatest Invention Makes Us Richer, Smarter, Greener, Healthier, and Happier.* London: Penguin Books, 2012.

Gleik, James. *The Information: A History, A Theory, A Flood.* New York: Pantheon Books, 2011.

Goethe, Johann Wolfgang von. *Italian Journey.* New York: Penguin Publishing, 1816 [1992].

Guiso, Luigi, Paola Sapienza, and Luigi Zingales. "People's Opium? Religion and Economic Attitudes." *Journal of Monetary Economics* 50 (2003): 225–82.

Harari, Yuval Noah. *Sapiens: A Brief History of Humankind.* New York: Harper, 2015.

Hayek, Friedrich. *The Road to Serfdom.* Chicago: University of Chicago Press, 1944.

Harrod, Roy. *The Life of John Maynard Keynes.* New York: Macmillan, 1951.

Heisenberg, Werner. *Physics and Beyond.* London: George Allen & Unwin Ltd, 1971.

Hessler, Peter. *Country Driving: A Journey Through China from Farm to Factory.* New York: HarperCollins, 2010.

Hirschman, Elizabeth C. "Differences in Consumer Purchase Behavior by Credit Card Payment System." *Journal of Consumer Research* 6 (1986): 58–66.

Hitsch, Gunter J., Ali Hortaçsu, and Dan Ariely. "Matching and Sorting in Online Dating." *American Economic Review* 100 (2010): 130–63.

Hochschild, Adam. *King Leopold's Ghost: A Story of Greed, Terror, and Heroism in Colonial Africa.* New York: Mariner Books, 1998.

Hoff, Karla, and Priyanka Pandey. "Belief Systems and Durable Inequalities: An Experimental Investigation of Indian Caste." World Bank Policy Research Working Papers, 2004.

Hofstede, Geert. *Culture's Consequences: International Differences in Work-Related Values.* Beverly Hills: Sage Publications, 1984.

Iyer, Syria. "The New Economics of Religion." *Journal of Economic Literature* 54 (2016): 395–441.

Jefferson, Thomas. *The Writings of Thomas Jefferson.* Edited by Andrew A. Lipscomb and Albert Ellery Bergh. Washington: Thomas Jefferson Memorial Association, 1813 [1905].

Jensen, Robert and Emily Oster. "The Power of TV: Cable Television and Women's Status in India." *Quarterly Journal of Economics* 124 (2009): 1057–94.

Jisheng, Yang. *Tombstone: The Great Chinese Famine, 1958–1962.* New York: Farrar, Straus and Giroux, 2012.

Johnson, Samuel. *The Letters of Samuel Johnson, Volume II: 1773–1776.* Edited by Bruce Redford. Oxford: Oxford University Press, 1773 [1991].

Johnson, Steven. *Future Perfect: The Case for Progress in a Networked Age.* New York: Penguin Press, 2012.

Johnson, Steven. *How We Got to Now: Six Innovations That Made the Modern World.* New York: Riverhead Books, 2014.

Johnson, Steven. *Where Good Ideas Come From: The Natural History of Innovation.* New York: Riverhead Books, 2010.

Jones, Eric. *The European Miracle: Environments, Economies and Geopolitics in the History of Europe and Asia.* Cambridge: Cambridge University Press, 1981.

Jones, Michael A., Philip J. Trocchia, and David L. Mothersbaugh. "Noneconomic Motivations For Price Haggling: An Exploratory Study." *Advances in Consumer Research* 24 (1997): 388–91.

Kafka, Franz. *The Trial.* Berlin: Verlag Die Schmiede, 1925.

Kahneman, Daniel. *Thinking, Fast and Slow.* New York: Farrar, Straus, and Giroux, 2011.

Keesing, Roger M. "Theories of Culture." *Annual Review of Anthropology* 3 (1974): 73–97.

Kerouac, Jack. *On the Road.* New York: Viking Press, 1957.

Keynes, John Maynard. *Essays in Persuasion.* London: Macmillan, 1931.

Keynes, John Maynard. *The General Theory of Employment, Interest, and Money.* London: Macmillan, 1936.

Khandker, Shahidur R. "Microfinance and Poverty: Evidence Using Panel Data from Bangladesh." *World Bank Economic Review* 19 (2004): 263–86.

Kilmer, Joyce. *Trees and Other Poems*. New York: George H. Doran Company, 1914.

Kiszewski, Anthony, Andrew Mellinger, Andrew Spielman, Pia Malaney, Sonia Ehrlich Sachs, and Jeffrey Sachs. "A Global Index Representing the Stability of Malaria Transmission." *American Journal of Tropical Medicine and Hygiene* 70 (2004): 486–98.

Knack, Stephen. "Groups, Growth and Trust: Cross-Country Evidence on the Olson and Putnam Hypotheses." *Public Choice* 117 (2003): 341–55.

Knack, Stephen, and Philip Keefer. "Does Social Capital Have an Economic Payoff? A Cross-Country Investigation." *Quarterly Journal of Economics* 112 (2007): 1251–88.

Knoop, Todd. *Global Finance in Emerging Market Economies*. London: Routledge, 2013.

Kocher, Martin G., Todd Cherry, Stephan Kroll, Robert J. Netzer, and Matthias Sutter. "Conditional Cooperation on Three Continents." *Economic Letters* 101 (2008): 175–78.

Kopits, Elizabeth, and Maureen Cropper. "Traffic Fatalities and Economic Growth." *Accident Analysis & Prevention* 37 (2005): 169–78.

Kuran, Timur. "Why the Middle East Is Economically Underdeveloped: Historical Mechanisms of Institutional Stagnation." *Journal of Economic Perspectives* 18 (2004): 71–90.

Kurzweil, Ray. *The Singularity Is Near*. New York: Penguin Books, 2006.

Lancaster, Carol. *Foreign Aid*. Chicago: University of Chicago Press, 2007.

Landes, David. *The Wealth and Poverty of Nations*. New York: W. W. Norton & Company, 1998.

La Porta, Rafael, Florencio Lopez-de-Silane, Andrei Shleifer, and Robert W. Vishny. "Trust in Large Organizations." *American Economic Review* 87 (1997): 333–38.

Leblang, David A. "Property Rights, Democracy and Economic Growth." *Political Research Quarterly* 49 (1996): 5–26.

Lehn, Kenneth. "Information Asymmetries in Baseball's Free Agency Market." *Economic Inquiry* 22 (1984): 37–44.

Levinson, Arik. "Technology, International Trade, and Pollution from US Manufacturing." *American Economic Review* 99 (2009): 2177–92.

Lindbeck, Assar. "Hazardous Welfare-State Dynamics." *American Economic Review* 85 (1995): 9–15.

Lynton, Linda. *The Sari*. New York: Harry N. Abrams, Incorporated, 1995.

Malthus, Thomas Robert. *An Essay on the Principle of Population*. London: J. Johnson, 1798.

Marlowe, Frank W., J. Colette Berbesque, Abigail Barr, Clark Barrett, Alexander Bolyanatz, Juan Camilo Cardenas, Jean Ensminger, Michael Gurven, Edwins Gwako, Joseph Henrich, Natalie Henrich, Carolyn Lesorogol, Richard McElreath, and David Tracer. "Costly Punishment Across Human Societies." *Science* 312 (2006): 1767–70.

Marshall, Alfred. *The Correspondence of Alfred Marshall, Economist.* Edited by John K. Whitaker. Cambridge: Cambridge University Press, 1996.

Marshall, Alfred. *Principles of Economics.* London: MacMillan & Co., 1890.

Marx, Benjamin, Thomas Stoker, and Tavneet Suri. "The Economics of Slums in the Developing World." *Journal of Economic Perspectives* 27 (2013): 187–210.

McCloskey, Deirdre N. *The Bourgeois Virtues: Ethics for an Age of Commerce.* Chicago: University of Chicago Press, 2006.

McGregor, Robert. *The Party: The Secret World of China's Communist Rulers.* New York: Harper Perennial, 2010.

Megginson, William L. *The Financial Economics of Privatization.* Cambridge: Cambridge University Press, 2005.

Meredith, Martin. *The Fortunes of Africa: A 5,000-Year History of Wealth, Greed, and Endeavor.* New York: PublicAffairs, 2014.

Michalopoulos, Stelios, and Elias Papaioannou. "The Long-Run Effects of the Scramble for Africa." *American Economic Review* 106 (2016): 1802–48.

Miguel, Edward, Shanker Satyanath, and Ernest Sergenti. "Economic Shocks and Civil Conflict: An Instrumental Variables Approach." *Journal of Political Economy* 112 (2004): 725–53.

Mitchell, David. *Cloud Atlas.* London: Sceptre, 2004.

Mokyr, Joel. *The Gifts of Athena: Historical Origins of the Knowledge Economy.* Princeton, NJ: Princeton University Press, 2003.

Mokyr, Joel, Chris Vickers, and Nicolas L. Ziebarth. "The History of Technological Anxiety and the Future of Economic Growth: Is This Time Different?" *Journal of Economic Perspectives* 29 (2015): 31–50.

Montesquieu. *The Spirit of Laws.* Anonymous, 1748.

Morrison, Andrew, Dhushyanth Raju, and Nistha Sinha. "Gender Equality, Poverty, and Economic Growth." Policy Research Working Paper No. 4349. Washington, DC: World Bank, 2007.

Mullainathan, Sendhil, and Eldar Shafir. *Scarcity: Why Having Too Little Means So Much.* New York: Times Books, 2013.

Nasar, Sylvia. *Grand Pursuit: The Story of Economic Genius.* New York: Simon & Schuster, 2011.

Nietzsche, Friedrich. *Human, All Too Human: A Book for Free Spirits.* Cambridge: Cambridge University Press, 1878 [1996].

Norenzayan, Ara, and Azim F. Shariff. "The Origin and Evolution of Religious Prosociality." *Science* 322 (2008): 58–62.

North, Douglas. *Institutions, Institutional Change and Economic Performance.* Cambridge: Cambridge University Press, 1990.

Obama, Barack. *Dreams from My Father.* New York: Times Books, 1995.

Olken, Benjamin. "Do TV and Radio Destroy Social Capital? Evidence from Indonesian Villages." *American Economic Journal: Applied Economics* 1 (2009): 1–35.

Orwell, George. *Keep the Aspidistra Flying.* London: Victor Gollancz Ltd, 1936.

Overton, Mark. *Agricultural Revolution in England: The Transformation of the Agrarian Economy 1500–1850.* Cambridge: Cambridge University Press, 1996.

Özkan, Türker, Timo Lajunen, Joannes El. Chliaoutakis, Dianne Parker, and Heikki Summala. "Cross-Cultural Differences in Driving Behaviours: A Comparison of Six Countries." *Transportation Research* 9 (2006): 227–42.

Peltzman, Sam. "The Effects of Automobile Safety Regulations." *Journal of Political Economy* 83 (1975): 677–726.

Perry, Alex. *The Rift.* New York: Little, Brown, and Company, 2015.

Pietra, Rivoli. *The Travels of a T-Shirt in the Global Economy: An Economist Examines the Markets, Power, and Politics of World Trade.* Hoboken: Wiley Publishers, 2009.

Piketty, Thomas. *Capital in the Twenty-First Century.* Cambridge, MA: Harvard University Press, 2014.

Pinker, Steven. *The Blank Slate: The Modern Denial of Human Nature.* New York: Viking Press, 2002.

Pounds, Norman J. G., and Sue Simons Ball. "Core-Areas and the Development of the European States System." *Annals of the Association of American Geographers* 54 (1964): 24–40.

Pritchett, Lant. *The Rebirth of Education: Schooling Ain't Learning.* Washington, DC: Brookings Institution Press, 2013.

Proust, Marcel. *In Search of Lost Time: The Prisoner Vol. 5.* Paris: Grasset and Gallimard, 1923.

Putnam, Robert D. *Bowling Alone: The Collapse and Revival of American Community.* New York: Simon & Schuster, 2000.

Preston, Samuel H. "The Changing Relation between Mortality and Level of Economic Development." *Population Studies* 29 (1975): 231–48.

Pritchett, Lant H. "Desired Fertility and the Impact of Population Policies." *Population and Development Review* 20 (1994): 1–55.

Rainer, Helmut, and Thomas Siedler. "The Role of Social Networks in Determining Migration and Labour Market Outcomes: Evidence from German Reunification." *Munich Reprints in Economics* 19783, University of Munich, Department of Economics, 2009.

Rajan, Raghuram G., and Arvind Subramanian. "Aid and Growth: What Does the Cross-Country Evidence Really Show?" *Review of Economics and Statistics* 90 (2008): 643–65.

Ravallion, Martin. "How Long Will It Take to Lift One Billion People Out of Poverty?" *World Bank Research Observer* 28 (2013): 139–58.

Ricardo, David. *On the Principles of Political Economy and Taxation.* London: John Murray, 1817.

Ridley, Matthew. *The Evolution of Everything: How New Ideas Emerge.* New York: Harper, 2015.

Ridley, Matthew. *The Rational Optimist: How Prosperity Evolves.* New York: Harper, 2010.

Rothwell, Jonathan, José Lobo, Deborah Strumsky, and Mark Muro. "Patenting Prosperity: Invention and Economic Performance in the United States and its Metropolitan Areas." Brookings Institution (2013): 1–49.

Ruef, Martin. "Strong Ties, Weak Ties and Islands: Structural and Cultural Predictors of Organizational Innovation." *Industrial and Corporate Change* 11 (2002): 427–49.

Ruskin, John. *Unto This Last and Other Writings.* Edited by Clive Wilmer. New York: Penguin Classics, 1860 [1986].

Samuelson, Paul. "The Keynes Centenary." *The Economist* 25 (1983): 19–21.

Samuelson, William, and Richard Zeckhauser. "Status Quo Bias in Decision Making." *Journal of Risk and Uncertainty* 1 (1988): 7–59.

Sandel, Michael. *What Money Can't Buy: The Moral Limits of Markets.* New York: Farrar, Strauss and Giroux, 2012.

Saunders, George. *The Braindead Microphone.* New York: Riverhead Books, 2007.

Schultz, Paul T. "School Subsidies for the Poor: Evaluating the Mexican Progresa Poverty Program." *Journal of Development Economics* 74 (2004): 199–250.

Schumpeter, Joseph. *Business Cycles.* New York: McGraw Hill Book Co., 1939.

Schumpeter, Joseph. *Capitalism, Socialism, and Democracy.* New York: Harper & Brothers, 1942.

Schumpeter, Joseph. "The Communist Manifesto in Sociology and Economics." *Journal of Political Economy* 57 (1949): 199–212.

Sen, Amartya. *Development as Freedom.* New York: Anchor, 2000.

Sen, Amartya. *Poverty and Famines.* Oxford: Oxford University Press, 1999.

Sigler, Joseph, "Review of *Economic Philosophy* by Joan Robinson." *Journal of Political Economy* 71 (1963): 192–93.

Smith, Adam. *An Inquiry into the Nature and the Causes of the Wealth of Nations.* London: W. Strahan and T. Cadell, 1776.

Solow, Robert. "A Contribution to the Theory of Economic Growth." *Quarterly Journal of Economics* 70 (1956): 65–94.

Sontag, Susan. *Susan Sontag: Essays of the 1960s & 70s.* Edited by David Reiff. New York: Library of America, 2013.

Spinrad, Norman. *The Druid King.* New York: Knopf, 2003.

Storr, Anthony. *Feet of Clay: Saints, Sinners, and Madmen: A Study of Gurus.* New York: Free Press, 1996.

Stover, Leon E. *The Cultural Ecology of Chinese Civilization.* New York: Mentor Books, 1974.

Suddle, Kashifa, Sjoerd Beugelsdijk, and Sander Wennekers. "Entrepreneurial Culture and its Effect on the Rate of Nascent Entrepreneurship." In *Entrepreneurship and Culture*, edited by Anreas Freitag and Roy Thurik: 227–44. New York: Springer, 2010.

Sullivan, J. P. *The Satyricon.* New York: Penguin Classics, 1984.

Svensson, Jakob. "Eight Questions about Corruption." *Journal of Economic Perspectives* 19 (2005): 18–42.

Swift, Jonathan. *Gulliver's Travels*. London: Benjamin Motte, 1726.

Tanzi, Vito. "Quantitative Characteristics of the Tax Systems of Developing Countries." In *The Theory of Taxation for Developing Countries*, edited by David Newbery and Nicholas Stern: 205–41. New York: Oxford University Press, 1987.

Tanzi, Vito, and Howell H. Zee. "Tax Policy for Emerging Markets: Developing Countries." *National Tax Journal* 53 (2000): 299–322.

Temple, Jonathan R.W. "Generalizations that Aren't? Evidence on Education and Growth." *European Economic Review* 45 (2001): 901–18.

Thaler, Richard. *Misbehaving: The Making of Behavioural Economics*. London: Allen Lane, 2015.

Theroux, Paul. *The Last Train to Zona Verde*. Boston: Mariner Books, 2014.

Thoreau, Henry David. "Life Without Principle." *Atlantic Monthly* 12 (1863): 484–95.

Török, Lásló. *Herodotus in Nubia*. Boston: Brill Academic Publishers, 2014.

Treisman, Daniel. "The Causes of Corruption: A Cross-National Study." *Journal of Public Economics* 76 (2000): 399–457.

Tversky, Amos, and Daniel Kahneman. "Judgment under Uncertainty: Heuristics and Biases." *Science* 185 (1974): 1124–31.

Twain, Mark. "Chapters from my Autobiography." *North American Review* vol. 598, 1906.

Twain, Mark. *The Innocents Abroad*. Hartford: American Publishing Company, 1869.

Twain, Mark. *Pudd'nhead Wilson*. New York: Charles L. Webster & Company, 1894.

Tynan, Kenneth. *The Diaries of Kenneth Tynan*. Edited by John Lahr. New York: Bloomsbury, 2003.

U.S. Energy Information Administration. Annual Energy Outlook 2015. Washington, DC: U.S. Department of Energy, 2015.

Vanderbilt, Thomas. *Traffic: Why We Drive the Way We Do (And What it Says About Us)*. New York: Knopf, 2008.

Vigna, Paul, and Michael J. Casey. *The Age of Cryptocurrency: How Bitcoin and Digital Money Are Challenging the Global Economic Order*. New York: St. Martin's Press, 2015.

Wacziarg, Romain, and Karen Horn Welch. "Trade Liberalization and Growth: New Evidence." *World Bank Economic Review* 22 (2008): 187–231.

Wagner, Adolf. "Extracts on Public Finance." In *Classics in the Theory of Public Finance*, edited by Richard A. Musgrave and Alan T. Peacock. London: Macmillan, 1958.

Waley, Arthur. *Three Ways of Thought in Ancient China*. Palo Alto: Stanford University Press, 1939.

Wang, Feng, and Xuejin Zuo. "Inside China's Cities: Institutional Barriers and Opportunities for Urban Migrants." *American Economic Review* 89 (1999): 276–80.

Weber, Max. *The Protestant Ethic and the Spirit of Capitalism.* New York: Scribner, 1930.

Weber, Max. "The Three Types of Legitimate Rule." *Berkeley Publications in Society and Institutions* 4 (1958): 1–11.

Wheelan, Charles. *Naked Economics: Undressing the Dismal Science.* New York: W.W. Norton & Co., 2010.

Whitman, Walt. *Specimen Days and Collect.* Philadelphia: Rees, Welsh & Co., 1882.

Wordsworth, William. *Lyrical Ballads.* London: J. & A. Arch, 1798.

World Bank. *Cost of Pollution in China: Economic Estimates of Physical Damages.* Washington, DC: World Bank, 2007.

World Health Organization. *Comprehensive mental health action plan 2013–2020.* Geneva: World Health Organization, 2013.

World Health Organization. *World Malaria Report 2010.* Geneva: World Health Organization, 2010.

Wrong, Michelle. *In the Footsteps of Mr. Kurtz: Living on the Brink of Disaster in Mobutu's Congo.* New York: Harper Collins, 2001.

Zak, Paul J., and Stephen Knack. "Trust and Growth." *Economic Journal* 111 (2001): 295–321.

Index

Absolute poverty, 10
Acemoglu, Darin, 49, 114–115, 125, 128
Adjacent possible, 173
Adverse selection, 208–210, 265, 281
Afghanistan, 263
Africa: agricultural marketing boards, 109; colonization strategies in, 79, 155; compared to East Asia, 87; cotton market, 189–190; food production, 89; import substitution policies, 188–189; international trade, 86–88; mobile phone technology, 180, 185–186; Sub-Saharan Africa, 2, 17, 50, 81, 86, 87, 89, 260; wildlife management, 253–254. See also *specific nations*
Aggressive driving, 33–34
Agricultural marketing boards, 109
Agricultural production, 52, 68, 89, 108–109, 118
Agricultural productivity, 241, 242
Agricultural subsidies, 102
Agriculture, 189, 203
Aid illusion, 264
AIDS/HIV, 124, 179
Airline industry, 266–267
Air pollution, 89–90
Air travel, 247–253
Akerlof, George, 128, 198, 207–209

Amara, Roy, 188
Amara's Law, 188
Amazon.com, 204, 205–206
Ambani, Mukesh, 9–10
Anchoring bias, 214–215
Animal spirits idea, 212–213, 256
Animist religious beliefs, 142
Antilia mansion, 9–10
Antiviral drugs, 179
Apartheid system, 4–5
Argentina, 42–43, 110–112
Aristotle, 124
Arts, 162–163, 164
Asia, 86–88. See also *specific nations*
Assembly line, 68, 169
Asymmetric information, 207–211, 218, 220, 221, 281
Atahualpa, 148
ATM machines, 74–75
Attribution bias, 214
Austerity measures, 113
Authoritarian political systems, 47, 116, 140
Autocracy and famines, 72
Availability bias, 214

Backpacking trips, 229–230
Banerjee, Abhijit, 80, 128
Banking services, 7–8
Banks, 107–108, 111, 119, 184

Bao Steel, 119–120
Bargaining strategies, 200
Barro, Robert, 126, 143
Barter economies, 216
Bauer, Peter, 264–265
Beauty, experiencing, 227–230
Becker, Gary, 156
Behavioral economics, 212–215, 221, 234, 253, 259
Bengal famine of 1943, 71–72
Biases, 214–215, 221, 252
"Big events," 115–116, 118, 122
Birth rates, 70, 71
Bitcoin, 219–220
Black Plague, 77
Blixen, Karen, 272
Botswana, 33, 41–42, 61, 121–124, 125, 145, 191–192
Brain drain, 176
Brazil, 110
BribeNigeria.com, 45
Bryson, Bill, 225, 230
Buck, Pearl, 102
Business cycles, 256
Business registration, 79–80

Cantonese shopkeepers, 146–147
Cap and trade programs, 248–249, 257
Cape Town, South Africa, 2
Capital, 81, 85
Capital and labor, tradeoff between: as complements not substitutes, 75–76; distortion of labor markets and investment decisions, 79–81; educational institutions, 81–82; environmental degradation, 89–92; incentives and institutions, 71–73, 76–77; introduction to, 61–63; legal systems, 82–84; macroeconomic instability and employment instability, 84; population control, 92–93; population growth, 69–71; productivity and economic growth,

64–67; productivity and inexpensive labor, 73–77; technology, role of improvements in, 68–69
Capitalism, 132, 181–182, 268, 269
Carbon emissions, 248–249
Car horns, 34–35
Caste system, 134, 141
Catholicism, 141–142
Centralized corruption, 48–49
Centralized power: in Botswana, 121–122; in China, 244; corruption and, 99; in democracies, 126; pluralism and, 279
Central planning, 105–107, 116, 117–121, 142
Charter cities, 128–129
Chase, Chevy, 271
Chicago Board of Trade, 203
Chicago School of Economics, 156, 164
Child labor, 82
China: car horns, 34–35; congestion taxes, 58; driving behavior, 52–53; eminent domain, 254–255; financial repression, 191; geography, 243–244; Great Chinese Famine of 1958–1961, 72; growth miracle, 117–121; *hukou* (household registration) system, 120; land-leasing system, 164; monetary policy, 12; one-child policies, 67, 92–93; pollution, 238–239; public goods, 54–55; religion, 143; state-owned banks, 107–108, 119; state-owned enterprises, 119–120; technology blocking, 184–185; tourism, 255; traffic policing and corruption, 45–46; transportation system, 38
Christianity, 155
Cities and technology, 174–177
Classification theory, 139–140, 147
"Clean slate" hypothesis, 128

Climate, 241–243
Climate change, 91–92, 248–249, 282
Clinton Foundation, 179
Clubs, 154
Coase, Ronald, 248, 250–251
Coase theorem, 247, 248–254,
    257–258, 269, 281–282
Code of Hammurabi, 77
Collectivism, 37, 139, 140
Colonization, 49–50, 78–79, 87–88,
    122, 142, 148, 155, 188
Commodification, 203
Commodity money, 217
Communication, 25
Community, sense of, 40
Competition, 20–21, 181
Complementary knowledge, 176
Compounding, 21, 66
Confirmation bias, 214
Conflict, 47, 101–102
Conflict and diversity, 148–165;
    culture and trust, 150–155; ethnic
    diversity, 153–154; game theory,
    151–153; globalization, 158–163;
    impact of culture on economics,
    155–158; religion, 154–155
Conflict trap, 102
Confucianism, 141, 142, 143
Congestion taxes, 57–58
Conglomerates, 151
Congo, 103
Contamination bias, 214
"A Contribution to the Theory of
    Economic Growth" (Solow), 21
Cooperative behavior, 40–41
Cooperative equilibrium, 40–41, 218
Cooperative outcome, 57, 58
Corruption, 43–47; in Argentina,
    111–112; centralized power, 99;
    driving behavior, 52–53; famines
    and, 72; foreign aid, 264–265; legal
    systems, 82–84; in Macau, 262;
    political dysfunction, 48; vs.
    taxation, 114; in Zimbabwe, 97

Costa Rica, 266
Cotton industry, 74
Cotton market, 189–190
Cowen, Tyler, 160, 161
Creative destruction, 181–182
Cross-country migration, 176–177
Crypto-currency, 220
Cultural destruction, 159–161
Cultural determinism, 51
Cultural differences, 51–59
Cultural differentiation, 133
Cultural dimensions index, 139–140,
    147
Cultural diversity, 132, 136, 158–163,
    175–176
Cultural evolution, 156–157
Cultural materialism, 136, 156
Cultural norms, 279–280
Cultural Revolution, 118
Cultural stability, 160
Culture, 131–165; conflict and
    diversity, 148–165; definition of,
    135–138; economists on, 132–134;
    entrepreneurship and risk taking,
    146–148; gender roles, 143–145;
    human behavior, 134–135; impact
    on economics, 155–158;
    institutions, 134, 163–164;
    measurement and classification,
    138–140; openness to new ideas,
    145–146; origins of, 136–138;
    religion, 141–143; trust and,
    150–155; virtuous and vicious
    cycles, 163–164
Currency, 217–219
Currency exchange rates, 11–12, 13,
    120
Curse of knowledge, 209

Dai Bingguo, 118
Dark Ages, 160
Darwin, Charles, 116, 168, 226,
    273–274
David Copperfield (Dickens), 15

Dawkins, Richard, 216
Dead capital, 84
Deaton, Angus, 264
De Botton, Alain, 197
Debt, 110–113
Decentralized corruption, 48–49, 102
De facto behavior/norms/laws: in
    China, 52; collectivism, 140; vs. *de
    jure* laws, 134; fair wages, 259;
    haggling, 205–206, 222;
    institutions, 51; introduction to,
    36–39; legal systems, 101; overview
    of, 277; personal space, 254;
    punishment, 42–43, 251; tax laws,
    112
Defoe, Daniel, 64–65
De jure laws, 36–39, 41–43, 51–52,
    101, 112, 134, 140, 277
De Maistre, Xavier, 284
Democracy, 72, 124–127
Demographic transitions, 92–93
Deng Xiaoping, 118
Dependency ratio, 92
Descriptive norms, 36, 38–39, 40–41,
    44, 135, 277
De Soto, Hernando, 83–84
Dhaka, Bangladesh, 55, 58
Dharavi slum, India, 2–4, 6, 99–100
Diamond, Jared, 50, 77, 240
Dickens, Charles, 4, 15
Diminishing marginal returns, 23–25,
    65–66, 69, 170
Discrimination, 144, 149
Diversification, 260–261
Doing Business (World Bank), 79–80
"Double-hit" accidents, 52–53
Dreams from My Father (Obama), 169
Drivers in other countries, 31–59;
    cooperative behavior, 40–43;
    cultural differences, 51–59;
    enforcement of laws and
    corruption, 43–47; game theory,
    39–40; historical path-dependence,
    49–50; institutions, 35–39;

introduction to, 31–35; political
    dysfunction, 47–49; public goods,
    54–58; safety innovations, 59
Driver training and licensing, 46–47
Dubai, 268–269
Duflo, Esther, 80, 128
Dutch disease, 261–262

East Asian financial crisis, 12
Easterly, William, 72–73, 127
East Germany, 117, 151
EBay, 204
E-commerce, 205–206
Economic crises, 84
Economic development: cultural
    changes, 158; impact of nature,
    240–244; impact on nature,
    237–240; trust and, 157
Economic diversity of cities, 175–176
Economic empowerment zones, 6
Economic environments and
    technology, 192–194
Economic freedom, 125
Economic growth, 21–22;
    beneficiaries of, 103–104; "big
    events," 115–116, 118, 122;
    democracy, 124–127; incentives
    and institutions, 71–73, 76–77;
    Malthus's theory of, 65–67;
    population growth, 69–71;
    productivity, 64–67; technology,
    170–171
Economic opportunities in slums, 6–7
Economic theory: asymmetric
    information and adverse selection,
    281; centralized power and
    pluralism, 279; cultural norms,
    279–280; descriptive and injunctive
    norms, 277; key aspects of,
    275–276; labor productivity, 278;
    natural environment, 282; need for,
    273–275; public goods and the
    Coase theorem, 281–282;
    technology, 280; theory and

observation, 282–286; wealth and poverty, 276–277. *See also* Incentives; Institutions; Market failure.
Edison, Thomas, 173
Education, 21–22, 81–82
Einstein, Albert, 1, 21, 167, 168
Electronic currency, 219–220
Eliot, T. S., 271
Elites, and economic growth, 101–104
Elizabeth I, Queen, 76, 182
Emerson, Ralph Waldo, 225, 233
Eminent domain, 54, 182–183, 254–255
Empathy, 273
Employment instability, 84
Encomienda system, 78
Energy, 25
Energy-intensive economies, 260–261
Enforcement of laws and corruption, 43–47
Enlightenment, 146, 155, 160
Entrepreneurial skills, 28
Entrepreneurship, 6, 146–148, 191
Environmental degradation, 89–92
Environmental Performance Index, 238
Epidemiological transition, 17
Ethnic diversity, 149–150, 153–154
Ethnic homogeneity, 153
Ethnicity, 148–149
Ethnolinguistic fractionalization, 148–149, 153–154
Eurasian societies, 50, 77, 240
European geography, 243
European Monetary Union, 113
Euro-zone debt crisis, 112–113
Evolution, theory of, 168, 173, 226, 273–274
Excessive debt, 110–113
Exchange rate controls, 207
Exchange rate policy, 120
Extreme poverty, 1–2, 7, 15–16

Fairness, 40
Family conglomerates, 151
Family planning decisions, 144
Famines, 66, 71–73, 106, 117–118
Faulkner, William, 49, 115
Feedback loops, 127
Ferguson, Niall, 190–191
Fertility decisions, 71
Fertility rates, 70, 144
Fiat money, 217–219
Finance, 216–217
Financial instruments, 216–217
Financial markets, 110, 208
Financial repression, 190–192
Finland, 42
Fitzgerald, F. Scott, 283
Fluid nations, 161
Food and culture, 162
Food production, 89
Forced sterilizations, 67
Ford, Henry, 68, 169
Foreign aid, 72–73, 127–128, 263–266
Framing bias, 214, 252
France, 80–81
Freedom, 14–15
Free market system, 105
Free-rider problem, 171, 281
Freud, Sigmund, 237
Friedman, Milton, 125
Friedman, Tom, 109

Game theory, 39–40, 56–57, 151–153, 200
Gandhi, 162–163
Gates, Bill, 173
GDP. *See* Gross Domestic Product (GDP)
Gender bias, 11
Gender roles, 143–145
Genocide, 148
Geographical determinism, 241–242
Geography, 240–244
Gini coefficients, 8

Global Financial Crisis of 2009, 261, 268
Globalization, 157, 158–163
Global tourism, 158–159
Global warming. *See* Climate change
Goethe, Johann Wolfgang von, 131
Gold standard, 217
Gosplan, 106
Government bureaucracies, 54–56, 79–81
Government influence on growth, 95–129; Botswana example, 121–124; China example, 117–121; correcting market failure, 104–109; democracy, 124–127; ensuring a stable and free environment, 101–104; growth miracles and disasters, 114–121; *Gulliver's Travels* example, 100–101; macroeconomic policy, 109–113; pluralism, 103–104; promoting tourism, 267; public welfare promotion, 98–100; reforming institutions, 127–129; size vs. quality, 113–114; technology blocking, 184; trust, 151; Zimbabwe example, 95–98
Grameen Bank, 145
Great Britain, 122
Great Chinese Famine of 1958–1961, 72
Great Famine, 117–118
Great Leap Forward, 72, 117–118
Greece, 112–113
Greene, Graham, 195
Green Revolution, 236
Greentoe, 206
Gross Domestic Product (GDP): currency exchange rates, 11–12, 13; freedom, 14–15; gender bias, 11; health, 16–17; income levels across countries, 11–12; introduction to, 10–11; law of one price, 12–13; as measurement of well-being, 11; multiplier effect, 256; poverty rates,

15–16; purchasing power parity (PPP) exchange rates, 13–14
Group lending, 145
Growth miracles and disasters, 114–121
Gulliver's Travels (Swift), 100–101
Guns, Germs, and Steel (Diamond), 240

Haggling, 197–223; asymmetric information, 207–211, 218, 220, 221; behavioral economics, 212–215, 221; cost of, 201, 203–204; definition of, 199; economic factors, 201–203; game theory, 200; good-specific factors, 207–211; introduction to, 197–199; money and, 215–219; perception of as unfair, 204–205; prices and, 199–201; social and psychological aspects, 206–207, 212; succeeding at, 221–223; transaction costs, 201–202, 251; trust and, 206
Hassle cost, 204
Haves and have-nots, 1–29; economic growth, 21–24; income inequality, 8–10; income measurement, 10–14; institutions, 27–29; other measures of economic well-being, 14–17; slums, 2–8; technology, 24–27; theories, 18–21
Hayek, Friedrich, 105–107, 114, 142, 232
Health, 16–17
Health care insurance, 282
Heisenberg, Werner, 274
Herodotus, 131–132
Hessler, Peter, 53
Himalayan Sherpa, 259
Historical determinism, 180
Historical path-dependence, 49–50
HIV/AIDS, 124, 179
Hofstede, Geert, 139–140, 147
Home, 271–286

Homestead Act of 1862, 79
Hong Kong, 128
Housing bubbles, 107–108
Hukou (household registration)
    system, 120
Human behavior, incentives and, 283
Human capital, 82, 85
Human ingenuity, 194–196
Human migration, 52, 53
Human nature, 27
Hyperinflation, 96, 98, 110–111

ICow, 186
Ideas, production of, 171–174
Ideology, 136
Import substitution policies, 87,
    188–189
Inca Empire, 148
Incentives: in centrally planned
    economies, 106; competition,
    20–21; corruption, 48; driving
    behavior, 52–53; economic growth,
    71–73, 76–77; human behavior,
    283; institutions, 27–29, 35, 43, 50;
    overview of, 276; punishment, 41;
    taxation, 57–58; technology, 178
Income: art and culture and, 162–163,
    164; democracy and, 124–125;
    variability of, 192–194
Income equality, 153
Income growth rates, 24
Income inequality, 8–10, 150,
    241–242, 262, 269
Income levels across countries, 23–24
Income measurement, 10–14
India: caste system, 134, 141;
    cooperative behavior, 41;
    decentralized democracy, 126–127;
    Dharavi slum, 2–4, 6, 99–100;
    international trade, 86; legal
    system, 43–44; Mumbai, 8–10, 32,
    38–39; personal space, 254;
    political dysfunction, 48; sacred
    cows, 136–137; technology

blocking, 182–184; tragedy of the
    commons, 57
Indulgence, 139, 140
Industrialization, 237–238
Industrial Revolution: cotton industry,
    74; cultural beliefs, 146; financial
    systems, 191; health, 16;
    institutions, 77–78; intellectual
    property rights, 178; labor
    shortages, 79; property rights, 83;
    urban migration, 68
Infant mortality rates, 16–17
Infeld, Leopold, 167
Inflation, 96, 98, 110–111, 218–219
Informal economy, 80, 81
Informal lending, 8, 108
Informal production, 100
Informational differences between
    buyers and sellers, 207–211
Information sharing, 209–210
Infrastructure, 54–58
Ingenuity, 194–196
Injunctive norms: in cohesive
    societies, 284; in communities and
    societies, 40–44; enforcing, 44,
    135; fairness and trust, 152; fair
    wages, 259; haggling, 204–205,
    221–222; institutions, 51;
    introduction to, 36–39; overview
    of, 277
The Innocents Abroad (Twain), 219, 255
Innovation, 69, 169–170, 175, 181,
    186, 194–196
*An Inquiry into the Nature and Causes of
    the Wealth of Nations* (Smith), 18, 64
Institutional evolution, 116
Institutions: in Botswana, 121–124;
    cooperative behavior, 39–43;
    cultural differences, 51–59;
    culture and, 134, 136, 163–164;
    democracy, 125–127; distortion of
    labor markets and investment
    decisions, 79–81; driving behavior
    and, 35–39; economic growth,

Institutions: in Botswana (*cont.*) 71–73, 76–77; education, 81–82; enforcement of laws and corruption, 43–47; game theory, 39–40; geography, 242–243; historical path-dependence, 49–50; incentives, 35; injunctive and descriptive norms, 35–39; international trade, 85–94; introduction to, 27–29; legal systems, 82–84; macroeconomic instability and employment instability, 84; Malthusian trap, 79; overview of, 277; political dysfunction, 47–49; public goods, 54–58; reforming, 127–129; tourist destinations, 263; trust, 151; vicious and virtuous cycles, 115–116. *See also* Government influence on growth
Intellectual property rights, 178–180, 184–185
Internal migrants, 120
Internationally traded goods, 12–13
International trade: in Asia and Africa, 86–88; barriers to, 109, 188–190; benefits of, 85–87; closing markets to, 85–94
Intuitive decisions, 213
Investment decisions, 79–84
Investment shortage, 3
Invisible hand of the marketplace, 64–65, 105, 138
Iowa, returning to, 284–285
IPaidABribe.com, 45
Irish potato famine, 93
Irrational behavior, 212
Islam, 142, 144, 155

Japan, 143
Jaywalking, 36
Jefferson, Thomas, 170, 172
Jerusalem, 154–155
Job elimination, 186–188

Jobs, Steve, 173
Johnson, Simon, 49
Johnson, Steven, 172, 173, 196
Juche economic system, 116
Judaism, 155

Kafka, Franz, 62
Kahneman, Daniel, 213
Kerouac, Jack, 32
Keynes, John Maynard, 95, 164, 212, 256, 275
Kgotla system, 122
Khama, Ilan, 123
Khama, Seretse, 122–123
Kilmer, Joyce, 226
Kim Il-Sung, 116
Kiribati, 91
Kleptocracy, 48, 97, 115, 124, 126, 127–128
Kliptown, 4–5
Knee Defender, 249, 252
Knitting machines, 76, 182
Korea, 116–117
Kuznets, Simon, 110–111

Labor: colonization strategies, 78–79; distortion of labor markets and investment decisions, 79–81; quantity and quality of, 21–22. *See also* Capital and labor, tradeoff between
Labor productivity, 278
Laissez-faire policies, 106, 268–269
Landes, David, 103, 141–142
Land-leasing system, 164
Landline telephones, 167–168
Language, 148–149, 153–154, 159
Latin America, colonization strategies in, 78–79
Law, Wagner's, 113, 114–115
Law of Diminishing Marginal Returns, 23–24, 170
Law of Diminishing Marginal Returns to Labor, 65–66, 69

Law of one price, 12–13
Leaking, ideas, 172–173, 180
Legal systems, 82–84
Lieh-Tzu, 61–62
Life expectancy, 16–17
The Life of Brian, 198, 206
Life satisfaction, 15
Liquid network, 196
Long-term orientation, 139, 140
Long-term unemployment, 208
Loss aversion bias, 213, 234, 252
Luddites, 76, 182

Macau, 262
Macroeconomic instability and
  employment instability, 84
Macroeconomic policy, 109–113
Malinvestment, 23, 105, 107
Malthus, Thomas, 65–71, 73, 226,
  274
Malthusian trap, 73, 76–77, 79, 88,
  174, 226
Mandela, Nelson, 4
Mandeville, Bernard de, 18
Mao Zedong, 117
Market economics, concerns about,
  231–233
Market failure, 54, 101, 104–109,
  278–279
Marketing boards, 108–109
Marshall, Alfred, 19–21, 155–156
Martin, McChesney, 110
Marx, Karl, 19, 66, 132, 156
Marxism, 187
Masculinity, 139, 140
Masire, Quett, 123
Matching, ideas, 172–173, 180
Maximum price, 199, 201, 202
McCleary, Rachel, 143
McCloskey, Deirdre, 26
Mechanization, 73–76
Megacities, 53–54
Mental health disorders, 237
Mercantilism, 18, 19

Microeconomics, 175–176
Microfinance, 144–145
Microinstitutions, 128
Migrant workers, 269
Migration, 176–177, 236
Minority rights, 47–48
Mishkin, Frederic, 191
Mitchell, David, 245
Mobile banking, 186
Mobile phone technology, 180,
  185–186, 196
Mobutu Seso Seko, 103
Modernization theory, 145–146
Mokyr, Joel, 187
Monetary policy, 12
Money as asset, 215–220
Monopolies, 171–172
Moore, Gordon, 172
Moore's Law, 172–173
M-Pesa mobile transactions, 186,
  220
Mugabe, Robert, 97–98
Multiple equilibria, 40
Multiplier effect, 256–257
Mumbai, India, 8–10, 32, 38–39.
  See also Dharavi slum, India
The Mystery of Capital (De Soto),
  83–84

Narco cultura (narcotics culture), 134
Nasar, Sylvia, 19
Nash, John, 56
Nash equilibrium, 56–57, 58, 153
Natural determinism, 240–242
Natural environment, 282
Natural resources and tourism, 257,
  260
Nature, 225–244; impact of economic
  development, 237–240; impact on
  economic development, 240–244;
  introduction to, 225–227; overview
  of, 282
Nature travel: to escape technology,
  230–233; to experience risk,

Nature travel (*cont.*)
   233–236; experiencing beauty,
   227–230; to get in touch with the
   land, 236–237
Negative externalities, 11, 57, 238,
   248–249
Negotiation, barriers to, 251–252
Neolithic Revolution, 16, 50, 77, 236,
   238
Neo-mercantilist, 189
Networked ideas, 173–174
New ideas, openness to, 145–146
Newton, Isaac, 195
New York City, 46, 58
New Zealand, 34, 41
Nigeria, 45, 49–50
Noncooperative equilibrium, 153
Noncooperative outcome, 56–57
North, Douglas, 83, 178
North America, colonization strategies
   in, 78–79
North Korea, 116–117, 190

Obama, Barack, 169
Observation, 282–286
Observer bias, 133, 143, 163
One-child policies, 67, 92–93
One-lane bridges, 41
One-party democracies, 126
On the Road (Kerouac), 32
Openness to new ideas, 145–146
Open-source software, 178
Opportunity cost, 201
Orwell, George, 1
Ottoman Empire, 144
Overconfidence bias, 214
Ownership, lack of, 248–249
Ownership bias, 213, 252

Parasitic diseases, 241–242
Patents, 171, 178–180
Patent trolling, 179–180
Path-dependence, 115–116, 155, 173
Peasant Revolt, 77–78

Peltzman, Sam, 59
Peltzman effect, 59
Personal autonomy, 232
Personal space, 254
Pharmaceutical products, 179
Physical capital, 22–24
Pluralism, 103, 126, 279
Poincaré, Henri, 173
Political dysfunction, 47–49
Political patronage, 111–112, 119
Pollution, 89–91, 119, 182–183,
   238–240. *See also* Carbon
   emissions
Poor Economics (Banerjee and Duflo),
   128
Poor Law of 1834, 93
Population control, 88–90, 92–93
Population density, 2–3
Population growth, 66–67, 69–71,
   88–89, 238
Positive externalities, 11, 54, 245,
   248, 260
Potential surplus, 201
Poverty: contribution of geography,
   241–243; driving behavior, 51–52;
   extreme, 1–2, 7, 15–16; foreign aid,
   264–266; GDP and, 15–17;
   geographic concentration, 176–177;
   in mercantilism, 18; need for
   entrepreneurial skills, 28; overview
   of, 276–277; psychological costs of,
   150; relative vs. absolute, 10; risks
   of living in, 7; in slums, 3–7;
   variability of income, 192–194
Poverty trap, 176–177, 180
Power distance, 139–140
PPP (purchasing power parity)
   exchange rates, 13–14
Present bias, 214, 217
Price discrimination, 205
Priceline, 206
Prices, 105–106, 199–201, 232, 252
Principle of Population (Malthus), 226
Principles of Economics (Marshall), 20

Prisoner's dilemma, 152–153
Private game parks, 253–254
"The Problem of Social Cost" (Coase), 248
Production methods, 86
Productivity, 20–23; of agricultural labor, 89; child labor, 82; economic growth and, 64–67; inexpensive labor, 73–77; population growth, 69–71; technology and, 68–69
PROGRESSA program, 82
Property rights, 82–84, 101, 248–250, 252–255, 257
Protectionism, 86, 109
Protestant Reformation, 141
Proust, Marcel, 271, 272
Public goods and services: assigning property rights to, 253–254; carbon emissions, 249; free-rider problem, 171; government and, 104; institutions and, 54–58; nonexcludable and nonrivalrous, 245–246; overview of, 281–282; pharmaceutical products, 179; shortages of, 3; technology, 171; technology blocking, 182–184; tipping, 260; tourism, 257; travel and, 246
Public health services, 3–4, 7, 183
Public sanitation, 182–184
Public transportation, 38–39
Punishment, 40–42
Purchasing power, 110
Purchasing power parity (PPP) exchange rates, 13–14

Rand, Ayn, 181–182
Rational actor model, 134–135, 212–213, 234
Rational altruism, 156
Reasoning processing, 213
Recession, 256
Reciprocity, 152
Regulation, 182

Relative poverty, 10
Relative value, 216
Relativity, theory of, 173
Religion, 141–143, 144, 154–155
Rent, 6, 9
Rent-seeking behavior, 124
Reputation, 210, 221
Resource curse, 260–263
Resource-intensive economies, 260–261
Rhodes, Cecil, 122
Ricardo, David, 187
Risk, 233–236
Risk aversion bias, 213, 234
Risk avoidance, 139, 140
Risk taking, 146–148
Risky economic environments, 192–194
The Road to Serfdom (Hayek), 105
Robinson, James, 49, 114–115, 125, 128
Robinson Crusoe (Defoe), 64–65
Romer, Paul, 25, 128
Ruskin, John, 230, 231
Russia, 110
Rwanda, 148, 155

Sacred cows, 136–137
Sandel, Michael, 158
Saunders, George, 31, 161
Schumpeter, Joseph, 181–182, 191
Scientific method, 275
Self-reliance, 231
Seller's curse, 209
Sen, Amartya, 14–15, 71–72
Settler mortality rates, 49–50
Sex-selected abortions, 93
Shanzhai goods, 184–185
Sierra Leone, 42, 109
Simple majority-rule political system, 102
Singapore, 128
Skilled workers, 176
Slavery, 78–79, 144

Slumdog Millionaire, 3

Slums: conditions in, 3–7; Dharavi slum, India, 2–4, 6, 99–100; as economic empowerment zones, 175–176; government incentives, 99–100; rent in, 6, 9; sense of unease in, 7; Soweto, South Africa, 4–6; visiting, 2–4

Small interest groups, 101–102

Smith, Adam, 18, 64–65, 85, 105, 132, 137–138, 155, 170, 192, 232

Sociability, 231

Social bonding, 206–207

Social capability, 146

Social Darwinist view, 28

Social norms: culture, 135; descriptive and injunctive norms, 277; fertility decisions, 71; government influence, 98, 127, 157; haggling, 204, 205, 206, 221–222; indulgence, 139; personal space, 254; in ultimatum game, 157, 251. *See also* Injunctive norms

Social structures, 195–196

Solow, Robert, 21, 25–26, 170

South Africa, 73

South America, colonization strategies in, 78–79

South Korea, 116–117, 190, 269

Sovereign debt, 110–113

Soviet Union, 106

Soweto, South Africa, 4–6, 99

Space when traveling, 247–248, 249–250

Spain, 73, 148

Special enterprise zones, 118

Specialization, 65, 82, 85, 151, 192–194, 231–233, 260–261, 281

Speed limits, 36–37

Spending multipliers, 256

Spinrad, Norman, 167, 175

Stable and free environment, 101

State-owned banks, 107–108, 119, 184

State-owned enterprises (SOEs), 107, 119–120, 184, 188–189, 191, 266

Status quo bias, 252

Steel industry, 185

Stereotypes about drivers, 33

Stewart, Potter, 95

Stigler, George, 283

Store of value, 216

Storr, Anthony, 138

Sub-Saharan Africa, 2, 17, 50, 81, 86, 87, 89, 260

Sustainable growth, 126

Swadeshi movement, 162–163

Swan, Joseph, 173

Swift, Jonathan, 100–101

Tata group of companies, 151

Taxation, 57–58, 104, 112, 114

Technological backwardness, 185–186

Technological diffusion, 167–169, 280. *See also* Technology; Technology blocking

Technology, 24–27, 59; cities, 174–177; definition of, 169–170; differing levels of, 180–186; economic growth, 170–171; environments for, 178–180; escaping to nature, 230–233; human ingenuity, 194–196; overview of, 280; pollution, 90–91; population growth and, 69; production of ideas, 171–174; role of improvements in, 68–69

Technology blocking: barriers to international trade, 188–190; differing levels of technology, 180–185; financial repression, 190–192; job elimination, 186–188; risky economic environments, 192–194

Technology ladder, 168

TFP (total factor productivity), 25–26

The Theory of Moral Sentiments (Smith), 137–138

Theroux, Paul, 2

The Third Man, 195

Thoreau, Henry David, 233–234

Thusang Basadi (Women's Finance House), 145

Tiberius, 178, 182

Tipping, 259–260

Total factor productivity (TFP), 25–26

Total surplus, 199–200

Tourism industry, 246, 255–260, 267–270

Tourist destinations, 260–263, 268

Traffic, 32–33; congestion, 55–58; fatalities, 35, 46; lights, 42–43; tickets, 41–42

Traffic policing, and corruption, 45–46

Tragedy of the commons, 56–57, 104, 253, 257

Transaction costs, 201–202, 218, 220, 241–242, 251, 254–255

Transportation, 25

Transportation infrastructures, 246–253, 255, 266

Traveling: barriers to, 190; new perspectives, 272–274

Traveling economics, 245–270; Coase theorem, 247–253; effect on local employment, 258–260; foreign aid, 263–266; future of tourism, 267–270; indirect impacts of, 258; introduction to, 245–247; public goods, 245–246; tourism industry, 255–258, 266–267; tourist destinations, 260–263

Travel spaces, 249–253

"Trees" (Kilmer), 226

The Trial (Kafka), 62

Trujillo, Honduras, 128

Trust, 150–155, 157, 206

Tversky, Amos, 213

Twain, Mark, 14, 131, 219, 245, 255, 272–273

Tynan, Kenneth, 47

Tyranny of the majority, 102, 124

Tyranny of the status quo, 182

UAE (United Arab Emirates), 268–269

Uber, 267

Ultimatum game, 40, 151–153, 157, 205, 251

Uncertainty avoidance, 139, 140

Underground lending markets, 108

Unemployment benefits, 81

Unemployment rates, 73, 75–76

United Arab Emirates (UAE), 268–269

United States, 10, 34

Unproductive property rights, 84

Urban migration, 53–54, 68, 236–237

Used car market, 207–209

U.S.S.R., 106

Usury, 142

Vacation, 271

Vicious cycles, 115–116, 163–164

Virtuous circles, 121, 157, 163–164, 280

Virtuous cycles, 115–116, 128

Volunteer organizations, 154

Voyage around My Room (de Maistre), 284

Wages, 73–77, 258–259

Wagner, Adolf, 113

Wagner's Law, 113, 114–115

Wallace, Alfred Russell, 173

Wealth, 176–177, 276–277

Wealth of Nations (Smith), 18, 64

Weber, Max, 98, 132, 138, 141, 143

Welfare state, 158

Well-being, measurement of, 11

Welles, Orson, 195

West Germany, 117, 151

The White Man's Burden (Easterly), 72–73
Whitman, Walt, 162
Why Nations Fail (Acemoglu and Robinson), 114–115
Wildlife management, 253–254
Women. *See* Gender bias; Gender roles

World Health Organization, 179
World Values Survey, 146, 147, 153, 157

Yunus, Muhammad, 145

Zimbabwe, 95–98, 109, 110
Zombie ideas, 172, 178

About the Author

Todd A. Knoop, PhD, is the David Joyce Professor of Economics and Business at Cornell College. He has taught economics in many different countries on four continents and is currently seeking an opportunity to teach economics in Antarctica. He is the author of multiple articles as well as the books *Business Cycle Economics: Understanding Recessions and Depressions from Boom to Bust*, *Global Finance in Emerging Market Economies*, *Recessions and Depressions: Understanding Business Cycles*, and *Modern Financial Macroeconomics*.